Essential Skills of Social Work Practice

Also Available from Lyceum Books, Inc.

Advisory Editor: Thomas M. Meenaghan, *New York University*

Evidence-Based Practices for Social Workers: An Interdisciplinary Approach
Thomas O'Hare

Research Methods for Social Workers: A Practice-Based Approach
Cynthia A. Faulkner and Samuel S. Faulkner

Social Work Evaluation: Enhancing What We Do
James R. Dudley

Cross-Cultural Practice: Social Work with Diverse Populations
Karen V. Harper and Jim Lantz

Endings in Clinical Practice: Effective Closure in Diverse Settings
Joseph Walsh

Therapeutic Games and Guided Imagery: Tools for Mental Health and School Professionals Working with Children, Adolescents, and Their Families
Monit Cheung

Mental Health in Literature: Literary Lunacy and Lucidity
Glenn Rohrer

Clinical Assessment for Social Workers: Quantitative and Qualitative Methods
Catheleen Jordan and Cynthia Franklin

Toward Evidence-Based Practice: Variations on a Theme
Joel Fischer

Essential Skills of Social Work Practice

ASSESSMENT, INTERVENTION, EVALUATION

THOMAS O'HARE

LYCEUM
BOOKS, INC.

Chicago, Illinois

© Lyceum Books, Inc., 2009
Published by LYCEUM BOOKS, INC.
5758 S. Blackstone Ave.
Chicago, Illinois 60637
773 + 643-1903 (Fax)
773 + 643-1902 (Phone)
lyceum@lyceumbooks.com
http://www.lyceumbooks.com

6 5 4 3 2 1   09 10 11 12

ISBN 978-0-933478-50-0

Psycho-Social Intervention Scale © 2007 by Thomas O'Hare

Library of Congress Cataloging-in-Publication Data

O'Hare, Thomas. Essential skills of social work practice :
    assessment, intervention, evaluation / Thomas O'Hare.
        p.   cm.
    Includes bibliographical references.
    ISBN 978–1-933478–50–0
    1. Psychiatric social work.   2. Social service. 3. Social work education.   I. Title.
HV689.O42   2008
361.3'2—dc22   2008016970

Manufactured in Canada

Contents

APPENDICES

Preface

Essential Skills of Social Work Practice is designed to help social work students learn both the basics of effective psychosocial practice and how to use informed critical thinking to advance their skills over a professional lifetime. Basic practice skills are important for two reasons: first, they are necessary for working effectively with clients who experience mild to moderate psychosocial distress; second, they are the building blocks of advanced evidence-based practices, which are now required in work with more seriously troubled clients. As such, this book serves as both a foundation practice text and a bridge to learning advanced social work practices. The literature on advanced interventions is more thoroughly reviewed and described in *Evidence-Based Practices for Social Workers: An Interdisciplinary Approach* (O'Hare, 2005).

This text is divided into three parts. Part I addresses the core foundations of social work practice. Chapter 1 provides an overview of the three interrelated functions of effective practice: assessment, intervention, and evaluation. Chapter 2 explores the application of informed critical thinking to social work practice. This approach to professional development requires initiative, intellectual maturity, and a respect for the human behavior sciences; it thus serves as a counterweight to theoretical orthodoxy, tradition, postmodernist ideology, and other forces in the profession that reject empirical testing. Chapter 3 examines the basic ethical and liability concerns of social work practitioners, and emphasizes how using knowledge supported by evidence can help maintain high ethical practice standards and avoid malpractice lawsuits.

Part II explains and describes essential practice skills in greater detail. Chapter 4 examines how to conduct comprehensive assessments and use evaluation methods, two closely linked functions. Chapter 5 provides an overview of supportive skills, those core aspects of the intervention that build the working relationship and facilitate client engagement in the intervention process. Chapter 6 describes therapeutic coping skills, those more action-oriented skills that enhance the client's ability to cope with cognitive, emotional, and behavioral challenges. Chapter 7 examines case management skills, those activities of social work practice that are essential for working with multiproblem clients and coordinating complex intervention plans.

Part III explains how essential skills can be combined and applied to specific problems and disorders experienced by individuals, couples, children, and their families. Each of these five chapters includes a brief case study with an illustrative psychosocial assessment, intervention, and evaluation plan. These cases are fictional but inspired by clients seen by the author over many years of social work practice. Students should critique, argue, and strive to improve on these comprehensive plans, as well as apply the format with real clients in their practice internships. Chapter 8 addresses serious mental illnesses and mood and anxiety disorders in adults. Chapter 9 covers substance abuse and personality disorders. Chapter 10 focuses on skills used with distressed couples. Chapter 11 explains how to work in the context of family interventions with children who experience internalizing disorders (e.g., depression, anxiety), and chapter 12 does the same for externalizing disorders (e.g., conduct disorders and attention deficit/hyperactivity disorder). Although not exhaustively inclusive of psychosocial problems, these chapters describe essential skills and interventions that can, with some modification, be readily applied to most problems that social workers are likely to encounter in direct practice settings. Collectively, these are the competencies that social workers now need to master to help clients solve problems, enhance adaptive capabilities, and cope optimally with serious psychosocial challenges in their everyday lives.

The book also contains several appendixes designed to be useful aids for beginning practitioners. Appendix A includes the Psychosocial Intervention Scale (PSIS), developed by the author to help practitioners conduct an inventory of the skills and interventions they use with their clients, critically consider their rationale for selecting a particular combination of skills, and monitor how their skill selection changes over time with each client. Appendix B contains the Comprehensive Service Plan, designed to help beginning practitioners collect, summarize, and synthesize qualitative assessment information, make quantitative ratings of client well-being across multiple domains, and make informed recommendations for their intervention based on a complete multidimensional and functional assessment. The plan also encourages the development of simple evaluation indexes to monitor client progress. Appendix C outlines basic research guidelines to help students become better consumers of human behavior research and outcome studies, the source of social work's professional knowledge base. Together, these three tools are intended to help students use informed critical thinking to develop competence in social work assessment, intervention, and evaluation.

As beginning social workers develop their knowledge and skills through both classroom learning and practice experience, it is this author's hope that they will go beyond this text and learn advanced evidence-based practices relevant to their chosen field. By mastering the essentials, social work students will be better prepared to continue their professional development, to keep abreast of advances in practice research, and to remain active, critical learners throughout their careers.

Tom O'Hare
Sutton, Vermont

PART ONE

Conceptual Foundations of Essential Social Work Practice Skills

CHAPTER ONE

Overview: Defining and Linking Assessment, Intervention, and Evaluation

THE TEACHING OF BASIC or essential skills has a long tradition in social work and the allied helping professions. The sources that have influenced the development of the essential-skills curriculum in social work programs over the past century include theory, practice wisdom and tradition, and more recently, empirical research on the processes of psychosocial interventions and their relationships to client outcomes (e.g., Compton & Galaway, 1999; Hill & O'Brien, 2004; O'Hare, 2005; O'Hare & Collins, 1997; Orlinsky, Grawe, & Parks, 1994; Perlman, 1957; Richmond, 1918; Rogers, 1951; Shulman, 1999; Truax & Carkhuff, 1967; Woods & Hollis, 1990). Many other practice scholars, too numerous to name here, have contributed to the vast body of literature on how to help people in serious psychosocial distress. Until recently, however, little work has been done to provide a conceptual model of social work practice that incorporates a broad array of interdisciplinary influences from social work, counseling, clinical psychology, and the other allied helping professions and that emphasizes the skills supported by the preponderance of current process and outcome research.

Building on the prior accomplishments of the previously mentioned practice scholars, the current chapter (1) outlines a conceptual model of social work practice skills that is informed by practice experience and tested through research methods, and provides a foundation for constructing evidence-based practices in contemporary social work, and (2) incorporates essential assessment and evaluation skills into that model.

Practitioners who work with individuals, couples, families, and small groups experiencing psychosocial difficulties and disorders are primarily concerned with three key professional functions: assessment, intervention, and evaluation. Assessment requires that the practitioner have a competent

3

grasp of the relevant knowledge base pertinent to the client's presenting problems and a keen understanding of the client's difficulties and adaptive strengths as conceptualized from each client's unique point of view. Interventions comprise combinations of essential skills drawn from three major categories: (1) support, which engages the client in a working relationship and facilitates the intervention process; (2) therapeutic coping, which enhances the client's ability to cope with life's stressors, reduce symptoms of serious disorders, and solve problems; and (3) case management, which improves social and instrumental supports and coordinates complex services. A practitioner ideally develops an intervention plan by consulting the relevant practice research and then flexibly implementing the approach to fit the client's needs and circumstances. A practitioner evaluates an intervention by employing key measures of the client's difficulties at assessment and repeating those measures at key intervals during the intervention, at termination, and if possible, within six months to one year following the termination of services. The measures should include quantitative and qualitative indicators of the client's problems (e.g., depression) or intervention goals (e.g., improved relationship with parents, reduced alcohol use), so they can be used to monitor client progress and determine (to some degree) whether the intervention was successful.

Figure 1 is a model representing the reciprocal relationships among assessment, intervention, and evaluation. As Figure 1 depicts, assessments are grounded in human behavior research, guide treatment selection, and provide a baseline for evaluation of one's own practice. A practitioner selects an intervention on the basis of supporting outcome research but flexibly adapts implementation to individual client's problems, needs, and circumstances. Interventions across all treatment modalities comprise combinations of supportive, therapeutic coping, and case management skills. The practitioner then monitors the client's progress and evaluates treatment over time with both qualitative and quantitative indicators. Ongoing client change further informs the assessment. This process continues in a cumulative and interactive manner until termination of the case.

The skills combined to conduct assessment, intervention, and evaluation range from the simple to the complex. Becoming an effective advanced practitioner means first learning the essentials and then applying them to more challenging and complex problems over time as one gains additional knowledge and experience. This chapter briefly describes each essential aspect of practice and how all the aspects are interrelated. First, a brief

FIGURE 1. ESSENTIAL SKILLS OF SOCIAL WORK PRACTICE: ASSESSMENT, INTERVENTION, EVALUATION

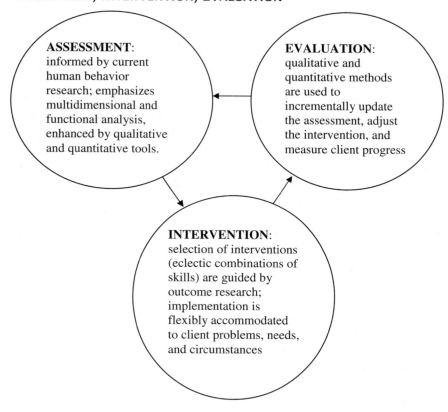

review of traditional practice theories is in order for two reasons: to understand their contributions to contemporary practice and to understand why each alone does not provide an adequate foundation for effective practice.

A Review of Traditional Practice Theories

Many practice scholars would agree that three or four major theories have guided social work over the second half of the twentieth century: psychodynamic; cognitive behavioral; family systems; and a collection of relatively atheoretical phenomenological approaches known as humanistic, constructivist, narrative, solution focused, existential, and client centered.

Some of these approaches have had important influences on contemporary practice, yet each by itself provides an inadequate foundation for understanding human behavior, conducting a complete assessment, explaining the processes of change, or offering intervention methods that are universally effective. In addition, some of these models have not been adequately tested, and others, when tested, have failed to show substantial benefits to clients.

Practice theory (also known as *orientation* or *school of thought*) is a catchall phrase that represents a collection of different types of theories and assumptions associated with a general intervention approach. The term *practice theory* refers to three different practice dimensions: (1) assumptions and theories about human behavior in the social environment (human behavior theory); (2) assumptions and theories about how people change (change-process theory); and (3) a collection of practice skills, techniques, and strategies intended to help people reduce psychosocial distress, reduce symptoms of psychological disorders, and improve coping capabilities (i.e., enhance individual strengths). Collectively, these activities are referred to as an "intervention" (Figure 2).

The first dimension of a practice theory addresses the following questions: Why do people behave as they do? How do human beings develop into happy and productive members of society or become unhappy or troublesome to others? What biological, psychological, social, cultural, and environmental factors affect people over time, and how do these risk and resilience factors interact to result in positive or negative adaptation across different areas of people's lives? Obviously, such questions are complex, and the research methods for answering them can be complicated as well. Nevertheless, a considerable amount of knowledge has been developed and cataloged that helps us understand some of the factors that contribute to major mental illnesses, addictions, childhood disorders, domestic violence, and so forth. The knowledge base of human behavior in the social environment is derived from the findings of multivariate research and provides a foundation for conducting informed assessments with clients. Human behavior theories are now understood to be complex and multivariate, and they incorporate a range of biopsychosocial influences. Thus, human behavior theories that overemphasize one factor or another (e.g., bad genes, bad mothering, bad learning experiences, dysfunctional thinking, stressful environment) are not considered sufficient to adequately explain the causes of human problems and cannot be relied on exclusively to support adequate assessments.

Human development is influenced by the complex interactions of both risk and resilience factors over time. Risks and resiliencies can originate

FIGURE 2. OVERVIEW OF THE TRADITIONAL PRACTICE THEORY MODEL

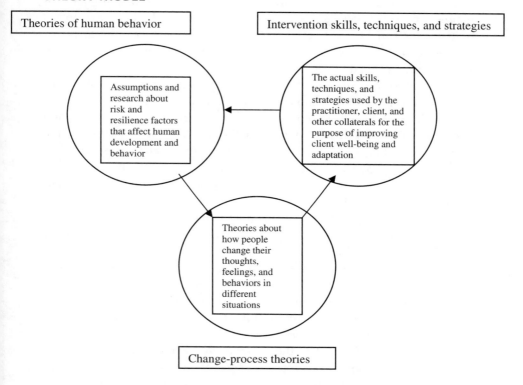

from and be expressed as biological, psychological, social, and environmental factors. They can also be conceptualized as two ends of a continuum that represent the influences of both individual psychosocial pathology and adaptive strengths. For example, if a biological predisposition to depression or substance abuse is a risk factor, having parents with no such history or parents who have modeled how to successfully cope with depression can be considered a strength or a form of resilience. The same can be said of positive versus negative psychosocial influences from one's family (e.g., good vs. negative modeling behavior of parents), quality of education, or other social or socioeconomic influences on one's life. As these examples imply, both risks and resiliencies can also be categorized as causal factors, change-process factors (i.e., mediating factors), or developmental or treatment outcomes. Biopsychosocial risks and resiliencies can affect human development (e.g., ability to handle stress), affect the process of change in treatment (e.g., ability to handle critical feedback and try new behaviors), or be the outcome of healthy psychosocial development or the result of an intervention (e.g., the degree to which a client learns to cope with bouts of depression or use social supports). Obviously, any and all of these forms of behavior can be considered either a risk factor or resilience factor depending on how, to what degree, and under what circumstances an individual expresses them.

The second area of knowledge required to support a practice theory derives from research on human-change processes. Change-process theories are human behavior theories that focus on how people change, and like human behavior theories in general, they are likely to include contributions from the biological, psychological, and other social sciences. This category of theory development addresses questions such as the following: What are the psychosocial mechanisms by which people change their behavior or situation for the better? What personal or environmental factors affect how people change? What are the biopsychosocial mechanisms that must be activated for people to achieve lasting change with or without formal psychosocial intervention? Answers to these questions can help us understand how people achieve success over their addictions; reduce impulsive behaviors such as self-mutilation; reduce symptoms of depression or psychosis; gain confidence to conquer anxieties and other fears; or simply become better communicators, problem solvers, more effective parents, or more loving partners.

Depending on the practice theory employed, change has been shown to result from a number of processes, such as increased mastery or self-efficacy; reinforcement from an external source; biological changes brought about by exercise or medication; or situational factors such as finances, improvement in a relationship, spiritual enlightenment, or the removal of some externally oppressive force. The reasons people change are complex and currently poorly understood in the behavioral sciences. Although theories abound, evidence to support specific change-process theories remains inconclusive at best. How these change processes can be activated to help clients overcome problems and enhance their adaptive capabilities is the focus and purpose of psychosocial interventions. However, although it is well known that some psychosocial interventions are effective, and that some are more effective than others for specific problems, much less is currently known about how these approaches help people change.

The third dimension of a practice theory, the intervention methods, are defined by the activities of the practitioner, the client, and the practitioner-client interactions—activities that help a client solve a problem or improve overall psychosocial well-being by activating some or all of the change processes discussed previously. Interventions comprise a collection of skills, intervention techniques, and overall strategies that help clients move toward their goals. Practice skills, collectively, are the efforts that constitute the intervention, and it is the use of these skills that can be defined, observed, and evaluated.

Although underlying human behavior and change-process theories are critically important matters, it is the actual skill combinations (i.e., the intervention) that can be more readily defined, taught, supervised, tested, and evaluated to determine whether they effectively help clients reduce symptoms, enhance coping abilities, and improve overall life circumstances. Thus, when adopting a practice theory, it is important to clearly distinguish the following separate but related parts: human behavior theory (i.e., the factors that cause the problem), change-process theory (i.e., the factors that explain how people change), and the intervention itself (i.e., the skills the practitioner uses to help the client). Confusion of these parts has often led to erroneous claims and abject confusion in the social work practice literature on the respective roles of theory and practice.

The Current State of Prominent Practice Theories

Although most practice theories and traditions have made positive contributions to effective social work practice, they all have both strengths and limitations. Some of the problems with current practice theories are the following: (1) scientific evidence often does not support the theoretical assumptions; (2) there may be some merit to the underlying theory, but the intervention methods have not been adequately tested or shown to be effective; and (3) the practice theory, in general, is not broad based enough to support a comprehensive approach to treating a wide range of psychosocial problems. Some social work practice theory texts do not use a critical framework to help students judge the relative validity of these theories but rather present practice theories as though they are all, more or less, equal and should be evaluated on their intuitive appeal to the student or the instructor. However, professional practice in all helping professions now demands more critical analysis of evidence in support of theories and practices. Although a thorough critique of each of these theories is not possible here, what follows is a brief overview and summary critique of the more prominent practice theories used in social work practice today.

Psychodynamic Theory

Psychodynamic theory has long been a mainstay for practitioners because of its intuitive appeal and its apparent explanatory power to illuminate how people develop psychologically (human behavior theory), how they change (change-process theory), and how practitioners attempt to help them (intervention techniques). Human behavior theory (according to psychoanalytic thought) is somewhat complex and actually represents a collection of somewhat different theories (e.g., Freud, 1938; Kernberg, 1976; Kohut, 1971). More recently, some psychodynamic social work practitioners have shown interest in relational theory, a reconstituted form of psychodynamic theory that also borrows from Bowlby's (1980) and Mahler, Pine, and Bergman's (1975) theories on childhood attachment. In brief, most psychodynamic practitioners work on the assumption that people develop internal representations of themselves and adaptive capacities (e.g., ego functioning, defenses) largely as a result of early childhood experiences associated with interactions with their primary caretakers, particularly their mothers. These internal representations and ego functions affect the way they cope with human relationships and other environmental stressors over time. Primarily as a result of these early influences, people develop interpersonal relations that either are generally growth enhancing or increasingly problematic. Much of the theoretical emphasis in psychoanalytic theory and its variants (e.g., ego psychology, object relations theory, self-psychology, attachment theory, relational theory) is on the way early childhood experiences establish relationship patterns (internalized models) that, in large part, determine interpersonal functioning over the life span. Assuming that clients have difficulties in intrapsychic and interpersonal functioning, they may seek treatment.

Although psychodynamic theorists and practitioners have rightly emphasized the importance of early childhood development, the core assumption that specific disorders can be predicted as a function of the timing and type of developmental disruption has not survived scientific scrutiny. Early disruptions in nurturance have not been shown to accurately predict the development of major mental illnesses, substance abuse, or specific emotional and behavioral disorders. However, cross-sectional and, more important, longitudinal studies have supported the conclusion that, to one degree or another, such problems are largely a result of the combined effects of genetic predisposition; early childhood experiences; and familial, social, environmental, and cultural influences that interact and reverberate over time. Thus, the important contributions of psychodynamic theoreticians and researchers have been greatly modified and incorporated into a more multivariate developmental framework.

Regarding intervention methods, psychodynamic practitioners have made important contributions to effective practice by emphasizing the importance of developing and maintaining a sound working alliance and creating a therapeutic environment in which the client can work through psychological injuries incurred in previous relationships. By using therapeutic techniques such as explanation and the interpretation of transference, practitioners attempt to help their clients better understand (through the change processes of insight and corrective emotional experience) how their past experiences affect them in the present. Through explanation and interpretation, practitioners attempt to help clients better understand their difficulties and learn to cope with their current relationships in a more enlightened and fulfilling way. Although some have questioned the specific efficacy of interpretation (Weiss, 1995), a contemporary model of evidence-based practice owes much to the psychodynamic emphasis on the working alliance, which is a cornerstone of effective practice.

Cognitive-Behavior Therapy

Cognitive-behavior therapy (CBT) evolved from three sources: scientific approaches to reasoning and cognition, classical and operant behavior theories, and social cognitive theory (Bandura, 1986, 1999; Beck, 1976, 1996). Aaron Beck's cognitive theory of depression has had a substantial impact on the evolution of CBT. For cognitive therapists, cognition is primary. Thus, for people to change their distressing thoughts about themselves, others, the world about them, and the future, they need to question and refute dysfunctional (i.e., irrational) ways of thinking: "If someone doesn't like me, then, it must be that I am no good"; "If I don't get into the school of my choice, I'm never going to be a success"; "I saw some students talking and laughing in the cafeteria; they must be making fun of me"; "If she leaves me, I will have to kill myself"; and so forth. By way of intervention technique, cognitive-behavior therapists guide the client in a critical examination of dysfunctional thinking (see the section "Critical Thinking" in chapter 2). The crux of gentle inquiry is to challenge the client to answer the question: "Where is the evidence to support your view that, for example, you can't live without her, or that everyone is laughing at you?" However, the goal of CBT is not to simply help clients reason their way out of their dilemma but to set up real-world tests to disconfirm or debunk the irrational belief (i.e., a process known as behavioral disconfirmation). The result of disconfirming dysfunctional beliefs can be highly reinforcing, and with increased self-confidence (i.e., self-efficacy), clients feel that they can continue to make progress with their particular difficulties.

Although cognitive practitioners focus on helping clients challenge irrational beliefs through critical thinking, traditional behaviorists emphasize gradually changing behaviors to positively reinforce change (i.e., increase the likelihood of change). Although behavioral interventions have shown generally positive results, they are unsatisfactory for some because they tend to downplay the cognitive component, or the client's view. Theoretically, behavioral models fell short because research has shown that external reinforcement procedures, though facilitative of change, are not always necessary or sufficient to produce change. Neobehaviorists and, later, social cognitive theorists like Albert Bandura began to take a more explicit scientific interest in the role of cognition in relationship to behavior and reinforcement. Social cognitive theory incorporates cognitive and behavioral theories but emphasizes the role of learning without immediate external reinforcement and stresses the importance of increasing self-efficacy, thus bolstering the belief that one can cope with challenging situations. Social cognitive theory provides a somewhat-integrated model for human behavior theories in that it emphasizes the interrelatedness of cognition, physiological responses (e.g., anxiety reduction), behavior change, and their reciprocal relationship in the social environment.

As a result of the combined influences of research in cognition, conditioning theories, and social cognitive theory, change processes in cognitive behavioral interventions now emphasize changing dysfunctional thinking, anxiety reduction methods, and the reduction of dysfunctional thinking through behavioral disconfirmation (i.e., practice in real life), with a resultant increase in one's belief that one can successfully cope with similar problems in the future (i.e., increased self-efficacy). Intervention methods used by cognitive-behavior therapists are quite eclectic, depending on the problem, and include directly addressing cognitive distortions by critically examining those thoughts (i.e., Socratic questioning); using covert (i.e., in the imagination) and in vivo (i.e., live) rehearsal, role-play, and practice of new behaviors; direct modification of physiological arousal (e.g., exercise, relaxation, and mediation techniques); improved problem-solving and communication skills; and the use of reinforcement techniques to improve one's own or another's (e.g., a child's) behavior.

To illustrate the combined influences of cognitive, behavioral, and social cognitive theory, consider the scenario of the young woman who suffers from severe shyness and general lack of self-confidence. After critically analyzing "the evidence" (or lack thereof) to support her view that no one likes her and everyone laughs at her, the young woman and the practitioner collaboratively plan weekly tasks to initiate brief conversations with some people in her class. The practitioner helps the client reduce her social anxiety through simple breathing techniques and provides guidance through role modeling and rehearsal to work on improving her conversation skills. After a few in vivo attempts (i.e., actual real-life experiments), she is likely to have had one or two successful conversations, and the expectation that people are always talking about or ridiculing her begins to dissipate. As a result of these reinforcing experiences, she grows in self-confidence, is less concerned about being laughed at, and presents herself as more confident (i.e., greater self-efficacy) and therefore more likable to others. In this way, current approaches to CBT have combined the developments of cognitive, behavioral, and social cognitive theories over the past forty years to result in a flexible and often creative evidence-based approach to practice.

Cognitive-behavior theory has spawned a wide array of effective interventions that have influenced and been combined with other interventions to ameliorate serious problems, including major mental illnesses, depression, anxiety disorders (including panic disorder with agoraphobia, obsessive-compulsive disorder, and posttraumatic stress disorder), eating disorders, substance abuse and addictions, borderline personality disorder, and the full range of childhood emotional and behavioral disorders. No other intervention methods can rival the totality of clinical outcome research that supports cognitive-behavior therapies.

Nevertheless, despite its success, the cognitive-behavioral model has limitations. Until recently, CBT theoreticians and practitioners often gave short shrift to the importance of the therapeutic relationship despite the evidence underscoring its importance as an effective dimension of psychosocial interventions. In addition, change-process research has not clearly supported theoretical assertions regarding how or why people change (e.g., increased self-efficacy, reduced dysfunctional thinking). Other interdisciplinary contributions are needed to enhance CBT approaches: developments in biological sciences regarding the brain and behavior, the addition of family intervention skills to broaden and improve assessments and intervention effectiveness with childhood disorders, an increased focus on processes associated with the therapeutic alliance, and a broader appreciation for environmental factors regarding the impact of cultural and socioeconomic influences. Nevertheless, cognitive-behavior therapies have set the benchmark for methodologically sound clinical outcome research, have provided practitioners with well-established effective interventions for a wide array of adult and childhood problems, and have become increasingly eclectic by incorporating multiple methods and modalities in its skill repertoire depending on the client's disorder or problems-in-living. Needless to say, empirical developments in cognitive-behavior theory highly influence most evidence-based practices today.

Phenomenological Therapies

Since the 1950s, a variety of relatively atheoretical therapies evolved, to some extent, as a counterweight to the dominant approach at the time— psychodynamic therapy—and, more recently, as a reactionary response to empirically supported interventions in general. These include existential (e.g., Frankl, 1963; May, 1969), narrative (e.g., Berg, 1999), humanist (e.g., Goldstein, 1986), solution-focused (e.g., O'Hanlon & Weiner-Davis, 1989), strength-based (e.g., Saleeby, 1996), and other similar phenomenological and experiential approaches. The term *phenomenological* generally refers to an attempt to describe the pure experience of the client, unfiltered and unfettered by psychological theories, research findings, or the practitioner's perspective. These approaches attempt to engage clients on their own psychological turf and work with their own inner experience (i.e., phenomenology) to define the problem and seek solutions. To varying degrees, phenomenological practitioners generally avoid, diminish, or reject outright theory-driven research on human behavior and feel that practice research somehow distorts or sullies client experience and the creativity and spontaneity of the client's change experience. This position might be considered a limitation in the current professional environment because practitioners are expected to provide research-based justification for their choice of intervention.

As for practice methods, the approaches generally incorporate a range of counseling techniques and pragmatic problem-solving approaches to help clients express their own unique view of problems and to construct potential solutions for them. Sometimes expressive, creative, or otherwise experiential techniques are employed to aid in this process. These techniques might include drawing, writing poetry, keeping diaries or journals, and using dramatic demonstration or other creative modes of expression. How these methods are arrived at is, perhaps, somewhat spontaneous or intuitive, and clear or testable guidelines for implementation are usually not provided. In fact, such approaches are often difficult to define, and few research-based guidelines are available to either clarify or justify the use of these methods with specific problems. However, a key strength of phenomenological approaches is the emphasis on exploring and understanding clients' experience from their unique perspective and working with clients' strengths to develop intervention methods rather than impose interventions on clients.

Client-centered therapy (also called "person-centered therapy"; Raskin & Rogers, 1995; Rogers, 1951) was also developed as a relatively atheoretical approach to interpersonal helping that focused on the client's inner experience. However, counseling and psychotherapy-process researchers later refined and further developed its key concepts over many years. As a result, client-centered therapy stands apart from other phenomenological approaches in that it has spawned the research foundation of modern psychotherapy process-outcome research. Rogers and his colleagues emphasized the inherent transformational abilities of the client and the practitioner's abilities to express empathy, authenticity, positive regard, and respect for the client. Developing the working relationship on the basis of these principles remains a cornerstone of the psychosocial helping professions to this day. Client-centered counseling made unique and long-standing contributions to psychosocial practice as a result of the hundreds of studies conducted to define, measure, and test the efficacy of his basic helping concepts. Thus, the evidence for the essential role of the working relationship and the core helping skills of client-centered practice remain quite strong (Hill & O'Brien, 2004; O'Hare, Tran, & Collins, 2002; Orlinsky et al. 1994; Truax & Carkhuff, 1967).

In summary, proponents of narrative, existential, solution-focused, and other atheoretical approaches emphasize understanding clients' inner experience and helping the client to use their innate abilities, skills, and strengths to find lasting solutions to their difficulties. As such, they provide an important foundation for working with a wide array of clients, but because of the lack of clear treatment guidelines, they must often be complemented with evidence-based approaches especially when working with clients who have moderate to severe psychosocial difficulties and disorders.

Family Therapies

Family therapies are actually a diverse group of practices designed to treat individual, couple, or family problems by including some or all members of the family in the intervention. However, family therapies vary widely in both theoretical foundation and intervention methods. Thus, family therapy is not really a coherent theoretical approach as much as it is a framework within which various theories and practices are applied to understand and deal with families in distress. To be more specific, it makes more sense to stipulate which type of family therapy is the focus of interest: psychodynamic family therapy, behavioral family therapy, humanistic family therapy, and so on.

Nevertheless, there appear to be some broad assumptions common among family therapies (Becvar & Becvar, 1996; Nichols & Schwartz, 2006). First, working with family members is often a more effective approach because practitioners can see how family members interact as a system and can better understand how those interactions affect the problems of the identified client (i.e., the person, usually a child, who is presented as having or expressing the problem of immediate concern). Second, changes in the behavior of one family member tend to cause changes in other members. Third, the family system is made up of subsystems (e.g., parents, siblings, other alliances) that help maintain problems or can be keys to solving them. Fourth, changing the way the whole family behaves can help maintain changes over time because it is difficult for individuals to change within a family if other members undermine those changes, deliberately or unintentionally. Last, family problems often have a way of being transferred from one generation to the next.

Behaviorally oriented family therapy (including some strategic and structural approaches) has been extensively studied and shown to be effective for a variety of vulnerable clients including families with a member who suffers from schizophrenia, substance use disorders in a parent or adolescent, conduct-disordered children and adolescents, emotional disorders in children, eating disorders, anxiety, and depression, among others. Behavioral family practitioners emphasize the identification of problem behaviors, carry out a functional assessment of how family members interact, track the positive and negative consequences of those behaviors, and help family members change the way they communicate and problem solve to resolve difficulties and reinforce more constructive forms of interaction. These approaches incorporate basic family therapy principles (e.g., interactions, subsystems) but also use core behavioral approaches: cognitive examination of beliefs, practicing new behaviors in the consulting office and at home, promoting mutually reinforcing behaviors among family members, focusing on clear goals, and evaluating outcomes. Behavioral family therapies have also been used to work with families in which one member has a serious disorder such as a major mental illness or addiction to alcohol or other drugs. Evidence to support behaviorally oriented family and couples therapies is substantial, and the approaches are now strongly recommended for work with both emotional and behavioral problems in children and adolescents (Northey, Wells, Silverman, & Bailey, 2003), substance abuse problems (O'Farrell & Fals-Stewart, 2003; Stanton & Shadish, 1997), and mental illness (Dixon, Adams, & Luksted, 2000), among other family-related problems. Beyond working with the immediate family, behavioral family systems approaches have also been applied within a broader ecosystems model whereby the practitioner works with the family and other members of the community: law enforcement, schools, and other important collaterals with a vested interest in improving the welfare of the family. Multisystemic therapy (Henggeler, Schoenwald, Borduin, Rowland, & Cunningham, 1998) is one exemplary approach.

Change-process theories in family therapies reflect the underlying theoretical assumptions of that particular type of family therapy. So, for example, psychodynamic family therapy relies heavily on relationship development and interpretation; behavioral family therapy emphasizes helping clients interact in ways that are more reinforcing. However, as with individual interventions, theories about how families change remain somewhat speculative. Thus, the only clear guidelines currently available for judging the relative efficacy of various family therapy interventions are drawn from the relevant practice outcome research on working with families. With a few exceptions, the bulk of research has been done on behaviorally oriented family therapies.

An Interdisciplinary Evidence-Based Approach to Social Work Practice

Various schools of practice have made important contributions to contemporary effective social work. The combination of a sound working alliance, respect for the client's experience and strengths, the use of effective coping skills, and case management strategies provide a coherent framework for effective practice with a wide array of psychosocial challenges. Given that no individual practice theory is sufficiently comprehensive to understand our clients and intervene in their problems, a more systematic interdisciplinary framework is needed to inform social work practice. The approaches applied in this framework, however, must now be supported with guidelines based on practice research. What follows is a brief overview of the essential assessment, intervention, and evaluation skills now required for effective social work practice. These skills will be examined in greater depth in part 2 of this book, and how these skills can be flexibly combined to form evidence-based practices will be addressed in part 3.

Assessment

A Range of Assessment Strategies

In social work practice, *assessment* is a general term that refers to a range of strategies used to describe, analyze, categorize, measure, and otherwise help practitioners better understand their client's difficulties (Bellack & Hersen, 1998; Franklin & Jordan, 2003; O'Hare, 2005; Sadock & Sadock, 2003). There is a wide, varied literature on assessment but little agreement regarding what assessment is. For example, in conducting an assessment with a depressed client (here, Bob), a practitioner may do one or more of the following:

- Qualitatively describe Bob's difficulties solely on the basis of his own perception and understanding of the problem (Bob might say, "I feel like I'm being crushed by the weight of the world").
- Apply a psychiatric diagnosis (major depression, 296.00)
- Rate the severity of Bob's problems in one or more areas of his life (on a four-point scale, where 0 = "none," 1 = "mild," 2 = "moderate," 3 = "serious," and 4 = "severe")
- Analyze a sample of Bob's daily behavior in detail to identify factors that seem to be associated with his depression (e.g., after discussing Bob's day-to-day struggles at length, the practitioner may try to help him connect the dots by pointing out the following: "It appears that you feel worse after you have consumed a lot of alcohol over the course of a couple of weeks, you've missed work, and your wife is angry at you for neglecting her and your children. Your kids don't sound too happy with you either. Could your depression be, at least in part, a consequence of heavy drinking and the consequences related to drinking?")
- Observe the interactions of family members to determine how problems are caused or maintained. In a family visit, the family expresses feelings to one another about Bob's drinking and neglect of his obligations at home and work. The social worker observes the communication patterns, body language, the tone of their expressions, and so on

All of these methods of assessment have useful qualities to recommend them, and they all have limitations because, as described earlier, the human behavior theories on which they are based have limited explanatory power. Therefore, to apply only one form of assessment is likely to prove inadequate in most cases. Thus, a pragmatic approach to assessment would combine some of the more useful aspects of different methods and capitalize on the guidance of research literature when relevant.

The Critical Role of "Person" Factors

Although practitioners should approach assessment with the understanding that all clients are unique, one should also consider the important roles of sex, age, race, ethnicity, culture, language, socioeconomic level, sexual orientation, and other client-identifying characteristics that are often grouped as demographics; however, I prefer (for lack of a better phrase) to call them *personal identity factors*. In the context of human behavior theory and research (in addition to some degree of common sense), these factors often provide important clues to variation in types and severity of problems among both individuals and client groups. For example, on average, men consume more alcohol than women, women are much more likely to meet diagnostic criteria for clinical depression than are men, clients from racial minorities are more likely to feel reluctant to engage in treatment in an agency staffed predominantly by whites, a recent immigrant may have little understanding of what behavioral norms are expected in a therapy clinic, and so on. Although one should avoid stereotyping people by such personal identity factors, they often help guide assessment strategies by pointing out known risk and resilience factors that, on average, may represent some groups of clients more than others. However, the factors should be determined by research findings (e.g., culturally relevant approaches to treating mental illness) and in-depth appreciation for the experience of each client, not by folk wisdom or the practitioner's personal experience. Clients with similar racial, ethnic, or cultural backgrounds, for example, may have different personal views on the meaning of those characteristics. How to engage clients on these important issues (e.g., cultural competence) will be more thoroughly addressed in chapter 4.

Sources of Assessment Information and Methods for Gathering It

A comprehensive assessment strategy requires gathering salient information, ideally from multiple sources and using multiple information gathering methods. Sources of assessment information are those people or databases that provide information that helps the practitioner better understand clients' problems, strengths, and other salient facts about their situation. Other people who provide assessment information directly or indirectly (e.g., physician's record) are referred to as *collaterals* or *collaborators*. Such sources include the client, family members or other relatives, school personnel, law enforcement or criminal justice workers, and other medical or human service professionals, among others. Relevant information about the client may be obtained from these parties or from pertinent reports.

Methods of information gathering encompass those techniques employed to obtain information from various sources. The most commonly employed method for gathering assessment information is face-to-face interviews, which are based primarily on the client's self-report. This method may be relatively unstructured, but most interviewers have some key information that they plan to examine, such as the client's mental status, quality of relationships with family or others in the community, general health status, use of alcohol or other drugs, and so forth. Given that the interview is somewhat structured, it is referred to as a *semistructured interview*. Because a large amount of essential assessment data can be gathered in the semistructured format, the practitioner wants to hit all the main points but can do so with considerable flexibility to accommodate the client's pacing, priorities, style of communication, and unexpected disclosures. With practice, a skilled social worker can amass a considerable amount of important qualitative information in a fairly short period of time (for different aspects of interviewing techniques, see chapter 4).

Other information-gathering methods include direct observation of clients (e.g., social worker observing a child with a behavioral problem in school or a treatment facility) and the use of clinical rating scales and similar quantitative instruments (to be discussed subsequently). For a behaviorally troubled child or adolescent, obtaining various points of view from several family members as well as teachers and an attending physician or the child's tutor or coach is likely to give a more complete assessment picture. In addition, combining large amounts of qualitative information from semistructured interviews and quantitative information from clinical rating scales can provide a rich and useful assessment and basis for ongoing monitoring and evaluation of each case. Above all, practitioners must remember that no client or collateral (collaborator) is interviewed without the informed consent of the client (or guardian), and when the data are collected, every effort is made to protect the client's confidentiality (for further discussion, see chapter 3).

Making Sense of Assessment Information

A practitioner may gather pages of assessment information from the client, family members, and others involved in his or her care. What to make of all this information, however, is another matter. As noted earlier, there are a variety of different theoretical approaches to assessment based on different assumptions about the nature of client's problems (e.g., a disease, a behavior problem, dysfunctional thinking). Yet, considering all the different models of assessment, there are two overarching themes that encompass them: first, the basic premise that clients' problems are caused by multiple biopsychosocial influences, both past and present, and that these problems manifest in multiple areas of a client's life: psychological, social, physical, and economic, among others. These characteristics of problems (i.e., having multiple causes and manifesting multiple psychosocial effects) constitute multidimensionality.

Second, although clients with similar problems (e.g., addictions, depression) manifest similar characteristics and difficulties, each client experiences those problems differently, which becomes evident when practitioners conduct detailed assessments of the client's day-to-day life. A detailed analysis of an individual client's thoughts, feelings, behaviors, and situational factors that influence their behavior will reveal a complex interplay of vulnerabilities and strengths that affect the problem. These factors do not occur randomly but tend to follow a pattern. Even clients with major mental illnesses have good days and bad days, strengths and deficits that appear to coincide with improvements or declines in their condition. Troubled families in which conflict is frequent and intense also experience times of relative tranquillity when parents or siblings seem to get along, some affection and cooperation is apparent, and serious problems abate. These patterns revealing both problematic and more adaptive experiences need to be identified so practitioners and their clients can accentuate adaptive behaviors and try to diminish behaviors that seem to maintain problems or precipitate crises. This unique patterning and sequencing of behaviors and related factors addresses the functionality dimension of an assessment. The detailed analysis of factors that seem related to a client's daily experiences is referred to as *functional analysis* because the purpose is to tentatively determine and better understand how the problem functions (i.e., how it works). Taken together, contemporary assessment informed by both current research and client experience is referred to as *multidimensional-functional (MDF) assessment* (O'Hare, 2005; for details on how to conduct an MDF assessment, see chapter 4).

Using Clinical Rating Scales and Other Measurement Tools for Assessment and Evaluation

Evaluation of every case begins during the assessment phase. Although the rationale for evaluation and the use of various evaluation designs will be discussed further on in this chapter, it is important at this point to discuss the use of indexes and scales. What follows is a brief overview of the different types of instruments employed in everyday practice to enhance qualitative assessment and to lay a quantitative foundation for monitoring client progress.

Measurement instrument is, perhaps, the most generic term that encompasses a range of tools for measuring the frequency, intensity, or duration of various client problems. These tools range from the simple (e.g., counting the number of swear words Johnny uses each day) to the complex (e.g., scales that measure quality of life). They may also measure one or more domains of client experience (e.g., thoughts, feelings, behaviors). Measurement tools are not intended to substitute for a comprehensive qualitative assessment, but they serve as a useful adjunct to provide a quantitative baseline of client well-being in one or more areas (e.g., level of depression, anxiety). Scales also are a handy monitoring tool for gauging client progress during and after intervention. Measurement tools have some advantages over qualitative assessment in that the data collected from many clients in the same program can be aggregated and used for program evaluation, something that is much less practical with large volumes of qualitative reports. When used repeatedly on large numbers of clients, scales can provide important tracking information to determine whether a client or group of clients is improving, staying about the same, or getting worse. In addition, most measurement tools can be tested for two critical qualities: the consistency with which they measure some aspect of human behavior (i.e., reliability) and the accuracy with which they measure that behavior (i.e., validity). These matters will be discussed more in-depth in chapter 4.

There are generally four types of measurement tools used in everyday practice: (1) diagnostic categories, (2) simple indexes, (3) unidimensional scales, and (4) multidimensional scales. Although diagnosis is generally not considered a form of measurement, in fact, it is. Categorization is a basic and somewhat useful form of measurement (i.e., nominal measurement), and the *Diagnostic and Statistcal Manual of Mental Disorders*, fourth edition (DSM-IV), also allows for some degree of measuring the severity of the condition. Although diagnosis is an important part of an assessment, especially when dealing with serious mental illnesses, there are considerable limitations to using the DSM-IV, and psychiatric diagnosis is no substitute for a complete assessment.

Simple indexes may be among the most basic and useful tools for quick assessment and continuous monitoring of client progress. Assuming the client's accurate self-report or others' observational reports, indexes provide straightforward, useful information and are generally considered reliable and accurate with most clients (unless there is good reason to believe that the client has motive to distort information). Some examples include number of drinks consumed daily, number of good days a conflicted couple reports, number of days a young person attends class (or number of days truant), a student's overall grade point average, number of times a young woman with schizophrenia initiates a conversation in the community, level of intensity of panic attacks, intensity of depression on any given day, duration of time-out for an oppositional child, number of days sober for a mom trying to regain custody of her child, and so on. The variety of measures that a practitioner can create to specifically suit a client's needs or situation is limitless. One needs only to accurately define a problem of concern and decide whether the best way is to measure its frequency (i.e., how often it occurs), intensity (i.e., severity of the problem), or duration (i.e., how long it lasts). Sometimes these indexes are referred to as *self-anchored scales* when they measure the client's subjective report (e.g., severely depressed) rather than an observable measure (days absent from work).

Unidimensional scales are instruments that use multiple items to measure the same concept. Valid scales are typically developed by interviewing a representative sample of people that includes those who do and those who do not experience the given problem to one degree or another. For example, a scale for measuring depression may contain twenty items, some of which might include "I feel blue," "I don't know if I can go on living," "I have little interest in things that I used to enjoy," "I don't sleep very well," "I feel guilty," and so on. Items like these have been shown to correlate statistically with a diagnosis of clinical depression. Depending on the purpose of the scale, the items may be measured by frequency (e.g., all of the time, most of the time, some of the time, seldom, none of the time), intensity (e.g., extremely, moderately, a little), or duration (a day, a week, a month, a year). Most scales measure all the items on the same rating system, though that is not always the case. In addition, some scales contain items that are scored in the opposite direction (e.g., "I feel happy" may be an item in a depression scale). If the client rated that item as "seldom," then that item would indicate some degree of depression for that client. The benefit of scales is that they use multiple items that enhance reliability (consistency) and validity (accuracy). The client's level of depression is gauged not on his or her response to one item but on responses to many items. In addition, the use of a scale improves the likelihood that practitioners will not forget to address key items, such as one that measures the frequency or intensity of suicidal thoughts. In this way, the adjunctive use of a scale improves the consistency and accuracy of assessments by indicating client responses to potentially high-risk behaviors.

Multidimensional scales share the same qualities as unidimensional scales but measure multiple aspects of a problem. As are unidimensional scales, they are designed and tested to optimize reliability and validity but are used to measure more complex problems. A scale that measures quality of life, for example, may use five items to measure each of the following: satisfaction with living situation, health, psychological well-being, relationships, and spirituality. For ten domains of living, a total of fifty items may be used (five for each). Each domain can be scored individually to measure a specific domain (e.g., family satisfaction), and an overall global-life-satisfaction score might be used by combining all subscale measures. In addition to several quality-of-life scales, multidimensional scales have been designed to measure psychiatric symptoms, addiction severity, posttraumatic stress, childhood disorders, and many other areas relevant to social work practice.

Practitioners may decide to use only one type of measurement or a combination of measures. The selection of instruments may vary from client to client, or a program may use one uniform instrument package at client assessment and during intervention and postintervention to evaluate a program. Some instruments are proprietary; that is, they can be used only with the permission of the scale creator (often for a fee), but there is a growing array of scales that are readily available in the public domain for no cost. Practitioners can locate these fairly easily, as they are often compiled in reference books in the library or on various Web sites. Practitioners should also place a high value on a scale's utility (i.e., practical use). In addition to being reliable and valid, scales should be relatively brief so that they can be incorporated into routine assessment or evaluation without placing undue demand on the client or on agency staff.

Assessment, overall, is both a qualitative and quantitative effort. A competent MDF assessment must be thorough, be grounded in current human behavior research, and describe the unique aspects of the client's day-to-day experiences. Scales should be used to augment the assessment and lay a foundation for evaluation. Summarizing assessment data succinctly is a challenge, and linking this information to the overall service plan requires further knowledge regarding effective practices, the subject to which we now turn.

Intervention

Defining Effective Interventions

Interventions are combinations of skills applied by practitioners, their clients, and collateral participants (e.g., family members, teachers) and implemented for the purpose of reducing symptoms, resolving problems, enhancing adaptive capabilities, and improving the overall psychosocial well-being of the client. Interventions include skills and combinations of skills that help clients achieve important intervention goals (e.g., lower depression, enhance couple's communication, increase prosocial behavior in behaviorally disordered children, improve school performance, reduce symptoms of psychosis). Later chapters will examine practice skills and their application to specific problems in greater detail.

In brief, hundreds of studies by clinician-researchers have revealed that a wide variety of practice skills provide effective care. However, careful analysis of different practice approaches has revealed that these skills can be categorized under three major headings (Lambert & Bergin, 1994; O'Hare, 2005; Orlinsky & Howard, 1986; Orlinsky et al., 1994):

- *Supportive or facilitative skills*: Efforts to engage clients in a therapeutic relationship and facilitate client change
- *Therapeutic coping skills*: Intervention efforts that engage clients in actively changing the way they think, feel, and behave to solve problems, enhance adaptive strengths, cope better with life's challenges, and reduce symptoms of serious disorders
- *Case-management skills*: Efforts that help clients deal with social and environmental barriers, gain access to needed resources, enhance social supports, and coordinate efforts of various service providers

As with other professional activities, beginning or basic interventions may comprise one or two key skills to address mild to moderate problems, whereas more complex and advanced interventions are more likely to be combinations of skills that have been shown to be effective in controlled practice research. Thus, the emphasis here is on learning those basic or essential skills that alone or in combination provide the best chance of ameliorating a client's psychosocial distress and improving the client's problem-solving and coping abilities over time. Combinations of skills shown in controlled practice research to be effective with moderate to severe psychosocial problems and disorders are now referred to as *evidence-based practices* (Goodheart, Kazdin, & Sternberg, 2006; Nathan & Gorman, 2007; O'Hare, 2005; Stout & Hayes, 2005; Thyer, 2004). These approaches now define the benchmark for competent social work practice.

Supportive, therapeutic coping, and case management skills are applied in unique ways depending on the client's problems, challenges, and needs. For example, the application of empathic listening (a supportive skill) with a seriously thought-disordered person is quite different from its application with a person experiencing a normal but difficult grief reaction. Using role-play, problem solving, or graduated exposure (therapeutic coping skills) to

help a young man reduce obsessive-compulsive rituals is quite different from using the same techniques to help a couple improve their communication and parenting skills. Coordinating the efforts of several providers and advocating for client benefits (case management skills) take on a different character whether one is working on a child abuse case or attempting to help a severely disabled elderly person. Essential skills in social work practice share a common research and practice base but take on unique application depending on the client's problems and needs. The definition of a coherent set of skills that can be used individually and in combination is essential for teaching, implementing, supervising, evaluating, and researching social work interventions.

Optimally Combining Essential Skills

Although essential practice skills can be used individually for discrete problems, they are often combined as evidence-based practices. For example, after employing supportive and facilitative skills to engage a troubled couple who have been fighting bitterly and are considering divorce, the practitioner may use both supportive and therapeutic coping skills to help them examine their interactions with each other in a more calm and less reactive manner, to have them take turns listening carefully to each other without interrupting, to ask them to show that they can identify each other's needs, to communicate their thoughts and feelings in a more sensitive manner, and to work on sharing household and other responsibilities. Case management activities may not be required at all in such a case. In contrast, for a young mentally ill mother who recently had her two children removed from her home under suspicion of neglect, supportive and facilitative skills may be more challenging to implement given the client's suspicions and other cognitive distortions related to her illness. Therapeutic coping skills might include psychoeducation about her illness, the importance of taking medication to ameliorate her symptoms, coaching her in better parenting skills, and teaching stress-management skills to help her deal better with trauma-related anxiety and depression. Case management skills would likely be required to help the client maintain her benefits and access to mental health care, to coordinate services, to help her manage her money, and to advocate for her with the courts and child welfare department. Most if not all cases will employ some combination of essential supportive, therapeutic coping, and case management skills, but the skills will be applied in different ways depending on the individual challenges facing the client. How these skills are combined and implemented is guided by both clinical outcome research and the use of the practitioner's judgment in concert with client input and continuous evaluative feedback.

However, to simply recommend that treatment be tailored to client needs means little if there are no empirical practice guidelines to plan the intervention. (Even the most innovative tailors and designers learned from patterns before they then learn to creatively deviate from them in a thoughtful way.) Although practice typically includes some trial-and-error efforts, exclusive reliance on practice wisdom or one's presumed creative powers is neither adequate nor necessary in professional social work practice and may even result in substandard interventions. Evidence-based practice guidelines can help practitioners reduce some of the guesswork in treatment planning with clients who struggle with a wide array of problems, from major mental illnesses to addictions, eating disorders, anxiety, traumatic reactions, depression, and emotional and behavioral problems in children. Evidence-based practices are made up of varying configurations of essential skills. These configurations of skills have been packaged to provide practitioners with research-supported intervention guidelines to better serve their clients. However, before practitioners can effectively learn evidence-based practices, they must master the essential supportive, therapeutic coping, and case management skills explained in these chapters. The Psycho-Social Intervention Scale will be described at the end of this chapter to help practitioners evaluate their own use of essential social work practice skills and to consider how to combine them to help different clients.

Applying Essential Skills to Family Interventions

The term *treatment modality* refers primarily to the configuration and relationship of clients who participate in the intervention. The traditional service modalities are individual, couple, family, and group work. Other than designating the number and relationship of the participants, these modalities do not refer to any particular practice theory or intervention approach. For example, as noted earlier, the term *family therapy* refers to interventions conducted with some or all members of a family. There are many different forms of family therapy, and the skills applied are likely to vary considerably depending on theoretical assumptions and the specific intervention methods. *Group therapy* refers to working with the members of a group of persons who are generally not related in a familial way to one another. Group therapy can be unstructured or structured, directive or nondirective, psychoeducational or therapeutic, psychodynamic, behavioral, Gestalt, and so on. Regardless of modality, the interventions comprise some combination of essential skills. Supportive, therapeutic coping, and case management skills are applied across all modalities, and their combination determines whether the intervention will be effective.

Despite the differences across major schools of family therapy, they do share several common assumptions and intervention methods (Becvar & Becvar, 1996; Nichols & Schwartz, 2006). Family therapies are characterized by recognizing family hierarchies, structures and alliances, the importance of interaction and communication patterns, the role of the identified client, and the significance of generational influences. However, these aspects of family therapy apply more to ongoing assessment of family functioning than to the intervention skills used. With regard to intervention, supportive skills apply to family therapies in the following way:

- Joining with the family; that is, engaging and developing a working alliance with some or all family members
- Developing intervention goals and role expectations of both practitioner and family members
- Using accurate and empathic listening to each member in turn
- Demonstrating respect and positive regard for all members
- Using motivational interviewing methods (e.g., not arguing, rolling with the resistance)

Therapeutic coping skills include the following:

- Psychoeducation
- Encouraging and modeling constructive communication
- Exploring dysfunctional beliefs family members have toward one another or other extended family members
- Using stress-management techniques with some or all family members
- Helping family members express intense feelings in more constructive ways
- Role modeling; rehearsing; and practicing better communication, problem solving, or carrying out of specific tasks
- Demonstrating how to apply reinforcement between partners (e.g., increase caring behaviors) and between parents and their children (i.e., improved parenting skills)
- Engaging in self-monitoring so family members can anticipate problems, apply what they have learned to interrupt problems, and evaluate their progress over time.

More specifically, when helping parents deal with emotionally and behaviorally troubled children and adolescents, therapeutic coping skills can be adapted accordingly:

- Teaching of basic behavioral parenting skills (e.g., demonstration of nurturance through caring behaviors and play, positive disciplining skills through clear directives; balancing rewards for prosocial behaviors and mild sanctions for unacceptable behaviors)
- Use of modeling and role play to demonstrate to a child how the parent wants things done (e.g., cleaning up the room, getting settled down to study, playing with siblings)
- Demonstration of how to monitor a child's progress and shape behavior by stringing together a series of rewards and sanctions to reach long-term goals

Social workers should learn to apply therapeutic coping skills at all levels (e.g., individual, couple, family). Sometimes these skills can be applied one level at a time, and other times concurrently. For example, if a child has a serious behavioral disorder that parental conflict exacerbates, the intervention may have to address each level in turn. First, the couple may have to learn to communicate better and deal with some of their own interpersonal problems as partners (e.g., money concerns, alcohol abuse, infidelity). Second, the social worker may have to focus on helping them collaborate to improve their parenting skills (e.g., setting limits, rewarding and sanctioning behaviors consistently instead of undermining each other). Third, the social worker may then focus on helping the child cope with emotional distress (e.g., learning to accurately identify feelings, finding more constructive ways to cope with anger). Last, the social worker may apply some of these core skills (e.g., communication, psychoeducation) when dealing with the larger social system (e.g., parenting education, classes in local schools). However, these skills are likely to be combined with case management skills as in the following examples:

- Networking and coordinating interventions with the school administration, school psychologist, and classroom teacher to generalize the child's improvements from home to the school
- Helping parents and teachers work from the same page to help the child maintain behavioral and academic improvements
- Advocating for a parent's rights in court-ordered cases
- Helping a family bolster social and instrumental supports to reduce isolation and provide for basic financial needs and ensure eligibility

for other benefits if available (e.g., public health insurance for children)

Although essential supportive, therapeutic coping, and case management skills apply as readily to family interventions as to individual cases, their application can be more challenging when working with a seriously troubled family.

Applying Essential Skills to Group Work

Working with groups in social work practice takes different forms. Perhaps the more common approaches include traditional psychotherapeutic interventions (Yalom, 2005) and behaviorally oriented groups for working with clients who experience other specific problems or disorders (e.g., Bieling, McCabe, & Antony, 2006). Groups are also used for early intervention prevention programs, such as youths at risk for substance use or other high-risk behaviors. Traditional psychotherapeutic groups tend to emphasize personal disclosure and expression of feelings, and they address the way group members interact with the practitioner and other group members to engender insight and improved relationships. Although such groups are not well researched, it is reasonable to assume that some clients are likely to benefit from these experiences. The essential skills applied include supportive skills (e.g., empathic listening, encouraging expression of feelings) and therapeutic coping skills (e.g., improving communication skills, examining conflicted thoughts and feelings regarding relationship problems). Although case management skills might be applied (e.g., referral for medication), they are less likely to be emphasized in insight-oriented group therapy.

Psychoeducational groups are commonly used for a wide range of purposes. Some examples include high school students learning to cope effectively with pressures to have sex and use alcohol and other drugs, parents learning to cope more effectively with their mentally ill young adult children, teaching young single moms how to balance the duties of motherhood while pursuing their education, and helping the elderly cope with depression and loneliness. The list of potential uses for psychoeducational groups is long. Although psychoeducational groups rely primarily on didactic methods, the use of supportive skills is critical. Practitioners still need to connect with their audience; listen carefully to their concerns; and communicate positive regard, respect, empathy, and genuineness. They also need to engender motivation in group members to apply what they learn in their daily lives. Psychoeducation is also a key therapeutic coping skill. Providing information is a rather direct way to alter cognitions (i.e., change beliefs, expectations, and attributions). Young-adult group members attending a psychoeducational group regarding sexual behavior and the use of alcohol and other drugs are often poorly informed about the risks associated with date rape and transmission of infectious diseases, as well as what is required to prevent pregnancy. Although providing information alone is often insufficient to dissuade people from engaging in high-risk behaviors, evidence suggests that it is an essential component.

Behaviorally oriented groups are often used with clients who demonstrate more serious difficulties, such as co-occurring mental illness and substance abuse, substance abuse groups with convicts who have been released from prison, domestic violence (e.g., anger management) groups for offenders, conduct-disordered adolescents, young women diagnosed with eating disorders, or group work with persons diagnosed with borderline personality disorder. Behavioral groups also emphasize the application of essential supportive skills to develop a working relationship with clients, facilitate communication, and enhance motivation. However, behavioral groups are also likely to place a heavy emphasis on a wide array of therapeutic coping skills: challenging dysfunctional cognitions (e.g., regarding substance use, using violence to cope with conflict), practicing self-regulation regarding impulses connected to intense emotions (e.g., self-mutilation, domestic violence, binge-purging by the bulimic client), learning behavioral coping skills through role-play and rehearsal (e.g., saying, "No thanks" to an offer of alcohol or other drugs, seeking social supports when the impulse to strike out in anger is provoked), using communication and problem-solving skills to improve relationships, and learning stress-management skills to enhance an overall healthier lifestyle. In working with clients who experience more serious problems such as these, case management skills are also likely to be used extensively to coordinate services among providers, hospitalize clients in crisis, act as liaison for court-ordered interventions, advocate for a mentally ill client, and enhance social and instrumental supports when needed.

Before becoming proficient at using more advanced family and group interventions, practitioners must first master essential supportive, therapeutic coping, and case management skills. Once these building blocks of effective interventions are mastered, practitioners can learn and effectively implement evidence-based practices with individuals, couples, families, and groups.

A Note on Culturally Competent Practice

Although all practitioners want to provide services that clients consider respectful and congruent with their own cultural background and beliefs, the concept of culturally competent practice remains largely theoretical and untested. For starters, *cultural background* is a heterogeneous term that precludes an easy one-to-one matchup between a client's race or ethnicity and a specific approach to assessment and treatment. Although culturally informed engagement processes (i.e., working alliance) used early on in the intervention may be critical to successful client engagement, there is currently no body of empirical evidence to guide practitioners in designing or adjusting interventions to fit the client's cultural background in a way that measurably improves current evidence-based practices. However, practices shown to be effective in controlled research (e.g., many cognitive-behavioral treatments) have been shown to work comparably well across racial, ethnic, and cultural lines (Whaley & Davis, 2007). Although many published treatment studies include people from various racial and cultural backgrounds, there is a pressing need to recruit more people of diverse ethnic backgrounds in practice research.

Despite the lack of controlled research on culturally competent practice, it stands to reason that one can enhance the working relationship with clients and better engage them in treatment if clients feel that the practitioner understands and respects their cultural perspective. Being a culturally competent practitioner is, in part, about educating oneself about the client's cultural background and using skills in a way that is culturally congruent with client expectations (Sue, 2007). It also refers to possessing a genuine awareness of one's own cultural background, strengths, limitations, and biases, and learning about client assimilation and acculturation challenges in the host country: how specific policies affect the client's reference group, what services are available, and what experiences a client has had with racism and discrimination (Lum, 2007). Given the current state of knowledge, practitioners can be culturally competent by engaging clients during the assessment on matters of cultural identity (i.e., what their cultural identity means to them) and by implementing practices that have been shown to be effective in the current outcome research with the understanding that most clients are likely to respond well to these. In a similar way these engagement considerations extend to other personal identity factors: sexual orientation, religious and spiritual beliefs and practices, and other matters. By using the supportive, therapeutic coping, and case management skills in this book in a culturally sensitive and informed way, practitioners can become truly culturally competent.

Evaluation

Evaluating One's Own Practice

Asserting that one claims to use essential skills or implement them in some combination as an evidence-based practice does not guarantee intervention success. The third major component of social work practice is evaluating one's own practice (Bloom, Fischer, & Orme, 2006; Siegel, 1984). There are various ways to do this. The most feasible way to evaluate a single case (i.e., individual, couple, or family) is to define and measure one or more key problems during the initial assessment phase, to define the intervention employed, and to monitor changes in the measures periodically over the course of the intervention and again at termination. This approach is sometimes referred to as a *passive-observational* or *naturalistic* approach to evaluation because no special controls are employed that might otherwise interfere with the usual delivery of services. No artificial baseline periods are planned, no comparison cases are used, and no treatment conditions are altered in a planned manner. This approach can be implemented by using some indexes discussed earlier in this chapter or by supplementing them with one or more validated scales. In some agencies, scales now are readily incorporated into the routine clinical documentation required of practitioners (e.g., assessments, treatment plans, progress notes). Changes over time (e.g., reduced depression in an elderly man, improved school performance in a child, more loving behavior between partners) indicate positive changes in the client. What this improvement cannot readily deduce is whether the intervention was responsible for the change. For naturalistic single-subject designs, one simply cannot draw such conclusions with a high degree of confidence. Nevertheless, if practitioners implement an evidence-based practice, they know that they have used an intervention with a reasonable likelihood of helping the client because it has previously been shown to be effective in controlled research trials with many clients experiencing similar problems.

Other more complex single case designs have been discussed at length in the literature on evaluating one's own practice, but these approaches have little practical application for everyday social work interventions. These designs involve controlling the implementation of the intervention in stages or making other predetermined changes to the intervention at various intervals to see if variations of the intervention affect client outcomes. They are, in fact, single-subject controlled experiments that lend themselves to clinical research, not routine practice (Kazdin, 1978, 1998; O'Hare, 2005). These approaches are called *controlled single-case experimental designs* and will be discussed in greater depth in chapter 4.

It is also possible to use naturalistic evaluation strategies with large numbers of clients to evaluate a whole program or a smaller program within a larger agency (e.g., a battered women's group within a mental health agency). In this situation, those participating in the program would record their levels of distress using valid scales during the assessment phase (e.g., to measure depression, anxiety, substance use, self-esteem) and repeat these measures at various intervals during the intervention (e.g., monthly) and at termination. These data can then be used to evaluate the improvement in each client individually and, when data from many clients are aggregated, provide some measure of improvement for the group or program as a whole. Although, as with the single-subject design, one cannot be certain that the improvements were a result of the program, one can place more confidence in the results if large numbers of clients improve and if past research findings indicate strongly that people with similar problems would probably not have improved without intervention. Naturalistic program evaluation will also be discussed in more detail in chapter 4.

Evaluation data from a single client, a group of clients, or a whole program does not prove that the interventions employed are the best or even that they are primarily responsible for client improvement. However, if done consistently well, evaluation can provide a strong indication that practices are implemented effectively at both the individual level and the program level. These data can then be used to identify strong or weaker points in the program, and if analyzed thoughtfully, they can provide a basis for program improvement through purposeful supervision and staff training. Many agencies now have quality-assurance programs that use evaluation methods to improve services to clients.

Monitoring and Evaluating the Use of Essential Intervention Skills: The Psycho-Social Intervention Scale

The Psycho-Social Intervention Scale (PSIS) is a self-evaluation practice tool designed to help social workers:

- Become familiar with essential practice skills
- Evaluate the use of these skills on a case-by-case and session-by-session basis
- Examine how to combine various practice skills to form broader intervention strategies
- Monitor how the use of different practice skills changes over time with an individual client, couple, family, or group

- Examine how practitioners use different combinations of skills depending on the primary problems presented by a client
- Compare the combinations of skills used with existing manualized evidence-based practice guidelines

Used in this manner, the PSIS is a self-teaching and self-evaluation tool designed to help social workers critically examine and better understand how and why they select different combinations of supportive, therapeutic, and case management skills depending on clients' needs. For example, let's say a social worker is providing an intervention for a seriously mentally ill person with a co-occurring substance abuse problem. The outcome research suggests that developing a good working alliance, using a motivational approach, enhancing coping skills, and encouraging social supports (e.g., a dual-diagnosis group) would be a promising approach. However, if the practitioner indicates on the PSIS that he or she is focusing primarily on discussing the client's past relationships and offering interpretations to provide insight into why the client abuses alcohol, these data would indicate an approach that the current outcome research does not support. The social worker's supervisor might then recommend some readings or additional training for the practitioner to become familiar with state-of-the-art practices.

The PSIS is a modification of the Practice Skills Inventory (PSI) (O'Hare & Collins, 1997; O'Hare, Tran, & Collins, 2002), a tool developed in several research studies to measure supportive, therapeutic coping, and case management skills. To make the PSI more comprehensive and useful for practitioners, new items were added to reflect skills used in recently developed evidence-based practices (see appendix A).

The individual items of the PSIS were designed to be somewhat general so the scale could have broad application to social work service settings and different client problems. For each item, practitioners should specify in their own words (in the lines under each item) what specific skill they are using—the skill that corresponds to that particular item—and then rate the emphasis that they place on the use of that particular skill as one part of the overall intervention plan. For example, under item 20, a practitioner might specify that he or she will help a shy adolescent practice (first, through role play with the therapist) how to start up and maintain a friendly conversation with someone he or she wants to get to know in school. That would be a specific and unique application of that particular skill. Key questions to consider when using the PSIS are as follows: Are the skills that I am using with this client reflecting best practices for this particular problem area? How am I modifying this particular evidence-based practice to suit this specific client? How is the client responding to the intervention overall? Practitioners and their supervisors can then compare the profile of specific skills used to those recommended in the practice-outcome research.

Pulling It All Together: Documenting the Comprehensive Service Plan

Together, documenting the completed assessment, describing the proposed intervention methods to be used, and stipulating the indicators and scales to be used in the evaluation constitute the Comprehensive Service Plan (CSP; see appendix B). Most social workers and agencies are required to document their services to clients. This documentation takes many forms and is far from standardized. The format of assessment and intervention plans vary by program, funding source, accreditation guidelines, and state and federal regulatory requirements. However, some basics are suggested here. First, documentation is required, and is necessary and important for a variety of contractual, legal, risk management, and ethical reasons. Second, although service documentation is often (and sometimes justifiably) considered a time-consuming and expensive nuisance, this author maintains that documentation can enhance social work practice in a number of ways: when conceptually well designed, service-plan documentation can improve the validity (i.e., accuracy, thoroughness) and reliability (i.e., consistency) of assessment, clarify the goals, objectives, and methods used in the intervention, and detail the methods used for monitoring and evaluation. Third, a well-conducted assessment, intervention, and evaluation plan is essential for guiding individual service for clients, and aggregated data from individual service plans can provide a sound basis for evaluation. In general, these processes are sometimes referred to as *developing a contract* with the client. This contract is closely tied to the important ethical and legal concepts of informed consent and confidentiality (discussed in chapter 3).

The CSP also includes items from the Psycho-Social Wellbeing Scale (PSWS); O'Hare, Sherrer, Connery, Thornton, LaButti, & Emrick, 2003; O'Hare, Sherrer, Cutler, McCall, Dominique, & Garlick, 2002). These items are used to quantitatively rate each area of the multidimensional-functional qualitative assessment. The adjunctive use of quantitative ratings in routine assessment is becoming common practice in human service agencies in response to increasing demands for routine evaluation from both private and public payers. Although qualitative data are critical for evaluating individual client progress, qualitative data cannot be aggregated (summed up and averaged) in any practical way for reporting to payers or to state and federal agencies. Quantitative ratings can also be used to monitor and evaluate individual client progress across many domains, but data from many clients can be aggregated to provide a database for program evaluation. Beginning practitioners should first make a thoughtful qualitative assessment and then, with all available client information, use the PSWS to rate how well or how impaired the client is in that particular area of well-being. Over time, if the client progresses, improvement will be reflected in higher ratings for individual domains and overall psychosocial well-being. Other scales and indexes should be used to supplement the PSWS according to agency needs and the types of problems for which social workers provide interventions. Many reliable and valid instruments are now available in the public domain and over the Internet (for the PSWS and other useful instruments, see O'Hare, 2005).

After collecting, analyzing, and discussing the information collected from the client, family members, consultants, and others, practitioners often end up with a lot of data. Reducing this information to a concise and useful CSP is an essential social work skill, and becoming proficient at it takes practice. After a full assessment, the practitioner must then collaborate with the client on the development of a formal intervention plan. Under the column "Problems" in the CSP Summary (appendix B), the practitioner should briefly describe those difficulties that the intervention is likely to address. Some efforts should be made to create a problem hierarchy. Under the "Goals" column, practitioners should briefly state what the agreed-on outcomes should be for each problem. Objectives are stepping stones toward each goal. Objectives are the linchpin of interventions: they are often activities that clients carry out as part of the intervention to move closer to their goals. For example, an objective toward a goal of stopping illegal drug use might be "Attend two Narcotics Anonymous meetings this week." Or an objective for a socially anxious adolescent girl might be "Strike up a conversation with that boy in the cafeteria at least once this coming week." Accomplishing this objective might bring the young adolescent a step closer to her goal of being more involved socially, but it is also part of a formal intervention (practicing her social skills). Under the "Intervention" section, the practitioner should describe both the formal title of the intervention (e.g., interpersonal psychotherapy) and specifics (e.g., to meet once weekly). Finally, under "Assessment/Evaluation," practitioners should note any indexes or formal scales they are using to help track client progress and evaluate the effects of the intervention. They should also describe who will collect the data and at what intervals. In chapters 8 through 12, brief case-study illustrations with completed CSPs will help students learn how to develop their own service plans with the outline in appendix B.

CHAPTER TWO

The Relationship between Research and Practice

IN GENERAL, SOCIAL WORKERS tend to be compassionate people who want to help others in distress, help them learn to cope better with life's challenges, and help them improve their quality of life. Compassion, curiosity, the ability to form helping relationships, the ability to help others problem solve and cope, and the initiative to coordinate multiple services are essential characteristics of the effective social worker. However, we also know that compassion and good intentions are not enough to qualify us as professional practitioners. Social workers also need to command up-to-date knowledge regarding the problems they treat, be able to select intervention methods supported by a body of research evidence, implement those interventions with good judgment, and, as best we can, evaluate our efforts. To use the existing professional knowledge base effectively, it is essential that social workers understand how to use research findings and employ critical-thinking skills to conduct competent assessments, sound intervention planning, and meaningful evaluation. Social workers who think critically use sound reasoning supported by relevant research evidence to make the best judgments they can when assessing client difficulties, planning interventions, and evaluating outcomes.

On the basis of many years of experience teaching both social work research and practice courses, I have noticed (in my own qualitative research) that students generally view practice as quite separate from research. In general, students seek out practice courses with enthusiasm and take research courses as a bitter pill only because they are mandated to do so. This impression is a bit disturbing, but it reflects the long tradition in social work education of portraying practice knowledge as resulting almost exclusively from practice wisdom, that is, theory-informed experience that authoritative practitioners dispense. Although such clinical observations often plant the seed for future developments in theory and practice, it is now understood that theories and interventions must be tested and supported by a body of research. To become knowledgeable about contemporary theories and practices, practitioners must become better consumers of research (not necessarily researchers themselves) to command up-to-date knowledge of their clients' problems and the practices that are likely to achieve optimal results.

Human behavior theories and practice models are now understood to be valuable to the extent that they are based on critically reviewed research findings. In the context of the helping professions, the contemporary human behavior sciences address two main questions: Why do people develop and behave as they do? What psychosocial interventions are effective at improving the individual and collective human condition? Human behavior research predominantly addresses the first question in the form of cross-sectional and longitudinal surveys that test human behavior theories. For example, whether child abuse and neglect are risk factors for future problems is a question that drives hundreds of related research questions and is a major focus of modern research efforts. Human behavior research addresses the second question primarily through controlled practice research. For example, whether psychoeducation and behavioral family therapy with case management can reduce the long-term effects of child abuse and neglect is a question about intervention effectiveness (not about the causes or effects of child abuse). Much research continues in this area as well. However, although these two question are related by theme, they are really two separate questions (causes of human problems vs. how to ameliorate them), and research efforts regarding the questions follow two separate but related paths. The sequence of developing questions about human problems and interventions is illustrated in Figure 3.

Addressing these two types of questions follows a similar pattern. Practitioners and researchers (and often, practitioner-researchers) pose questions about the nature of a problem or a type of intervention. The new theory or intervention method then must be well defined and tested in a series of studies. Last, whether the evidence resulting from these research processes actually supports the theory or this new form of practice is determined by the findings of the studies and their methodological quality. Researchers and research-practitioners who engage in this process conduct these studies in the relatively transparent world of blind peer review, and over time, the collective results of a series of related studies emerge in scientific journals. Ultimately, the data tell the story; in other words, the chips are allowed to fall where they may. Theories and practices should live or die by the quality of the evidence that supports them.

FIGURE 3. DEVELOPING AND TESTING THEORIES AND PRACTICE MODELS

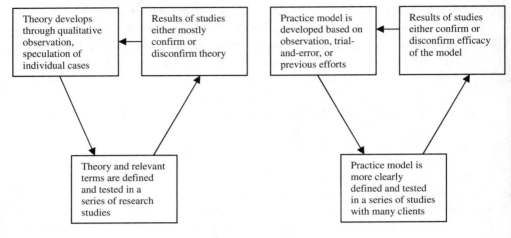

Now, this process is not perfect, nor does it happen overnight. Fortunately, there already exists a large body of theory-driven human behavior research findings that support social work assessment in many areas of practice. Similarly, there is a very large and growing body of controlled research findings on effective practice (i.e., evidence-based practices [EBPs]) to provide solid guidelines for treatment planning. Although there is a long way to go on both fronts (which will keep researchers busy for a long time), the understanding is that "you go with what you've got." Translation: practitioners are ethically obliged to use the existing research knowledge base as their guide and to fill in the gaps with informed judgment as best they can.

The current chapter has two purposes: to provide a brief overview of how human behavior and practice research can inform our work as practitioners and to discuss how the use of critical-thinking skills can help improve our ability to implement the current knowledge base effectively. Having both a sound knowledge base and knowing how to use it are two closely linked qualities of competent helping professionals. Figure 4 illustrates these processes.

Figure 4 illustrates the iterative process of accessing and using knowledge (i.e., research findings) regarding valid assessment and effective intervention, and critically evaluating the implementation of that knowledge. Information about the client, which we might acquire directly from the client and others who know him or her, is usually not self-explanatory. In

FIGURE 4. USING RESEARCH FINDINGS TO SUPPORT PRACTICE

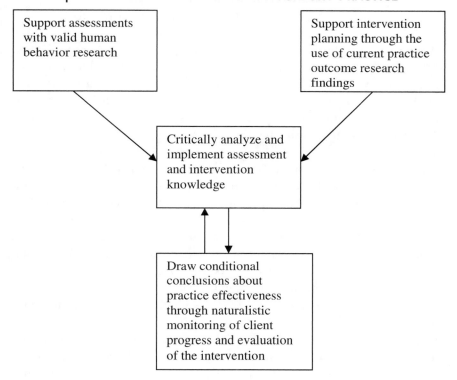

other words, such raw data do not automatically explain the client's difficulties or readily determine the best course of intervention. In a similar vein, simply being a good critical thinker is of little use to practitioners if they do not have the knowledge or skills to conduct informed assessments or select effective interventions. Thus, both knowledge and clear critical thinking are necessary for effective practice. The combination of possessing knowledge and knowing how to use it defines the social worker who is an informed critical thinker. Last, when knowledge is applied in real practice, feedback from clients further informs our ongoing assessment and gives us some indication as to whether the intervention is working. Thus, information gained by observing and listening to the client and important collaterals in his or her life will further shape the decision-making process during the course of the intervention. But these course corrections will also be guided by expertise, not mere instinct, intuition, or uninformed speculation.

The Foundation of Valid Assessment:
Human Behavior in the Social Environment

There are essentially two sources of knowledge regarding client problems: (1) the unique narrative experience of the client and (2) knowledge of human behavior derived from theory-driven research. The first approach emphasizes inductive reasoning. The second emphasizes deductive reasoning. These are complementary forms of reasoning. Relying solely on the client's narrative to inform the assessment and the intervention without accessing a verified body of knowledge makes as little sense as relying completely on generalizations from research without considering a client's unique problems and adaptive strengths. Both sources of information are essential for engaging in competent and ethical practice. Understanding the client's personal narrative provides a partial but essential understanding of cognitive, emotional, behavioral, and situational factors that are unique to that client. Collaterals (e.g., significant others) also provide unique observations from their viewpoint. (Practitioners who work with couples often hear startlingly different accounts of the same event from each partner—one often wonders if they live in the same house!) However, unique client experience is usually insufficient as a basis for assessment because the meaning of the client's experience must be informed by human behavior knowledge specific to the client's particular problems to understand its relevance and relative significance. For example, should a client claim to be an omnipotent superhero who can fly without the aid of aircraft, the practitioner would have to be knowledgeable about serious mental illnesses or mind-altering substances to understand the significance of such a claim. If another client is becoming gradually withdrawn, gives up activities he or she formerly enjoyed, and begins expressing themes of hopelessness, the knowledgeable social worker would not merely empathize and "be in the moment" with the client but would also understand the behaviors (well documented in the research) as indications of high suicide risk. Understanding the subjective experience of clients requires that practitioners are knowledgeable about human problems such as mental illness, childhood disorders, substance abuse, domestic violence, eating disorders, and other problems.

Social workers confront a wide array of human behavior theories and practices. How do we, as practitioners, determine which theories of human behavior are most valid and which interventions are most likely to be effective? It is understood in the applied social sciences that no theory is likely to ever be 100% accurate, and no psychosocial intervention is likely to be

100% effective. What researchers try to do is understand what risk and resilience factors cause or mitigate human problems (e.g., mental illness, addictions, eating disorders) and estimate which practice approach is likely to work best for a given type of problem. For example, although the exact causes of schizophrenia are not known, researchers are fairly certain that biological factors in the limbic system (part of the brain stem) and problems in the regulation of neurotransmitters account for some symptoms. Although no specific social stressor has been shown to cause schizophrenia, stress can exacerbate the illness and make it more difficult to treat. These explanations are now considered more likely or less wrong than, say, the vacillations of mood attributed to the "schizophrenogenic mother" (the prevailing view for many social workers in the twentieth century) or demonic possession (which continues as a prevailing view in some cultures). Although science has yet to fully explain the causes of schizophrenia, practice researchers have demonstrated that some psychosocial interventions can greatly alleviate the suffering of those with major mental illnesses. As in medicine, one need not know everything about the causes of a problem to treat it effectively. Thus, a good working definition for *knowledge* in the practice professions is not a guarantee of certainty but a measurable reduction in uncertainty. Although this lack of certainty may be unsatisfying to some, standard social science research methods are the best tool we have to test out our theories and practices. And the better the research methods, the more confidence we can put in our knowledge base. Thus, how the quality of evidence regarding human behavior is judged leads us to another axiom: "the quality of evidence for supporting theory and practice is only as good as the methodology that produced it."

As noted earlier, many books on social work clinical practice continue to present theories uncritically. Because of this "choose what you like" approach to theory selection, a number of myths have been cultivated regarding the role of theory in social work practice. These myths include the following:

- There is no way to judge the validity of human behavior theories, so one theory is just as good as any other.
- Theories are just imaginary constructions of influential and powerful people.
- Theories are simply metaphors about human behavior, so they do not reflect objective reality.
- The selection of theories is just a matter of personal value preferences.

These inaccurate representations of human behavior theory have led many students to adopt substandard approaches to assessment. Theories of human behavior regarding serious problems such as major mental illnesses, substance abuse, trauma, anxiety disorders and depression, eating disorders, childhood emotional and behavioral disorders, domestic violence, and so forth, are essential in formulating valid assessment procedures. Among behavioral and social scientists, it is well understood that a body of research evidence must support such theories (i.e., models that attempt to explain the factors that cause human problems). Social scientists now largely agree on a number of useful assumptions regarding human behavior theories:

- Human behavior sciences are interdisciplinary—there are no clear demarcations among anthropology, psychology, evolutionary biology, sociology, and so on—and the knowledge from these disciplines must be increasingly integrated and synthesized to achieve a more complete understanding of human behavior.
- Human behavior is complex and caused by a wide range of biological, psychological, environmental, cultural, and other social factors that include both risks and resiliencies, limitations, and strengths that affect human behavior and adaptation over time.
- A variety of individual personal factors (e.g., age, gender, race, ethnicity, cultural background) affect these biopsychosocial processes.

How Human Behavior Research Supports Assessment

For assessment to be valid, it must be informed by contemporary, theory-driven human behavior research. Human behavior research supports valid assessment in the following ways:

- It provides base-rate estimates (i.e., incidence and prevalence) of specific disorders and problems in the community (e.g., knowing that depression may run as high as 20% in the general population, schizophrenia about 1%, alcohol dependence at 7%, and multiple personality at 0.0001% are all useful data and provide practitioners with realistic expectations regarding the prevalence and incidence of serious forms of psychopathology and other behaviors); epidemiology helps practitioners from being overly responsive to the emergence of mental health fads (e.g., a sudden surge in the rates of multiple personality disorder).

- It provides rates of co-occurring problems. For example, we now know that children with conduct disorder have a high likelihood (50% or more) of demonstrating key symptoms of attention deficit/hyperactivity disorder as well, and that people with serious mental illness have a 50% chance of experiencing a substance abuse problem in their lifetime. Knowledge of co-occurrence helps practitioners avoid the tunnel vision of diagnosis in their assessments.

- Human behavior research identifies key risk and resiliency factors (both developmental and current) that are likely to contribute to the client's problems or predict recovery. These factors may be cognitive, physiological, familial, social, environmental, cultural, and so on. For example, there are several risk factors that increase the likelihood that a client will commit suicide, including a sense of hopelessness, recent losses, and substance abuse, among others. Dealing with suicidal clients is not infrequent in social work practice. It behooves the astute practitioner to know what researchers know about the risks for suicide attempts. Learning these risk factors the hard way (by experience alone) is risky for both clients and practitioners. We also know that children who are diagnosed as conduct disordered are more likely to become antisocial adults, but most do not become antisocial adults. Thus, knowing risk-factor probabilities helps practitioners avoid over- and underestimating risks and related problems when we conduct assessments.

- Human behavior research provides estimates of the relative strength of risk and resiliency factors. Beyond knowing which risk factors are relevant, research can also provide guidelines to consider the relative weight of those risks compared to others. For example, the genetic risk factor for schizophrenia (for a client with one parent with the disorder) is understood to be greater than any known psychosocial risk (e.g., familial stress). However, environmental stressors may play a relatively stronger role in depression. Practitioners who ignore the relative weight of factors that contribute to their clients' problems are likely to conduct inadequate or inaccurate assessments. Incomplete or misinformed assessments are likely to lead to the wrong intervention plan.

- Human behavior research explains the multidimensional nature of client problems—research on eating disorders, for example, helps us understand that young women with binge-eating disorders experience distress in several modes: cognitive distortion about the way they see themselves, physiological problems (e.g., electrolyte imbalances) from repeated vomiting, and disordered behaviors with regard to eating habits and appetite regulation. Women with eating disorders also seem to have more difficulties in interpersonal relationships. A complete assessment needs to address all these dimensions (among others).

- Human behavior research provides support for some theories and invalidates others. Research has dramatically changed the way some problems have been conceptualized. For example, theories regarding the etiology (cause) of panic disorder have moved from assumptions about early parenting habits (e.g., abandonment fears in the infant/toddler) to biological causes that environmental stressors or other physiological factors may trigger and reinforce (e.g., substance abuse).

- Human behavior research provides an empirical and theoretical foundation for instrument development. Scales that measure important aspects of human experience (e.g., depression, self-esteem, hope for recovery, self-efficacy in meeting challenges, childhood fears) must be well researched and validated before they can be used in assessment, evaluation, or research. The knowledge base that informs the development of such scales originates in human behavior research that incorporates the self-report of hundreds or thousands of people from all walks of life.

Human behavior theories evolve and accumulate as a result of many different research designs. No design is inherently better than another, but each design must be understood in terms of what it can and cannot logically demonstrate within a reasonable degree of confidence. Qualitative research typically draws on small samples of clients to obtain in-depth, highly detailed, and nuanced descriptions of client problems and intervention processes. These are good strategies for exploratory research and evaluation. Keeping an open mind to see what comes of this can often generate important and interesting questions. Yet qualitative research is not confirmative, and conclusions are almost always tentative. Cross-sectional surveys can be used to obtain data from hundreds or thousands of clients as part of large representative samples to estimate the type and nature of human problems, including mental illnesses, substance abuse, or general attitudes or opinions toward important social issues. Longitudinal surveys look at how risk factors affect people over time. Small-group experiments can demonstrate how people behave in different circumstances when some important factor is introduced. Collectively, all research strategies help fill in the complex picture regarding how biological, psychological, and social factors interact within and between people over time. Theories of human behavior in the social environment are validated by using all of these methods to build a sound body of knowledge, but the weight of evidence is applied to designs that provide a stronger basis for making cause-effect inferences (i.e., longitudinal designs) and those that provide a basis for broad generalization of findings (i.e., cross-sectional designs with large samples).

Theory development and testing is critical to the development of valid psychosocial assessment for this reason: a theory is only as good as the research evidence that supports it. An accompanying corollary is also critical: an assessment can be only as valid as the theory that supports it.

In summary, human behavior research provides the foundation for conducting valid assessments. All social science research methods have their place in the seamless continuum of rational inquiry into human problems and adaptation. To be competent as practitioners, social workers need not become researchers themselves, but they do need to cultivate a deep respect for human behavior research and make every effort to keep up with research developments in their respective area of interest: serious mental illnesses, substance abuse, child abuse and neglect, and so forth. Figure 5 illustrates the relationships among theory, research, and assessment.

How Practice Research Informs Practice

Much of what has been said here regarding research applies equally to practice research and its implications for everyday practice. Interventions may be somewhat related to or even derived from a human behavior theory, but the actual methods employed must be tested in their own right. There are a number of designs used to test interventions, and they all have strengths and weaknesses. Some of these designs are uncontrolled (e.g., no use of comparison groups, participants are not assigned to treatment conditions) and are similar to the evaluation designs discussed in chapter 4. However, most professional bodies accept that randomized controlled designs (RCTs) provide the strongest evidence that an intervention will result in substantive positive benefits for the client. The RCT designs provide the current guidelines for evidence-based practices.

The rationale for using controlled practice designs is quite straightforward: one cannot determine whether an intervention is effective unless

FIGURE 5. THE RELATIONSHIPS AMONG THEORY, RESEARCH, AND ASSESSMENT

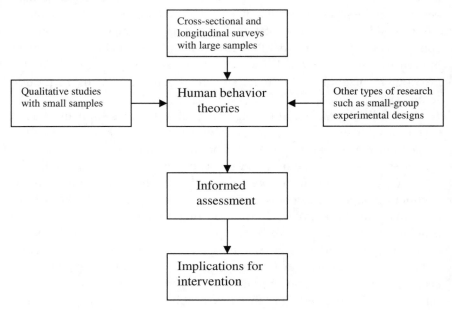

the intervention is compared to no intervention or to some other intervention under controlled conditions with clients who share similar problems in comparable degree of severity. Controlled conditions mean that the clients are clearly defined with regard to their personal characteristics (e.g., gender, age), their problems are defined and measured with one or more valid instruments, the intervention is clearly defined, the practitioners are well trained in the methods to be employed, and meaningful client outcomes are defined. In other words, in a fair comparison, the intervention that results in the best outcomes in repeated trials is considered the most efficacious. Controlled trials are the most valid method practitioner-researchers have to determine whether an intervention works at all (when compared to no intervention) and whether one intervention results in better outcomes than another intervention. In short, RCTs are designed to answer the following question: all things being, more or less, equal, does the intervention result in substantial improvements for clients? Although there are many variations of the controlled trial, Figure 6 shows the basic paradigm.

Clients with significant degrees of problems (e.g., depression, alcoholism) are typically recruited from the community or from clinic populations. These study participants should also meet some minimum criteria

FIGURE 6. THE RANDOMIZED CONTROLLED TRIAL PARADIGM

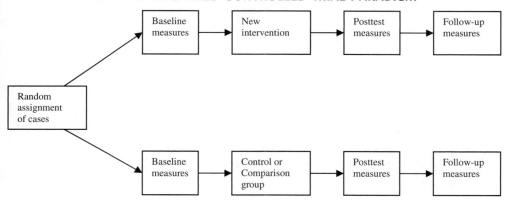

for the problem to be treated (e.g., usually diagnosis and/or a cutoff score on one or more scales). Random assignment is a key factor in controlled trials because it minimizes the chances that clients improve (or do not improve) on the basis of their own treatment expectations or other characteristics that might determine the selection of one treatment condition over another. Professionals who are blind to the treatment condition of the client assess clients in both the new (i.e., experimental) intervention and the control or comparison group using the same battery of reliable and valid scales to measure the problems or treatment goals of interest. This method reduces bias. Often, measures are completed directly by clients as well, or some combination of client self-report and clinical judgment is used.

People trained in each respective approach carry out the interventions. Strictly speaking, clients in the control group initially do not receive any intervention but do receive intervention later on. However, most studies of intervention use comparison groups—that is, alternative interventions—often ones that might otherwise be received in everyday practice settings (i.e., treatment as usual). After treatment has been completed, both groups are again assessed using the same (and sometimes additional) measures to determine whether they improved on several outcomes as a result of the intervention. Ideally, follow-up measures should be taken at six or twelve months (and sometimes up to five or six years) to determine whether the results of the interventions actually hold up over time. The overall rationale for the RCT is, as much as possible, to conduct a fair test of the experimental intervention compared with no treatment or some alternative intervention. Ethical standards regarding informed consent and confidentiality are strict and highly scrutinized before and during such studies. After two or more replications of such studies demonstrating that an intervention is effective with clients who meet valid criteria for specific problems or disorders, the intervention is considered an evidence-based practice. To date, no other research methodology has been offered that provides as rigorous a test of what works, with whom, and under what circumstances. Authors of research reports of controlled trials should provide sufficient detail of all aspects of study design and procedures so that other researchers can replicate the study.

Now, demonstrating that an intervention is efficacious under controlled circumstances such as RCT is no guarantee that it will be implemented well in everyday social work treatment environments. Evaluation designs, discussed in chapter 4, can be used to see that evidence-based practices are implemented well. Nevertheless, there is much that can be learned from RCTs, and practitioners are well advised to use collective RCT results to guide intervention planning. From critical reviews of the outcome research on RCTs for a given problem (e.g., anxiety disorders, drugs, major depression), social workers can learn

- What interventions have the most thorough track record of success for a particular client problem
- Whether there are comparable alternatives
- Whether the intervention is effective with certain groups of clients more than other groups
- How much impact one should reasonably expect from the intervention
- What is the average length of time to see substantial results
- Whether the whole intervention or parts of an intervention may be sufficient for most or all clients with a given condition
- The sustainability of positive results, likelihood of relapse, and recommendations for follow-up booster visits

Of course, before using an EBP (evidence-based practice), one should become familiar with the approach (there are many good practice texts available that define the methods in detail) and obtain training and supervision in the approach from someone with the requisite qualifications. Hopefully, before too long, social work curricula will regularly offer EBPs as required coursework for second-year practitioners-interns.

Informed Critical Thinking in Social Work Practice

Assuming that one develops the skills to read and understand research, drawing conclusions from several research reports and applying that knowledge to better understanding and helping clients requires the ability to apply knowledge in a critical and logical manner. Critical-thinking skills are essential for social work practitioners to consistently and accurately apply the knowledge base of human behavior, conduct competent and valid assessments, select and implement effective practices, and evaluate their own practice. What are critical-thinking skills? These are cognitive skills that allow us to draw reasonable inferences and sensible conclusions from sometimes ambiguous observations and data (Gambrill, 1990; Nisbett & Ross, 1980; O'Hare, 2005; Tversky & Kahneman, 1974). Although social workers have often been advised to "trust their gut" or "go with their instincts," the hallmark of effective professionals is the critical application of scientific evidence to inform their assessments and intervention plans. However, applying the social work knowledge base to individual situations is not easy and requires that social workers are aware of some inherent biases in human reasoning.

Cognitive researchers have identified a range of critical-thinking errors that we all make from time to time. These critical thinking errors apply to all professionals as well. There are four main tendencies toward errors in judgment that both practitioners and researchers should be aware of: (1) to see explanations for human problems as relatively simple when in fact human behavior is generally complex, (2) to confuse correlation (or even coincidence) with causal relationships, (3) to draw firm conclusions from dramatic examples or the experiences of only a few people, and (4) to make arbitrary judgments about the significance of a problem or situation without the aid of valid benchmarks. Although these four biases are overarching themes, more specific types of thinking errors and relevant examples will be discussed subsequently, along with how we can use relevant research to reduce these errors when conducting social work assessment, intervention, and evaluation.

Theories that stress one factor as the cause of psychosocial problems tend to be good examples of oversimplification. For example, when a practitioner concludes that a young man in his twenties who has a drinking problem, is depressed, and has only transitory relationships with women must have been neglected emotionally as a child, this conclusion overlooks a host of other possible factors that may contributed to his less-than-happy young-adult life. These include genetic and cultural factors that may have increased his tendency to drink excessively and be depressed, an abusive parent or guardian, early losses, having been overindulged by parents who did not care enough to hold him accountable for his actions or provide genuine rewards for real accomplishments, long-term struggles with learning disabilities, traumatic events such as military combat or having been victimized as the result of a crime, having had a head injury as a result of a motorcycle accident, or other medical conditions. The list of possibilities is quite long. At a minimum, practitioners should be open to conducting full and complete assessments (including input from other professionals) before drawing simplistic, one-factor conclusions (e.g., poor self-esteem).

One of the more seductive thinking errors involves reasoning based on post hoc, or after-the-fact, reasoning. The tendency toward post hoc revisionism is referred to as hindsight bias. Let's say that a young woman, age eighteen, is admitted to a community mental health center. There may be some evidence that she has schizophrenia, but because she is still young, the doctors are not sure. Nevertheless, she has been living on the street for some time and requires the additional psychosocial supports that a community support program can provide. During her intake, there is some evidence to suggest that she may have been involved in some minor crimes such as selling small amounts of marijuana, shoplifting, and occasionally getting into physical fights. One day, a female case manager visits her in a supported housing apartment. During the visit, the client gets angry at the case manager, picks up a kitchen knife, and stabs the worker. The case-worker dies.

The agency administration, lawyer, and practitioners meet the following day. Indeed this is a tragic event, yet all members of the group have a different view of the situation and feel the need to place responsibility on someone else, because some are concerned about lawsuits or charges of criminal neglect. At one point, the director of the program yells at the person who did the initial intake and admitted the young client into the program: "You should have known that she was going to be dangerous and recommended a more secure setting. It's your fault!" Of course, the intake worker feels angry at being accused, guilty, and resentful about being unfairly singled out. She is erroneously and unfairly blamed for this tragic incident.

The old saying is "hindsight is 20–20." The fact is, unless one has a crystal ball and can see into the future, no one would have bet that the young client would ever have murdered anyone. Predicting low-frequency events when there is no history of similar behavior is at best a guessing game. If every client in a mental health center who had used illegal drugs or had an occasional fight as an adolescent was confined on the grounds of being too dangerous, mental health centers would be empty, and most clients would be locked up in secure facilities. In everyday practice, social workers do not have the luxury of projecting themselves into the future to make practice decisions. They have to conduct their assessments and make intervention recommendations based on the best evidence they have at the time. Those who present themselves as experts by reflecting on what should have or could have been done engage in hindsight bias, an argument that provides only the illusion of expertise. On the other hand, if the young woman had a documented history of violence and it was ignored by a worker who thought, "She seems nice. I don't think she'll do it again," then one would have a case for having ignored invaluable data (i.e., past violence is a good predictor of future violence).

As with many people, practitioners sometimes confuse correlation with causation. An elderly man, for example, comes to a clinic for depression. The social worker takes a thorough history and notes that the man has been drinking six to eight beers a day. The social worker concludes, therefore, that the man is drinking too much because he is depressed. Not so fast! All we know is that the man drinks too much and that he is depressed. These two things may certainly be correlated, but it would be premature to conclude that his drinking is the result of his depression. That is one possibility. The social worker's more experienced supervisor (who keeps up with the research on dual diagnosis in the elderly) also considers the possibility that the man is depressed, in part because he is drinking too much. The client also has a history of depression (even when he had not been drinking), has recently lost his wife, and has recently received troubling results from a medical examination, along with other health problems. It is often tempting as a practitioner to infer causality between two proximate behaviors. Although a causal connection is possible, other factors must be considered. How do we avoid jumping to conclusions in this manner? We conduct thorough assessments and use available research to support assessment hypotheses.

Young practitioners are often told that practice experience will eventually guide their careers. This is only partly true. As noted earlier, experience based on unsubstantiated theories does not constitute expertise; experience must be informed by relevant research evidence. However, in the understandable desire to develop a feeling of professional competence, less experienced practitioners are often tempted to develop practice guidelines from exposure to only a few cases. As a result, inexperienced practitioners often cite dramatic stereotypes to support their assessments or choice of an intervention for a client. The reasoning goes something like this: "I once worked with a client who had a certain problem and responded well to this treatment approach. Therefore, I think that this other client, who has a similar problem, will also benefit from the same approach." This "if it worked for him, it will work for her" reasoning illustrates the overgeneralization from too small a sample, in this example, a single case. Practitioners should draw from a tested knowledge base regarding the assessment and intervention with a problem to support one's strategy. The client's unique input will also be an essential part of intervention planning. Although considering both the research and the individual client's views are no guarantee of success, this more informed method will yield better results in the long run than will relying on one or a few dramatic or available case examples.

A similar problem in reasoning also involves overgeneralizing, not from too few cases, but from readily accessible information to inform assessments or select interventions. Experienced practitioners have all met colleagues who seem to consistently use only one theory to inform their assessments (e.g., all clients have either pre-Oedipal or Oedipal conditions) or employ only one form of intervention ("it's all about the relationship!"). These practitioners rely almost exclusively on what they know and have failed to broaden their repertoire of assessment and intervention knowledge. They have wedded themselves (and their clients) exclusively to one treatment model and use that model with all their clients. This theory or intervention model is, for all intents and purposes, all the information they have readily available to them.

Another example of using only information that is readily available is to conduct assessments by relying exclusively on information provided by the client. Although this may be adequate for minor adjustment concerns for which the client has little reason to withhold or distort information, this approach is generally considered lacking because there are other sources of information that one may need to obtain an accurate and complete picture of what is going on with the client (e.g., other treatment records, family members, law enforcement). Erroneous assessments that rely on readily available information can also take the form of basing an assessment only on a client's record from another agency, relying on another practitioner's assessment (from one cursory intake interview), or relying only on one family member's observations about a client's difficulties. Assessments should be grounded in both a relevant knowledge base about the client's problems and a careful process of data gathering from the client and other sources to provide a more complete picture of the client and his or her situation. Relying solely on easily accessible information, particularly when one is overworked in a busy agency, can lead to inaccurate assessments and substandard treatment recommendations.

One way to mislead oneself into thinking that one is usually correct in one's assessments, selection of interventions, or evaluations is to consider only information with which one agrees: to consider only information that supports one's chosen opinion and to avoid observations or evidence that refutes one's beliefs or convictions. This form of reasoning bias is selective attention. Given that new research findings relevant to assessment and intervention with mental illnesses, trauma, childhood disorders, eating disorders, domestic violence, and other serious problems emerge continually, it is surprising that so many experienced practitioners maintain the same assessment and intervention models for very long periods of time—sometimes for decades! If one only selectively attends to the theories and practices that one likes, then one never has to be troubled with examining new ways to engage in social work practice.

Consider, for example, a female client diagnosed with panic disorder and agoraphobia. If she happens to be referred to a practitioner who believes that all anxiety disorders are caused primarily by childhood trauma (e.g., physical or sexual abuse), the client is likely to spend a lot of time answering questions about her childhood and any traumatic events that occurred. The time they spend together in sessions may focus almost exclusively on what the client recalls or does not recall from early childhood. The practitioner may be so predisposed to the view that anxiety disorders can be caused only by early childhood trauma that, when the client insists that she cannot remember these events, the practitioner concludes that this inability to remember is proof positive of child abuse! When thinking critically, practitioners avoid the tendency to draw conclusions based solely on familiarity with a theory and instead explore what current research suggests about the problem and relevant risk factors. In the case of this young woman, possible explanations for her troubles include depression and anxiety disorders that run in the family, exacerbation by the use or abuse of alcohol or illegal or prescription drugs, panic triggered by a recent stressful or traumatic event (e.g., sexual assault, sudden death of a loved one, an accident), childhood physical or sexual abuse, some combination of these, or some other explanation. Critical-thinking practitioners keep an open mind regarding theories and stay abreast of the relevant research regarding human behavior theories and effective interventions.

Social work practitioners make judgments regarding the seriousness of human problems all the time. Gauging the severity of a client's problems and strengths is an essential step toward assessment and setting priorities for both programming and intervention planning. Anchoring refers to how we gauge the degree of a problem along a continuum (e.g., mild, moderate, severe or low, medium, high). These judgments often involve questions such as the following: Is hard spanking a culturally accepted form of discipline in a particular community or is it a form of child abuse? Is my elderly client just thinking about suicide or is he or she really going to try it? Is the consumption of five beers every day considered a drinking problem, or is this client becoming dependent on alcohol? Does a client's witnessing of a fatal accident constitute a traumatic event or was it just momentarily stressful? Is Jonny's habit of jumping out of his desk in class once a day a sign of ADHD, or is he just a bit rambunctious? Obviously, the answers to these questions will determine, in part, the assessment and the intervention plan.

Practitioners constantly make judgments about the seriousness or significance of clients' thoughts, feelings, and behaviors. In a general sense, this practice of gauging the importance or severity of client difficulties is a rough form of measurement. The only question is, How consistently and accurately do practitioners measure the seriousness of a client's behavior to judge its relative significance? Judging the relative importance of client problems (or how well they are doing) involves benchmarking frequency, intensity, or duration of a client's thoughts, feelings, or behaviors relative to previous client experiences or to the experiences of others in the general population or similar client population. To judge whether a client has only mild suicidal ideation or is at imminent risk to kill him- or herself is obviously an important question and involves informed clinical judgment. Anchoring requires base-rate knowledge (i.e., evidence from research and a thoughtful assessment of past client experiences) regarding the client's key problem.

One might think that judging suicidal intent is merely a matter of common sense. However, the benchmarking skill for judging mild or serious suicidal ideation can vary not only among social work practitioners but also within the same practitioner over time. For example, if one works in an agency that specializes in depression, suicidal ideation may be observed often in many clients. Over time, a practitioner may become somewhat desensitized to signs of suicide. After all, clients say things like "I can't go on any more," or "I feel hopeless about the future," with a fair degree of frequency, yet most clients do not make serious suicide attempts. A less experienced practitioner may find him- or herself overreacting to every client utterance that suggests suicidal intent, whereas a more experienced practitioner may find his or her sensitivity to suicidal intent inadvertently erode over time as a result of overexposure. A practitioner's anchoring point regarding what constitutes mild, moderate, or severe suicidal intent may be quite different from other practitioners or may change over time as a result of individual practice experience.

Making judgments about the seriousness of a client's problems or their degree of adaptive capabilities is not merely a matter of trusting one's instincts. There is a considerable amount of research that can help us reduce the effects of anchoring and make informed judgments about the seriousness of client problems. In the case of suicide risk, a list of known risk factors is widely recognized, including a client's sense of hopelessness, history of depression, previous suicide attempts, heavy drinking or abuse of other drugs, and owning weapons, among other factors. One way to mitigate the anchoring effect is for practitioners to consistently use a valid suicide-risk assessment scale. Although no scale can guarantee 100% accuracy, using a valid knowledge base to support one's clinical judgments can go a long way toward instilling consistency and accuracy and reducing the tendency of one's anchoring point to drift from one end of the continuum (underestimating) to the other (overestimating).

The same principle applies to making clinical judgments about other problems. For example, anchoring bias can occur in similar fashion with assessment for child abuse and neglect. After witnessing hundreds of cases of abuse and neglect, and feeling pressured to expedite large numbers of cases, a social worker's anchoring point for serious risk of abuse may drift gradually toward the severe end of the continuum (in other words, the practitioner's tolerance for what constitutes abuse increases). This phenomenon may account for why overburdened child welfare workers, who may not be equipped with good risk-assessment tools, find themselves overlooking cases in which children are seriously at risk. Despite the best of intentions, social workers are human, and estimates of the seriousness of client problems can drift over time. The more those judgments can be based on sound risk assessment data, the more accurate they are likely to be. Reliable and valid evidence can enhance clinical judgment.

Somewhat related to the issue of anchoring is the failure to employ accurate base rates of a problem, sometimes by becoming infatuated with rare phenomena. If anchoring refers to making judgments about severity of problems, accurate base-rate data is the relative frequency with which particular problems occur in the community, including the incidence (how often certain cases occur in a year) and prevalence (how often they occur in a lifetime). These data are readily available for many problems including major mental illnesses, substance abuse and addiction, domestic violence, eating disorders, and so on. Nevertheless, because of a tendency of some practitioners to overrepresent the likelihood of rare phenomena or novel diagnoses (e.g., satanic ritual abuse, multiple personality disorder), some less experienced social workers have been influenced to look for more exotic or unusual explanations for people's problems rather than consider more probable explanations. For example, a young man who manifests psychotic symptoms in a hospital emergency room can either be having his first episode with a major mental illness or be experiencing drug-induced hallucinations. Considering that a sizable proportion of young men use hallucinogenic drugs, the social worker conducting the screening would be wise to rule out the use of these drugs before committing the young man to a psychiatric facility, as only a very small percentage of the population develop serious mental illnesses that involve non-drug-induced psychoses. The likelihood of the symptoms being caused by drugs instead of a mental illness are approximately ten to one. Accessing more information about the client's activities and overall functioning on that day and in the weeks leading up to the crisis would be in order before jumping to the conclusion that he was, in fact, suffering his first psychotic episode. In situations where the facts are ambiguous or in short supply, or where client self-report is compromised for some reason, practitioners should rule out more likely explanations first before jumping to conclusions that could lead to inaccurate assessments and the wrong intervention.

Other similar judgments or measuring problems include engaging in dichotomous thinking (e.g., client is alcohol dependent or not) rather than measuring behavior on a continuum (e.g., client is not alcohol dependent, but his or her drinking is negatively affecting work, home life, and mood). Sometimes using a psychiatric diagnosis (by its very nature) leads to dichotomous thinking (is client borderline or not?) rather than focusing on the client's distressing thoughts, feelings, or behaviors, and assessing whether they require intervention.

Sometimes practitioners deal with the challenges and ambiguity of practice by saying things like, "Social work is more an art than a science." Perhaps a better way to deal with the ambiguity and indeterminacy of working with clients is to accept that there is much we do not know about client problems and effective interventions. What can we do to increase the accuracy of our judgments? We can make the effort to become as knowledgeable as we can about the problems we deal with and the interventions we provide in our field of practice by keeping up with the latest evidence-based assessment and intervention methods, and we can practice good reasoning skills to apply that knowledge.

Characteristics of the Social Worker Who Thinks Critically

To critically evaluate human behavior and practice research, social workers need to be able to think critically; to think critically, they must be knowledgeable about human behavior and practice research relevant to their field. These two essential elements of social work practice are necessary and reciprocal. As a final point, I would like to note some personal observations of critical-thinking colleagues based on more than thirty years of experience and observation in the helping professions as practitioner, researcher, and instructor.

1. Critical thinkers are not inclined to be dogmatic or rigid in their professional beliefs. They tend to be humble in their professional opinions because they understand the limitations of our knowledge of human problems and the limitations of current psychosocial interventions. They generally understand that professional opinions are based primarily on well-considered evidence, not on personal feelings, personal experience, ideology, or one's personal values or political opinions.

2. Critical thinkers are generally curious and open to new advances in the field, and are less inclined to cling rigidly to more familiar and comfortable theoretical or practice traditions.

3. Critical thinkers tend to welcome peer review of their own work and do not shy away from challenges to their opinions.

4. Critical thinkers tend not to take criticism personally but view research and practice efforts as part of a whole enterprise shared with their peers—other critical practitioner-scholars.

5. Critical thinkers share a healthy skepticism toward unsubstantiated claims regarding theories and untested or unproven practices: they are not easily taken in by untested theories or practice fads no matter how attractive they may seem on the surface.

6. Critical thinkers tend to provide measured responses to questions regarding theories and practices such as, "Some evidence suggests . . ." or "I don't know" or "I'll have to review the research on that."

7. Critical thinkers are not afraid to change their minds when the evidence warrants such a change.

8. Critical thinkers tend to be specific when providing a professional opinion and understand that one must provide evidence to support one's opinions.

9. Critical thinkers tend to avoid vague emotional or value-laden arguments to support their methods but refer to theories and practices that are supported by a body of peer-reviewed evidence.

10. Because critical thinkers do not overly personalize their professional opinions, they tend to make enjoyable and productive colleagues. They tend to focus on the important work at hand: thoughtfully providing informed and effective social work services to clients and keeping up with new research findings to inform practice.

Summary

Social workers must acquire and develop the knowledge and skills to become competent consumers of human behavior and practice research relevant to their field. By keeping up with the literature and applying this knowledge critically, social workers can maintain their professional competence, continually hone their expertise, and stay on the cutting edge of their profession over the course of a professional lifetime.

CHAPTER THREE

Essential Ethics in Social Work Practice

SOCIAL WORK ETHICS, as they relate specifically to practice, are guidelines, values, and principles that engender respect for clients and colleagues, protect clients' rights to privacy, ensure informed client participation when receiving social work services, and encourage competent practice methods. For example, protecting a client's confidentiality means being mindful of with whom one discusses a client's case (e.g., a supervisor vs. a friend); ensuring informed consent means discussing the nature of the intervention with a client and obtaining his or her willing participation in the planning and implementation of treatment; last, using competent practice methods means obtaining adequate training and supervision and keeping up with relevant advances in practice research.

There is every reason to believe that the majority of social workers are caring, committed professionals who strive to behave ethically in all their professional activities. However, occasionally practitioners hear stories from colleagues; read them in the newspaper, professional newsletters, or on the Internet; or see reports on television. A mental health professional, sometimes a social worker, is accused by a professional body or licensing board of unethical conduct, sued for damages by a client in civil court, or charged with criminally negligent practice. The examples include charges that a practitioner

- Inadvertently divulged confidential information to a colleague in the lunchroom
- Showed up for work impaired by alcohol or other drugs once or twice a month
- Had sex with a client as part of an "emotionally corrective" therapeutic experience

- Conducted a creative rebirthing therapy by coercing a child to fight her way out of a sack to reexperience the birth trauma (the child dies as a result of the experience)
- Encouraged a client with whom one is uncovering repressed memories to cut off all ties to his or her presumably abusive family
- Convinced patients that their problems are caused by trauma that occurred in a past life, or during satanic ritual abuse, or as the result of having been abducted by aliens
- Provided treatment for a client after diagnosing him or her as having more than five hundred distinct personalities
- Got even with restrictive insurance companies by billing them for group therapy conducted in one's backyard hot tub with five of one's closest friends
- Terminated treatment with a client on short notice because he or she had become overly dependent and troublesome (coincidentally, just as the insurance ran out)
- Ignored a client's homicidal or suicidal threats and interpreted them as passive-aggressive manipulation

These are all examples of unethical, negligent, and criminal activities that practitioners, including some social workers, have engaged in. Some of these are extreme examples, yet social workers can be charged with unethical or illegal conduct for less serious transgressions as well. The purpose of this chapter is to help beginning practitioners become aware of key ethical dimensions of social work practice and how to avoid liability risk by using practice-relevant evidence to inform assessment, intervention, and evaluation.

The NASW Code of Ethics

The Code of Ethics of the National Association of Social Workers (NASW) covers many areas related to professional conduct of social workers, including social workers' ethical responsibilities to their clients and colleagues; ethical, professional behavior in practice settings; and ethical responsibilities to society. Although all areas of ethical responsibilities are important, the emphasis in this chapter is on those matters that most directly affect practitioners' work with clients. Social workers should keep a copy of the code and related texts available and review the guidelines periodically (see NASW, 2007; see also Dolgoff, Loewenberg, & Harrington, 2005; Reamer,

1998, 2006; Strom-Gottfried, 2007). Because matters of ethics often coincide with legal and liability issues, questions regarding such matters should be referred to qualified attorneys.

Privacy and Confidentiality

Social workers must respect clients' right to privacy and should solicit only information from clients that is germane to providing the service (Houston-Vega & Nuehring, 1997; Reamer, 2003). Social workers cannot disclose information about clients to anyone, including other practitioners or third-party payers, without the express written consent of the client. Even when ordered by courts, social workers should strive to protect the confidentiality of clients if they deem the disclosure to be potentially harmful. The social worker may request that the court withdraw the order, focus the request as narrowly as possible, or keep the disclosed information under seal and away from public scrutiny. Social workers should take every caution to protect electronic or written information (e.g., written records, computer files, e-mails, tapes, phone messages) from being revealed to others by maintaining vigilance over secure storage of relevant material. Destruction of client records should follow statutes, usually stipulated by state departments of health. Confidentiality is one of the foundation ethical principles for social workers and has been robustly supported by the courts (see, e.g., *Jaffee v. Redmond*, in Appelbaum, 1996) and federal legislation, specifically the Health Insurance Portability Accountability Act of 1996.

Clients also have a right to examine their own records. However, if practitioners feel that such examination may cause undue distress or psychological harm to the client, they can refrain from letting the client see the entire record or the part of the record they consider potentially harmful. However, the practitioner must record the reason for refusing to let the client see the record. The social worker should also sit with the client and discuss the content revealed in the record to answer questions and clarify its content (e.g., the meaning of a diagnosis). If a client is allowed access to the record, the social worker should take steps to protect the confidentiality of others identified therein.

Social workers may disclose confidential information when appropriate with valid consent from a client or a person legally authorized to consent on behalf of a client. Disclosure of private information is ethically and legally permissible to prevent serious, foreseeable, and imminent harm to the client or to another identifiable person. Social workers often cite the famous *Tarasoff* case (*Tarasoff v. the Board of Regents of the University of California*, 1976) to support their understanding of the duty to warn another person who may be at risk of imminent harm from a client. In *Tarasoff v. the Board of Regents of the University of California*, a psychologist failed to adequately warn a person known to the psychologist's client that she was in imminent danger of being harmed by the client. The client later killed Tatiana Tarasoff. The psychologist was found liable for not warning Tarasoff of the danger. Since then, the *Tarasoff* decision is frequently cited to remind practitioners of their duty to warn by making a reasonable effort to protect any person when there is evidence of a client threatening imminent harm against that person. In a *Tarasoff*-like situation, social workers are legally obliged to breach confidentiality and do what they deem prudent and necessary to warn the intended victim. However, even in circumstances in which the client or another person is in danger (e.g., suicidal risk), the practitioner should disclose only the information that is necessary to achieve the desired purpose (i.e., protect the client or someone else). Such situations minimally include known incidents of child abuse, abuse of an elderly person, or imminent threats of violence to anyone.

Early in the working relationship, social workers should outline the client's rights to confidentiality and discuss circumstances under which the social worker can divulge information to third parties without the client's expressed permission.

Whenever feasible, social workers must inform the client about the disclosure of confidential information and the potential consequences of disclosure. This guideline is applicable to situations in which the client has given written consent or the law compelled the social worker to report information against the client's wishes. Social workers who treat minors should consult legal authorities in their states on the limits of confidentiality in order to make informed judgments on when to disclose confidential information to parents if they believe it would be important to do so.

When working with multiple individuals (e.g., couples, families, groups), social workers should seek to honor confidentiality among members, but they must make it clear that they cannot prevent clients from revealing confidential matters to one another or to people outside the group. In short, social workers should keep one rubric firmly in mind at all times regarding confidentiality: practitioners should not release information to anyone unless the practitioner knows that he or she is on firm ethical and legal grounds to do so. If there is any doubt about confidentiality regulations, consultation with an attorney is advised.

Conflicts of Interest

It is paramount that social workers keep the well-being of their clients as the main focus of interventions. Occasionally situations arise in which work with a client competes or potentially conflicts with other agendas. For example, a social worker provides psychotherapy for a client whose mother is a real estate agent in town. The social worker happens to be looking for an affordable home, and discussion ensues during one of the sessions about where to find a good deal. The client now becomes a potential ongoing source of valuable information to the practitioner, and the client's insider role now becomes a distraction to the treatment process. The social worker begins to schedule meetings more frequently to keep up with emerging prospects for a good deal or offers free sessions if the client can find her a home.

Or consider the following: a social worker is working with a young woman through a difficult period of her life. The young woman happens to reveal that her uncle, with whom she is close, is on the board of trustees of a local university to which the social worker is applying for admission to a doctoral program. The client offers to put in a good word for the practitioner. Although the situation occurs out of pure coincidence, the social worker reduces the customary fee and continues to work with the client even though her psychological state has improved and she is no longer in need of services.

These situations are problematic for one basic reason: the purpose of the original contract between the social worker and the client has been muddled. The purpose of the professional relationship with the client is for social workers to use their knowledge of psychosocial problems and their intervention skills to help clients resolve problems and cope with their lives better. The social worker provides a professional service, and the client pays for that service. Nothing more is relevant to the relationship. Other matters such as potential benefit to the social worker's personal, social, or financial well-being (beyond the satisfaction of helping others and getting paid for the service) goes beyond the professional relationship and potentially erodes the benefit of the service to the client. The NASW Code of Ethics properly exhorts social workers to identify and avoid such conflicts of interest whereby the purpose of the professional encounter competes with some other need of the practitioner or where the benefit to the client is somehow compromised (Houston-Vega & Nuehring, 1997; Reamer, 2003, 2006; Strom-Gottfried, 2007).

Personal Demeanor: Sexual Relationships, Physical Contact, and Sexual Harassment

The NASW Code of Ethics clearly states that social workers should not participate in, condone, or be associated with dishonesty, fraud, or deception. However, social workers have an obligation to maintain professional demeanor that goes beyond not breaking the law. These situations include not allowing personal problems including mental health, substance abuse, and interpersonal or social problems to negatively affect their ability to perform professional duties toward clients. If social workers become aware of these impairments, they should seek whatever professional help is necessary to ameliorate the problem and ensure that they are able to carry out their professional responsibilities adequately.

Social workers should not engage in sexual relations with their clients or others close to the client under any circumstances. Social workers, not clients, clients' relatives, or close acquaintances, are responsible for maintaining boundaries. The burden of proof also lies with social workers to demonstrate that sexual relations with former clients did not cause harm or result from manipulation or coercion. Social workers should also not provide services to people with whom they have had a prior sexual relationship. Social workers should never attempt to solicit sexual contact in any form from a client. Any such behaviors could be considered sexual harassment.

Social workers should not engage in physical contact with clients where psychological harm may result. Cuddling, caressing, or otherwise physically nurturing clients are strongly discouraged. Incidental touching such as handshakes or helping an elderly client from a chair are not ordinarily a problem, but other forms of touching (e.g., hugs, pats on the back) should be done with discretion. Clients may interpret even the most well-intentioned contact as a gesture laden with some unintended meaning. Interpretation of physical contact may also carry unknown cultural meaning, and practitioners should be aware of these gestures. Clear, professional boundaries should be maintained at all times. Warmth, compassion, and encouragement can be communicated effectively without physically touching clients.

Interruption and Termination of Services

Generally, social workers should provide only those services that clients need. Termination of services should occur when the client can no longer benefit from the service or when the service is no longer needed. In doing so, social workers should avoid abrupt termination of services (i.e., abandonment). Social workers can terminate services with a client if the client stops paying for contracted services as long as the client does not pose an imminent danger to him- or herself or another person.

Social workers are obliged to maintain the continuity of services and must make arrangements to continue service for clients should the service be interrupted by the practitioner's unavailability, illness, or death. Every effort should be made to anticipate termination of services and plan for orderly cessation of services, transfer to another practitioner, or referral in a way that is agreeable to the client.

Informed Consent and Ensuring Competent Practice

Social workers should claim competence only in providing services for which they have had proper training along with associated licensing, certification, supervision, and professional experience. The NASW Code of Ethics is ambiguous, however, in guiding practitioners in the use of intervention methods for which recognized standards do not exist. Rather, the code exhorts practitioners to use their judgment and obtain proper training, supervision, and consultation. This injunction, nevertheless, begs this question: if no such recognized standards exist, then on what knowledge criteria are the training, supervision, or consultation based?

Although the code is somewhat ambiguous regarding the criteria employed to define practice competence, its authors exhort social workers to

accept responsibility or employment only on the basis of existing competence or the intention to acquire the necessary competence . . . [and to] . . . strive to become and remain proficient in professional practice and the performance of professional functions. Social workers should critically examine and keep current with emerging knowledge relevant to social work. Social workers should routinely review the professional literature and participate in continuing education relevant to social work practice and social work ethics. Social workers should base practice on recognized knowledge, including empirically based knowledge, relevant to social work and social work ethics. (NASW, 2007, 401(c))

Practitioners are guided by the code to provide clients with informed consent regarding the type of practices they offer the client and to provide services to clients only in the context of a professional relationship. The problem analysis (assessment and diagnosis) and intervention plan should be discussed with the client in language that is clear and understandable, and clients should be educated about the nature of the intervention, likely benefits from it, and any possible risks of harm associated with the intervention. Financial matters and associated limitations imposed on the intervention (e.g., cost of treatment, insurance matters, amount of treatment covered) should also be explained clearly to the client. Key to the matter of informed consent is the obligation of the social worker to discuss the type of intervention to be used, what benefits are likely to accrue for the client, and what inherent risks may be incurred. Although there is some ambiguity in the scientific and legal communities as to what knowledge base is adequate for justifying the use of certain forms of social work practice, a sound body of peer-reviewed research provides a much stronger argument than do untested therapies or practices supported by anecdotal clinical evidence (e.g., uncontrolled case studies). Courts are increasingly referring to evidence-based practices (i.e., interventions shown repeatedly to be effective in randomized controlled trials) as the criteria against which the adequacy of practitioners' interventions will be judged.

Conducting Evaluation and Research

The NASW Code of Ethics also exhorts social workers to engage in reviews of current practice research and engage in evaluation of their own practice. Keeping up with current knowledge relevant to their clients' problems and effective practices is an essential social work skill that will help maintain professional competence within the current standards of care. Evaluating one's own practice can take a number of forms, from simply monitoring the progress of one's own clients to participating in agency program evaluation initiatives. In any case, practice, evaluation, and research activities share a common ethical rubric:

- Clients should be informed as to the nature of practice, evaluation, and research efforts.
- These activities should be participated in voluntarily whenever possible.
- Confidentiality of all data (e.g., progress notes, quantitative data from scales and indexes) should be protected.

When practitioners engage in research that goes beyond routine evaluation of agency services, they must obtain permission and follow the guidelines of an institutional review board (IRB), commissioned to examine the nature of the evaluation or research and to ensure client safety, informed consent, and confidentiality. Such participation of clients is voluntary, and they are free to withdraw at any time. Clients are also provided with support should they suffer any undue distress from the evaluation or research activities. Whether the activities of social workers are practice, evaluation, or research, they should commit themselves to the core ethical principles of competence, informed consent, and confidentiality (Houston-Vega & Daguio, 1997; Reamer, 1995, 2006; Strom-Gottfried, 2007).

Practitioners and researchers also share the responsibility of receiving adequate informed consent from clients after explaining the nature of the intervention or the research-evaluation project, and of indicating whether there is any potential for psychological distress. Practitioners and researchers are also required to be responsive should clients become distressed in the course of an intervention or research and evaluation procedure. With increasing frequency, practice and evaluation activities are simultaneous (e.g., use of clinical scales as part of assessment and clinical review procedures), which often renders the intervention and evaluation distinction moot for practical and ethical purposes. A sensible policy is for social workers to concentrate on applying good ethical principles whether the professional activity is defined as practice, evaluation, research, or a combination of these.

Malpractice and Liability in Social Work Practice

Although ethics provide important and useful guidelines for sound professional practice, social workers must also be familiar with basic legal requirements, usually regulations published by the health authority in states where they practice. "Professional malpractice is generally considered a form of negligence" (Reamer, 2003, p. 3). In general, *malpractice* means that social workers have provided a service in a way that diverges significantly from the standard of care; that is, the way other competent professionals would act under similar circumstances (Beutler, Clarkin, & Bongar, 2000). Malpractice does not imply that the practitioner intended to act in an unethical or malevolent manner. It can be an innocent mistake (e.g., inadvertently discussing confidential information with someone not authorized to hear it), a mistake in diagnosis or assessment (e.g., not diagnosing a DSM-IV major mood disorder or failing to identify known suicide-risk factors), or an egregious breach of proper care (e.g., sleeping with a client to "nurture" the inner child"). Malpractice generally occurs when a legal duty has been breached (e.g., confidentiality); when the practitioner failed to carry out his or her duty either through omission or commission of an improper act; or when the client was harmed psychologically, emotionally, or physically by the social worker's actions (Reamer, 2003).

Malpractice suits often involve allegations of improper treatment. These situations are usually related to practitioners who do something improper or who fail to do what they should do within the standard of care. Malpractice lawsuits related to improper treatment may stem from failure to receive adequate informed consent, failure to provide adequate assessment and intervention, or breaching of proper practitioner-client boundaries. The literature on liability matters is complex and requires a thorough understanding of legal issues. Reamer's (2003) text *Social Work Malpractice and Liability* provides an excellent introduction to these and related matters. In addition, his book *The Social Work Ethics Audit: A Risk Management Tool* (2001) is a useful guide for both private practitioners and agency administrators in reviewing and improving policies that can reduce liability risk; improve the overall ethical climate of practice; and reduce the likelihood of lawsuits for breaches of confidentiality, divergences from the standard of care, and other unethical actions. However, for our purposes, the main focus here is on basic considerations to avoid malpractice lawsuits through adequate assessment and intervention methods.

Avoiding Breaches of Informed Consent

Informing clients about the nature of the intervention and obtaining voluntary consent (in most cases) is relevant to services with both adults and children. Although in most situations practitioners must obtain the written permission of parents or guardians of minors, the requirements vary by state law and apply differently to emancipated minors, or those who have obtained independence before the usual age of emancipation. As noted earlier, the NASW Code of Ethics enjoins social workers to explain the interventions to be used in clear and understandable language. This means that social workers should be explicit about the type of intervention they intend to use, the nature and limitations of that intervention, whether there is any risk of harm, and any available alternatives (Houston-Vega & Nuehring, 1997; Reamer, 2003). Clients should be closely involved in, and agree to, the development of an intervention plan. Even with court-mandated client treatment, every effort should be made to engage clients in the intervention-planning process and to provide them with some degree of choice and participation.

Let's say a client arrives at a social worker's office with a clearly diagnosed panic disorder. She is understandably terrified by the shortness of breath, fits of trembling, feeling sick to her stomach, and feeling as though she is about to lose her mind. The client recently had to pull off the highway while driving over a suspension bridge because she felt her arms going numb, a feeling that increased her terror. Although a combination of antidepressants and antianxiety medication had been prescribed, the client was still experiencing the attacks and was becoming more and more reclusive and afraid to go outside. Her mobility was greatly decreased, and though she had found some alternative ways to get to work and school (e.g., taxis, friends), these options were too expensive or, at best, time limited. The client was feeling desperate and felt she had no recourse other than to receive mental health care that would alleviate her symptoms and help her get back on track.

The social worker met with her supervisor, and they discussed the assessment and diagnosis of the client's condition. The supervisor, convinced that childhood trauma was causing the client's panic disorder, advised the social worker to develop a working alliance with the client, identify the root cause of fear, and help the client work it through with the help of a proper interpretation.

The social worker left the session with the supervisor with an uneasy feeling. Recently, she had read in a professional journal review article that cognitive-behavioral treatment and graduated exposure combined with medication offered the client the best chance of a speedy and lasting recovery compared to other known interventions. However, the supervisor had not mentioned this approach. The social worker was new on the job and reluctant to challenge her supervisor's recommendations. Her supervisor had a tendency to speak in an authoritative tone, did not seem to like being questioned about his clinical decisions, and seemed perturbed when any of his colleagues mentioned evidence-based practices. What should the novice social worker do? Could she give accurate and full information to the client about the type of intervention she was about to provide? Would she incur any liability risk if she failed to point out the availability of this other well-researched approach? Would the chief executive of the for-profit agency be angry with her if she referred the client to another agency that did provide the current best practices?

Obviously, providing information to clients about effective practices would put the social worker in jeopardy. Nevertheless, providing adequate information requires that social workers be knowledgeable about both the problems they treat and the interventions they use. Knowledge of effective interventions must be obtained through social work education, training in field experiences, and ongoing supervision in postgraduate employment. Social workers who become aware of the relative effectiveness of some interventions over others should pursue training in those methods if they choose to continue providing interventions for clients with those problems.

Consent for treatment should be voluntary (although there are exceptions to this general rule), documented in the client record (although verbal consent is sometimes accepted), and the client must be mentally capable of providing voluntary consent (a matter that the courts sometimes have to determine). Clients generally have the right to withdraw consent for services, and social workers should request that the client sign a form that details the risks the social worker feels the client may incur by terminating the intervention prematurely. Generally, in cases of emergency where clients are at risk (e.g., involuntary commitment) or put someone else at imminent risk (as in *Tarasoff*, noted earlier), social workers may intervene without the client's informed consent.

Reducing Liability Exposure with Competent Assessments

Although there is considerable ambiguity in the professional literature regarding what constitutes an adequate assessment, social workers should become competent in using methods of assessment that fall within the profession's standard of care. There are a number of assessment schools of thought that a substantial number of social workers accept. Thus, should a social worker be informed by psychodynamic theory, cognitive-behavioral theory, family systems theory, and so on, the courts generally do not pass judgment on which theory or assessment framework is the right one. Despite legal and scientific ambiguities, social workers, at a minimum, should be familiar with the criteria in the DSM-IV, as this text is generally accepted and used by most mental health professionals regardless of theoretical orientation. The criteria for diagnoses provide helpful guidelines for assessing serious mental illnesses and associated risks (e.g., impulsivity, suicidal intent). Other approaches to assessment may be helpful as well, and social workers should pay attention to key areas of assessment where the client's well-being or the well-being of others may be at risk. Should a client express a good deal of anger at an individual with no apparent threat, this matter needs to be addressed at length and documented. Should a client express suicidal thoughts, these matters should be addressed in further detail, and social workers should become familiar with known risk factors for suicide identified in the research literature. In general, social workers should strive to provide a comprehensive and consistent approach to assessment that includes an assessment of mental status, family and social problems, and substance abuse, as well as daily functioning at work, school, and in the community. High-risk behaviors such as substance abuse or impulsive behaviors that endanger themselves or others, or verbal threats should be duly noted and addressed at length with the client and, if need be, with others. Suicidal ideation should be thoroughly evaluated using known risk factors reported in the research literature, and such an evaluation should be documented in the client record. Assessments that focus on observable or reported facts should be given priority over assessments based primarily on a high degree of inference (e.g., interpreting dreams, unconscious motives, drawings, children's play behavior). If the social worker has serious doubts about the adequacy of an assessment, he or she should seek expert consultation and document what was discussed (for details about conducting assessments, see chapter 4).

Intervention Plans That Reduce Liability Risks

Social workers can also be legally liable for not providing interventions that meet the standard of care. This situation can arise in several ways, including engaging in practices for which the social worker does not have adequate training, performing an intervention poorly with harm resulting to the client, and engaging in practices that are not supported by a significant proportion of the professional community. Because there are many therapeutic practices that have not been well researched but that, nevertheless, more than a few therapists practice, determining what constitutes the standard of care according to the court can be an ambiguous matter. However, the courts have awarded judgments to plaintiffs (i.e., clients or relatives who sue their therapists) for having been subjected to fringe therapies that resulted in harm. Such practices as rebirthing therapy, conducting past-life regressions, and recovered-memory therapy are interventions of questionable value to clients and have resulted in social workers being sued, at times, with damages awarded to the clients or their relatives.

Although scientific debate continues regarding the value of more mainstream therapies, the courts will generally accept these, and judgments will focus on whether the approaches are applied with adequate skill within the standard of care. Nevertheless, social workers are best advised to employ interventions for which there is a substantive body of peer-reviewed controlled research (i.e., evidence-based practices). Practitioners should be conservative in their choice of interventions and err on the side of restraint by pursuing training and supervision in methods that are well supported in the practice-research literature. Practitioners are required to document their intervention plans and provide progress notes in sufficient detail to demonstrate that the interventions were skillfully applied. This strategy reflects the spirit of the NASW Code of Ethics and is best for both the client's well-being and the practitioner's legal protection.

The code also enjoins practitioners to keep up with emerging practice knowledge. To stay current and fully appreciate the emergence of new practices, social workers must be able to critically read and understand practice evaluation and research reports in such a way that they can distinguish unsubstantiated fad therapies from practices supported by methodologically sound research (for basic guidelines on reviewing practice research to develop this skill early on, see chapter 2). Although social work faculty carry some degree of responsibility for what they teach students, once students become licensed practitioners, they are fully responsible for the practices they employ with clients.

Properly Terminating Services

Informed consent and developing a good working relationship with the client should mark the beginning of intervention, but how interventions end is equally important. Termination of treatment should, under the best of circumstances, be planned and discussed and should proceed with the knowledge that the client achieved some or all of his or her goals, is satisfied with the service received, and would know how to return to treatment or seek additional treatment in the future if needed. Social workers will find that such endings occur regularly and are often satisfying for both the worker and the client. Sometimes, however, things do not end smoothly. If a client, for whatever reason, terminates abruptly or prematurely, the social worker (if given the opportunity) should discuss the client-initiated termination with the client and document his or her own efforts to understand the client's needs and offer referral services. In extreme cases, should a client pose a danger to the community (e.g., a dangerous client escapes from an in-patient psychiatric hospital), the authorities must be notified.

Additional liability risk occurs when the practitioner fails to make him- or herself available to the client, extends service beyond what is required, or abruptly terminates services without adequate justification. Once a social worker begins to work with a client, there is an ethical expectation that he will follow through with the intervention until service is completed or until he can no longer provide intervention that will benefit the client. There is also an understanding that the limitations of the initial contract for payment also applies (e.g., insurance covers only ten sessions), but these matters must be discussed at the beginning of the intervention if this information is available. If a social worker feels that he or she can no longer work with a client for whatever reason, these reasons must be discussed with the client and plans made to terminate and refer the case to someone else if the client is still in need of treatment. A social worker who decides to stop seeing a client because the client can no longer afford to pay the cost or because the client has become uncooperative places the social worker at risk for a lawsuit. In general, social workers should plan for termination well in advance, document the discussions, confer with colleagues, and offer referral elsewhere if needed when the intervention ends (Houston-Vega & Nuehring, 1997; Reamer, 2003).

Informed consent, adequate assessment and intervention, and proper termination of services are core concerns regarding liability risks. However, social workers can be sued for other reasons as well, such as the following:

- Having sex with clients or former clients
- Providing therapeutic interventions for former sex partners
- Breaching confidentiality
- Failing to report suspected abuse of a child or elderly person (i.e., mandated reporting)
- Reporting abuse in bad faith, meaning that the social worker did not demonstrate that he or she had good reason to believe there was evidence of abuse

In all these cases, regularly reviewing the NASW Code of Ethics, knowing agency policies and relevant state regulations, making every effort to document efforts to provide adequate care that is supported in the practice-research literature, and consulting with supervisors and experts can go a long way toward preventing violations of ethics or exposure to lawsuits.

Ethical Considerations for Working with Involuntary Clients

The NASW Code of Ethics rightly enjoins social workers to respect client autonomy and self-determination. At every turn, practitioners should strive to optimize that principle with their clients. However, social workers are increasingly called on to work with clients who have committed serious crimes, hurt people in their own families and communities, and are at risk to hurt others again. Thus, social work ethical principles also enjoin practitioners to consider potential harm to the public when making assessment and intervention decisions about clients. The *Tarasoff* decision represents a relatively obvious situation in that the practitioner must respond to an imminent threat of harm to others ("I'm going to kill her when I get home!"). However, social workers often serve clients where the risk to others does not appear imminent but nevertheless remains a genuine, albeit indeterminate, concern. Social workers are increasingly called on to work with "involuntary" clients. These are clients who have behavioral problems related to mental illnesses; are addicted to illegal drugs; or have been physically or sexually abusive to their partners, children, or others in the community. These and other categories of committed, court-ordered, or involuntary clients now constitute a large proportion of people served by social workers. The ethical mandate for working with involuntary clients requires a skillful balance between protecting the rights of clients and protecting the rights of the often anonymous public. Knowledge of research regarding known relapse and recidivism rates in the community is essential when contributing to court decisions as expert witness or client advocate regarding a client's disposition (e.g., prison, treatment, some combination of treatment and close monitoring). Working specifically with court-mandated clients requires that social workers balance empathy for their clients with compassion for their likely (anonymous) victims (i.e., protect the innocent).

Behavior-change professionals (including social workers) in the mental health, substance abuse, child welfare, and other fields, along with many professionals in law enforcement and the criminal justice system, share common goals of reducing antisocial behaviors in clients and simultaneously protecting the public from their harmful actions. Although public policy debate often lurches between the extremes of lockup and providing treatment, more thoughtful observers have begun to see some potential for productive accommodation between the two extremes for certain clients. Although clients are responsible for their actions (except in rare cases such as gross medical impairment), society and the criminal courts recognize mitigating circumstances (e.g., mental illness, addiction) and, more important, the potential for more effective approaches that combine the strengths of effective psychosocial change efforts and the leverage of the criminal justice system (Nygaard, 2000; O'Hare, 2005; Wexler, 1991). Helping a client become a more prosocial, productive member of society are goals commensurate with both the criminal justice system and the human services professions. Although a sound idea in principle, the effectiveness of approaches such as outpatient civil commitment and early-release diversionary substance-abuse treatment for convicted offenders must be judged by sound evaluation and outcome research, not by ideology, value statements, personal convictions, or the sheer venality of political pandering.

Clients who participate in programs such as these are often referred to as *involuntary* clients, but the term is somewhat of a misnomer on at least two levels. First, clients who participate in therapeutic programs and are simultaneously court-monitored to ensure their purposeful and regular participation (i.e., compliance) are often given a choice to participate in the programs. The person convicted of a nonviolent drug-related offense may be offered the opportunity for a briefer prison sentence if he or she elects to participate in a therapeutic community for drug addiction and agrees to continue treatment (e.g., halfway house, outpatient) after release. The

seriously mentally ill person who repeatedly decides not to take antipsychotic medication may be given a choice of in-patient hospitalization or
commitment to supervised outpatient care (i.e., outpatient civil commitment). Legal guidelines associated with these decisions and other related
dilemmas (e.g., estimating risk to others in the community) are complex
matters that need to be addressed in court by attorneys, other client advocates, and expert witnesses. A key element in making decisions about
diversionary treatment in the community versus incarceration involves sci-
entifically informed (i.e., evidence-based) risk assessments about the probability of recidivism and the nature of the potential criminal act (e.g., a
convicted burglar buying and using drugs again versus an aggressive sexual predator raping, torturing, and killing a four-year-old child). Suffice it
to say that these are sometimes difficult matters to resolve, and mistakes
will follow from either overrestriction of the civil rights of some clients or
failure to confine or closely supervise people who pose a high degree of
danger to the general public. Nevertheless, social workers must come to
grips with their own ethical standards with regard to balancing clients'
rights and public safety.

Second, not all clients pressured to accept or comply with treatment are
completely resistant to the idea of change. Many involuntary clients are
quite willing to engage in treatment and (perhaps faced with worse alternatives) give their best effort to make positive changes in their lives. From
the social worker's point of view, although such clients may, indeed, be
leveraged by the courts with contingencies related to rehospitalization or
reincarceration for noncompliance with treatment, practitioners can often
offer clients a fair amount of latitude and flexibility with regard to how
they participate in treatment and pursue their treatment goals. So, while
they may appear to be coerced, many involuntary clients do have a choice
with regard to type of intervention, and social workers can help these clients develop treatment plans and goals that offer some degree of autonomy
and flexibility within the mandated treatment framework (O'Hare, 1996;
Rooney & Bibus, 2001).

Arthur Caplan, the bioethicist, makes a reasonable argument for the
ethics and morality of coerced treatment for convicted felons addicted to
narcotics: although these clients may not be mentally incompetent according to law, they are often grossly lacking in autonomy as a result of their
protracted addictions, and coerced treatment (provided for a limited time)
can help restore that autonomy (Caplan, 2006). Wynn (2006) notes that
mandated treatment is an accepted policy in most countries despite different definitions of psychosis, different rates of coercive treatment, and different laws governing client rights and coercive treatments. According to

Wynn, there are two main reasons for using coercive psychiatric treatments: to reduce suffering in patients (e.g., a person with schizophrenia who, as is characteristic of the disease, is very ill but denies the illness and refuses medication) and to protect others from possible harm. Although the empirical literature is mixed regarding the effectiveness of coercion in the long run, it must be guided by balancing four main principles: respecting client autonomy, acting responsibly in the patient's best interest, avoiding harm to the client in any way, and providing quality care for all clients (i.e., justice; Wynn, 2006). However, despite the intended beneficence of mandated care, coercing a client to receive mental health treatment might result in further treatment avoidance by clients who would otherwise benefit from voluntary treatment. The barriers of mandated care are often compounded by other barriers to care, including poverty, drug addiction, and lack of transportation, among others (Van Dorn, Elbogen, Redlich, Swanson, Swartz, & Mustillo, 2006). Most informed and thoughtful writers on the subject of mandated treatment recognize that arguments for and against involve a complex interplay of legal, ethical, and clinical argument. Overly aggressive use of mandated treatments and categorical refusal to even consider the use of mandated care in extreme cases tend to be seen as fringe positions on the matter. Ultimately, the benefits and costs to both the client and society must be determined by much-needed empirical research on mandated treatments.

Using Research Findings to Avoid Breaching Ethical or Legal Practice Guidelines

Civil and criminal legal actions against social work practitioners are usually related to alleged breaches in the standard of care, and outcome research is beginning to have greater influence in court decisions regarding what constitutes the standard of care. These concerns have increased the anxieties of some clinicians, administrators, evaluators, supervisors, and quality-assurance professionals. Questions arise such as the following: Do assessment protocols reliably capture high-risk behaviors? Are we using the best intervention approaches available to help clients? Are recently graduated social workers properly trained in evidence-based approaches when they begin their first professional jobs? If their professional education does not include evidence-based practices, what liability exposure do agencies incur, and how much remedial training can agencies afford to provide to bring new practitioners and their supervisors up to speed? Are instructors in schools of social work liable if their students employ non-evidence-based practices with adverse consequences for their clients? Although these questions involve potentially complex legal arguments, instructors, practitioners, and administrators should, at a minimum, be more circumspect in what approaches are endorsed in the classroom and in agencies. To quote Barbara White, former president of NASW and former chair of the NASW Insurance Trust: "A social worker's best protection is a solid understanding of the standard of care as it applies to practice" (Houston-Vega & Nuehring, 1997, p. xiv). Because competent, critical reviews of the outcome research are increasingly defining the standard of care, one can readily argue that treatment not based on careful and thoughtful reviews of the literature is more likely to lead to ineffective and perhaps unethical practices, and possibly to wider exposure to lawsuits (Meyers & Thyer, 1997; O'Hare, 2005; Thyer, 2004).

In addition to reviewing the relevant research literature, Reamer (2003) recommends several other steps social workers can take to buttress their decisions and reduce the likelihood of being found negligent in practice: consult expert colleagues and obtain supervision from someone who has the relevant credentials and expertise, review the NASW Code of Ethics, know relevant laws and policies (e.g., confidentiality regulations), document one's decision-making steps, and obtain legal consultation.

What follows are a few basic guidelines to help social workers do their best work and avoid pitfalls that can lead to charges of unethical behavior and criminal malpractice or civil lawsuits. Although these suggestions are not to be construed as legal advice, making reference to sound assessment and practice guidelines will generally help practitioners do their best work, avoid inadvertent errors in judgment, and provide a rational basis for their practices:

Assessment and Evaluation

- Conduct a thorough assessment using multiple sources and methods (see chapter 4).

- Conduct a thorough mental-status exam including a thorough assessment of any suicidal ideation.

- Examine all areas of the client's life in addition to the specific target problem, including health status, substance abuse, work or school functioning, and family and community relationships. If you do not query about the client's well-being across multiple domains, they may not volunteer the information and important assessment data might be overlooked.

- Inquire as to previous mental health and substance abuse treatment and its outcome.

- Examine other conflicted relationships, including any history of abuse or violence. Inquire in detail about any evidence of potential harm to children or elderly people in the client's life, whether the danger be the result of the client's or another's behavior.

- Conduct a thorough assessment of their immediate relationships (e.g., couple, family, children, extended family members with whom they have regular contact).

- Tactfully inquire about past criminal behavior, arrests, and imprisonment.

- Conduct a thorough functional assessment; that is, ask questions about day-to-day details to identify risk factors associated with the client's problems.

- Document a DSM-IV diagnosis and provide supporting evidence for that diagnosis.

- Use scales and indexes that have a published track record of reliability and validity in the clinical research literature. These measures can provide additional support for the overall qualitative assessment.

- Given the proper informed consent, obtain as much corroborating information as possible about the client and his or her difficulties. Ask to interview partners and family members. Go beyond the client's immediate social circle and obtain copies of records with client consent (e.g., legal, mental health, health) to get a full picture of the client's presenting problems.

- Be thorough, document your observations, and discuss any matters of concern with colleagues, supervisors, and other experts as needed.

Intervention Methods

- After a comprehensive assessment, examine the current research on effective practices and discuss these matters with your client and supervisor.

- Describe to the client what is known about available effective practices and explain what you believe to be the best choice.

- Encourage the client to collaborate with you in the development of an individualized intervention plan.

- Explain to the client why you think the plan will be helpful, the likely benefits, and any risks, and give the client a chance to air any questions or concerns.

- Write the intervention plan with the client, and document the agreement to participate in the plan.

- As the plan is implemented, keep accurate progress notes and use qualitative and quantitative means to monitor the client's progress.

- Should problems arise, consult supervisors and experts if the client does not seem to respond well to the intervention.

- If the client does not improve in a reasonable amount of time, discuss options and possible referrals for another opinion if necessary.

- Always keep termination processes in mind, and discuss the client's progress at each visit.

- As the client approaches the end of the intervention, discuss after-care plans and referrals for follow-up should they seem necessary.

In summary, practitioners should stay abreast of current research literature regarding valid assessments and effective practices, be open with clients about the recommended interventions, communicate opinions in clear and plain language with clients, document essential intervention activities and client responses to them, seek consultation as needed, and always keep the client's well-being foremost in mind.

The profession of social work will face increasing challenges to reconcile clinical practice, research, and evaluation with social work ethics as health-care policy continues to evolve. Changes in mental health policy and administration have implications for several areas of the law including access to managed-care treatment in the face of service denials, increased involuntary interventions, more attention to defining and measuring psychological and social outcomes, confidentiality issues related to the development and use of massive data banks designed for the routine monitoring and evaluation of clinical practice, and other changes in treatment technologies and the economic structures needed to run them. Social workers will have to become more involved in developing evidence-based practice guidelines for the profession to maintain professional viability and autonomy and compete with the other professions (Howard & Jenson, 1999; O'Hare, 2005).

PART TWO

Essential Practice Skills

CHAPTER FOUR

Conducting the Assessment and Planning the Evaluation

A THOROUGH AND INFORMED ASSESSMENT helps the practitioner and client better understand the client's problems and adaptive capabilities (i.e., strengths), provides an understanding of the role of personal identity factors with respect to the individual client or family, serves as a guide to the development of the intervention plan, and provides a foundation for monitoring the client's progress and evaluating the intervention. Valid assessment of clients' difficulties and strengths must be based on a thorough qualitative review of the client's own experiences over time, the observations and concerns of those involved in the client's life, and a solid grasp of human-behavior research relevant to the client's specific difficulties (e.g., depression, addictions, domestic violence). The current chapter describes the essentials of multidimensional-functional (MDF) assessment, a comprehensive approach to problem analysis that combines a firm grounding in contemporary human-behavior theory and research with a respect for each client's unique problem construction and situation. Many practice traditions across the helping professions have contributed to contemporary social work assessment (Bellack & Hersen, 1998; Franklin & Jordan, 2003; O'Hare, 2005; Sadock & Sadock, 2003). However, one can argue that two major concepts subsume the best qualities of those approaches: multidimensionality and functionality.

Before beginning this chapter, a caveat is in order. Competent assessment is closely tied to competent interviewing and engagement skills; that is, the early stages of the intervention process. This chapter focuses on the conceptual content one should master to conduct a thorough assessment. The next chapter will cover the supportive, interviewing, and engagement skills necessary to carry out the assessment and continue the intervention.

It is important to know what information to obtain before addressing how to engage the client in the reciprocal process.

Key Organizing Concepts of a Valid Assessment: Multidimensionality and Functionality

There are a range of different approaches to assessment in social work. Traditional psychiatric assessment (i.e., diagnosis) is based on a disease-oriented model and emphasizes disorder within the individual. Systems-oriented assessment emphasizes interactions between and among individuals, family members, and the community. Cognitive-behavioral assessment focuses on how an individual's thoughts, feelings, and behaviors interact reciprocally with people and conditions in the environment. Narrative, constructivist, humanist, and other phenomenological approaches emphasize the unique experience of each client, and the inherent ability of each person to adapt and come to their own solutions. Psychodynamic assessment focuses on the effects of early childhood events and their assumed long-term impact on shaping unconscious motivation and interpersonal relationships.

Practitioners driven by ideology rather than critical thinking tend to take reactionary approaches in promoting one kind of assessment (e.g., pitting the psychopathology model against the strengths model, or family systems against individual assessment). However, adherents to all these forms of assessment have made positive contributions to better understanding our clients' troubles. Nevertheless, the contributions of these assessment models must be sorted out critically and informed by research rather than ideology and personal preference. Psychiatric diagnoses are essential when identifying bona fide mental disorders such as schizophrenia and major mood disorders, but the psychopathology model does not accurately represent serious problems that are primarily psychosocial in origin (e.g., domestic violence). Systems models highlight interactions between and among individuals within families and communities, but they often fail to adequately recognize individual psychopathology when it does exist (e.g., bipolar disorder). Cognitive-behavioral assessment stresses the role of faulty thinking in relation to feelings and behaviors but is enhanced when individual functioning is considered in a broader family and community context. Constructivist and other phenomenological practitioners stress the importance of a client's unique experience, but their deemphasis (and, in some cases, rejection) of knowledge of psychopathology renders them unprepared (and perhaps unqualified) to deal with serious mental and behavioral disorders. Last, psychodynamic theoreticians emphasize the importance of early childhood experience and its impact on the development of close relationships, but their specific theories regarding psychosocial development and psychopathology have not stood up well to scientific scrutiny. What is needed is an assessment framework that is comprehensive, multidimensional, reflects current scientific knowledge of human behavior, and incorporates the best that these various models have to offer.

As the term *comprehensive* implies, a sound assessment involves a considerable amount of data gathering that generally covers the following areas:

- Individual well-being, including cognitive, emotional, and behavioral functioning
- General health status and ability to attend to activities of daily life
- Family and other proximate interpersonal relationships
- Social functioning and environmental supports including community ties and level of integration with social organizations (e.g., school, social agencies)
- Academic, occupational, and other relevant role functioning

The assessment process includes (1) gathering information about the client's experiences relevant to his or her problems and coping abilities and (2) understanding the significance of that information within the context of contemporary human-behavior research that is specifically relevant to the client's presenting concerns. Although a thorough assessment often results in a large amount of information regarding the client and his or her circumstances, the final assessment summary should be fairly succinct and focus on the problems of greatest significance and the potential for positive change.

Assessment is multidimensional in two respects: first, clients' problems are complex; that is, multidimensional. Many factors, biological, psychological, and social, contribute to the causes of clients' problems. To more fully understand a sexually abused child's fears, a mentally ill person's delusions, an addicted person's anxieties, or an obsessive person's preoccupation with orderliness, practitioners must have a grasp of the relevant research that informs our understanding of these conditions. Second, clients' problems are multidimensional in the sense that the problems and adaptive strengths usually manifest across multiple interacting domains of living: psychological, interpersonal, community, occupational and educational, health, and other domains of daily living. Social work has a long tradition of framing clients' problems within the context of interacting psychosocial systems. However, these broad frameworks lack explanatory power to support assessment with specific problems (e.g., mental illnesses, child abuse and neglect, anxiety disorders). Thus, ecosystems models and similar models must be informed by current research findings specific to that problem area (Wakefield, 1996). For example, to fully understand the nature of a mentally ill client's thought disorders and interpersonal deficits, the practitioner must have a grasp of the relevant research on mental illness. For a practitioner to more fully understand a battered woman's passivity, depression, and apparent helplessness, a solid familiarity with the research on domestic violence and co-occurring substance abuse would be required. General frameworks may outline the perimeter of human-behavior problems, but knowledge specific to any given problem is required to more fully understand the significance of each client's situation.

Estimating the severity of client problems and adaptive capacities across multiple domains does not in itself result in a complete assessment. Practitioners must also conduct a functional analysis of the client's key problems. Knowing what the problems are does not mean that practitioners understand how they work over time and across situations. What is meant by "how they work"? Problem analysis is functional to the extent that it attempts to describe how the various factors related to a client's problems interact in everyday life. For example, although research on substance abuse informs us in a general way about the causes, course, and consequences of addictions, each client will manifest his or her struggles in a unique way. For one client, daily stressors, problems coping with anxiety, and interpersonal conflict may precipitate binge drinking. For another person, antecedents to drug use may be associated with otherwise-positive social encounters (e.g., parties) even though the consequences may be negative (e.g., mood disturbance, poor school or work performance). A child struggling with symptoms of attention deficit/hyperactivity disorder (ADHD) and problems at home may have trouble concentrating in the classroom and staying in his seat. At other times, when conditions are more tranquil at home, he may have an easier time getting some of his homework done and may respond more readily to praise from his teacher. The functional assessment is important to complement the multidimensional assessment for this reason: although we know much about mental illnesses, addictions, child abuse, ADHD, and other problems, the causes, course, and consequences of the problems will be different for each client.

There are a number of key concepts related to functional analysis that can help map out each client's experience with problems and better understand each client's adaptive capabilities. These include (1) temporal sequencing and patterning of thoughts, feelings, behaviors, and social-environmental events related to the client's problem; (2) measurement of the frequency, severity (intensity), or duration of specific problems; (3) identification of contingencies (i.e., antecedent events, responses to those events, and resultant consequences; that is, rewards and punishments) that influence the client's behavior; (4) setting of priorities among different problems; (5) establishing progressive hierarchies to gradually address intervention objectives; (6) understanding the client's construction of the problem and expectations for change; (7) focusing on problems that are amenable to change; and (8) defining problems in a way that is sensitive to change over time.

The Five Steps to a Complete MDF Assessment

Determine the Sources of Data

Social workers often rely almost exclusively on client self-reports for their assessment information. In some cases, the client's description of his or her problems may be sufficient, as in situations when the client presents mild to moderate stressors or situational problems with little reason to hold back or dissemble about salient information. Even under these circumstances, clients often provide an incomplete picture. Individual clients may be quite ambivalent about their reasons for coming to see a social worker, may not fully understand what is troubling them (and are, therefore, unaware of relevant factors affecting them), or may distort or withhold information they deem embarrassing. Involuntary clients (e.g., substance abuse, child abuse allegations) may understandably minimize or deny important aspects of their behavior because they fear reprisal (i.e., confidentiality does not come with a 100% guarantee). Individual partners may give an honest yet one-sided view of their relationship problems; children and adolescents are likely to paint a rosy view of their school situation or problems at home; seriously mentally ill people simply may not be able to give a sensible account of what has happened to them. Social workers have an obligation to go beyond the client's view of the problem and obtain additional information from other sources to corroborate and complete the psychosocial assessment. Other sources include family members; community members such as teachers, other professionals, and coaches; and medical and legal records, among others.

Decide on the Methods for Obtaining Data

Qualitative and quantitative assessment can be conducted in a variety of ways. Face-to-face interviews with clients, family members, and other collaterals are the most frequently employed method for obtaining assessment data. The information obtained includes both self-report of individuals and their reports about others, including the client. Although client self-report is essential, the information and perspective provided by significant others can be invaluable to understanding what is going on with the client and those immediately around him or her. Face-to-face interviews can be fairly unstructured, semistructured, or highly structured. Unstructured interviews are best when there is little predetermined agenda and the interviewer is open to exploring possibilities offered by the client or others who may have important viewpoints on the client's problem. However, social workers usually approach an interview with a client or a collateral source with some assessment framework in mind, and a thorough psychosocial assessment implies some degree of structure designed to capture salient psychosocial information. This is referred to as a *semi-structured* approach to assessment. Highly structured interviews might be used when there is a specific and specialized reason for an interview, such as to investigate child abuse or conduct a thorough mental-status exam for a competency court hearing, whereby the practitioner uses a standardized instrument that has been well tested for reliability and validity. Structured interviews are also often used in clinical research to enhance reliability in data collection and measurement. Any or all of these approaches may be used in an assessment that uses face-to-face interviews.

In some cases the best approach to data gathering may be observation of clients' behavior in their environment (e.g., home, hospital ward, school, consulting office, summer camp). Of course, as with all assessments, observation requires informed consent from clients and/or their parents or guardians. However, unobtrusive observation of a client can be invaluable, as clients generally forget that they are being observed and can demonstrate problem behaviors and adaptive strengths that the practitioner can observe live (i.e., in vivo). Live observation has at least one major advantage over client self-report in that the social worker can make a more objective appraisal of some problem behaviors than if he or she had to rely on the client's reported perception of his or her own behaviors. Consider a social worker trying to understand why a child keeps getting into fights at school. Simply asking that child why he or she gets into fights with others at school is likely to yield rather biased results. The social worker may get a more accurate picture observing the child at play during lunch and recess.

A child who presents him- or herself as a victim in a face-to-face interview may appear to be the bully during in vivo observation.

For younger children, many child therapists attest to the usefulness of drawings, toys, games, and dolls as a method of assessment. Research evidence suggests that these methods are an excellent way for practitioners to help engender rapport with the child, to help the child to express him- or herself, and to explore the child's reports of problems or events in his or her life. However, because research has not supported the view of interpretation of the symbolic nature of children's play or children's drawings as a valid form of assessment, or that it adds much to an otherwise competent assessment, these should never be used to diagnose a child.

If in vivo observation is not practical, having clients demonstrate (i.e., role-play or act out) a problem situation can be the next best thing. Clients who have trouble with social anxiety or communication skills, for example, can demonstrate how they negotiate a social situation either on their own or with the help of a social worker who stands in as a proxy for a client's significant other. Role-playing can provide valuable insights not available to the client through self-reflection. Asking a parent to role-play with his or her child how the parent disciplines or encourages the child to do a chore or finish homework may be telling beyond the parent's self-report. Role-playing can serve as both a valuable assessment tool and a valuable behavior-change method (i.e., a form of rehearsal), as we will see in subsequent chapters.

Having a client engage in self-monitoring of thoughts, feelings, and behaviors across various situations for a week or two (e.g., keeping a diary of eating-disordered behaviors; having a parent or teacher keep a chart noting a child's homework completion) can contribute to the functional assessment of the client's day-to-day struggles. All of these assessment activities may include the collection of qualitative data, quantitative data, or (preferably) both types of data with the adjunctive use of charts, diaries, indexes, and scales, which will be explored in greater depth later in this chapter.

In general, the more sources of information and methods of data collection that are in an assessment, the more accurate the picture that will emerge about the client's struggles, the severity of those problems, the client's strengths, and other challenges and situational factors related to the problem. However, such a comprehensive strategy is not always feasible, and practitioners must sometimes choose the method that seems optimal under the circumstances. Sometimes client self-report is sufficient if there is good reason to believe that the client's self-report is accurate. In other circumstances, client observation may be best; in others, corroborating information may provide more accurate data than even the client's own self-report.

CONDUCTING A THOROUGH MDF ANALYSIS

Given that there are numerous sources and methods for collecting assessment data, we now move to an examination of the actual content of the MDF assessment.

Agencies typically require some basic background information about clients. Often an intake worker who does not conduct the primary intervention gathers this information at the first visit. Other times, the social worker who intends to continue working with the client may collect basic background information as part of the formal assessment. In any case, agency policies usually determine the type of information collected, such as the client's name, sex, marital status, race, religion, income source, insurance coverage, and so forth.

Background information can be understood on two levels. Some of it is simply client-identification data or demographics (e.g., age, sex, race), and can usually be readily determined in the initial interview. However, matters such as sexual orientation, religion, family composition, race, ethnicity, and other person characteristics may be very important to the client's identity and are often associated with complex layers of meaning. These matters should be approached in a more thoughtful and informed manner. Matters of sexual orientation, feelings about one's racial identification, subjective ethnicity, or matters of spirituality or religious practices are often of great significance to the client, and the practitioner can revisit them after addressing the preliminaries of the first intake. These matters will be addressed further on in this section.

THE PRESENTING PROBLEM

During the first visit, clients generally expect to discuss the reasons that brought them into the agency; that is, the presenting problem. Practitioner queries such as "What brings you in to see us today?" or "What seems to be troubling you?" are acceptable and routine openers. Practitioners should listen carefully to the way clients describe their problems from their own point of view. Often simple prompts such as "Uh-huh" or "Please, go on" are sufficient for encouraging clients who are anxious to talk about their difficulties or distress. Other clients, such as those who are very depressed or have been mandated for treatment, may be less forthcoming and may require a bit more prompting and structuring (for more on basic interviewing techniques, see chapter 5).

Practitioners, however, should feel ready to ask simple follow-up questions to encourage further details in an attempt to more fully understand the client's problems and concerns as they see them. Practitioners should be willing to express genuine curiosity about the client's difficulties and ask questions in a matter-of-fact style. Basic queries should include who (e.g., Who did what? Who was there? To whom are you referring? Who else was involved?), what (e.g., What happened? What happened before and after? Then what happened? What were the consequences?), where (e.g., Where did this occur? Where did you go?), when (e.g., When did that happen? What time of day? What day of the week, month, year?), and why (e.g., Why do you think they did that? Why did you have to go? Why did you decide to go for help?). In the initial stages of the assessment, it is probably best to avoid openly making judgments or drawing conclusions about the client's difficulties. Only after more data gathering, ideally with input from more sources, can practitioners begin to work with clients to connect the dots regarding the factors that seem to be related to their presenting complaints.

PSYCHOSOCIAL HISTORY WITH AN EMPHASIS ON PROBLEM TRAJECTORY

History taking is an essential part of a thorough assessment. Most practitioners agree that the client's history is informative with regard to identifying psychosocial risk factors (e.g., abuse, trauma, childhood disorders) and adaptive strengths and provides a sense of trajectory regarding the onset of difficulties, changes in problems over time, and the client's successful efforts to cope with those problems. Obviously, the relevance of past experiences will vary, in part, depending on the age of the client and how he or she perceives the importance of past events.

It is important to obtain a general history of the client's life. This history taking should result in a linear time line of key normative and problem events. Often, many clients' histories are relatively benign, and most milestones (e.g., starting school, first date, leaving home, marriage) pass uneventfully. However, within that time line, events may have occurred that provide important clues to emerging problems. Most notably are those that portend serious mental disorders, such as serious withdrawal or bizarre behaviors in high school or early childhood behavior problems such as setting fires, mutilating animals, or abusing inhalant chemicals. Other times, the report of a client's history reveals that few notable events have been interrupted suddenly by a traumatic, out-of-the-blue event, such as being raped or witnessing a fatality that resulted from a crime or accident. Although some practitioners might place too much emphasis on the minutiae of a client's past, a reasonably well-informed psychosocial history should cover key points in a client's life with special notice to difficulties in normative psychological development or particularly stressful or unpredictable events, as well as the client's attempts to cope with those challenges. Practitioners should note evidence of significant sequences of events, evidence of strengths or problems, and obvious patterns related to the client's presenting complaints.

Although retrospective reports can be fraught with distortions, memories of past events are often quite accurate and are usually important for understanding the client's current difficulties. However, memories can erode with time, and recollections may have only limited relevance to a client's current difficulties. Both the client's subjective experience of his or her personal history and research on risk factors can be helpful in determining the salience of historical events. Corroborating data from significant others (particularly when dealing with children and young adolescents) is essential for accurate history taking. The background data for involuntary clients should also be supported by other sources, including medical, legal, and other social service records.

Overall, a basic psychosocial history should minimally include the following:

- Place and circumstances of birth and early childhood
- Childhood developmental milestones
- History of family composition and quality of family life
- School experiences
- Relationships with peers and others in the community, from latency through adolescence
- Reports of abuse, trauma, extreme psychosocial stressors (acute and chronic) or any indications of serious emotional or behavioral disorders
- Work and academic history
- Health history and related treatments
- Emancipation experiences (e.g., leaving home; early adulthood)
- Romantic and sexual relationships
- Early, middle, and late-adult life experiences, as required

It is important to understand that assessments with very young children require a solid background in contemporary developmental child psychology. Understanding a young child's behavior at each stage of development requires some basic knowledge of the child's cognitive abilities and an understanding that abilities may vary from one child to the next (Bjork-lund, 2000). The assessment method employed with the child (e.g., look-ing at pictures, playing with dolls) should fit the child's level of understanding, though much assessment of children can be done by obser-vation in specific contexts (e.g., family, school, peer groups) and by obtain-ing collateral data from parents, day-care workers, teachers, and others. Early memories of family life (both positive and negative), early school experiences, friendships, community, and accomplishments, as well as losses, adolescent experiences with peers, friends and romantic relation-ships, and scholastic and work experiences can provide a rich tapestry for better understanding how the client came to develop his or her current adaptive strengths and how the client began to experience current difficulties.

Practitioners should work with clients to develop a time line of the prob-lem, whether it covers days, months, or years. Clients can be helped to remember what happened over time by anchoring their memories with key events (e.g., When did you move to that neighborhood? Is that before or after your father passed away? Was that your freshman year in high school? In what year was your first child born?). Often, key events can trigger a chain of other memories that link to the client's difficulties. Devel-oping a time line with regard to the problem, and linking key people and events to variations in the problem, can yield important clues to under-standing how the problem works (i.e., the functional analysis).

Practitioners can also begin to make some preliminary assessments regarding which factors in the client's life are more remote and unrelated to the current difficulties, which are more proximate (i.e., more closely related to the client's distress); which are acute (i.e., intense and short term), and which are chronic (i.e., of longer duration and either constant or intermittent). Tentatively pointing out to the client the factors that appear more significantly related to the current difficulties often helps engage the client in the process of thinking about the current situation more analytically and helps place the primary complaint into a broader life-span perspective.

As part of history taking, practitioners should also pay attention to cli-ents' attempts to resolve their problems through their own initiative, by seeking help from others, or through professional means. Psychological and social difficulties are often recurrent and sometimes resistant to change, and people often struggle with them over long periods of time. Practitioners should take careful note of any experiences when clients made an effort to resolve their own difficulties and had some success in those efforts.

THE INDIVIDUAL ASSESSMENT

After collecting basic background data and psychosocial history, the more analytical part of the assessment begins (i.e., What does all this information mean?). Although assessment is best understood in a social context, it is important to focus a considerable part of the overall assessment on the well-being of the individual and to gradually broaden the individual assessment to include family and social relationships. This initial focus on the individual should identify thoughts, feelings, and behaviors of the individual that are relevant to problems and adaptive abilities. This approach incorporates the mental-status exam, which includes diagnosing for serious mental disorders.

Cognitive disturbances are often a sign of more serious psychiatric disorders. These disturbances may include hallucinations (e.g., seeing, hearing, smelling, or feeling stimuli that do not exist), delusions (i.e., having fixed false, implausible beliefs), disorientation, bizarre behavior or speech, memory problems (short or long term), serious confusion, and symptoms of serious cognitive impairment. One or more of these symptoms may indicate any number of serious mental disorders, such as schizophrenia or bipolar disorder; organic brain disorders, such as Alzheimer's disease; a chemical- or substance-induced condition; or a medical condition such as a brain tumor. Conducting a thorough and accurate assessment and diagnosis of serious cognitive disturbances requires considerable training and experience and is best conducted in collaboration with a medical specialist in psychiatry and/or neurology. Beginning social workers, however, should obtain some basic understanding of the symptoms and related conditions from a course in psychopathology, develop the ability to identify these symptoms to make proper referrals, and be prepared to work with referred clients who experience these symptoms. Analysis of cognitions should focus on both the content of thought (i.e., the nature of the client's beliefs; convictions; and attitudes toward him- or herself, others, and the world) and thought processes (e.g., reasoning abilities, how client arrives at conclusions).

Nearly everyone has experienced feelings of depression, anxiety, anger, and other distressing feelings. Emotional disturbances are of particular significance in an assessment when the client's emotional state is particularly acute (i.e., sudden and extreme) or chronic to the degree that the client's emotional expression goes beyond normative expectations given the client's situation or particular circumstances. Emotional disturbances usually become problematic when they interfere with a client's close relationships or broader social or occupational functioning. Sudden and severe depression may result from a sudden tragic or traumatic event, such as a sudden loss, frightening medical diagnosis, a major disappointment, or another stressful event. On the other hand, a serious bout with depression (which often runs in families) can come on gradually, almost imperceptibly even to those who know the client well, and can cause considerable degradation in the person's sleep and overall energy level, loss of optimism and initiative, loss of pleasure in life, withdrawal from loved ones, poor work performance, and even suicidal thoughts and attempts.

Anxiety symptoms can be equally debilitating. The causes of anxiety (as with depression) can be complex in origin and result in symptoms such as chronic worry and dread or obsessive concerns that cause dysfunction in daily life. Serious anxiety can result in sweaty palms, a racing heartbeat, and shortness of breath with feelings that one might faint or lose control. Clients with anxiety often begin to avoid situations in which they feel afraid, and the situations may multiply to the point that a client begins to avoid work or social gatherings altogether. Anxiety problems may occur out of the blue or as a result of extreme stressors or traumatic events. In any event, anxiety problems are often not discrete and may accompany other problems, such as depression, substance abuse, and other serious mental illnesses that include cognitive disturbances.

Behavioral problems are more discrete, observable actions on the part of the client that cause him or her and/or others distress. Behavior problems can range from mild to severe and can be related to mental disorders, substance abuse and addictions, deficits in impulse control and poor interpersonal skills, personality disorders, conduct disorder and criminal activities, or other difficulties in self-regulation. Some behaviors may be primarily troublesome for the individual, such as compulsive hand washing for the person with an obsessive-compulsive disorder or avoiding going outdoors for the person suffering from agoraphobia. Behavioral problems may also be troublesome for others including family members and others in the community. These problems may include violence, drug abuse, or other criminal activities. Practitioners should consider how well clients engage in everyday activities, such as abilities to express themselves effectively and work at things patiently and tendencies to verbally or physically lash out at others; run away; harm themselves; or exhibit a proneness to impulsive, criminal, or drug-abusing behavior.

The assessment should not focus exclusively on behaviors considered negative or dysfunctional, even though those are the behaviors that usually bring clients into treatment. It is also important to identify and highlight the client's coping abilities and adaptive strengths, which may include a strong work ethic or evidence of a solid relationship. Clients who have struggled with depression, anxiety, or abusive relationships may have had their share of problems and difficulties coping, but they may also have developed strong survival strategies and the will to persevere. The practitioner can harness these abilities to help clients address their current difficulties and ongoing problems.

Social work practitioners are not expected to conduct medical exams or diagnose physical disorders. However, conducting a general health history is often part of a routine psychosocial assessment. Clients often know quite a lot about their health status and are willing to share much of that information, including reports of previous and current diagnoses, treatments, and use of any medications. Such information is important because medical conditions and psychosocial well-being are often closely intertwined. It is important for the social worker to know that a client's medication can result in depression or that the client is drinking alcohol against a doctor's advice. Medical conditions may affect clients' daily functioning and have a negative impact on their ability to care for themselves (e.g., daily hygiene, going shopping, climbing stairs, driving). Whether a client can feed, clothe, and otherwise care for him- or herself are important data to gather as part of the assessment. Last, social workers should know that collaboration with the client's doctor (with client's written consent) is a two-way street: social workers need to communicate periodically with doctors to better understand the client's condition and to inform the doctor of any significant changes in the client's psychosocial condition. The biopsychosocial nature of client problems is often better addressed through interdisciplinary collaboration.

An individual assessment often includes a DSM diagnosis. In the introductory chapter of the *Diagnostic and Statistical Manual of Mental Disorders* (APA, 2000) the authors make it clear that a psychiatric diagnosis assumes that the primary causes of the client's difficulties are within the client. Although there may be some validity to this assertion, particularly with serious mental illnesses, social workers are well aware that many of clients' problems are familial or societal in origin. At least those factors external to the client play a large role, and that is why it is recommended that practitioners conduct a thorough MDF assessment along with documenting a DSM diagnosis. Nevertheless, it is important to provide a diagnosis for clients for at least two reasons: (1) there is value in diagnoses in that they provide a common nomenclature recognized by other professionals, and (2) practitioners are often obliged to provide a diagnosis for administrative, legal, and insurance purposes. Having said that, practitioners should do the best job they can to accurately apply diagnoses with strict adherence to the DSM criteria.

As client problems are identified, practitioners may also have to use more specialized forms of assessment. For example, a social worker may identify depression in an elderly person but may require additional training or consultation with another specialist to identify the underlying emergence of Alzheimer's disease; a child with behavioral and learning difficulties may need additional specialized testing with a school psychologist to determine whether he or she is suffering from autism or attention deficit/hyperactivity disorder; a teenager with an eating disorder and possible drug problem is likely to require a medical exam to determine whether he or she is experiencing other somatic disturbances. In brief, a thorough psychosocial assessment can raise important questions that require further examination by another professional. These matters may be overlooked in an incomplete assessment. A rule of thumb for social work practitioners should be "When in doubt, refer out" (for further assessment and diagnosis).

To illustrate the individually focused part of the assessment, consider a client, Jill, a fourteen-year-old female adolescent who recently started school in a new community (she just moved with her mother and stepfather). An individual assessment reveals troubled cognitions (e.g., "Nobody likes me; I don't fit in"), emotional disturbance (e.g., anger, worry, depression), and some behavioral difficulties (e.g., fighting with other girls, scratching up her arms, suspected drug use). Jill's health is otherwise good. Her background history reveals little psychosocial disturbance other than some chronic tension between her and her stepfather, which began about four years ago. Although she shows no signs of serious mental disorder, there is cause for concern and probably some links among her negative view of herself and others, her emotional upset, and her disturbing behaviors. Diagnoses to be considered after a thorough assessment might include oppositional-defiant disorder, substance abuse, and dysthymic disorder.

As Figure 7 illustrates, Jill's troubled thoughts, emotional distress, and problematic behaviors are reciprocally interacting, which means that they are mutually self-perpetuating. Because it is difficult to determine where this cycle begins and ends, individual assessment does not emphasize a linear analysis but provides a working model of the client's internal experience, which can be addressed by interventions on multiple levels: changing thinking, coping with feelings, and modifying behaviors. However, this brief illustration of an individual assessment, though helpful, does not give

FIGURE 7. A MODEL ILLUSTRATING ASSESSMENT OF THE INDIVIDUAL CLIENT

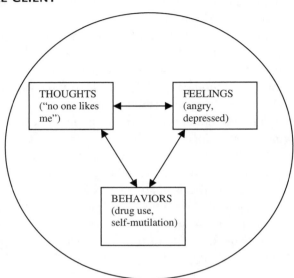

us the whole picture. To more fully appreciate her difficulties and circumstances, we must place Jill's individual assessment within a broader family and social context.

FAMILY ASSESSMENT

Assessing couples and families is also part of a complete MDF assessment. Couples and families must also be assessed on multiple dimensions, and understanding family interactions (e.g., behaviors, communications) is an essential part of the functional assessment (i.e., how the problem works). What problems is the family experiencing? How severe are the problems? What adaptive coping skills and strengths does the family have? And what behavioral patterns, interactions, and sequences define the family's difficulties and efforts to resolve those problems? These are key questions for an MDF approach to family assessment.

Although there are a variety of family therapy theories, most are relatively untested and remain somewhat speculative and abstract. Nevertheless, some generic practical guidelines have emerged from a combination of couples and family research and the practice wisdom of family therapists. These key concepts are, more or less, common to most family therapy assessment models (as noted in chapter 1) (Minuchin, 1974; Nichols & Schwartz, 2006). These concepts include the following:

- The family system: The whole of the family is greater than the sum of its individual members.
- Family structure and hierarchy: Identifying family roles and who has influence (e.g., power, authority) and who does not.
- Family subsystems: Alliances within a family that can be viewed as a system within a system, including siblings, parents, or alliances between parents and children. Subsystems may be functional or problematic.
- Boundaries (rigid vs. enmeshed) between family members or subsystems: Boundaries may be rigid (where family members create nearly impassible blockages between them) or enmeshed (where family members may be overly involved with one another in presumably dysfunctional ways).
- Systemic interaction and communication patterns: How members interact, the types and styles of behaviors, the consequences of those behaviors, and the overall emotional tone associated with these interactions (e.g., anger, caring, contempt, competition).
- The behavior of individuals in context: Individual behavior is better understood within the context of family interactions.
- Triangulation: A family member becomes a vehicle for family conflict (e.g., a couple is angry at one another and fights for a child's allegiance); triangulation often causes difficulties for the individual deliberately or unwittingly targeted by other family members.
- Intergenerational patterns: Family problems can be passed on from one generation to the next (e.g., a female child who grows up in an alcoholic home takes on parental roles by monitoring her own parent's drinking problem; she may develop a drinking problem of her own and her children adopt the same parental role toward her). History taking for one or two generations can provide the family and practitioner with a better understanding of recurrent generational difficulties. It should be kept in mind, however, that these problems can be transmitted through a combination of both genetic and psychosocial risk factors.
- Family developmental trajectory: The normative or problematic passage through typical family milestones: early marriage, young children, high school years, emancipation of children and empty-nest years for the parents, the arrival of grandchildren.

The assessment strategies associated with more effective family therapies tend to reflect the key aspects of MDF assessment of both individual behaviors and family interactions (Birchler & Spinks, 1980; Duncan &

Parks, 1988; Mueser & Glynn, 1999; Northey, Wells, Silverman, & Bailey, 2003). Figure 8, an assessment schematic, owes its influences to both structural and behavioral family-systems models. In my experience, many practitioners use similar approaches when assessing families, and new practitioners should be encouraged to adopt similar assessment strategies. The symbols in Figure 8 are intuitively straightforward. Key characteristics or problem descriptions can be noted within the circles representing each family member. Single-pointed arrows suggest a positive influence (e.g., support) from one person to another. Double-pointed arrows suggest mutual support or reciprocal influence. Dotted lines suggest a loose or tenuous relationship between persons. Lines with hash marks suggest barriers or conflict between family members; the more hash marks, the more blockage or conflict. Because there are no standardized or well-tested graphic displays of family assessment, practitioners should take what liberties they

FIGURE 8. MODEL ILLUSTRATING AN APPROACH TO FAMILY ASSESSMENT

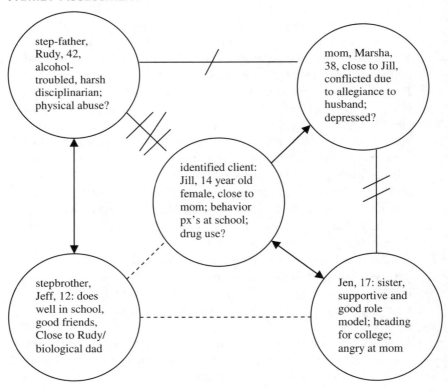

need to capture family dynamics in a concise but descriptive way (e.g., I like to use lightening bolts to suggest severe conflict between individuals).

In Figure 8, it appears that there is mild conflict between Rudy and his wife, Marsha, but severe conflict between Rudy and Jill. Jill is the emotionally troubled fourteen-year-old introduced earlier. Jeff, Rudy's biological son, is close to his dad, and Jill has a mutually supportive relationship with her sister, Jen. But affection and support toward her mom are not reciprocated, and Jeff has only tangential relationships with his two stepsisters. It is also useful to consider the existence of subsystems within the family. In Figure 8, Jen and Jill seem to be well bonded, as are Jeff and his stepfather. But key alliances that form a wholly supportive family are absent. For example, Rudy and Marsha are really part of two major subsystems: their role as a couple and their shared role as parents. Neither of these two subsystems appears to be operating well at the time of the assessment. Subsystems between parents and children and among children seem to suggest some fragmentation within the family.

In conducting a family assessment, it is important to recognize that most families today do not fit the conventional nuclear model (e.g., two parents, two kids, and a dog or cat). Many families have one parent present, possibly another biological parent intermittently in the picture, perhaps a stepparent or live-in partner who shares some parenting duties, or perhaps extended family members, and so on. The definition of what constitutes a family has become considerably blurred relative to the more conventional view, and social workers should be flexible with regard to labeling or defining exactly what constitutes a family. Perhaps a useful definition of *family* is as follows: people residing together for a shared purpose of mutual love and support. Although this definition could refer to a well-functioning cult as well as a family, the concept of individual and collective well-being may serve as useful organizing principles when assessing a family and its members.

INCORPORATING CULTURAL COMPETENCE INTO THE CLIENT ASSESSMENT

Becoming knowledgeable about a client's cultural beliefs is essential to conducting a sound assessment and, simultaneously, to establishing a productive working relationship. As with most concepts relevant to the ongoing assessment, this knowledge informs one's judgment continually throughout the intervention process. Both individual and family-systems assessments should include an examination of racial, ethnic, religious, and cultural identity and their meaning as defined from the client's perspective. This meaning is likely to vary among individuals and families, and allegiances will vary in quality and intensity across generations. The meaning of ethnic, racial, and cultural identity will also vary by socioeconomic level.

Some of the earlier social work literature on diversity tended to oversimplify various characteristics and traits associated with different racial and ethnic groups. The fact is, though there may be some characteristics that are more prominent in some groups, practitioners should avoid broad generalizations about various racial or ethnic groups. Given an increasingly mobile world population, the concept of ethnic identity is quite malleable across generations and between racial and ethnic subgroups and individuals. For one thing, a growing number of people claim multiracial and multiethnic heritage. For another, the extent to which broad characteristics are uniquely attributable to any group is questionable and often borders on stereotyping. For example, some texts have suggested that the importance of family is more important to one racial or ethnic group than another. To the extent that this might be true, it is probably more a matter of degree, and there is little doubt that within that racial or cultural group there is wide variation in importance placed on family closeness and allegiance.

Rather than categorize, social workers should focus on the process of engaging clients in conversation during initial sessions about how they subjectively view their own racial, ethnic, and religious affiliations; history; and commitments. These views can vary considerably even within the same family across generations and often reveal a picture characterized by nuance and subtlety, not ethnic or racial caricature. Guidelines for assessing cultural allegiances might include identifying the birthplace of the client and family members over two or three generations; immigration experiences; differences in assimilation and acculturation experiences across generations; examining clients' use of language (preference for native or English, and in what contexts, such as work vs. home, they use each); examining the ethnic identity of friends and acquaintances; noting the various types of media they access (e.g., television, newspapers, Internet sites); and exploring clients' participation in cultural and religious events, as well as preferences for music, art, entertainment, and food. Practitioners can also gauge the extent to which clients have assimilated into American norms and how they feel about those who are not in their ethnic enclave (i.e., reference group; Shiraev & Levy, 2007; Uba, 1994). Rather than attempt to become experts in treating a wide array of cultural subgroups (an impractical solution), practitioners should strive to become knowledgeable about the culture of the families they work with, avoid their own cultural myopia, and explore each client's and family's unique perception of own cultural background without predetermined assumptions, biases, or prejudices (Sue & Sue, 1999). The process versus categorical approach to exploring ethnicity, race, and culture readily lends itself to working with a wide variety of clients should one find oneself working in a highly diverse community.

If a practitioner is interested in working with a racial or ethnic subgroup with whom he or she is largely unfamiliar, the practitioner can take some steps to become knowledgeable about the group's history, culture, traditions, and mores. Although some research suggests that clients appreciate seeing people like "them" when they seek social work services, this demographic matching is no guarantee of good rapport during the intervention. Beyond having staff who can speak various languages, other factors can impede a good working alliance: generational differences (e.g., a young practitioner is not sufficiently deferential to family elders; the client's dress and demeanor is too "Anglo"; the practitioner was trained to be aloof, a posture that most clients find cold if not offensive). Even practitioners who are two or three generations removed from the parent country may need to do some remedial work on their knowledge of their own reference group's history, cultural norms, language, homeland politics, and other topics that clients would expect from "one of their own." Conversely, there is not much evidence that if practitioners are not from the client's culture they cannot successfully engage the client on these issues. Practitioners can compensate for a lack of firsthand knowledge by learning about the client's culture, language, and traditions and by inquiring about the client's beliefs in these matters. These efforts can make the work extraordinarily enriching for the practitioner and help the client feel respected, more valued, and better understood.

THE SOCIAL SYSTEM ASSESSMENT

As part of a complete MDF assessment, both the individual and the family-system assessment should be integrated into a broader social-system perspective. This approach to assessment has been well established, for example, as part of evidence-based practices with behaviorally disordered adolescents (e.g., multisystemic therapy, developed by Henggeler, Schoenwald, Borduin, Rowland, & Cunningham, 1998). This approach links the family assessment to the wider community, including school, workplace, and relationships to other organizations, such as human service and health-care providers. There is an array of different approaches to graphically displaying these interacting social constructs, and they all derive from social work's traditional person-in-environment perspective. Nevertheless, a qualitative graphic display of interacting influences in the client's life (using the same symbols as in Figure 8) can be a useful tool for putting the client's challenges in perspective, identifying important social supports and environmental barriers, and conceptualizing how various social domains of a client's life interact.

Figure 9 shows a fairly simple qualitative systems model. Practitioners can use it to qualitatively record how well the client is doing in each of these important domains and to identify important people within the client's various social domains who support or are a liability to the client's well-being.

Figure 9 provides a somewhat impressionistic overview of Jill's problems in a broader community context. In the center, she is triangulated by family conflict. Although struggling academically, she receives some support at school and cooperates by seeing the social worker. Her stepfather's drinking problem has manifested itself at work and in the community, and he is in conflict with the Department of Child Welfare. Last, Jill has a mixed relationship with some peers: they provide emotional support but are a

FIGURE 9. MODEL FOR ASSESSING A FAMILY WITHIN THE COMMUNITY CONTEXT

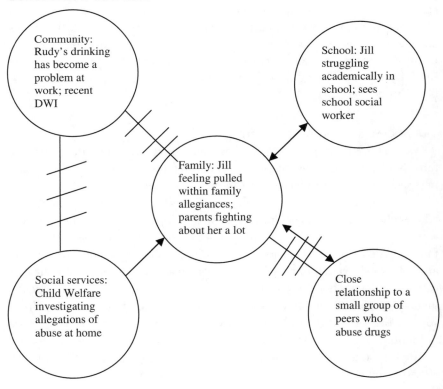

source of problems and conflict because of their mutual involvement with drug abuse.

SUMMARIZING THE MDF ASSESSMENT

After gathering a lot of information about client's individual, family, and social functioning from multiple sources using multiple methods, summarizing all these data succinctly can be a daunting task, even for seasoned practitioners. However, the MDF framework can help practitioners do just that if they emphasize two things: (1) focus on dimensions with which the client is experiencing the most problems (e.g., psychological, interpersonal, community, work), and (2) describe sequentially those individual, family, or social factors that appear to be closely related to the key problems (i.e., How does the problem work on a day-to-day level?).

A succinct summary of Jill's difficulties may be as follows: Jill is depressed, angry, discouraged about her grades, having behavioral problems at school, and may be exacerbating her problems with drug use (though the extent of drug use is not clear at this point); her parents' conflicts apparently have a negative effect on her, particularly her mother's failure to protect her from Rudy, who has been verbally and physically abusive in the past. Rudy's drinking is causing difficulties for the whole family. Nevertheless, Jill has a close relationship with her sister, who seems somewhat resilient in the face of the family troubles and has encouraged Jill to continue seeing the social worker. At some point soon, the social worker will have to confer with child welfare. Whether Rudy will seek help for his drinking problem and work on his marriage is an open question. Functionally, Jill's emotional and behavioral difficulties seem directly linked to family conflict, abuse from her stepfather, and her negative interactions with schoolmates and some teachers. These problems are not likely to abate until her parents begin to resolve their problems as individuals and as a couple and to collaborate to help Jill with hers.

After completing the MDF assessment, practitioners may feel that further assessment is warranted if a particular problem requires a more detailed look. For example, if it appears that Jill may be seriously depressed or more extensively involved with drugs, more focused assessment can be targeted at those problems by using standardized scales and/or a referral for further consultation. This additional information would be incorporated into the overall assessment when those data became available. Moving forward with an intervention without first further assessing the severity of specific problems is shortsighted and can lead to the wrong intervention strategy.

There are many brief, reliable, and valid scales that practitioners can use with their clients to further explore problems such as substance abuse, eating disorders, depression, anxiety disorders, childhood disorders, and marital distress. The scales are not intended to be a substitute for a complete qualitative MDF assessment, but they can be an important addition to it. Some of the scales are also designed to be used as evaluation tools when administered periodically before, during, and after the intervention to track client progress. Scales and related instruments will be discussed in more detail later in this chapter.

Consider the Implications of the Data for Intervention Planning

A good assessment provides important clues for intervention planning in several ways: first, it identifies what problems need to be addressed; second, it provides a measure of the severity of each problem; third, it helps to set priorities regarding the relative importance of problems; fourth, it helps us understand functionally how the problem works (thus providing clues as to how to activate positive change processes); and, fifth, it provides some basis for selection of intervention methods.

Perhaps the most important implication of a complete assessment is that it provides guidelines for the development of an intervention strategy. There are two main avenues of information that help develop the intervention plan. First, there is a large body of clinical outcome research now that provides useful guidelines for selecting interventions that are likely to be effective with a wide range of problems. The interventions are generally some combination of supportive skills used to develop a working relationship, coping skills that help clients learn to deal more effectively with their problems, and case management skills that enhance social and instrumental supports in the community and coordinate complex interventions. The optimal combinations of the skills that have been shown to be effective in controlled clinical research are referred to as *evidence-based practices*.

However, we know that applying these approaches in cookie-cutter fashion is neither realistic nor clinically wise, and moreover would not be acceptable to many clients. Evidence-based practices need to be applied with some degree of flexibility to accommodate clients' needs, wishes, and special circumstances. Nevertheless, outcome research provides important guidelines in the selection and adaptation of the approaches to individual clients, but the whole process depends first and foremost on having conducted a thorough and accurate MDF assessment. Beginning with the next chapter, the remainder of this text will be largely devoted to describing the essential skills of social work practice and how these skills can be optimally combined to form evidence-based practices.

Delineate a Plan to Monitor Client Progress and Evaluate the Intervention

A thorough assessment provides not only a framework for better under-standing of the client's problems, strengths, and potential solutions but also a baseline for monitoring client change and, to a more limited degree, support for the evaluation of the intervention. Thus, the assessment and formulation of the evaluation plan happen at the same time and provide the foundation for intervention planning. It is important that practitioners and clients clearly define the problems qualitatively so that they can be reassessed periodically during the course of the intervention and again at termination of treatment. Examples of qualitative evaluative questions that emerge from the assessment include the following:

- Does an elderly depressed and withdrawn male client become less depressed and more involved with family and friends over the course of the intervention?
- Does a young woman struggling with a binge-eating disorder reduce binging and purging and reduce her alcohol consumption?
- Does a schizophrenic young man become less thought disordered, begin to interact with others in his social club, and begin to shower and launder his clothes more regularly?
- Does a young conflicted couple become better able to discuss their problems more constructively and make progress toward sharing and compromise?

TYPES OF MEASURES USEFUL FOR ASSESSMENT AND EVALUATION

Although qualitative indicators of client progress are generally useful, they can be somewhat vague and often inconsistent. A practitioner's esti-mate of what constitutes moderate depression, for example, may vary over time with a client or between different clients, or practitioners may dis-agree about what *moderately depressed* actually means. Quantitative mea-sures can enhance qualitative assessment and evaluation. Scales and simple indexes can provide unambiguous baseline data (i.e., the initial measurement of key client problems). Once this measurement is made, it becomes the benchmark against which to judge future progress. Quantita-tive measures provide a sensible complement to the qualitative assessment and evaluation for two reasons: (1) they are more exact and may be based on well-established scales, and (2) the data can be aggregated (pooled with other client data) and used to judge the performance of a whole program (i.e., program evaluation), a process that many agencies now require.

Quantitative instruments can range from the simple to the complex, but those that are more practical and amenable to daily service delivery are emphasized here. These include simple indexes, unidimensional scales, and multidimensional scales. Single-item indexes measure one specific problem, such as number of drinks consumed per day, number of minutes a child spends doing homework, severity of depression, number of days homeless, and intensity of intimacy a couple shares. These are important and straightforward indicators that are also sensitive to change; thus, they can provide both a good baseline measure at assessment and an important indicator of progress during intervention and at termination. Because of their ease of use, practitioners can use multiple indicators as needed. Simple indicators are generally considered reliable and reasonably valid if the data source is deemed a trustworthy, reasonably objective observer. The simple index is, perhaps, the most frequently relied-on indicator of client progress in clinical practice.

When deciding on what to use as an index, practitioners should consider two important points: the dimension of human experience to be measured and the type of scaling that will measure that dimension. There are four basic dimensions or expressions of human behavior that practitioners can observe: a client's thoughts (cognitions; via verbal report); feelings, affect, and emotions (via verbal report and observation); behaviors (via verbal report and observation); and physiological indicators (via verbal report and observation). Although the dimensions interact in complex ways, it is important to distinguish them when considering the design or selection of a specific index. Ideally, one should measure all of them. Consider the person who has a serious anxiety problem. The client may report having frightening thoughts (e.g., "I feel like I am losing my mind") or feeling overwhelmed (e.g., feelings of inability to cope and extreme dread), may indicate physiological arousal (e.g., racing heartbeat, light-headedness, stomachaches), and may manifest behavioral problems (e.g., avoiding work, driving, and social contact). The practitioner and client may choose to select one or more of these indexes to monitor the client's progress and evaluate the outcome of the intervention. The following changes would suggest improvement: for cognitions, lowered intensity of the client experiencing feelings of losing his or her mind; for feelings, reduced feelings of dread; for behaviors, more frequent contact with family or friends and better work attendance; for physiological indicators, a general lowering of somatic symptoms.

The second consideration in designing simple indexes is the type of measurement scale. There are no hard-and-fast rules in selecting the type of measure, so discussing with the client the best way to measure the specific problem is a good method. Indexes are typically measured in one of three ways: frequency, severity (intensity), or duration.

Frequency indicates how often the event occurs (e.g., How many days per week do you drink alcoholic beverages? How many panic attacks do you have per week? How many times did you yell at your child this week? How many days of school did your son miss in the past month?).

If one is concerned with the severity (intensity) of a problem, consider the following examples: How severe has your depression been since last month? How close do you feel to your spouse right now? How frightened are you about making that speech in front of your whole class next week? Intensity can be measured with simple scales such as low, moderate, and high, or by asking a client to rate the intensity of the problem on a ten-point scale.

Indexes of duration can be simply measured on the clock (e.g., seconds, minutes, hours, days, weeks). How long have you been depressed? How long has it been since you've relapsed (or, alternatively, have been sober)? How long can your son concentrate on his homework at night without being distracted?

Thus, when selecting a quantitative measure for baseline assessment and monitoring client progress, practitioners should consider three key questions: (1) What is the problem to be measured? (2) What dimension of human behavior will be the focus (e.g., thoughts, feelings, physiological responses, behaviors)? and (3) What type of scale will be used (e.g., frequency, intensity, duration)? Table 1 below may be a useful guide in determining the best way to construct an index that can be used as part of assessment, ongoing monitoring, and evaluation.

In Table 1, the practitioner and client should discuss which approach is most useful. A person with an anxiety problem might decide that severity of thoughts of "losing my mind" measured on a ten-point scale would be helpful, that duration of feelings and physiological symptoms might be best measured in hours per day, and that frequency of contacts with family and friends would be a meaningful indicator of lessening behavioral withdrawal. The strength of using simple indexes is in their apparent validity, ease of use, and the fact that they can be tailored to meet a client's unique treatment goals.

Although simple one-item indexes are quite versatile and intuitively useful, practitioners are increasingly likely to use unidimensional and multidimensional scales in routine practice. Unidimensional scales measure one

TABLE 1 A GUIDE TO CREATING SIMPLE BEHAVIORAL INDEXES

	Frequency	Severity	Duration
Thoughts			
Feelings			
Physiological			
Behaviors			

concept (e.g., depression, self-esteem) but use multiple items to do so. Such scales have some advantages over one-item indexes because they are likely to have greater reliability and validity because they use ten, twenty, thirty, or more indicators. Different scaling devices are used to measure the items in a unidimensional scale. Three of the more common measuring devices are Likert-type scales (e.g., strongly agree, agree, disagree, strongly disagree), severity scales (e.g., low, moderate, high), and yes/no scales (known as *dichotomous measures*). A brief scale to measure a couple's satisfaction in a relationship, for example, might look like this:

I enjoy spending time with my partner.
strongly agree (4)   agree (3)   disagree (2)   strongly disagree (1)

I like to share household responsibilities.
strongly agree (4)   agree (3)   disagree (2)   strongly disagree (1)

I believe we share a common vision for the future.
strongly agree (4)   agree (3)   disagree (2)   strongly disagree (1)

I think we enjoy visiting with each other's families.
strongly agree (4)   agree (3)   disagree (2)   strongly disagree (1)

I enjoy making love with my partner.
strongly agree (4)   agree (3)   disagree (2)   strongly disagree (1)

Although each item might serve as an important index to gauge improvement in the couple's relationship, the collective strength of five (or more) indicators would provide a better overall measure of progress; the higher is the overall score, the greater is the progress. Some problems might progress more than others. Many couple-satisfaction scales have twenty or more items. Most problems that clients experience have multiple aspects to them, so it makes sense to measure problems such as the intensity of couple satisfaction with many indicators.

Multidimensional scales are similar to unidimensional scales in that they use multiple indicators. But, as the name indicates, they measure several dimensions of a more complex concept. A more sophisticated couple-satisfaction scale, for example, might have five items for each domain or subscale—for example, intimacy, parenting, dealing with extended families (in-laws), sharing household duties, money matters, and recreation—for a total of thirty items (five items for each of six domains). Each subscale or dimension of couple satisfaction would be scored separately, and an overall score would be provided as a global satisfaction score for the relationship. The advantage to a multidimensional scale is that it provides a more complex view of the relationship and allows for a more detailed assessment and evaluation of progress in different dimensions of the couple's relationship. For example, the couple may do well with regard to matters of parenting and finances but have serious conflicts with regard to intimacy and getting along with in-laws.

Overall, the use of quantitative measures in practice can increase consistency and accuracy in the initial assessment and monitoring of client progress, but only if they have been tested for reliability and validity. A scale has good internal reliability when respondents complete the individual items of a scale in a way that is consistent with the concept being measured. For example, consider the following three items, which are part of a hypothetical thirty-item scale measuring depression:

I think of killing myself . . .
    a lot (3)   somewhat (2)   a little (1)   not at all (0)

I feel happy . .
    a lot (3)   somewhat (2)   a little (1)   not at all (0)

I feel sad . . .
    a lot (3)   somewhat (2)   a little (1)   not at all (0)

If this scale has good internal consistency, one would expect that if the client answers "a lot" in response to the query "I am thinking of killing myself," one would also expect that the client would respond at least "somewhat" or " a lot" to the item "I feel very sad." One would also expect that the client would respond "a little" or "not at all" to the item "I feel very happy." If the client answers the same to all three items, this would seem counterintuitive (as the general mood cannot be both happy and sad at the same time), and if the client responded in this contradictory way for all the items, one would expect the results to show a low level of internal consistency. However, if the client indicated that he or she was very sad, very suicidal, and not at all happy, the scale would likely show high internal consistency (assuming this pattern was consistent for the other twenty-seven scale items).

Another form of reliability that is of key importance in everyday practice is interrater reliability. Let's say that two practitioners are working with the same client, and both have access to the same assessment data. One practitioner suggests that the client shows only mild suicidal ideation, but the other practitioner insists that the client is very suicidal. One would consider their judgments to be at a poor level of agreement. That is not to say that one is right and the other is wrong. Aside from the issue of accuracy (i.e., validity, to be discussed below), scales need to demonstrate good interrater consistency (interrater reliability). If two practitioners use a suicidal-intent scale with the same client in two different interviews, the results should be reasonably consistent. In fact, use of scales that have been tested for interrater reliability tends to enhance agreement among practitioners because it puts them on the same page.

However, mere demonstration that a scale has good reliability does not mean that it is a valid scale. Scales can have good reliability but be inaccurate. Consider a scale that measures all the signs and symptoms of alien abduction syndrome: high anxiety, a feeling of having gone on a faraway trip but without knowing where you have been; a sense of having been medically examined against your wishes; a feeling that someone is coming to take you away on another long trip to a faraway place whether you like it or not, and so forth. Practitioners can be trained to consistently rate these signs with clients who believe they have been, in fact, abducted by aliens. In other words, such a scale can be shown to have good reliability, but without hard scientific evidence that aliens occasionally abduct some of us, it would be hard to argue for the scale's validity.

Validity is a matter of degree and is measured by how well the scale corresponds to more observable and objective measures of the phenomenon. There are four types of validity: face validity is an intuitive confirmation based on expert opinion (e.g., are the three items of degree of suicidal intent, happiness, and sadness indicators of depression?). Content validity is determined by judging whether a sufficient number of indicators represent the concept (depression). Although three items are illustrated here, they would not be sufficient to measure depression. Presumably other items would include things like "I feel hopeless," "I have trouble sleeping," "I am pessimistic about the future," and so forth. Construct and criterion validity are, perhaps, the most difficult to demonstrate, and require a variety of statistical techniques to show that a range of indicators accurately corresponds to the scale items. Although scale development and testing (i.e., psychometrics) is complicated and requires special research skills, practitioners need not be experts in this area. Many reference books containing reliable and valid scales are now available to practitioners for use as aids in conducting more focused assessments and evaluations of practice.

STRATEGIES FOR EVALUATING ONE'S OWN PRACTICE

Evaluation methods used in everyday practice share common characteristics: a clear definition and valid measure of the problem, as well as a well-defined intervention (for the practitioner to know what he or she is evaluating). Qualitative evaluation may be the easiest and most intuitively appealing. Basically, the practitioner obtains a detailed accounting of the client's views of the problem, provides some form of intervention, and judges the client's progress on the basis of the client's self-report and observations of others (including the practitioner).

Another approach to routine evaluation of individual cases is single-subject design. The simplest approach involves using quantitative indexes (as discussed previously) to provide a baseline measure of the problem, provide an intervention, and after some period of time (e.g., six sessions), repeat the measure to determine whether the client has made progress in response to the intervention. This process describes the classic ABA design illustrated by the following:

> A (take a baseline measurement)
> B (provide the intervention)
> A (measure the client's problem again)

There are variations on this theme in single-subject design, which involves planned changes in the treatment to determine whether the client responds differently under different treatment conditions. For example, the practitioner may start off with basic relationship skills for two months (intervention B) and later add specific problem-solving methods (intervention C). The reasoning here is that if the client changes in response to different treatment conditions, then he or she must be responding to the treatment itself. Such an evaluation design might be represented as ABCA, where C represents a planned change in the intervention (e.g., the addition of problem-solving skills). Although there are considerable limitations to drawing the conclusion that the client's change actually resulted from the change in treatment, these problems of internal validity in research design will not be addressed here. What can be said is that planned changes in an intervention made for the sake of testing the effectiveness of routine practice is neither practical nor feasible in everyday social service settings. Planning different evaluation methods for each client (when you are carrying a caseload of sixty cases or more in an agency) is generally considered impractical. In addition, more complex single-subject designs are intended to be used in controlled research with innovative treatments. As such, special informed-consent procedures including the permission of an institutional review board are required before conducting single-subject experimental studies.

What is acceptable in daily practice is what should be referred to as single-subject naturalistic evaluation. *Naturalistic* means that the practitioner collects assessment and evaluation data as part of routine practice but does not conduct planned changes in treatment conditions as part of that evaluation. Services are provided as they normally would be, but scales may be used to measure change in the client's condition. The single-subject design ABA can be used as a naturalistic single-subject evaluation. Naturalistic program evaluation operates in much the same way, except that practitioners would use a common set of measures for all clients in a specific program (e.g., substance abuse clinic) to determine whether the program as a whole was effective.

In summary, evaluating one's own practice may include the use of qualitative or quantitative judgments (measures) on a routine basis and can inform practitioners as to whether clients are improving, staying the same, or getting worse. Answering questions about the validity of underlying theories, how clients change, or whether the change resulted from the actual intervention is more difficult and requires more rigorous and methodologically sophisticated research and evaluation designs.

Summary

Conducting a thorough MDF assessment and evaluation plan provides the foundation for effective intervention. The assessment is informed by contemporary human behavior research, provides a unique functional analysis of the client's problems and strengths, and is supported by the use of quantitative measures, which also provide a basis for monitoring client progress and evaluating the intervention. Perhaps the most important reason to conduct a thorough MDF assessment is to provide guidance for the selection of effective interventions. The next three chapters will examine the building blocks of interventions (i.e., essential skills).

CHAPTER FIVE

Supportive Skills

THE SKILLS OF HELPING that facilitate engagement with clients; put them at ease; establish a trusting and empathic working relationship; provide comfort, understanding, compassion, and encouragement; and further facilitate the implementation of the assessment and intervention are referred to here, for the sake of simplicity, as *supportive skills*. As noted earlier, the research on the working relationship and basic counseling skills is voluminous, and the evidence for the importance of a sound working relationship is impressive (e.g., Hill, Nutt, & Jackson, 1994; Hill & O'Brien, 2004; Horvath & Greenberg, 1989; O'Hare, 2005; Orlinsky & Howard, 1986; Orlinsky, Grawe, & Parks, 1994; Rogers, 1951; Truax & Carkhuff, 1967). Implicit in the ability to develop and maintain a good working relationship and to engage and motivate clients in the change process is the need for practitioners to master basic interviewing skills (Hill & O'Brien, 2004; Shulman, 1999; Sommers-Flannagan & Sommers-Flannagan, 2003). Although practitioners and theoreticians of good will often disagree about the meaning or theoretical significance of the working relationship, most social workers agree that a sound supportive relationship and essential interviewing skills are a critical dimension of effective care.

The Basic Elements of Supportive Skills: Listening and Communication Skills

Interviewing skills are, perhaps, the most elemental of the helping skills. They are not only essential for the effective use of supportive, therapeutic coping, and case management skills but also necessary to conduct valid assessments and evaluation. Thus, basic interviewing skills lay the foundation for effectively implementing all social work practice functions. Basic interviewing skills include asking important questions, listening accurately, seeking clarification, accurately identifying feelings, and recounting client experiences. Skillful interviewing creates a level of discourse that encourages clients to be forthcoming about their difficulties, enhances collaboration, and enhances clients' adaptive capabilities. To better understand clients, practitioners must make their best efforts to enter and understand the client's subjective world to better understand who they are, what experiences they have had, how they see themselves and others, how they understand their current difficulties, what they want to achieve, and what they need to do to improve their lives.

At all stages of service provision, from first contact to last, interviewing skills (1) develop and maintain a working relationship with the client; (2) help obtain as accurate a picture as possible of what the client thinks, feels, and does; (3) deepen the practitioner's understanding of the role of people and events that affect the client, both through the client's eyes and by interviewing significant others; (4) encourage the client to engage in the intervention process; and (5) assist the client in monitoring his or her own progress and evaluating the impact of the intervention as best as he or she can. How interviewing skills are used may vary from client to client on the basis of age, the client's presentation style, the client's psychological and intellectual capacities, and the practitioner's own personal style. Nevertheless, there are some basic interviewing skills that have been well researched and honed by years of practice experience. They will be briefly reviewed here before considering other supportive and facilitative skills.

Types of Questions Used in the Helping Interview

There are different types of questions one can use to help clients generate personal narrative and obtain the information necessary for understanding a client's difficulties and adaptive capabilities. A good general approach is to ask questions initially that are somewhat general and then work toward more specific questions that focus on greater detail. This deductive trajectory from the general to the specific is helpful not only in the first few interviews when the practitioner conducts a thorough assessment but also in later interviews when clients are actively engaged in working toward solutions to their problems. Most of what follows regarding basic skills applies to older adolescents and adults. This chapter will also address adapting essential supportive skills to working with children.

Open-ended questions are quite general and allow clients wide latitude to talk about themselves and their situations. By using minimal prompts and little structure, open-ended questions provoke clients to take the initiative to discuss what they think is important. In the first visit, for example, a practitioner may simply begin, "So, what brings you into the clinic today?" For some clients, this opener may be more than enough. At some point, the practitioner may have to interject some modest amount of structure in the discussion to obtain necessary information to conduct the formal assessment (see appendix B). However, for verbally active clients, a little structure and occasional prompts ("So, tell me a little more when you first felt depressed") may be sufficient.

Closed-ended questions offer a more limited range of answers and encourage clients to provide more definitive answers to specific topics. "So, did you drink alcoholic beverages this weekend?" may be a follow-up to a client's vague report on how he or she has been coping since being discharged from a rehabilitation facility. If the client responds in the affirmative, closed-ended, follow-up questions might include "So, how many drinks did you have?" With a court-ordered client, a practitioner might ask: "Have you tried to see your spouse since she had a restraining order taken out on you?" Closed questions are intended to limit the range of possible answers, in this case, to yes or no.

Specific questions are intended to focus the interview in greater detail on important subjects regarding the client's thoughts, feelings, behaviors, or details of a situation or event. These questions are intended to fill in the gaps of a general narrative about especially important events (e.g., "When did your husband hit you? Was this the first time? No? Then, how many times had it happened before? How did he hit you? Was it a slap or a punch? Did he ever use an object or a weapon? What kind of injury did you sustain? What happened after the event was over? Did you call the police? Was anyone else there to witness what happened?). Although in some situations, the interview may sound a bit like an interrogation, this is typically not the case if a sound working relationship has been formed with the client and the practitioner communicates empathic concern. The details of clients' problems and experiences may be critical to understanding exactly what has been going on for them. At times, talking about the events out loud may be the first time a client has had a chance to process thoughts and feelings about a stressful or traumatic event. The opportunity to discuss the events in detail in the presence of an empathic and trusted listener can be inherently therapeutic.

Detailed querying is also critical when recounting a client's experiences in implementing the intervention outside of the fifty-minute hour. Most effective interventions involve a client's active participation in the treatment during everyday life, whether the purpose is working on communication skills with his or her partner, improving parenting skills with an oppositional child, taking one day at a time to stay clean and sober, or trying to master social anxiety. When client and practitioner meet in session, recounting the client's efforts to implement the intervention in everyday life usually involves some reconstruction of events to gauge whether the client is making progress (e.g., "What opportunities did you make to work on your social anxiety this week?" "For how long did you carry on your conversation with that new woman in your office?" "Did you ask her out for a cup of coffee?" "How did your lunch date go?" "Did you ask her about what she likes to do in her free time?" "What did she say?").

Some counseling texts refer to interviewing styles as either directive (structured) or nondirective (unstructured). The fact is that effective interviewing requires a thoughtful use of both. Nondirective interviewing relies more on open-ended questions, creates ambiguity regarding expectations of the practitioner, and gives clients free rein to take the discussion where they want to go. A directive style introduces more structure into the interview, uses more closed questions that limit response options, and is more purposeful to the task at hand. As for the client recently discharged from rehabilitation, mixing closed and open questions might sound like the following: "So, you had about fifteen drinks on Saturday afternoon. Can you tell me what was going on with you emotionally at that time?" (open question). Then, "Did you make any attempt to cut short your relapse?" (closed question) and "How did you feel about your slip the next day?" (open question). Using only one interviewing approach or the other makes little sense in social work practice. The exclusive use of a nondirective approach would result in puzzling ambiguity and leave many clients eventually wondering what the purpose of the intervention was. Conversely, an exclusive reliance on a directive style would likely leave some clients wondering if the practitioner were even interested in what they thought or felt or were simply carrying out some predetermined agenda of his or her own. Directive and nondirective approaches should be mixed and follow both an inductive (broad information gathering) and deductive (drawing cause-effect conclusions) pattern. The purposes of each interview are guided by the goals of the intervention (previously negotiated between practitioner and client) and the phase of the intervention: completing the assessment, implementing the intervention, or conducting the evaluation. In general, sessions with clients should probably begin on an open-ended note and move toward a more structured purpose linked to treatment goals. Imbuing each interview with that kind of rhythm helps keep the purposes of the intervention at the forefront.

Adopt a Relaxed and Attentive Posture

Helping a client feel at ease is the result of several processes and is closely intertwined with good interviewing skills: careful listening so the client feels that he or she is being understood accurately, carefully delineating both the practitioner's and client's role; and being relatively nonjudgmental and focusing on an agenda to solve problems and enhance coping in everyday life. Practitioners must be genuine, authentic, and come across in a way that is congruent with who they are so that their professional demeanor does not come across as contrived. Clients feel more at ease when they understand the purpose of meetings and feel they have some input into the treatment agenda. Even court-ordered clients can be given some degree of choice and a sense of control over methods and treatment goals. Clients will also feel more at ease when they feel assured that the practitioner will uphold the informed-consent and confidentiality aspects of ethical practice (see chapter 3). Clients feel more at ease when practitioners communicate that they are knowledgeable, competent, and confident that they have the skills to help the client. Finally, clients feel more at ease when they sense that the purpose of the meetings is to focus exclusively on the agreed-on goals of the intervention and that there is no other competing agenda insinuated into the meeting. Said another way, the express purpose of the meetings is to help the client achieve his or her goals.

Most clients are at least a little nervous when interviewed by a social worker, particularly for the first time. They may suffer from a psychiatric disorder, be investigated for alleged abuse, struggle with a drug problem, or have recently been released from prison. The client may be relieved to have the opportunity to be seen, may be guarded or angry at being coerced into the visit, or may be indifferent. Some clients may suffer from psychoses and be somewhat delusional about the purpose of the meeting, and others may be so depressed they are almost unable to respond to questions. In general, it helps to begin by appearing relaxed and attentive. This presentation will communicate to the client that the practitioner is alert, ready and willing to be of assistance, and interested in hearing what the client has to say. Depending on the cognitive and emotional state of the client, practitioners should be ready to expend the necessary level of energy it takes to engage each client depending on how much initiative the client takes in the interview. The client recently court-ordered to the interview, for example, may be hostile and give only one-word answers, provoking the interviewer to work harder to engage the client in the assessment. An anxious client may speak rapidly, obsess over every minute detail of a story, or jump from one subject to the next. Practitioners might need to help these clients structure their presentation and focus on more substantive matters. The depressed client may be almost mute, necessitating that the practitioner work hard just to excavate even basic background information. Practitioners should consider being relaxed and attentive a good starting point, but they should be flexible and ready to engage the client according to his or her needs, abilities, and expectations.

Nonverbal Communication

For the most part, in Western cultures, making eye contact is a powerful form of communication in that it demands the other person's attention and communicates a form of psychological engagement. When you look into the client's eyes, it says that you are paying attention to them. However, not all clients are comfortable being stared at for a lengthy period of time. Clients who are shy or otherwise anxious, feel unduly scrutinized, are ashamed, or are hiding something they feel uncomfortable about may begin to chafe under a social worker's unwavering gaze. In some cultures, it may be simply impolite or even an affront to make steady eye contact. Practitioners should take notice to determine whether a client is comfortable making consistent eye contact; if not, practitioners should perhaps break off the constant gaze by taking occasional notes or looking down or away from the client between questions or points of discussion. Some practitioners have been known to position their chairs in such a way that they need not look directly at the client if the client seems uncomfortable. Being flexible about seating arrangements and providing choices for clients can help them be more comfortable during the interview.

If one pays attention to everyday conversation (in line at the check-out counter, at home with family, with friends, or at work), one would readily become aware that much of what passes for conversation is nonverbal. *Nonverbal behaviors* refer to nonword vocalizations and physical gestures that convey fairly specific meaning in everyday discourse. Nonverbals are, essentially, powerful shorthand vocalizations and gestures that facilitate communication. The classic *uh-huh* encountered in popular media portrayals of therapy is, indeed, a common utterance. It is simple, easily recognized in everyday conversation (though not in all languages), and is infinitely flexible to provide nuanced indication of interest in what the client is saying. *Uh-huh* can suggest keen interest, boredom, humor, disapproval, concern, or compassion with the slightest inflection. The same can be suggested about *hmm, aha,* or other nonverbal expressions. Practitioners should pay careful attention to these almost automatic utterances and note how clients respond to them, as their meaning can be ambiguous.

Other nonverbal utterances include facial expressions, another powerful form of communication. Generally, social workers do not receive the kind of training that, for example, professional actors do. So they may not be keenly aware of what they are communicating through facial expressions. But facial expressions can clearly communicate any of the following, often in a more primal and compelling way than words can: concern, compassion, disgust, anger, sarcasm, pity, ridicule, alarm, fear, and so forth. Spending some time in front of the mirror may not be a bad way for a practitioner to examine how he or she expresses the full range of emotions, and being aware of how one wears one's feelings on his or her face is critical to becoming aware of communicating emotional responses to clients. For example, after several months of this author working with a depressed young woman going through a divorce with an apparently difficult man, she remembered little about what I had said during our sessions but recounted in her last session: "All I had to do while talking about how things were going at home was to look at your face, and I knew that I wasn't the crazy one!" Fortunately, my ingenuous communications of alarm and puzzlement at their encounters validated for her that her husband's behaviors were somewhat extreme, unfair, and sometimes hostile, and that the failure of the marriage was not all her fault.

But nonverbal behaviors go well beyond facial expressions. Sitting back, relaxed with one's legs crossed comports with the earlier suggestion to be relaxed and attentive. At some point, however, such a posture would seem bizarre, when, for example, a client recounts a time when he or she was sexually assaulted or contemplating suicide. Physical posture communicates an emotional response, and practitioners must be aware of what they are trying to say with their physical presentation. Again, practicing in front of a mirror may help beginning practitioners define extra concern (e.g., leaning forward in a chair to listen with extra care), such as reeling back slightly with a single clap of the hands to express surprise at a fortuitous outcome or joy at a client's courageous breakthrough. Leaning sideways in one's chair and scratching one's head to communicate a bit of confusion can be an effective way of saying, "Your version of the story seems to contradict what you were telling me last week. Perhaps I'm not getting this right." Although traditional approaches to psychotherapy long extolled the virtues of adopting a somewhat impassive, blank-slate posture on which clients would project (displace) their deepest feelings about others in their life, this posture not only can seem contrived and artificial but also can be easily interpreted by some clients as apathy. Because most social work encounters are relatively brief (e.g., three to twelve visits), there is little benefit in creating such a level of ambiguity and confusion. When it comes to communicating with clients, practitioners should assume that everything they say or do, even silence, is a form of communication. The question is, What is it you are trying to say to your client, and is it in his or her best interest (i.e., does it help the client move toward intervention goals?)?

Reflection, Tracking, and Clarifying

Effective communication between two people is generally considered a process of developing mutual understanding of each other's thoughts, feelings, intentions, and behaviors. Most theoretical communication models are represented as feedback loops: one person communicates a message, and the other person receives it, analyzes it, and sends back a communication. The first person acknowledges the response and demonstrates that he or she understood the second person's response—and the cycle continues. Understanding someone you know well or are especially close to can seem almost automatic. At times, you feel that you can anticipate what that other person is about to say. Sometimes friends, family members, or intimate partners can communicate and be fully understood with a gesture. People sometimes talk at each other simultaneously (breaking all the rules of good communication), or finish each other's sentences and, amazingly, can still find mutual understanding at a deep level.

Working with clients is another story, and little should be taken for granted about clear communications. The helping relationship is a professional and somewhat contrived one whereby relative strangers are expected to divulge personal information in a relatively short amount of time at scheduled intervals. As such, professional helping interviews are a special kind of relationship and require more purposeful communication skills. Understanding what your client is trying to tell you and helping them understand your responses can be much more difficult, and these skills must be cultivated with much practice. Helping the client feel understood is a task that often must be accomplished in a relatively short amount of time, not over weeks, months, and years. Practitioners facilitate communication by demonstrating that they really comprehend what the client is trying to get them to understand. Practitioners are primarily responsible for seeing that the communication feedback loop is completed on a consistent basis. In addition to careful listening, the practitioner can ensure that the communication process is complete by consistently testing the clarity of the signal between practitioner and client.

Reflecting, tracking, and clarifying are related communication skills that are used to focus on one major goal: to gradually string together a clear, accurate, and understandable client narrative and to help the client confirm for him- or herself that you have understood. Reflecting, tracking, and clarifying are three related skills used to continually test the hypothesis that you, as practitioner, understand what the client says. *Reflecting* simply means repeating in a somewhat different way what the client said to see if your meaning is congruent with the client's meaning. This, of course, may take a bit of practice and may require a process of gradual approximation. Clients generally appreciate that you make the effort to accurately reflect what they say before you move the conversation forward. One way to quickly lose a client's tenuous commitment to the working alliance is to behave as though you knew what the client meant when, in fact, you did not. The client might sense that you did not understand him or her and failed to make an effort to clarify what was said because of apathy or distraction. Making a concerted effort to understand exactly what the client meant shows respect, empathy, and a real commitment to helping the client. Clients have to feel, first and foremost, that you are willing to try hard to listen and understand what they are saying from their point of view. Practitioners may develop their own points of view, and may later (after a working relationship has developed) share their perspective with the client. But, especially early in the helping process, practitioners must demonstrate that they are willing and able to listen and reflect back to the client an accurate understanding of what the client is trying to say.

Accurate reflection is more challenging with some clients than with others. Young children, for example, might not have the verbal capacity to express their thoughts and feelings or to describe others' behaviors or intentions clearly or accurately. Adolescents may use language that is comprehensible only to their immediate social group. Many clients may struggle with their host country's language. Other clients may have difficulties expressing themselves verbally as a result of poor education, learning disabilities, or other developmental disabilities. Clients suffering from serious mental illnesses might use idiosyncratic language or have difficulty expressing themselves because of a thought disorder. Practitioners, whatever the circumstance, should be prepared to be flexible and resourceful in finding ways to communicate with clients. In many circumstances, such as with younger children, people who primarily rely on a nonnative language, or people with specific problems with verbal expression, practitioners should be prepared to obtain specialized training so they can fully communicate with clients.

After demonstrating that you can accurately reflect what the client is saying, track what the client says, which means demonstrating that you can follow the narrative along from one point to the next. For clients who express themselves in clear, organized, linear fashion, tracking the narrative may be relatively easy. However, many clients encountered in social work practices struggle with emotional distress or cognitive impairments as a result of substance abuse, mental disorders, or other learning disabilities. Tracking what clients say may involve more than just following along, but it may take considerable effort on the part of the practitioner to help clients construct their narrative both temporally (i.e., connecting time and dates related to key events) and sequentially (i.e., sequencing cause and effect over time). This process of helping the client track the time line and causal sequence of events often requires some directive interviewing but must be done with a minimum of interference.

Clarifying combines the best of both reflection and tracking. Clarification is accurately communicating to the client that you understand not only specific facts or expressions of feelings but also how the client's experiences evolved over time and across situations. When practitioners clarify, they do not simply make sure that they understand each individual fact of the client's narrative; they show that they are beginning to get the big picture (i.e., put the facts in a broader context) and to connect the dots. The elements of your clients' experiences are related to all facets of their experience: thoughts, feelings, behaviors, and situations, especially those involving other people in their lives. As a result of clarification and understanding, an intricate picture of a client's experience begins to emerge. To use a more contemporary metaphor, accurate clarification of a client's experiences is similar to the emergence of a picture from a digital camera: the clearer is the electronic signal (i.e., the more pixels), the clearer is the whole picture. Clarification is, essentially, a descriptive exercise, not an interpretive one. A good test of whether you have achieved clarification is an unambiguous confirmation from the client, such as when he or she exclaims, "Yes, that's exactly what I mean!"

At times, practitioners must confront clients with known facts or the practitioner's professional opinion regarding something that potentially affects the client's well-being or the well-being of others. The term *confrontation* often brings to mind the stern or disapproving admonishments of an authority figure. In the working relationship, confrontation skills give clients accurate feedback for several purposes: (1) the practitioner might have information that points out incongruities or apparent falsehoods in what the client has stated and maintained (e.g., evidence of child abuse, drug use, violence toward a partner, other harmful or unethical behaviors); (2) the practitioner might feel the need to point out something about the client's behavior that puts him or her at risk (e.g., repeating behaviors that put the client at risk of harm in a relationship, behaviors that put the client at greater risk of relapse with drugs or psychiatric symptoms). There are many other reasons why practitioners sometimes have to express opinions to clients that they may resist accepting. For confrontation to be effective, however, a sound working relationship must be in place. For example, if a young woman with a history of dating verbally and sometimes physically abusive men says, "I know he's been violent before, but I really think I can change him!" the practitioner might respectfully muster the relevant facts of the client's past relationships and present them in a straightforward manner: "Abbey, from our previous discussions, it sounds to me like you're about to make the same mistake you've made several times before. Each time, you thought you could change abusive men by loving them. And each time, you have ended up being disappointed or, even, abused again. I think we need to examine more closely why you seem to believe you have this power to change abusive men and why you confuse their efforts to control you with love or passion. Maybe we should talk about this some more before you plunge ahead. What do you think?"

For a young man struggling to abstain from alcohol and other drugs, confrontation may take the following form: "Joe, you've been in and out of rehab three times now. Each time, you've made an attempt to hang out with the same group of guys that like to party a lot. How is this time going to be different?"

Practitioners should develop their own styles with regard to confrontation. However, confrontation is a skill to be implemented with a balance of straightforward honesty and sensitivity. Being ambiguous, tentative, or overly sensitive is likely to be both confusing and ineffective. Real compassion requires the ability to be honest and explicit when the practitioner judges that the client is ready to receive accurate feedback. Being sensitive does not mean being ineffectual. Navigating the path toward an effective confrontation takes practice, and confrontations should be used sparingly and only after a sound working alliance is established. Although the client role brings with it some expectation that the client will receive some feedback from their practitioner, that feedback needs to be communicated in a way that shows empathy for the client's ongoing struggle.

Adapting Basic Interviewing Skills to Work with Children

As a function of age and cognitive development, children see the world differently than do adults. Thus, interviewing children requires special skills and a solid understanding of what cognitive competencies they have at each age. Practitioners who work with young children should especially have a solid grasp of modern child developmental psychology. Particularly young children (younger than age six, more or less) often have very different ideas about human relationships, the passage of time, and difficulty sorting out the concrete from the abstract. Children may have good memories of specific events, but the experience of the interview itself may significantly affect the retrieval and understanding of the memories. Children also have many fears and anxieties, some realistic and some not. They are quite susceptible to the vagaries of their imaginations in response to things they are told by others, see on television, hear in bedtime stories, or see in the movies. The phenomenology of young childhood is quite different from that of older children, adolescents, and adults.

It should also be understood that there are different purposes to interviewing children in social work practice: clinical assessment (to describe the problem and understand the factors related to the problem to prepare an intervention) and forensic assessment (to determine whether a crime has occurred). Many of the basic principles of interviewing described in relation to adults apply to children as well: careful listening, empathic attunement, putting them at ease, reflecting, tracking, and clarifying are all essential skills for interviewing a child. However, perhaps even more critical information is obtained through observation of children not only in the consulting room but also in the classroom, at day care, and during structured after-school activities. Possibly the most critical information is acquired from parents, guardians, and other adults (e.g., teachers, coaches, other responsible caretakers) who have ample opportunity to observe the child.

Nevertheless, there are some essential data that can be obtained from young children in the traditional one-on-one interview. Focus on their agenda, not yours. Listen with minimal prompts as needed and allow the child to communicate his or her inner world and version of events from his or her own point of view. Wilson and Powell (2001) suggest some ground rules for basic listening, tracking, and clarifying with children. Practitioners should take care to communicate to a child the following: "Let me know if I misunderstand you," "Tell me everything you can about what happened," "Let me know if you don't understand something I've said and I'll try again using different words," "Saying 'I don't know' or 'I don't remember' is OK," "Tell me everything you remember but don't guess; just tell me what you are sure about," "Even if you think I already know something, tell me anyway," "Only talk about things that you know really happened," "You may use whatever words you want to use," "I promise I'll not get upset or angry at anything you say to me" (pp. 35–36).

A variety of aids can be enlisted to facilitate interviewing with a child, including the use of games, toys, and dolls (Morrison & Anders, 1999). When playing with children, use figures or toys that do not overly constrict play or themes that they might elicit. Put children at ease, get down on the floor at their level, and participate in a way that encourages them to play. Be a participant observer. Build rapport with the child, explore general themes, and then delve into promising areas with increasingly greater specificity. Be flexible in the way you approach the interview. Young children are not usually linear in communicating their story.

Research on the validity of using these methods suggests that simple games or activities that put children at ease and enhance communication with the practitioner are helpful. These activities include playing games or using dolls to re-create or remember events which may be a cause for concern (e.g., physical abuse, sexual abuse). However, practitioners should avoid drawing firm conclusions from children's utterances in response to symbolic play. Young children are suggestible, can be easily led, and often do not understand the significance of what the practitioner is driving at. Interpreting a child's unconscious motives or inferring abuse from symbolic play with toys, games, or drawings is risky, and there is little evidence that such interpretations are valid. Interpreting children's play or artwork is no substitute for more objective evidence when attempting, for example, to determine some external cause of their depression, anxiety, or other behavioral problem. As discussed in chapter 4, only through the collection of multidimensional data from multiple sources can a practitioner begin to make reasonable but tentative hypotheses about allegations of abuse, neglect, or other events that may negatively affect a child's mood or behavior.

Wilson and Powell (2001) provide some guidelines for the structure of the basic interview with children that reflect a similar approach to interviews with adults: establish a basic rapport, introduce the topic for discussion, elicit a free narrative account using open-ended questions, and use prompts minimally to keep the conversation on track. Practitioners should use simply worded, specific questions to clarify inconsistencies and obtain sufficient detail. The interviewer should then close with a brief summary and the interviewer should make an effort to provide the child with a chance to correct any mistakes or misunderstandings.

Putting Basic Interviewing Skills to Work: Developing the Working Alliance and Facilitating Change

Communicating Positive Regard and Respect

To successfully engage clients in a working alliance, communicating basic respect for them is essential. Treating a client with positive regard means that the practitioner communicates in words and behavior that he or she believes the client to have inherent value as a human being. Treating the client with respect means communicating through one's words, intonation, and other nonverbal expression that the client has inherent dignity and is worthy of concern and assistance. This assumption on the part of the practitioner may seem, at face value, to be an obvious prerequisite for practicing social work. However, practitioners, at times, should expect to find this assumption a challenging one to maintain with every client.

It has been commonly observed in the helping professions that some practitioners find that clients who are more verbal, better educated, and have better incomes seem to be more appealing to work with than are clients who are more marginalized or stigmatized in society. Voluntary, educated, and self-sufficient clients tend to be more personally engaging, are better socialized into the purposes and processes of psychotherapy services, are less likely to have serious mental illnesses, tend to place a priority on relationship problems, and are generally less stressful to work with. It is understandable that many practitioners cultivate their practice with clients who appear more amenable to voluntary, private social work services.

Some practitioners view clients who are less economically and educationally advantaged, are less sophisticated in the ways of talk therapy, are more likely to have serious mental health problems and chronic addictions, or have perhaps run afoul of the law as less desirable to work with. Many of these clients are considered involuntary, are less amenable to the role of client, and are more likely to be considered resistant and difficult to treat. Many of these clients have been in prison, and some have committed serious crimes, including domestic violence, physical and sexual abuse of children, rape, assault and battery, and gun-related offenses. Some practitioners may find that maintaining a position of positive regard and respect for clients who have engaged in serious antisocial behaviors or are otherwise stigmatized is very challenging indeed.

Practitioners, particularly those starting out in their social work careers, should be honest with themselves if they experience a strong degree of ambivalence regarding work with difficult-to-treat or antisocial clients. To work with involuntary clients, it is essential that practitioners sort through that ambivalence early on and be willing to distinguish clients' harmful behaviors from their inherently good qualities as people. Understanding the contributions of genetic risk factors, the developmental impact of years of physical or sexual abuse, and the enduring effects of other environmental stressors can sometimes promote empathy and help practitioners maintain respect and positive regard for the client. At some point, the client may have been a good son or daughter, friend, or parent or may have contributed to the community in some meaningfully positive way. However, differentiating people from behaviors (while holding them accountable for their offenses) may not be easy for some practitioners. Beginning practitioners who choose to work with clients who have engaged in harmful and antisocial behaviors should honestly explore their feelings about working with such "unattractive" groups and admit any serious reservations they might have. The social work profession serves many needy populations, and practitioners should work with clients with whom they can establish a commitment and consistently maintain a feeling of respect and positive regard.

Being Genuine and Authentic

Genuineness and authenticity are achieved when one's professional persona is congruent with who one really is as a person. Many clients can instinctively sense when a social worker is not being him- or herself, comes across as playing a role, or presents an image that simply does not ring true. Being authentic and genuine, however, does not mean self-confession or self-disclosure with a client. Being honest does not mean saying everything on one's mind. Such excesses on the part of the practitioner can actually make the client uncomfortable (e.g., "Who is the client here anyway?"). All practitioners are somewhat different in the way they present themselves, in their sense of humor, in their comfort level with different clients, and in their style of professional decorum (formal vs. informal). What matters most is that a practitioner maintains good boundaries with the client, communicates a genuine empathy, and keeps the professional purposes of the work together clearly in mind.

Communicating Empathy, Compassion, and Understanding

Communicating empathy means demonstrating verbally and nonverbally that you understand, as best you can, how the client feels. Clients are likely to sense whether what you say and how you say it truly communicates empathy. Empathy should not be confused with agreeing with what the client says or condoning a client's behavior. Empathy should also be distinguished from compassion, an expressed feeling that reflects a sense of shared, often painful human experience. You may express empathy for a man who has acted violently toward his family ("I can understand your sense of frustration and sense of powerlessness") without communicating compassion. On the other hand, a practitioner may be more likely to feel and communicate compassion for a client who has just lost a child to a terminal illness. Compassion goes beyond empathy, beyond merely communicating an understanding of the client's feelings and experience. Expressing compassion lets the client know that, as a person, you can imagine sharing in disappointment, loss, or other source of emotional distress.

Engendering Trust through Consistency and Attending to Client Needs

Many clients have had negative experiences with people in their lives. Many clients have been physically and sexually abused by people they otherwise trusted, betrayed by someone with whom they had an intimate relationship, abandoned by a mother or father, financially exploited, discriminated against, victimized by crime, rejected by fellow citizens after risking their lives for them in combat, or deeply harmed in some other way. Why should they expect a social worker to be any more reliable? Mutual trust is a condition between two people that must be developed, cultivated, and nurtured over time. It is not an assumed condition of the relationship between social worker and client. Trust implies constancy and congruency. Clients are more likely to trust social workers when they say what they mean clearly and directly, do not hide behind vague answers or use ambiguous, pseudo-professional language (i.e., psychobabble), do not pretend to know things for which they cannot give a well-informed answer, and consistently focus on clients' needs.

Practitioners can engender trust in a client by empathizing with the client's feelings regarding experiences in which he or she has been betrayed and by being trustworthy as a practitioner. Being worthy of trust means being consistent, reliable, and honest with your client, and always keeping the client's well-being in mind by keeping the main purpose of the intervention in the forefront.

Providing Encouragement and Enhancing Motivation

Clients come to receive social work services with different levels of motivation and readiness to make changes. Many clients experiencing personal problems, mental illnesses, substance use disorders, eating disorders, family problems, and the like, generally do not feel enthusiastic about asking for help. Some may not feel they have a problem and resent having been coerced into social work services through the child welfare, mental health, or criminal justice system. Some clients may be difficult to engage initially but often participate more when they feel they have some say in how the intervention will progress and realize that participation may yield some personal benefit.

Other clients are highly motivated: they want to feel better and want their situation to improve. Such clients are more readily engaged in the beginning, though considerable ambivalence might emerge later as they realize they may have to work hard to make some changes to feel better. Seriously depressed clients may have a hard time even getting out of bed in the morning, but they might feel the need to work hard because of obligations to those who depend on them. The person struggling with an addiction wants to stop drinking or using other drugs, but the initial success is often short lived. A young angry adolescent might be tired of getting into trouble but also does not want to give in to the demands of adults around him or her. The mother investigated by child welfare struggles with her commitment to give up smoking marijuana daily but does not want to lose custody of her children. All these clients know that they must make an effort to improve their situation, know that change might be hard, and struggle with their commitment to change.

In recent years, practice researchers have focused their efforts on reaching difficult-to-engage clients. Because of an increased emphasis in social work on work with involuntary (e.g., court referred, treatment mandated) clients, practitioners are more likely to deal with clients who do not believe that they have a problem, do not believe that psychosocial interventions are of any value, or simply disagree with practitioners about the nature of the problem or necessity for intervention. They may feel strongly (rightly or wrongly to some degree) that it is the system that is unfair.

Supportive and facilitative skills that focus on enhancing motivation are now considered essential for engaging clients in the early process of change (Miller & Rollnick, 2002). Perhaps one of the better-known assessment frameworks for identifying a client's readiness to change is that developed by James Prochaska and colleagues (Prochaska & DiClemente, 1984; Prochaska, DiClemente, & Norcross, 1992) at the University of Rhode Island. Their research team stipulates five stages of change: precontemplation, when clients do not agree that they have a problem, may see others as the cause of their difficulties, or may feel coerced into treatment by the courts or significant others; contemplation, when a client is aware of a problem and may want to find out whether therapy can help; preparation, when the client takes some initial steps toward change; action, when a client may take more significant steps toward working on the problem and actively seek help in the change process; and maintenance, when clients have already made changes with regard to a problem and have sought treatment to consolidate previous improvements. Clients may cycle through these stages of change or proceed in a trajectory of one step forward, two steps back. The stages-of-change model has been employed with a range of problems including smoking cessation, substance abuse, and other mental health and health-related problems.

As the stages of change imply, clients are usually not clearly in one stage or another and may feel considerable ambivalence in the change process (O'Hare, 1996). If stages of change suggest when clients are ready, motivational enhancement methods (designed to help clients move beyond ambivalence and through the stages of change) suggest how to help clients engage in the change process (Miller & Rollnick, 2002). Readiness to change is particularly relevant for working with involuntary clients, those more or less coerced into receiving social work services who practitioners often label as "resistant," "hard to reach," "hostile," and "unmotivated" (Rooney & Bibus, 2001). However, the voluntary versus involuntary dichotomy is far from absolute and is better considered a continuum. Strategies designed to help clients move through the stages of change include the following:

- Accept clients' initial reluctance: Empathize with clients' ambivalence about engaging in treatment or making changes, acknowledge that they may have been treated somewhat unfairly without suggesting that you think they are blameless with regard to their current difficulties, and acknowledge that not everyone benefits from social work intervention. Above all, do not argue or try to sell clients on the benefits of treatment.
- Avoid premature confrontation: Again, do not quarrel. Get the facts from clients and other relevant sources. Practitioners should objectively present their summaries to clients and give them a chance to respond and explain their point of view.
- Clarify one's dual role within the social service and/or criminal justice system: Be up front with clients. Let them know you empathize with the situation and want to help with concerns. However, you collaborate with the criminal justice system because a particular client has been convicted of child abuse, drug possession, domestic assault, or some other antisocial act. Communicate the expectation

that clients have an obligation to acknowledge the behavior (assuming the accusations are well founded), take responsibility for the behavior, and change the behavior. Social workers not only have an ethical obligation to protect society but also should use contingencies of the courts as therapeutic leverage to help clients meet agreed-on goals of the intervention (i.e., therapeutic jurisprudence).

- Explore clients' perspective on the problem: Encourage clients to suggest intervention goals and ways to pursue them. Recruiting clients as collaborators this way can provide them with some sense of control and choice in developing the intervention plan.
- List problems by priority: Start with one or two that are more readily resolved; then break each individual problem and objective down to manageable steps.
- Employ behavioral contracting: Collaborate on agreements, keep them specific, and track them to completion.
- Avoid overemphasis on clients' irrelevant self-disclosures: Gauge each client's need to open up but do not make it a condition of pursuing intervention goals.
- Anticipate obstacles to treatment compliance: Look down the road with clients and help them identify scenarios that may interfere with successfully reaching agreed-on goals.
- Involve significant others when at all possible: Encourage clients to recruit people in their lives who have a vested interest in the client's compliance with intervention goals.
- Actively enhance motivation: Help clients visualize the benefits of working toward intervention goals and consequences of returning to the previous problem behaviors, list the pros and cons of changing versus not making progress, and empathize with the difficulties of change but communicate optimism about positive change and the benefits that might accrue.

Enhancing Clients' Confidence and Morale

Improving self-confidence, overall morale, or self-efficacy with regard to coping with some specific problem is not something that a practitioner can readily impart to a client. Clients must earn that feeling from graduated experiences of success. Relating positive testimonials of other clients struggling with similar difficulties or reporting relevant outcome-research findings might be helpful ("You mean, I'm not hopeless?"), but there is no substitute for success. For positive success experiences to occur, however, practitioners must be skilled in clearly identifying the problem and helping clients break it down into manageable objectives. The intervention methods used must be targeted toward achieving modest but substantive objectives so clients can gradually gain back a true sense of confidence. This linking of client behavior and increased self-efficacy (i.e., the belief that one can cope in a given situation) is where the practitioner's ability to cultivate a supportive working relationship facilitates effective therapeutic coping skills. The working relationship, in many cases, makes it possible for clients to take the risks necessary to make real changes and experience success. The practitioner and the working relationship he or she cultivates become a catalyst for change.

Clarifying Roles of the Practitioner and the Client

The practitioner has the primary responsibility of being the expert; that is, the practitioner, not the client, is the one who has the requisite credentials, gets paid for the service, is liable for providing services within established standards of care, and is held accountable for delivering ethical and effective interventions. Clients expect social workers to be knowledgeable about the problems they treat and skilled in the interventions they provide. Thus, in the practitioner-client relationship, the practitioner is responsible for certain roles: conducting informed assessments, implementing interventions that have been shown to be effective in current outcome research, and evaluating the results of those efforts.

Although practitioners bear much of the responsibility for implementing professional services, clients have responsibilities as well. They should be expected to show up on time, make an effort to participate constructively in treatment, and cooperate with arranging for insurance and initially agreed-on out-of-pocket payments. Also, clients can forfeit their rights to confidentiality and informed consent when they threaten to harm themselves or other people during the course of the intervention.

Clarifying the role of the practitioner and that of the client, however, can be confusing at times. For example, for most social work agencies, maintaining fiscal integrity (i.e., balancing the budget) is critical for the agency to continue serving the public. Sources of income for agencies can span the continuum from private to public funding and often combine both sources. The manner in which these conditions influence practitioners, however, can influence intervention planning decisions. For example, in a busy clinic where a combination of state funding and private insurance pays for services, should the extent of coverage determine, in part, clients' length of stay? Even with the most ethical of behavior (e.g., avoiding conflicts of interest) on the part of practitioners and administrators, there are external influences that have a subtle but real impact on how social workers define their role in relation to clients.

Defining the client's role can be difficult at times. A more challenging situation concerns involuntary referrals. *Voluntary* and *involuntary* is a matter of degree—perhaps representing a level of willingness to engage in treatment. If a court-diversionary program, for example, offers a client the choice of drug treatment or jail, who is the client? The overloaded criminal justice system or the person who arrives for treatment? If a distraught and depressed middle-aged woman arrives for her first session, and it becomes clear that she is there because she does not know what to do about her alcohol-addicted husband but wants to get him to come for treatment, who is the client? If a young woman is referred for mental health treatment as a condition of having child custody reinstated by the courts via the approval of child welfare and mental health professionals, who is the client? Practitioners can help clients define their role by helping them sort out the reasons why they sought treatment and how those reasons are contingent on the behavior of other people in their lives or other institutions. Although many of these circumstances involve mixed motives in the client, these must be drawn out: "Is there any reason why you don't want to be here?" "Do you feel that you are being forced here against your will?" "Is there any reason why you think this might be helpful to you despite the fact that you don't really want to be here?" Helping clients sort out mixed agenda can go a long way toward helping them define their role as client, a necessary step in defining mutually agreed-on intervention goals and engaging in the change process.

Collaborating with the Client on the Assessment, Intervention, and Evaluation Plan

Defining practitioner and client roles also necessitates determining shared responsibilities. One of the most supportive aspects of effective helping is cultivating a shared feeling of collaboration, the sense that client and practitioner are "in this thing together." True, one does not want to ignore the power differential: the practitioner has the responsibility to implement effective care and has some prerogatives that the client does not (e.g., the practitioner can hospitalize clients against their will; the practitioner can breach confidentiality should a client threaten to harm him- or herself or others; the practitioner may be bound to report client information to the courts). However, the practitioner can underscore the importance of collaboration in the following manner: "We both agree that you want to work on

Topic A, and that we will first do that by trying Intervention B and then see how it goes." To transcend some of the ambivalence about receiving social work services, clients must feel that, on some level, they voluntarily participate in (and take responsibility for) the course of the intervention. This collaborative relationship, again, does not obviate the power differences in the relationship, but it does establish a common ground on which practitioner and client can base a productive working relationship.

As part of the intervention, however, the practitioner also recruits the client into activities. Clients provide the information to complete the assessment. Clients might also spend some time on their own completing assessment instruments, such as self-report scales, charts, or diaries to help with the assessment and monitor treatment progress. Practitioners might also have clients carry out some of the intervention during the time when they are not in session. For example, people struggling with addictions may attend mutual help meetings, psychoeducational classes, or a family gathering (later on in recovery)—at which they know family members are likely to drink—to practice relapse-prevention coping strategies. A family with a conduct-disordered adolescent may have to spend time in brief family meetings to negotiate guidelines for doing homework and increasing prosocial activities. Clients, in effect, become collaborators with practitioners to implement interventions successfully. They are not passive recipients of treatment. The shared feeling that exists between practitioner and client that they are collaborating on the assessment, intervention, and evaluation plan together is the glue that holds the working alliance together.

Maintaining Clear Boundaries

Defining clear boundaries and collaborating effectively on the intervention requires that the practitioner take the responsibility for maintaining clear professional boundaries over the course of the intervention. Boundaries are best kept in sight not by maintaining a pseudo-professional, aloof posture but by continuing to communicate empathy and respect and by continually focusing on the goals of the intervention contract. To stay on track, good working questions for every practitioner are, Is what I am doing in the meeting with the client today likely to enhance this client's progress? and, Am I helping the client move toward the agreed-on goals? Practitioners also need to model behavior that reinforces good boundaries to reassure the client about the respective roles of practitioner and client. Clients should be encouraged to express their feelings, participate in the intervention during the session, put what they have learned into action outside of sessions, and help evaluate whether things are getting better. In other words, for both practitioner and client, the mutual focus should be on getting the work done together.

Clients sometimes have strong feelings about their practitioner. How should practitioners handle these feelings? For a variety of reasons, the helping relationship creates, at times, an ambiguity about the nature of the relationship whereby the client may interject a variety of feelings (e.g., love, hate, anger, envy, jealousy, gratitude) into the relationship. The client may communicate these feelings in a variety of ways, both directly and indirectly. These feelings may spring from a variety of sources. In the psychodynamic tradition, feelings displaced or projected onto the practitioner (i.e., transference) were often assumed to be feelings that the client felt about his or her mother or primary caretaker in the past. Although one's parents may be a source of such feelings, there are many other possible sources as well, including how the person actually feels about the relationship with the practitioner (e.g., the client may be justified in feeling angry with the practitioner). Other sources of these feelings may stem from experiences the client had with some other person with whom they had or currently have a close relationship (e.g., spouse, friend, employer). Other legitimate feelings may be evoked from racial, cultural, or socioeconomic differences and tensions. A young African American man who has had negative experiences with white authority figures may feel suspicious and resentful about a white social worker; a woman who has been abused by men in the past may be predisposed to feel a mixture of anger and shame or other feelings toward a male practitioner; an older client may feel either nurturing or resentful feelings toward a younger social worker; a male client from a culture where women are dissuaded from achieving educational or professional success may feel disdain toward a female social worker. Because a professional helping relationship is not a naturally occurring relationship (e.g., friendship, marriage, parent-child, coworkers), ambiguities abound and clients will find a way to fill in those ambiguities, accurately or otherwise. It is the practitioner's job to explore those ambiguities and help clients deal with them realistically and with minimal distortion.

Likewise, practitioners make interpersonal misattributions (O'Hare, 2005) toward some clients. Practitioners can experience a range of feelings that potentially obstruct the helping process. These may include anger, disgust, sexual attraction, a parental need to nurture, and so on. Mild feelings of genuine affection or caring are usually not a matter of concern and may enhance the helping process. However, other feelings toward clients can become a serious obstacle to effective intervention. Anger can lead to punitive behavior toward a client, premature termination, or abandonment; attraction or infatuation can lead to overtures for sexual relations. Practitioners are obliged to identify for themselves what they feel, determine whether the way they deal with their feelings helps or hinders the working relationship, and take responsibility for feelings and subsequent behaviors toward the client. Practitioners often sort these matters out for themselves or in discussion with colleagues; if the problem is not readily resolved, the practitioner can seek professional consultation. Whatever method practitioners use to cope with these matters, keeping the client's well-being in mind should be the foremost priority. Maintaining clear boundaries means continually returning to the key question: Is what I am about to say or do in the client's best interest?

Summary

Supportive and facilitative skills incorporate basic interviewing methods in the service of cultivating a sound working alliance, enhancing motivation, and helping the client engage in a collaborative change process. However, although supportive skills are essential for establishing the working alliance, the practice process research has clearly shown that they are usually not sufficient for helping clients with more serious and complex problems. To conduct more advanced interventions with clients with moderate to severe psychosocial disorders, expert use of therapeutic coping skills is essential.

CHAPTER SIX

Therapeutic Coping Skills

ROOTED PRIMARILY IN THE COGNITIVE and behavioral therapies, therapeutic coping skills are used to help clients critically examine the content and process of thinking as it relates to their difficulties, better regulate distressing emotions, enhance their behavioral coping and abilities in challenging situations, and enhance their problem-solving skills (Butler, Chapman, Forman & Beck, 2006; Craighead, Craighead, Kazdin, & Mahoney, 1994; Dobson & Craig, 1996). These approaches originally evolved from an integration of cognitive and behavioral theories and practice research and were further shaped by advances in social-cognitive theory (Bandura, 1986, 1999). Cognitive-behavioral therapy (CBT) methods not only are the most researched intervention methods relative to other approaches but also show superior effectiveness in controlled trials for a range of specific disorders (Butler et al., 2006). Although specific CBT skills can be used as discrete interventions (e.g., examination of dysfunctional thinking, breathing retraining to cope with anxiety, exposure to overcome a specific phobia), they are typically used in combination to treat moderate to severe psychosocial disorders with individuals, couples, families, and groups. Rather than being passive recipients of treatment, clients are best served when therapeutic coping skills are implemented within a supportive and collaborative working alliance. The goals for using therapeutic coping skills are not for practitioners to effect cures but for clients to incorporate skills into their own coping and problem-solving repertoire to ameliorate specific problems and enhance overall adaptive capabilities (i.e., strengths). Subsequent chapters will describe applications of these skills to address specific problems.

Cognitive-Change Skills

Understanding clients' experiences, difficulties, and expectations from their perspective is an important starting point, one that has been underscored in basic counseling literature for decades. For some clients, particularly those with mildly stressful and usually transitory problems in living, listening to themselves talk out loud and being helped to feel understood may be sufficient for resolving some transitory difficulties. However, for clients with moderate to severe and complex difficulties, simply providing accurate listening and reflection is not likely to satisfactorily resolve their situation or enhance their ability to cope. More often than not, beyond understanding what our clients tell us, it is essential to help clients better understand how their problems are maintained so an effective intervention can be tailored to fit their needs. Efforts to inform and educate clients about their problems and potential solutions often include the use of skills aimed to directly effect cognitive change.

Psychoeducation may be among the most basic forms of cognitive-change techniques, and one that is typically either under- or overrated in terms of efficacy. Psychoeducation is, essentially, the imparting of well-established information for the purpose of preventing problems (e.g., drug-abuse prevention programs), coping with specific situations (e.g., grief counseling), or improving overall lifestyle (e.g., stress-reduction skills). Psychoeducation is employed across individual, family, and group modalities. An individual client who has experienced his or her first panic attack, for example, can benefit substantially from learning about the signs and symptoms of panic disorder to alleviate the fear of "going crazy" or "dying of a heart attack" (assuming the client is otherwise in good health). Young and inexperienced couples can benefit from some basic psychoeducation in communication and problem-solving skills during the often-challenging first years of marriage. Small and large groups of adolescents can obtain some benefit from basic lessons regarding safe sex and the risks associated with excessive alcohol use. Imparting information is certainly not a new strategy, but using it for targeted purposes to improve psychosocial well-being and health is often useful and sometimes effective when delivered in a timely manner to a receptive audience. Recently, for example, some studies have shown that online eating-disorder-prevention programs yield modest positive effects for many young women.

How does a practitioner provide psychoeducation as part of an intervention? Formats are quite flexible and can range from the impromptu and informal to a carefully planned curriculum that extends over several weeks or months. With an individual, couple, or family, questions might arise unexpectedly about the relationship of substance use to depression, what constitutes safe sex, what to do about a grandparent who is becoming extremely forgetful or appears to talk to people who are not present, how to relate to a brother who has schizophrenia, or how to help a daughter who has been diagnosed with attention deficit/hyperactivity disorder (ADHD). Providing psychoeducation to a client also requires that the practitioner be knowledgeable about the given area. If a client's questions are beyond the practitioner's area of expertise, then the practitioner can refer the client to a colleague, an agency, or an organization that can provide that service.

Psychoeducation, because of its didactic nature, is sometimes dismissed as less legitimate than other social work services. Often, however, providing clients with accurate, timely, and complete information is sufficient to meet their needs and can help them move toward a long-term solution to a problem. For larger groups that require a more formal psychoeducational curriculum, more planning and expertise in presentation may be necessary. As a complement to practice, many social workers enjoy providing psychoeducational services to larger audiences in local schools, hospitals, community centers, and religious congregations on some important topics of today: coping with Alzheimer's disease, how to approach a family member with a substance use problem, decisions on whether to adopt a child, and how to cope with and help a family member who suffers from chronic and severe depression. Psychoeducation provides a valuable and sometimes essential function by itself or as part of a multifaceted intervention.

Explanation and interpretation are, in one sense, a teaching function of social work practice. One might even consider it a form of psychoeducation. Helping clients better understand their depression, an addiction process, their difficulties controlling anger, or dynamics of a relationship problem requires that practitioners help clients hypothesize aloud about factors that might contribute to the problem or interfere with their ability to cope. Explanations and interpretations are usually tentative (i.e., hypothetical) because, on a case-by-case basis, it is difficult know with certainty exactly which factors cause or maintain an individual client's difficulties. Nevertheless, theorizing aloud about factors that cause and maintain the client's psychosocial difficulties (i.e., connecting the dots) is necessary for ongoing assessment and intervention planning. Practitioners' ability to help clients hypothesize about their problems in an informed way requires that practitioners are knowledgeable about the problems they treat and listen carefully to clients to understand their difficulties as they view them.

To understand, for example, what underlies a schizophrenic young man's incoherent ramblings, an addicted elderly man's reported sensations of bugs under his skin, a female domestic violence victim's feelings of hopeless defeat, an adolescent's explosive rage, or a child's compulsive ordering of a toy collection, social workers must have an up-to-date grasp of the relevant knowledge of these problems. Practitioners who rely on unsubstantiated theories are less likely to understand their client's difficulties and, therefore, are less likely to be of much help. For example, after one or two visits, an assessment reveals that a client is seriously depressed and suicidal. This is important descriptive information, but a more complete understanding of the client's depression necessitates more information grounded in current research: What factors seem to contribute to the client's depression? How did things get to this point? Has the client been depressed like this before? Is there a family history of depression? Has the client experienced serious trauma or stressors, including sudden losses or disappointments? Has the client been drinking alcohol to excess or been using drugs or medications? Has the client been physically ill? Have there been any serious interpersonal difficulties in the client's life? Educating the client about factors that potentially contribute to depression (i.e., explanation and interpretation) assumes that a practitioner is knowledgeable about the problem and can base his or her assessment and intervention recommendations on that sound knowledge base. Explanation and interpretation do not imply that the practitioner has all the right answers, but that he or she is sufficiently informed about the problems the client is experiencing to at least make educated guesses about what psychological, physical, social, or situational factors might contribute to the client's current difficulties. Practitioners should avoid explanations and interpretations based on unsupported theories.

When clients engage in self-monitoring, they collaborate in their treatment in a significant way. Rather than experience the intervention as something "done" to them, clients who engage in self-monitoring help carry out ongoing assessment and evaluation of the intervention. More specifically, when clients engage in self-monitoring, they

- Help define problems, goals, and objectives
- Help develop and use self-anchored scales to track progress (e.g., anxiety level on a ten-point scale; days clean and sober; days homework was completed)
- Complete self-report standardized scales for key problems
- Evaluate the apparent effects of the intervention on key presenting problems and have the opportunity to give feedback to the practitioner
- Participate in continued monitoring of long-term progress after termination

Self-monitoring is a highly flexible skill. In addition to having clients use standardized scales, practitioners can help clients create self-anchored scales; use qualitative diaries or journals; design quantitative charts (e.g., to track a child's academic and behavioral improvements); or develop other creative ways to monitor cognitive, emotional, or behavioral changes over time. As described in chapter 4, self-monitoring can use basic indexes to measure frequency (e.g., number of positive days for a couple), duration (e.g., days without serious suicidal ideation), or severity (e.g., level of depression). Clients often appreciate the specific and objective value of demonstrated progress that self-monitoring provides.

Assessing, challenging, and changing dysfunctional thinking have become essential skills for facilitating client change. As discussed earlier, practitioners should initially strive to encourage the expression of the client's personal narrative and understand it with as little interpretation or filtering as possible. For relatively mild forms of distress or transitory life difficulties, the use of basic counseling skills in this way is often sufficient to help the client resolve a dilemma. Clients often need to hear themselves talk out loud and often come to solutions on their own with little assistance from practitioners. However, for more serious problems, including substance abuse, major mental illnesses, conduct disorders, and antisocial and self-destructive behaviors, clients typically require a more robust intervention. Clients, for example, who believe in using severe corporal punishment on children or who abuse a spouse, scream obscenities in public to imaginary tormentors, carve images in their skin with broken glass, ruminate for hours about how to end their life, are too anxious to concentrate and complete homework, or are addicted to alcohol or other substances and commit crimes to support the habit need more than nondirective counseling. They need help in critically reevaluating some of the beliefs, convictions, and expectations that drive their behavior. Effectively challenging and critically examining dysfunctional thinking, however, is not likely to be helpful unless the practitioner has first established a solid working alliance with the client.

One can readily assert that practitioners from all schools of thought attempt to influence and change the way their clients think. Practitioners who deny this premise underestimate the power of silent listening, their own nonverbal communications, or how selectively attending to one topic of conversation or another influences the client's way of thinking. Practitioners, depending on their theoretical orientation, may go about the process of influencing their clients differently. Psychodynamic practitioners, for example, might theorize about how a client's early childhood attachments currently affect his marriage. Cognitive therapists might challenge a client's feelings of hopelessness by asking her to provide examples of positive things happening in her life. A strategic family therapist might ask siblings to engage in a role-reversal exercise to help each one see the problem from the other's point of view. A narrative-constructionist practitioner might encourage a client to generate alternative constructions of a problem and list three creative solutions to a current dilemma. Suffice it to say that talking interventions of all kinds attempt to help clients reflect critically on their difficulties and consider new ways to think about their problems and potential solutions.

Challenging clients' beliefs, however, is not premised on the notion that the practitioner is the final expert, the arbiter of objective reality, or subscribes to a statistical benchmark for what is normal. It simply means that, on a practical level, the clients' ways of viewing themselves and others seem to cause significant problems for them (and perhaps for others), and a reappraisal of those views might be necessary to arrive at meaningful solutions. In some cases, clients' views may be seriously immoral or illegal (i.e., harmful to the client or others), and social workers are sometimes ethically obliged to intervene, even when intervention requires a breach of confidentiality. In short, practitioners should respect every client's reality to the furthest extent possible. However, when a client's reality puts the client's or society's well-being at risk, social workers are expected to challenge the way clients think and, ultimately, influence the way they behave. Social workers strive to help mentally ill clients reduce command hallucinations to hurt others, reduce the likelihood of using harsh corporal punishment on children, engender hope that the person addicted to drugs can envision a clean future, and help the suicidal client consider that life might be worth living. Social workers try to help people change their minds about many things. Cognitive-change skills are one way to achieve that goal.

Cognitive therapy and research has provided the most explicit and well-researched approaches to addressing cognitive change, not just as a way to reduce dysfunctional thinking but also as a catalyst to improve emotional well-being and behavioral adaptation. Research has demonstrated that a client's difficulties are sometimes grounded in erroneous, distorted, or dysfunctional thinking regarding the client's self-image, relationships, the surrounding world, and the future. A negative schema (i.e., the cognitive model a client uses as a template to view him- or herself and others) can promote automatic negative thoughts and subsequently lead to systematic thinking errors and difficulties coping in life (Beck, 1976, 1996; Clark & Beck, 1999). For a female client with very low self-esteem, for example, automatic negative thoughts (in response to moderate stressors) might include the following: "Oh, I'm not that interesting; he'll never ask me out," and "I didn't deserve that promotion; I don't think I can do this job." A person with a pessimistic schema may be inclined to think, "It doesn't matter how hard we work at this relationship, it will end in divorce just like our parents," or, "With the way the world is—the economy, climate change, and terrorism—what's the point of getting my MSW? We're all doomed!"

Cognitive assessment addresses the client's cognitive world on two levels: the content of thought (i.e., what clients think) and the process of thinking (i.e., how critically a client thinks) (Clark & Beck, 1999; Gambrill, 1990; Nisbett & Ross, 1980; Tversky & Kahneman, 1974). The content of thought is important because it reveals the clients' views regarding themselves, the nature of their relationships, what they think about the world around them, and their expectations about the future. At the more extreme end, some clients suffer from serious mental illnesses, learning disabilities, or cognitive dysfunction from severe substance abuse problems. Cognitive distortions associated with those disorders can be severe and include hallucinations, delusions, and other thought disorders. With more ordinary problems, some clients are simply misinformed about certain matters or have erroneous beliefs or unreasonable expectations regarding relationships, health-risk behaviors, or coping with life. Although what is reasonable varies among individuals for cultural, political, religious, or other reasons, the focus here is on what constitutes obviously problematic or dysfunctional ways of thinking—problematic for the client, the client's family, or others.

Enhancing a client's cognitive coping skills also requires an examination of how the client thinks; that is, the client's critical-thinking processes. These are the same critical-thinking skills reviewed in chapter 2 with regard to using evidence to support professional decision making, but here they are applied to the way people view their problems and cope in everyday life. Although the use of critical-thinking skills does not guarantee happiness, as engaging in dysfunctional thinking does not necessarily result in serious problems, some key thinking errors seem to be associated with problems related to depression, anxiety, and other psychosocial disorders.

Some clients use dramatic stereotypes, emotional testimonials, or draw conclusions from readily available information to guide their own behavior. A client with a drinking problem, for example, might minimize the negative consequences of drinking by citing the fact that his or her father and grandfather were daily heavy drinkers and "lived well into their seventies." Although this fact may attest to the family's overall robust health, the client is focusing on an uncharacteristically good scenario and might also overlook other problems that resulted from years of heavy drinking, such as depression and domestic violence. Another client may cite the popularity of ultrathin celebrities as justification for routine binge purging and daily use of diuretics and ignore the risks of potential health problems caused by bulimia. Practitioners can gently challenge this self-serving tendency by helping clients access more objective and representative sources of information.

Some clients engage in dichotomous thinking, all-or-nothing thinking, or good versus bad thinking rather than viewing most experiences in life on a continuum and often more complex than they appear at first glance. Clients often apply such thinking to their own mental status (e.g., "Am I crazy or not?"), to relapse during substance abuse treatment ("I slipped; therefore, I am a treatment failure"), to raising a teenager ("She was a minute late from the dance, so I grounded her for a month!"), to work ("I didn't get the promotion—I am such a loser"), and to relationships ("He left me—I'll *never* find anyone who will love me again!"). Practitioners can help clients examine how viewing their situation in such extremes severely limits their options and a wide range of possible outcomes.

In a similar approach to extreme thinking, many clients overgeneralize from limited experiences or draw erroneous conclusions from only a few examples (i.e., small sampling of their own or other's behaviors). Having had a bad experience with a mental health professional, a client may opine, "All you therapist types are just a bunch of jerks!" A child who experienced teasing at their friend's birthday party might say, "I'm never going to a party again. Kids always make fun of me." An elderly person for whom supervised care is considered the best option might conclude from one visit to such a facility, "I'll never fit in with people like that. These places are all the same—they are just full of a bunch of old folks." Gently exploring other possibilities and encouraging more experimentation can sometimes help attenuate overgeneralizations based on only one or two experiences.

Another form of extreme thinking is "catastrophizing"—always expecting the worst. This form of cognitive distortion lies in a failure to consider accurate base rates for a variety of phenomenon. Awful and tragic things happen to people on a daily basis: people are affected by sudden onsets of terminal illnesses, car accidents, airline disasters, sudden loss of loved ones, and other dreaded events. Nevertheless, on any given day, these events are unlikely to occur in the lives of any single individual. Persons who are inclined toward anxiety and depression (which often co-occur) often spend more time ruminating excessively about the what-ifs than they do enjoying their lives. Philosophers exhort us to live in the present, but catastrophizing erodes individuals' abilities to cope with daily stressors and enjoy living in the moment.

Hindsight bias may be among the more common strategies for distorting reality and drawing erroneous conclusions. Many clients suffer from what are colloquially known as the *coulda-woulda-shouldas*, a bias caused by the illusion that hindsight is twenty-twenty. For example, a mother grieving the loss of a child to a rare illness accompanied by common symptoms such as headaches and stomachaches might torment herself with the belief, "If only I had taken her to the doctor sooner, she might have gotten proper treatment and lived"—despite the doctor's assurance that she did nothing wrong given the seemingly ordinary presentation of the child's symptoms at the time. Sometimes helping clients recall in detail what they were thinking and feeling at the time of the event and re-create the circumstances can help them understand why they did something at the time and dispel some of the false clarity and guilt associated with hindsight bias.

Selective attention occurs when a client focuses disproportionately on details that support only his or her point of view. As a result, the client might not take into consideration all the representative facts, including those that do not support his or her own opinion. Clients with agoraphobia, for example, note all the bad things (e.g., muggings, car accidents, earthquakes) that could happen if they start to leave their apartment and reenter the world but overlook the vast majority of the time when nothing of note happens. Selective attention, in this case, appears to be the consequence of a negative schema influenced by strong feelings of anxiety and the pessimism associated with depression. Consider another example: an angry spouse may selectively focus on all his or her partner's failings in the relationship but forget to consider other considerate and caring behaviors.

Clients often confuse correlation with causation. As a result, clients often present problems on the basis of their own assessments and find cause-effect relationships in their own and others' lives where there may be only coincidence. For example, a client may come in for treatment for severe depression and report that her grandmother recently died, and that she has recently been thinking about her own mother's death ten years ago. She may conclude that she has always been depressed: "You can't count on anyone sticking around for long. They always leave you." The client may feel strongly that this is the cause of her depression and report that she has read many books on loss issues by experts who support her view. The practitioner, on meeting the woman's husband and adolescent son, finds out that the client has been addicted to prescription tranquilizers and alcohol for many years. Although there is little doubt that loss and grief can be related to depression, long-standing and severe depression often has either a genetic or some other physiological base (e.g., chronic substance abuse). In this case, loss is probably more a correlated issue than a causal one for depression. Practitioners can help clients sort out those factors that are likely to cause and maintain their problems over time in contrast to other factors or events that might be coincidental.

Within the context of a sound working alliance, practitioners should strive to (1) explore in detail the content of clients' thoughts, (2) examine their cognitive reasoning processes, and (3) hypothesize how those beliefs and thinking processes reflect the client's overall cognitive schema. Practitioners can then gently challenge dysfunctional thinking through Socratic questioning. Socratic questioning is essentially the use of basic interviewing skills accompanied by empathy and support to encourage clients to justify their problematic thoughts, attitudes, and beliefs. The following dialogue with a depressed adolescent illustrates the practitioner's attempt to coax a rational examination of a client's anxieties regarding meeting new friends:

SOCIAL WORKER: Jim, you say that you will never fit in at your new school, that you will always be alone—tell me, what brings you to that conclusion?

JIM: I feel like I've always been alone. Nobody likes me. I have no friends.

SOCIAL WORKER: You have no friends now, but you told me about friends you had last year. What happened in the last year?

JIM: You know what happened. My parents moved after my sophomore year. Those f—ing idiots. I told them not to move. I lost all my friends.

SOCIAL WORKER: So, you're angry with your folks for moving. Now you're in a new school. Most of your classmates are tight with their own groups, and you feel like the outsider, like you don't belong. Do you think things will always be that way?

JIM: Seems like that.

SOCIAL WORKER: Seems like that, but do you really think you will never make new friends again?

JIM: I guess *some* day I might make some new friends. I've only been here three months. But everyone else is solid with their group.

SOCIAL WORKER: So, do you think there's no chance of making new friends at this point?

JIM: I guess there is a possibility.

SOCIAL WORKER: If there is a possibility, how might you go about getting to know people a little, or having a conversation now and then? That's usually the way it starts.

JIM: I guess I have to try and talk to people. But, I don't think they want to make new friends. I don't think they want me to talk with them.

SOCIAL WORKER: How do you know that?

JIM: They just seem busy.

SOCIAL WORKER: Busy.

JIM: Yeah. Busy. You know, during class, in the lunch room, in the hall.

SOCIAL WORKER: So, that means they don't want you to talk to them?

JIM: I guess not. But I don't like to interrupt.

SOCIAL WORKER: So, talking to people means you are interrupting them?

JIM: I guess I'm not sure how to start a conversation.

SOCIAL WORKER: How do other people start conversations?

JIM: I guess they just say, "Excuse me, did you get the homework assignment in the last class?" or something like that.

SOCIAL WORKER: Seems about right. So, have you tried that?

JIM: No, because I don't think they want me to.

SOCIAL WORKER: Has anyone said they don't want you to? Has anyone objected?

JIM: No. I just don't think they'd like it much.

SOCIAL WORKER: So, there is no real indication that they don't want you to talk with them, you just have this general expectation that they don't want you to try. Right?

JIM: Seems so.

SOCIAL WORKER: So, what evidence do you have that some people would not want you to talk with them?

JIM: I guess I really don't have any. I just happen to feel that way.

SOCIAL WORKER: Sounds like this situation has more to do with the way you feel about yourself than how other people feel about you, huh?

JIM: Maybe.

SOCIAL WORKER: Have you had *any* conversations with people since you started at that school?

JIM: Sure. Lots of times.

SOCIAL WORKER: Well, I guess I'm a little confused. So you *have* had conversations. Did any of them go well?

JIM: Yeah. Some.

SOCIAL WORKER: Good. Did you follow up with those people? Have you tried to talk with them again? You know, say "Hey, what's up?" Have you asked anyone if they'd like to get together after school?

JIM: *No.* I guess not. I figured if they wanted to, they'd talk to me.

SOCIAL WORKER: I see. So, because they didn't initiate the conversation, you figured they didn't want to talk to you.

JIM: I guess.

SOCIAL WORKER: Have you considered the possibility that maybe they think you don't want to talk with them?

JIM: No. I hadn't thought about that. I guess, maybe they think I'm the one who isn't too friendly.

SOCIAL WORKER: Sometimes, shy people are seen as aloof or stuck up. Is it possible that some people see you that way?

JIM: Yeah. I overheard someone say I was a snob. Maybe I'm the one giving off the bad vibe.

The social worker might continue to use Socratic questioning to help Jim sort out whether any real shortcomings of his own justify his lack of self-confidence or whether he is just anxious about being rejected and not fitting in. At some point, however, questioning and clarifying distortions will have to be used as a springboard to action by discussing some of Jim's anxiety about being vulnerable and meeting new people (i.e., expressing and identifying his feelings) and by risking a conversation (i.e., behavior change). The key point in implementing cognitive change, however, is identifying the core content of dysfunctional thoughts (e.g., "Nobody likes me"), identifying the thought process that maintains the belief (e.g., expecting the worst: "What if they tell me to get lost?"), and sensitively helping the client examine the belief, evaluate the evidence that supports it, and consider alternative views. Although cognitive change is important, it usually is only a prelude to change.

Emotional and Physiological Regulatory Skills

Although challenging dysfunctional thinking can be a helpful place to start, rational discussion is often insufficient to engender lasting change. Often, dysfunctional thinking is related to unresolved emotional difficulties, including depression, anxiety, chronic anger, and other forms of emotional distress. Although some cognitive theorists have opined that cognition is primary (meaning that thoughts come before feelings and behaviors), others have suggested that it is equally plausible that emotions sometimes precede and influence the content and processes of cognitions. Keeping in mind Figure 7, thinking, acting, and feeling are reciprocally related, and change can be initiated in any modality. Despite that change-process theories are not sufficiently developed, most theoreticians agree that thoughts, feelings, and behaviors are interrelated in a complex way, and emotional distress can strongly affect the way people think and act. Thus, identifying feelings, giving clients an opportunity to express those feelings thoroughly, and connecting distressing emotions to specific behaviors and situations is essential for clients to better understand how their emotions play an important role in maintaining problems and preventing resolution to those problems. In some respects, practitioners often need to provide a form of psychoeducation about how feelings work for both children and adults. Practitioners can do this by helping clients develop new ways to accurately recognize, constructively express, and cope with distressing emotions.

Resolving emotional distress and associated physiological changes (e.g., reducing anxiety, coping with depression, regulating anger) often pave the way for lasting change. Historically, most practice theoreticians have agreed that anxiety (e.g., fear, dread, apprehension) is a key impediment to change. Psychodynamic, behavioral, existential-humanistic, and other psychotherapeutic practitioners agree: a little anxiety can be healthful and promote change; too much anxiety reduces the potential for change and growth. Although these theoreticians often disagree about the roots of anxiety, most agree that anxiety must be brought into manageable limits for clients to begin the change process and for lasting change to occur.

Chronic anger and depression can exacerbate clients' difficulties and interfere with significant change. Other emotions such as envy and jealousy may be variations of or accompaniments to the more basic feelings of anxiety, anger, and depression. (Of course, do not forget about the more positive emotions such as joy and love, but excess of joy and love are rarely presented to social work practitioners as a problem). Researchers who study emotions assert that they are not synonymous with feelings, cognitive states, physiological responses, or behaviors. Emotions seem to encompass all of these modes of expression. When a practitioner asks a client, for example, "How do you feel about that?" the practitioner is asking not merely about the client's current emotional state but also about a whole cascade of events related to what the client thinks, how the client interprets his or her physiological state, and what behaviors the client engaged in as a result. As testament to the complexity of emotions, practitioners should be prepared for a range of responses to the question: "How do you feel about X?" Clients are likely to respond with answers that cover a range of thoughts, feelings, and behaviors: "I was so angry I thought I was going to hit her!" "I felt awful, like I was going to die," "I was so afraid I just ran," and "I was so nervous I just threw up!" Rarely will practitioners receive a simple answer identifying the pure emotional response for this simple reason: feelings are global responses that tie together all modes of human expression: thought, physiological response, behavior. The responses are also, in part, specific to the situation within which they occur. Feeling questions can, indeed, provide important, powerful, and compelling responses about a client's experience. If explored carefully, sensitively, and fully, the responses will provide important clues to factors that maintain client problems and suggest potential solutions.

Helping clients, initially, connect their thoughts, feelings, and behaviors is an essential step before moving on to behavioral change. Consider the following brief dialogue between a young woman, Melanie, who has just left home for the first time after a long, conflicted relationship with her parents, and her social worker.

MELANIE: I'm very upset, very angry, about having to leave home. I remember so many good things, but in the last year of so, things have become awful. All we do is argue.

SOCIAL WORKER: What have you been arguing about?

MELANIE: They keep trying to control me. They get angry if I stay out late with my friends. I'm twenty years old, for heaven's sake, why couldn't they cut me some slack?

SOCIAL WORKER: That was all they were concerned about?

MELANIE: No. They didn't like it if I'd been drinking, and my mom found some pot in my room. I don't smoke much, but she flipped out, saying I could get arrested if I got caught with it on me.

SOCIAL WORKER: So, your parents are objecting to some of the things you want to do, but you don't want to play by their rules any more. Do you think this situation can be resolved?

MELANIE: Not if I stay home. I mean, most of my friends are out of their parents' home, and I could share an apartment. Most of them are taking college classes like me. I guess it's time for me to leave. I'd probably get along with my parents better, and if I'm not doing this stuff under their nose we'd probably not fight so much.

SOCIAL WORKER: So, how do you feel about leaving home?

MELANIE: I guess I'm feeling a lot of things. I'm not really angry at my parents, but at times I am. I guess I'm feeling sad about it. I'm their only kid, so, I know it's been hard for them too. Mom and dad have been very good to me (she starts to cry). I guess I'll miss them a lot.

SOCIAL WORKER: It must be hard to be angry with them and, at the same time, feel like you're going to miss them. Do you feel anything else going on?

MELANIE: I feel so guilty leaving them. They've spent their whole lives focused on me. I'd hate to leave when we're fighting like this. And, what are they going to do when I leave home?

SOCIAL WORKER: Are you worried that they won't be able to take care of each other?

MELANIE (she laughs, wiping her tears away): I guess that doesn't make much sense. I know they'll be fine. I mean, I can visit them pretty regularly.

SOCIAL WORKER: So, you can keep an eye on them, right?

MELANIE: Yeah, right. It's more like so they can keep an eye on me, I guess.

SOCIAL WORKER: So, you are feeling angry at them for insisting that you live by their rules, sad about leaving your childhood home with all those great memories, and guilty about leaving your parents on their own. How do you suggest we sort out this jumble of emotions you are struggling with?

The social worker and Melanie continue to discuss a resolution plan, but before she can move forward, the practitioner focuses on helping the client clarify and sort out the client's jumble of feelings and emotions. Helping the client connect her thoughts and feelings, in this particular circumstance, is an essential part of imparting therapeutic coping skills. Once she has a better grasp of what she is thinking and how she feels about the situation, she can move more freely toward taking some constructive action.

In summary, practitioners of various theoretical backgrounds more or less agree that identifying clients' emotional states (feelings) is of critical importance for a number of reasons:

1. It helps clients give their feelings a name.
2. It helps increase their understanding about factors that affect the way they feel
3. It helps clients understand how their feelings are reciprocally related to the way they think (i.e., how thoughts affect feelings, how feelings affect thoughts)

4. It helps clients understand how their feelings affect behavior and how behavior affects feelings
5. Discussing feelings helps clients understand how their physiological state affects and is affected by their feelings
6. It helps clients understand how situations and interpersonal relations can affect and be affected by the way they feel.

No doubt, feelings (emotional states) both acute and chronic can be powerful influences on behavior, and practitioners need to help clients become more emotionally "literate" by examining how emotions tie in with thinking and acting across various situations.

Practitioners can help clients become more feelings savvy in a number of ways:

- Have clients identify and express their feelings: Ask clients how they feel about different experiences they report and help them identify those feelings accurately and put them into words, a process that may be surprisingly difficult for some clients.
- Help clients gauge how intense those feelings are: Some may be related to stressful or traumatic events; measuring and tracking those emotional changes over time will be important to help clients self-monitor their own subjective distress over time.
- Teach clients how to analyze their own feelings in relation to their thoughts, behaviors, and interpersonal situations: Many clients simply feel raw emotions and have difficulty thinking about their feelings; this step, however, is important if they are to learn to regulate distressing emotions more effectively.
- Once clients learn to identify, express, and think about their feelings, they will be better prepared to regulate emotional distress rather than simply respond to it: Clients can learn to accept that they feel intense emotions without having to respond to them by acting on them, sometimes in destructive ways (e.g., drinking, self-mutilation, lashing out at others); over time, clients can learn to anticipate circumstances that may trigger intense feelings and be better prepared to deal with that distress in a more constructive way (e.g., talking to someone, taking a walk, distracting oneself with some useful activity). Clients can learn to buy time to stop, think, and consider alternative ways to cope with distressing feelings.
- Help clients more accurately assess the behaviors and feelings of others in family and social situations: Often, distressing feelings

are triggered in specific social situations when dealing with other people, often people with whom one may have had considerable conflict in the past. Practitioners can help clients visualize meeting that person, anticipate the troubling emotions that might come up, and rehearse alternative responses to diffuse the situation or cope with those feelings directly should the client feel that he or she is ready (e.g., meeting an ex-spouse at a family gathering).

- Teach anxiety- and stress-reduction skills, including progressive muscle relaxation, breath control, and meditation: These skills directly address an often underestimated component of intense emotions, the physiological mechanisms associated with strong feelings (e.g., racing heart, sweaty palms, nausea, quivering knees, clenched fists). An array of visual presentations, audio recordings, and books are widely available on relaxation and stress-reduction methods, and practitioners should learn to use them for their own stress-reduction needs before using them to help clients learn how to cope with emotional distress.

Behavior Change Skills

Identifying dysfunctional thinking and clarifying one's feelings about a given problem or situation are essential steps but are often insufficient for engendering lasting change. Clients must also change their behavior, develop behavioral coping skills, and practice those skills over time (sometimes for life) to maintain the lasting benefits of psychosocial interventions. The challenge for social work practitioners is to help clients learn behavioral coping skills, incorporate them into their lifestyle, and generalize the skills to dealing with other problems that will inevitably surface. There is a range of behavioral coping skills that can be used as individual interventions but that are usually combined as part of more complex intervention plans.

After having developed a strong working alliance and helped the client sort through his or her problematic thoughts and distressing emotions, interventions should then move into a more active phase that focuses on behavior change. Developing or enhancing behavioral coping skills may be the most robust change agent for lasting improvement. These methods put the client's cognitive and emotional insights to the test and result in success experiences that increase client confidence (i.e., self-efficacy). The reinforcement engendered by gradual success increases the likelihood that clients will improve their coping capacities and adaptive strengths over time. To achieve lasting improvements, the depressed client may have to become more socially involved, the anxious client more daring, the addicted client more confident in saying, "No thanks," to alcohol and other drugs, and the conduct-disordered child more in control of his anger. All these changes are difficult to initiate and even more difficult to maintain over time. To achieve lasting change, clients need to learn new ways of behavioral coping, and then they need to practice, practice, and practice those new coping skills. There are no magical insights or easy routes to long-term change.

Modeling can be a powerful inducement to behavior change. Sometimes showing rather than telling a client how to try something different is a more effective intervention mode. Most people, particularly children, readily respond to the influences of modeling. Research on modeling behavior attests to its negative influence on promoting smoking, heavy drinking, and physical violence. Conversely, modeling can be used to promote prosocial and healthful behaviors, such as the following:

- Communication skills in a couple
- Parenting skills
- Drink-refusal skills
- Social skills in a person with major mental illness
- Conflict resolution skills in a conduct-disordered adolescent
- Anxiety-management skills

Modeling is a versatile tool and can be used as part of an overall intervention package. Modeling can be provided in several ways. Practitioners can demonstrate a behavior in the presence of the client and have the client try it. Professional videotapes are available to demonstrate various skills, such as how to effectively provide discipline to a behaviorally troubled child or how to overcome problems related to anxiety. Persons suffering from severe social phobia can benefit from watching models demonstrate conversational skills. Often, modeling is used as a prelude to role-playing.

In role-playing, both client and practitioner or clients in couples or family sessions participate in acting out scenarios that facilitate the learning of important coping skills. The practitioner may begin by modeling a parenting skill (e.g., giving directives to a child) and then asking the mother to role-play the skill with the child or with the "child" as played by the therapist, initially. Thus, the sequence goes accordingly: (1) model the way to give an instruction to a child (e.g., "Pick up your toys"), (2) role-play the behavior by alternatively switching roles with the parent playing both parent and child, and (3) have the parent practice the behavior with his or her child in the consulting office and at home (in both situations, ideally observed by the practitioner, though this opportunity is not always available).

Practitioners can be quite creative with role-playing. For example, when working with a client who has been recently discharged from detoxification for alcohol dependence, it might be helpful to the practitioner to play the role of the client's older brother, with whom he has always had a close relationship but one based largely on drinking. Should the client be planning a trip home for the holidays (where the family is likely to be imbibing liberally), the practitioner can play the role of the brother and become increasingly insistent with regard to pressing the client to have a drink. For the role-play to be realistic, the practitioner should become familiar with the people and circumstances before setting the scene. What kind of pressure is the brother likely to use? What kinds of ploys? What appeals to filial loyalty and the good old days? What phrases will the brother likely use to provoke or tempt the client to have just one? The more realistic the practitioner can make the role-play, the more emotionally compelling it is likely to be. Role-play can be used to effectively activate the client's thoughts, feelings, and behaviors within an at-risk situation that the client must master. Modeling and role-play are safe ways to provide the client with an opportunity to practice and fine-tune coping skills before confronting the real situation, one that can be potentially overwhelming.

At some point, rehearsal ends and clients must deal with their problems in everyday life. Graduated exposure is a powerful and effective technique designed to help clients confront their personal challenges in a step-by-step approach. There are essentially two types of exposure: covert and overt. In covert exposure, the client gradually confronts a personal challenge in a stepwise fashion in his or her imagination. In a sense, this is a kind of transitional step between rehearsal and confronting the problem in a real situation (i.e., in vivo). Although clients are best served by approaching their difficulties in real life, this option is not always practical. For example, say a social worker is treating a person with severe agoraphobia and panic attacks (specifically, fear of going into grocery stores for fear of having a severe anxiety attack and fainting). Although graduated exposure (gradually spending more time in the store) would be the ideal approach, the client is initially reluctant to try it.

A helpful preliminary step would be to use relaxation exercises and imagery exercises to make the experience as real as possible in the client's mind's eye or imagination. Systematic desensitization is, in effect, the combined use of relaxation techniques and covert graduated exposure (*covert,* because it is done in the client's imagination). In systematic desensitization, practitioners (1) teach the client basic relaxation exercises (e.g., meditation, breathing retraining, progressive muscle relaxation); (2) teach the client how to measure subjective units of anxiety (SUDS) by gauging the severity of anxiety on a one-hundred-point scale; (3) create a graduated hierarchy of the problem they will face. If the client, for example, is a sexual assault victim who has become housebound and is suffering from posttraumatic stress disorder (PTSD), she would need considerable assistance to learn how to manage and eventually overcome disabling anxiety to reenter the world from which she has seriously withdrawn. After teaching basic anxiety management skills and how to measure subjective distress, the client would covertly approach the following hierarchy in her mind's eye: first, go outside to the corner to mail a letter; second, go to the local supermarket; three, drive to work; four, drive past the town park where she was assaulted six months previously. Although these are the major milestones of increasing difficulty in the hierarchy, practitioners may find that they have to break down each step into even finer increments. During the exposure process, the client would imagine taking each step, focus on maintaining inner calm with relaxation exercises (e.g., deep breathing), and periodically report his or her level of anxiety when prompted by the practitioner. The technique is relatively easy to learn and clients generally respond well to it, but it must be conducted with care and sensitivity. To maximize its benefits, practitioners should be prepared to have the client tolerate each anxiety-provoking scene until the client feels that the anxiety has come down to a manageable level before moving on to the next scene. With repetition, clients often find considerable relief and then are better prepared to deal with their problems in vivo. Other approaches that use covert exposure (e.g., eye-movement desensitization and reprocessing [EMDR]) work on similar principles. Aside from preparing the client to gradually face the real thing, covert exposure can also be used as an effective assessment tool to determine those aspects of the experience that are likely to be the most challenging for the client. A wide range of other problems can be addressed with covert exposure as well, often as a prelude to in vivo exposure.

Although covert exposure and systematic desensitization are effective therapeutic tools for many client difficulties, eventually clients have to confront their problems in their daily lives. The next step is to engage the client in graduated in vivo exposure; that is, gradually mastering the problem in real life step-by-step. As with covert exposure, a detailed assessment (especially functional analysis) of the problem must precede the intervention. Client and practitioner must work carefully to construct a step-by-step plan to gradually confront the problem at hand while progressively increasing the challenge to the client. After each step in the hierarchy is mastered, the client moves on to the next step. The client suffering from PTSD and agoraphobic symptoms must gradually approach the supermarket, step inside, spend more time, eventually buy items, return to checkout, stand in line, pack the items, and leave. Taken one step at a time, accompanied by a coach or alone, and using relaxation skills (e.g., breath control), clients successfully overcome these difficulties. Sometimes the success comes in as two steps forward, one step back, but research on graduated exposure is positive overall. No other intervention, with or without the use of medication, is as effective. Although typically associated with anxiety disorders, graduated exposure is a sound working paradigm for other difficult problems: break the problem down to incremental steps, learn to manage one's internal distress, and deal with problems one step at a time while increasing the challenge after each successful effort.

The idea that success experiences increase client self-efficacy is based on the well-established principle of positive reinforcement. Reinforcement and contingency management methods are the planned use of rewards and sanctions to improve prosocial and other healthful behaviors. Reinforcement and contingency management methods can be used to help an individual improve their own self-regulatory strategies (e.g., control anxiety, improve social skills, maintain abstinence) or help clients influence the behavior of other people in their lives (e.g., improve parenting skills). In practical application, using reinforcement principles usually means rewarding those behaviors that move the client toward positive goals or using sanctions (i.e., negative reinforcement) to reduce unhealthful or antisocial behaviors.

Although practitioners may provide reinforcement through verbal rewards, clients are often taught how to reinforce their own behaviors or the behaviors of others. Parent-child management skills, for example, are based on the sensitive but straightforward use of rewards and mild sanctions to help a child improve social behavior or academic performance or to reduce unhealthful behaviors (e.g., autistic children who pull their own hair or bang their head repeatedly). Distressed couples and others with relationship difficulties can improve their relationships by learning how to verbally reinforce their partner's constructive behaviors (e.g., reduced argumentativeness, drinking less alcohol). The use of sanctions is the planned withholding of rewards (e.g., loss of television privileges or video game time for not completing homework). Generally, punishment (typically the use of verbal rebukes, chastisement, or social control as in the case of antisocial behaviors) is the least preferred type of reinforcement but is sometimes necessary if children or adults engage in behavior that may have serious consequences to themselves or others (e.g., playing with matches in the home, missing a planned meeting with a parole officer). Extinction (i.e., ignoring a behavior) is often an effective tool, particularly when the behavior is simply annoying and leads to no serious consequences if ignored. Petulant and whiney behavior in children (or a professional colleague) is best extinguished by ignoring it.

Positive reinforcement (e.g., rewards), negative reinforcement (e.g., withdrawal of something rewarding), punishment (e.g., mild rebukes, social control, confinement), and extinction (e.g., ignoring certain behaviors) are often associated with applied behavioral analysis (i.e., a functional assessment of antecedents, behaviors, and reinforcement) and behavior modification (i.e., the planned use of reinforcement to improve psychosocial adjustment). Because these approaches have their roots in conditioning theory and research, self-described deep practitioners have misrepresented these behavioral approaches as cold, technical, and unempathic in influencing human behavior. However, despite these erroneous connotations, the use of rewards and sanctions to influence another's behavior is simply a naturally occurring part of human relationships. The relevant question is as follows: can basic behavior principles be used in a thoughtful and sensitive way to improve one's own behavior, improve the quality of relationships, and influence the prosocial behavior of others? In everyday life, the planned and thoughtful use of reinforcement is reflected in the following examples: Partners who say "Thank you" to one another for unsolicited favors and everyday kindnesses; parents who say "Good work" to their children after they finish their homework or clean up their room, take a surly adolescent son out for pizza when he decides to say what is on his mind without the usual sarcasm, or putting special stickers on a completed assignment for a job well done by a child struggling with ADHD; and anyone who buys a mentally ill young woman a cup of coffee and tells her how well she has been doing in her new job, ignores the provocative and annoying behaviors of an antagonistic coworker, or revokes community-visiting privileges of a conduct-disordered young man in a diversionary addictions halfway house after relapsing.

Using rewards, sanctions, and punishment are part of everyday human interaction. When done in a thoughtful, planned, and compassionate manner, the results (when used in treatment or otherwise) can be quite compelling. What social cognitive theory has taught us is that reinforcement must be genuine and salient to the person at whom it is directed. Although reinforcement that immediately follows behavior can be helpful and facilitate positive changes, it is not necessary that it always be immediate. In some respects, reinforcement should be used to help clients move from requiring immediate reinforcement for improvements to working toward long-term self-generated rewards as the greater goal. Reinforcement may be generated externally (e.g., rewards given to a child for completing homework, an employee for doing good work) or internally (e.g., self-satisfaction of a job well done). Ideally, reinforcement may be best used when it becomes part of a person's self-regulatory behaviors: the ability to identify challenges, address them with confidence (i.e., self-efficacy), and feel the resultant personal sense of accomplishment that accrues with experience and persistence. One could suggest that the evolution from requiring external reinforcement to using self-regulatory skills to generate internal reinforcement parallels healthy psychological development from childhood to adulthood.

The use of contingencies (i.e., contingency management) is part of the planned use of rewards. The contingency is simply an *if-then* statement: "If you take out the garbage every day, then I'll do the dishes," "If you pick up your room, then we'll go out to the movies this Friday," "If you come to my family's reunion, then I'll go to your cousin's wedding," "If you stop mutilating your arms with broken glass, then the staff can increase your community privileges," and "If you violate your probation, then you will have to return to prison." Contingency-management approaches have been shown to be effective with clients court ordered to diversionary addictions treatment, conduct-disordered children and adolescents, work with couples, and children struggling with ADHD. Whether the idea is appealing or not, life is full of contingencies. Can they be compassionately and purposefully used to enhance client well-being? Absolutely! As with otherwise healthy relationships, the terms of rewards and contingencies in any relationship should be specific, honest, salient, and transparent.

Therapeutic coping skills often include efforts to improve communication skills. Implicitly or explicitly, the modeling and teaching of effective communication skills are often included in interventions with individuals, couples, families, and groups. Social work practitioners, by modeling communication skills, are in an influential position to demonstrate to clients how to (1) listen carefully and attentively, (2) rephrase what clients say to ensure that they understood exactly what was said, (3) express their own thoughts to the client, (4) have clients rephrase what the practitioner said to demonstrate that they clearly understood the message, and so on. Periodically, if this communication feedback loop is interrupted (i.e., if one or the other does not quite understand), the client or practitioner should feel free to stop and request clarification: "Excuse me, let me make sure I understand what you just said."

The teaching and demonstration of empathic communication skills may be among the more essential aspects of social work practice. Although all couples and families, for example, are likely to encounter problems from time to time, lasting improvement seems to occur when the members of a couple or a family are able to deal with those problems by communicating in a calm and respectful manner. A key finding in research with high-functioning couple relationships is not that they never experience problems but that they learn to express their disagreements in a way that does not provoke extreme anger, hurt, or resentment. The following mark good communications skills:

- Avoiding sarcasm, name calling, and being accusatory
- Taking personal responsibility for one's own thoughts rather than mind reading a partner's intentions or feelings
- Listening carefully and not interrupting the other person while speaking, and taking turns (allowing enough time for both to air their views)
- Staying focused on the subject at hand
- Agreeing to disagree at some point, should the issue seem unresolveable
- Accepting that not all matters need to be resolved (unless it is an absolute matter, such as a couple deciding where to live)
- Apologizing with sincerity when such admissions are called for
- Avoiding stonewalling (unreasonable stubbornness), a tactic that can readily lead to resentment, contempt, and a continued downward spiral in the relationship
- Planning to revisit a contentious issue at an agreed-on time when both partners are emotionally prepared to discuss it
- Rewarding the other person and letting him or her know that you appreciate efforts to communicate honestly and constructively

In a word, good communication skills demonstrate and foster mutual respect even if the matter at hand cannot be resolved. Social work practitioners are in a strategic position through modeling and using role-play, rehearsal, and homework assignments to promote effective communication skills. Research evidence in couples and family practice demonstrates that communication skills are an effective component of intervention.

Improving communication skills can bring clients one step further to adopting effective problem-solving skills as well. Good communications skills should be considered a prerequisite to problem solving (it is tough for a couple or for family members to solve problems if they cannot communicate effectively with one another). Problem-solving skills have been well researched over the past few decades and have become a mainstay for work with both adults and children (Bedell & Lennox, 1997; D'Zurrilla & Goldfried, 1971; Meichenbaum, 1974). Core skills of various problem-solving models are quite similar: (1) identify what the problems are, (2) brainstorm ideas for solutions, (3) develop a problem-solving plan that is specific and targeted at one problem at a time, (4) evaluate the results, make modifications to the plan, and try again as needed. This basic approach is quite flexible and can be applied to a wide range of problems. It can also be adapted for work with individuals, couples, and families.

After the client's target problems have improved, therapeutic coping skills can be used to generalize improvements to other problems. Improvement in one area (e.g., depression, addictions) can be a catalyst for other changes (e.g., improving overall health through exercise, relationships and family life, and work performance). To help clients generalize their gains and maintain long-term positive outcomes, it may be worthwhile to discuss enhancing the client's overall lifestyle. These changes might include changing diet or exercise, taking a course, taking up a constructive hobby, joining a mutual support group, and so on. If the changes require the advice of other professionals, social workers can refer their client as needed (e.g., to a physician before beginning an exercise regimen).

Summary

Therapeutic coping skills include a wide array of skills to optimize clients' thinking, feeling, and behavioral abilities. Designing a specific protocol and treatment plan for each client is a highly individual affair, and the protocol must be designed to specifically address each aspect of the problem from the client's point of view. Far from being a cookie-cutter approach, intervention plans using therapeutic coping skills require extraordinary sensitivity, empathy, and a commitment to tailoring the intervention to the client's needs. Coping skills interventions can be highly variable and often require considerable creativity on the part of the practitioner to target the client's challenges. Although treatment manuals are essential for laying out the core principles of evidence-based practices (i.e., tested combinations of essential skills), no two individual treatment plans are likely to be the same.

CHAPTER SEVEN

Case Management Skills

HUMAN BEHAVIOR THEORY provides a strong rationale for the use of case management skills. It has been long recognized in the research that, although there is considerable variability in how individuals respond and cope with stress, chronic social and environmental stressors are closely associated with poorer psychosocial and health outcomes (Dohrenwend, 1998). Holahan and Moos (1994) identify three main elements in a model of stress-environment coping: person factors (e.g., inherent deficits and strengths), stressful events (e.g., trauma, daily stressors), and physical and social environment (e.g., social and instrumental supports). Psychological stress has been defined as tension between the person and the environment that people perceive as taxing or exceeding their resources and endangering their well-being (Lazarus, 1999; Lazarus & Folkman, 1984). Coping is defined as the client's cognitive and behavioral efforts to manage internal and external stressors.

The thoughtful use of supportive and therapeutic coping skills can successfully alleviate many client difficulties and improve clients' coping capacities in both the short run and the long run. However, sometimes even the best efforts may not be sufficient for clients who have more enduring psychosocial challenges. Many clients, often those with more complex and severe difficulties, need a broader level of support and require coordination of multiple services. Such clients can benefit by the practitioner's addition of case management skills to the comprehensive service plan. Case management skills include the following:

- *Enhancing social supports*—a skill that goes beyond engendering a sound working relationship with the practitioner but also bolsters ties with family members, mutual support groups, and other community supports

- *Providing instrumental supports*—such as arranging for subsidized housing, procurement of health insurance, income supports, and other legislated entitlements, as well as providing supported employment and job coaching
- *Advocating for clients to ensure that their rights are protected*—assertively inquiring about benefits or appealing services denied, accompanying clients to court to assist attorneys in defending their rights, and intervening for clients with landlords, employers, or other community members
- *Networking and coordination*—including among service providers as well as brokering services and making referrals for clients

Despite the often-significant impact of applying these skills, case management is often represented as a less sophisticated approach to intervention than is office-based social work practice, such as psychotherapy. However, case management skills often enhance the effectiveness of other interventions and are essential for maintaining many clients' well-being in the community. Clients with serious disorders—such as severe and persistent mental illness (e.g., schizophrenia), chronic addictions, homelessness, developmental disabilities (e.g., mental retardation), problems associated with the elderly (e.g., depression, Alzheimer's disease, other disabling conditions), chronic physical disabilities, and charges of child abuse and neglect—often require multiple services in a multilevel approach. In such cases, case management can ensure continuity of services and maintain positive outcomes over time.

Social workers who use case management skills often coordinate a matrix of services involving several professionals: physicians and nurses, bachelor-level case workers, other social service workers (e.g., to ensure entitlements and related financial supports), public defenders, and professionals who provide other contracted psychosocial services (e.g., addiction treatment, psychotherapy). Social workers who provide multilevel case management must be qualified to perform the following functions:

- Conduct multidimensional and functional assessments, and be knowledgeable about the problems they treat
- Keep up to date on the availability of various services
- Take the initiative and provide leadership to maintain communication and continuity among various service providers

- Ensure that confidentiality regulations and other ethical standards are followed
- Promote efficiency in service delivery by avoiding redundancy and unnecessary use of services
- Evaluate the results of the overall intervention plan

To summarize, the effective implementation of case management skills suggests a high degree of knowledge regarding the client's problems, extensive knowledge of the broader social service arena, and the ability to work at multiple levels with a variety of professionals to bring about successful outcomes for clients with complex needs.

Case management is a term that has been used extensively in the social work practice literature in primarily two distinct ways: (1) to represent the selective use of discrete skills as described previously (e.g., enhancing social and instrumental supports, advocacy, networking) and (2) as a unifying framework for guiding interventions with multiproblem populations. With respect to discrete skills, case management skills can be combined with other mainstream interventions such as outpatient mental health therapies, medical social work, school social work, and nearly any other social work field of practice. When used as a comprehensive framework, the term *case management* represents more than the use of adjunctive skills secondary to some other primary intervention. Case management, as a comprehensive strategy, serves as an organizing structure to coordinate the implementation of multiple services that, collectively, target a common set of goals. Thus, the current chapter discusses case management skills individually and presents a unifying intervention model with two important groups of multiproblem clients: families in which there are allegations of child abuse and neglect and people with severe and persistent mental illnesses.

Case Management Skills Applied to Child Abuse and Neglect Cases

There are approximately one million confirmed cases of child abuse and neglect annually in the United States. These cases, which include overlapping incidents of physical abuse, sexual abuse, and child emotional and physical neglect, result in the deaths of more than two thousand children annually (Pecora, Whittaker, Maluccio, & Barth, 2000; Putnam, 2003). Assessment and intervention with suspected cases of child abuse and neglect require extensive multidimensional-functional (MDF) clinical assessment as well as forensic investigations to determine whether crimes have been committed. Risk factors for child abuse and neglect can include parental psychopathology or other vulnerabilities (e.g., mental illness, addictions, criminality, lack of parenting experience), environmental stressors (e.g., poverty, lack of support services), and, often, multiple interactions among these risk factors. Case management with families in which child abuse or neglect has been reported can range from occasional monitoring and psychoeducation to multilevel, multiservice interventions that include bolstering social and instrumental supports; ongoing monitoring of the case; providing couple and family therapies; liaising with criminal justice; and networking with multiple services, including mental health, substance abuse, and other social services. Specialized services for the child and/or other family members (e.g., mental health, substance abuse treatment) and more intensive home-based, multilevel treatment (e.g., intensive family preservation or family reunification services) may be available as well. Short-term institutionalization may be used for temporary treatment or respite care. If the safety of the child is a serious concern, temporary out-of-home placements may be recommended, such as foster and kinship care, residential care for the child, or termination of parents' rights and permanent removal of the child. Overall, research evidence suggests that child welfare interventions show mixed results, in part as a result of wide variations in type and quality of service delivery. However, stronger evidence suggests that the inclusion of parenting skills and behavioral family therapies (to be discussed in chapters 11 and 12) in a comprehensive case management model tends to improve outcomes (Kazdin & Weisz, 1998; Lutzker, Bigelow, Doctor, Gershater, & Greene; 1998; O'Hare, 2005; Smokowski & Wodarski, 1996; Wolfe & Wekerle, 1993).

Social Supports

Social supports are among the essential case management skills used in child abuse and neglect cases. As applied in cases of child abuse and neglect, social supports include improvements to the family's natural social network, increased links to other community resources, access to mutual-help groups, and assistance from other family members, among others. Practitioners should also make efforts to link clients to local social supports, such as parent-teacher associations, free parenting-skills workshops in local health or mental health agencies, mutual-help groups for people in recovery from alcohol or other drugs; sexual abuse support groups, and local religious institutions, among others. Practitioners should also try to connect troubled families with extended family members who might be willing to help, other community networks for sharing child-care services, carpooling arrangements to lower commuting expenses, and so forth. The availability of natural and public supports and services varies greatly by location, but providers should make every effort to find out what is available and explore the use of those resources with clients.

Social support has been shown to be critical for mitigating psychosocial distress. It is widely recognized in the child welfare field that the recruitment of informal supports (i.e., family, friends) when intervening with child abuse and neglect cases can be of considerable benefit (Lyons, Henly, & Shuerman, 2005). Lyons et al. (2005) demonstrated in a large sample of more than eight hundred mothers that informal supports showed some evidence of reducing depression and financial strain.

An example of a growing source of social support is what is now referred to as *public kinship care*. One-quarter or more of out-of-home placements in the public child welfare system are now arranged with the child's grandparents (U.S. Department of Health and Human Services, 2003a). Grandparents care for many other children informally; that is, without the intervention of the child welfare system. Whether the arrangements are made publicly or privately, grandparents not only provide social support but also are in considerable need of social support themselves. In a recent study, Goodman, Potts, and Pasztor (2007) noted that research evidence demonstrated that social supports coupled with financial supports resulted in improved psychological and physical health of grandmothers who are caregivers.

Instrumental Supports

Instrumental supports are essential to help bolster families in which there are allegations of child abuse or neglect. Evidence strongly supports the view that poverty is related to the quality of child care and to the psychosocial outcomes of children (e.g., Bagley & Mallick, 2000; Leschied, Chiodo, Whitehead, & Hurley, 2006). Although child abuse and neglect are not the exclusive domain of the poor, children are at greater risk for abuse and neglect when they grow up in poor, single-family households in which there is higher stress, violence, mental disorder, substance abuse, and fewer social and instrumental supports. Generally it is agreed that these risk factors are cumulative, and long-term outcomes for poor, neglected, and abused children are not as bright as they are for children in dual-parent households with higher psychological functioning, better social supports, and stable financial resources. Although the child welfare system cannot be an adequate substitute for adult caretakers who are constant, well-adjusted, and attentive to a child's emotional, physical, academic, and social needs, social workers can make a difference by assertively determining that clients are aware of their eligibility for available financial supports, including food stamps, state health programs for routine medical care, access to food banks or local charities, and other available resources. Clearly, instrumental supports are closely tied to social supports. Clients not only need the emotional support to cope with the child-care burden but also require basic financial resources to do so.

Although the debate continues as to the outcomes of welfare reform (Wells, 2006) few doubt the necessity of financial supports for many of those living in poverty, including single mothers and people with physical and mental disabilities. Single mothers, in particular, are at high risk for involvement with child protective services, and cash assistance appears to lower this risk. Educating clients about financial supports, facilitating access to such benefits, helping clients complete eligibility forms, and advocating for clients turned down for benefits are important case management functions for social workers. Although some social workers do not see the provision of these services as a core function of their practice, having a working knowledge of the laws related to them and eligibility standards for participants is important for social workers in most fields.

Advocacy

Advocacy on behalf of clients includes making attempts to represent the client's rights with landlords, the courts, public defenders, other agencies, neighbors, and other community members. Noting the lack of case management coordination in many child abuse and neglect cases, Smith, Witte, and Fricker-Elhai (2006) note the growing interest in the use of child advocacy centers (CACs) to enhance child protective services by improving coordination of forensic and clinical interventions as well as by reducing stress for the victim and other family members. More specifically, CACs use multidisciplinary teams (MDTs) of law-enforcement officers, investigators, prosecutors, mental health and medical personnel, and other professionals to centralize and coordinate the investigation of child abuse allegations with social, medical, mental health, and advocacy services. The use of an MDT aims to increase interagency cooperation, promote accountability, improve tracking of cases, and increase the efficient use of community services and resources (Smith et al., 2006, p. 355).

Noting the lack of empirical evidence supporting CACs, Smith et al. (2006) conducted a preliminary study comparing CACs with standard child-protective services in primarily sexual abuse cases and found that the addition of formal child advocacy resulted in increased involvement by law enforcement, increased medical exams, and more substantiation of cases than did standard child protection services. One might conclude from this preliminary investigation that CACs truly represent what good case management is supposed to be: centrally coordinated, comprehensive, accountable provision of multiple services. Clearly, advocacy can provide an important organizing principle in the implementation of effective case management services.

Networking, Coordinating, Brokering Services, and Making Referrals

Networking, coordinating, brokering services, and making referrals are especially critical skills in cases of child abuse and neglect. Such cases often require the well-integrated use of multiple services. Child abuse and neglect cases can conceivable require the coordination of mental health, substance abuse, legal, financial, and other social services. Although social workers can refer parents who have serious mental health or substance abuse problems to specialized services, social workers coordinating an overall family intervention can reinforce these efforts or, in the case of a lack of available services, be the main provider of these services. Practitioners can help a parent, for example, who is being treated for bipolar disorder, by discussing medication compliance, examining whether the client is aware of an increase in depressive or manic symptoms, and discussing the client's plans to reach out to either the social worker or psychiatric professional if the client notices a recurrence of symptoms. Clients who have undergone detoxification of alcohol or other drugs or who have been recently discharged from rehabilitation are likely to need help identifying triggers, or antecedents to starting to use substances again. The stresses and strains of daily parenting and maintaining sobriety often lead to relapse in multiproblem families, and parents are likely to need much support from the social worker to anticipate these daily at-risk situations, to deal with emotional distress, to stay motivated to maintain sobriety, to learn and use stress-management techniques to reduce the likelihood of relapse, and even to role-play scenarios to refuse offers of alcohol or other drugs. Social workers can help child welfare clients make connections between the quality of parenting skills and their need to maintain good mental health and sobriety. These skills are essential for helping multiproblem families achieve and maintain good outcomes.

As part of case management, practitioners should also be prepared to facilitate contingency-management programs with law enforcement and/or criminal justice to ensure adherence to drug-treatment protocol and to comply with other court-ordered mandates (e.g., refraining from all forms of domestic violence) as required to maintain custody of children or regain custody of a child in placement. These conditions may also include determining that the parent (or parents) is consistently using contracted mental health services as recommended. Social workers may also have to refer children for brief hospital or residential stays or for temporary foster and kinship care.

Comprehensive Approaches to Case Management for Child Abuse and Neglect Cases

Eco-behavioral or systemic approaches are multilevel, multiservice intervention methods built on a case management framework. Variations of these comprehensive models include some or all of the following skills:

- Bolstering of social and instrumental supports for families in crisis where abuse or neglect are of concern
- Making efforts to preserve the family unit rather than place the child outside the home
- Reunifying families by reintroducing the child to the family after having been temporarily placed outside the home
- Improving the parents' general living skills (e.g., safety, cleanliness, provision of adequate healthful food, general maintenance of the environment)
- Bolstering other adaptive skills (e.g., enhancing strengths)
- Improving child care (e.g., promoting emotional nurturance, physical care, adequate learning stimulation, and safety; improvements in other parenting skills such as positive discipline methods)
- Improving family communication and problem-solving skills
- Enhancing social supports and reducing isolation (e.g., joining a parenting group; becoming more involved with parents in the local school)
- Ensuring access to available environmental and financial supports (e.g., free health care for children offered in many states, other financial benefits)
- Referring clients for specialized services such as mental health or substance abuse services for adults or children
- Serving as a liaison with schools, health care, and criminal justice to ensure the coordination in provision of services
- Conducting ongoing evaluation of services with an emphasis on

multidimensional outcomes (e.g., parent's engagement in treatment, children's school attendance, emotional well-being)
- Serving as advocate for the family for eligible services, benefits, and protection of rights.

Variations on ecosystems approaches have a strong conceptual base and seem to intuitively make a lot of sense. Nevertheless, evidence on the effectiveness of some of these broad-brush programs has been mixed.

Case Management Skills Applied to Clients with Severe, Persistent Mental Illness

Clients who receive case management services in community mental health services typically meet the following criteria: (1) diagnosis with a severe, persistent mental illness (e.g., schizophrenia spectrum disorders, major mood disorders such as depression and bipolar disorder) and (2) demonstration of functional deficits that require the client to have ongoing community supports to reduce psychiatric crises and avoid unnecessary psychiatric hospitalizations. Many of these clients also have other co-occurring problems, including substance abuse and personality disorders. A growing number of such clients have also been involved with the criminal justice system. When taken together, each year, clients in community mental health case management programs number in the millions nationally.

Assessment with seriously mentally ill clients requires a thorough review of all psychosocial domains, especially with regard to mental status, interpersonal relationships, and community functioning. These clients also have a disproportionate number of serious health problems. Given the multiplicity of problems that community mental health clients present, intervention requires a comprehensive approach. In addition to psychiatric medication and occasional brief hospitalization, case management models have emerged as the organizing framework for delivering multiple services to clients with severe and persistent mental illnesses, many of whom are the most psychosocially debilitated people whom social workers care for.

Case management models were developed in response to federal initiatives begun in the 1960s (Drake, 1998; Sherrer & O'Hare, 2008) that promoted improved care for the mentally ill and an increased drive toward deinstitutionalization, a policy that has been unfolding since that time. Comprehensive community-based programs were developed to prevent client relapse in the community, to avoid rehospitalization, and to enhance psychosocial functioning in seriously mentally ill clients. Case management models were considered the vehicle for coordinating multiple services in the community-based programs.

Social Supports

Although case management skills with seriously mentally ill people are often packaged in comprehensive programs like Program for Assertive Community Treatment (PACT), the essential skills employed deserve a closer look. Because social withdrawal is a common symptom of mental illness and social stigma a common social response, the bolstering of social supports for mentally ill people has come to be understood as essential for long-term recovery. Social supports include a wide array of possibilities: improving clients' natural social network by connecting with family members; linking clients to other community resources, mutual-help groups, or client-run social clubs; and enhancing relationships with employers, landlords, and others in the client's natural social network. Helping clients connect with other mutual-help groups in the community can be a challenge, however. For example, clients with co-occurring substance use disorders may feel somewhat alienated from mainstream mutual-help groups such as Alcoholics Anonymous, Narcotics Anonymous, or similar groups. Social stigma exists in many of these groups as well. Case managers can work with clients to try to work through some of these barriers, or they can promote specialized support groups for mentally ill clients who cannot make the transition to mainstream organizations. In either case, social workers should attempt to promote acceptance in the community, to help clients develop social skills to transcend some of the barriers, and to provide opportunities for more socially debilitated clients to have access to specialized social supports to reduce social isolation, recover from addictions, improve medication compliance, and cope with other common difficulties that community clients experience.

Although facilitation of the supportive working relationship is typically discussed in the context of psychotherapeutic or counseling services, many clients with major mental illnesses do not regularly receive such services. However, the case manager, often a bachelor-level social worker or other mental health worker, is in a strategic position to provide such support. There is strong evidence that case managers' relationships with clients have a positive effect on clients' well-being (Coffey, 2003; Hopkins & Ramsundar, 2006; Ryan, Sherman, & Judd, 1994). Social supports that case managers provide seem to reduce client symptoms by enhancing participation in treatment and reducing high-risk behaviors that cause other problems. Mueser et al. (2002) contend that social supports that treatment staff provide may also reduce posttraumatic stress disorder symptoms and improve overall adjustment by further reducing exposure to traumatic events and providing an opportunity to experience an empathic trusting relationship. Because professional social support (i.e., the working relationship) has been repeatedly demonstrated to advance therapeutic efforts for clients with other disorders, there is little reason to believe that enhancing social supports through case management efforts would be any less relevant for enhancing both treatment engagement and overall outcomes (O'Hare, 2005). Teaching clients how to build, maintain, and improve their own social supports can also enhance the benefits of social supports. For example, illness management and recovery, a comprehensive approach to client skill building, is a holistic model of clients' long-term growth and life enhancement (Mueser et al., 2006).

Instrumental Supports

Instrumental supports for people with mental illness include income supports, housing assistance, supported employment, medical assistance, and referrals to services that address other basic needs. People with severe mental illnesses have substantially higher rates of homelessness and unemployment (Herman, Susser, & Struening, 1998). Unemployment and homelessness exert considerable stress on mentally ill clients, lead to reduced social supports, worsen their symptoms and overall functioning in the community, and put them at higher risk of being victims of crime. Supported housing has been shown to improve psychosocial functioning and medication compliance, to reduce stigma, and to improve relationships (Browne & Courtney, 2007). Although considerable efforts have been made in the past two decades to develop and maintain residential programs for severely mentally ill persons, homelessness remains a serious problem (Randolph, Ridgway, & Carling, 1991), and mentally ill people of color appear to be at even greater risk of homelessness (Kuno, Rothbard, Averyt, & Culhane, 2000). Because homelessness remains a significant national problem, schizophrenia must continue to be assessed and treated in the context of substantial social, environmental, and economic risk factors.

In past years it was believed that sheltered workshops or extensive preemployment counseling were required for clients with severe mental illness to remain employed. However, thinking in this area has changed in recent years. Evidence suggests that supported employment (i.e., direct placement into real, paying jobs without training beforehand), ongoing social support, and respect for clients' work preferences result in more successful job placement, more time worked, and higher wages earned (Bond et al., 2001; Gold et al., 2006). Supported employment is usually provided as a service within a broader case management program. Gold et al. (2006) describe the details of how supported employment is integrated into one successful, assertive community treatment (ACT) program:

> Employment specialists assessed each participant's past work experiences, current skills, and tolerance for type and intensity of job demands. Participants chose which jobs to pursue, although specialists strongly urged competitive jobs over work-adjustment experiences in protected settings. Together participants and specialists searched for competitive job openings and/or agreed to placement into new jobs "developed" jointly by specialists and local employers. Specialists provided time unlimited support before, during, and after periods of employment. Like ACT staff, they shared responsibility for meeting every participant's employment goals. (p. 381)

Although helping clients maintain employment over time remains a challenge for practitioners, significant progress has been made with supported employment programs. The results continue to demonstrate that this strategy is superior to prior methods, such as sheltered workshops.

Advocacy

Social workers advocate on behalf of clients in many situations. Difficulties in coping and dealing with low-socioeconomic status or social stigma remain serious barriers for people with severe, persistent mental illnesses. Media portrayals that presumptively characterize a violent person as mentally ill continue to reinforce a public perception that the mentally ill are dangerous. In fact, violent behavior is no more prevalent among the mentally ill than among the non–mentally ill, except for a subgroup of young, aggressive, substance-abusing male offenders with a history of violence (Tehrani, Brennan, Hodgins, & Mednick, 1998). Noncompliance with medication also contributes to aggressive behaviors (Swartz et al., 1998). In addition to better coordination of services among the mental health, substance abuse, and criminal justice systems, social workers often need to advocate for their clients to ensure that the various systems are according all rights, benefits, and due process available to them.

In the legal realm, social workers are often called on to advocate for clients. Often, this advocacy is conducted in court while accompanying the client's public defender. In making determinations about type of treatment, treatment commitment, or proper placement of clients, judges often want to know how the client has responded to treatment, how cooperative he or she has been with treatment, and whether the least restrictive intervention is likely to be adequate to ensure proper care for clients and to protect public safety. Advocating for clients with mental illness requires a keen awareness of clients' rights, a competent grasp of clients' psychosocial status, and the ability to balance the ethical mandate to protect clients' rights with the need to protect the public from harm should a client be potentially harmful to others.

Because of some clients' difficulties in reading and comprehending bureaucratic prose, difficulty concentrating because of intrusive thoughts, low energy resulting from depression, or fears resulting from paranoid ideation, social workers need to advocate assertively for clients to ensure that they receive all due consideration regarding eligibility for public financial supports, subsidized housing, and disability benefits. Many mentally ill clients are eligible for such benefits but would find the application and follow-through processes daunting, to say the least. Social workers can guide them through the process, help them make follow-up phone calls, and directly challenge and appeal circumstances in which clients are undeservedly turned down for applicable benefits. For some services, like housing, clients may require letters of recommendation—for example, should a landlord initially balk at a mentally ill client's application. Social workers should also make clients aware of potentially discriminatory practices and tenant rights, and they may intervene to secure some forbearance from landlords (e.g., if the client experiences a return of severe symptoms or has a personal crisis). Mediating such day-to-day issues is an important dimension of advocacy. Social workers might also advocate with child welfare officials to make recommendations for deliberations on a mentally ill parent's ability to care for his or her child. Advocacy may go beyond individual clients to broader public efforts to educate the community about mental illness, such as assuaging the misconceptions of locals about the construction of a new social club for mentally ill people. Advocacy groups such as the National Alliance for the Mentally Ill often invite social workers to make presentations and collaborate with them to advance the rights of people with mental illnesses.

Although many community mental health centers offer a wide range of services to clients with severe mental illnesses, some services must be contracted with other providers. Networking, coordinating, brokering services, and making referrals are essential case management skills for working with severely mentally ill clients. Such services include primary medical care, psychiatric hospitalization, detoxification services, legal assistance, and job and housing supports. Because mentally ill people are arrested more often than non–mentally ill persons, are often held without filing of formal charges, and do not receive adequate treatment for mental illness during incarceration, there have been increasing calls to improve the coordination of services across the mental health, substance abuse, and criminal justice systems (Fisher, Packer, Grisso, McDermeit, & Brown, 2000; Lamb & Weinberger, 1998). Social workers who work with people who have severe mental illnesses will find that the work is quite challenging and requires a high degree of expertise to adequately coordinate a wide range of different services.

Case Management as a Unifying Framework for Interventions

Perhaps the best-known paradigm for community case management models is the PACT model (Drake, 1998; Stein & Test, 1980). Other variations of this program include continuous treatment teams and mobile treatment teams. Although there is considerable variation in the structures of these programs, they generally include the following:

- Use of social supports to reduce isolation through regular contacts with case managers and promotion of affiliation with other community groups (e.g., client social clubs)
- Use of instrumental supports (e.g., arranging for disability benefits, health-care coverage, other income supports)
- Provision of ongoing support to obtain and maintain employment in the community
- Advocacy for the rights of clients, some of whom courts may mandate treatment for
- Coordination of multiple systems of care (e.g., psychiatric services, primary health care, psychotherapy and counseling services, supported housing services)

Comprehensive case management programs typically use a team approach, offer twenty-four-hour coverage and open-ended treatment, and attempt to keep a relatively low client-to-staff ratio. Although these models appear coherent and intensive on paper, the quality of their implementation varies from state to state (Mechanic, 1996; Mueser, Bond, Drake, & Resnick, 1998; Sherrer & O'Hare, 2008). Nevertheless, evidence suggests that these programs have shown solid gains in reducing hospitalizations and improving the overall psychosocial functioning of multiproblem clients (Mueser, Drake, & Bond, 1997; Mueser et al., 1998; Scott & Dixon, 1995; Sherrer & O'Hare, 2008). In addition, programs designed specifically to help mentally ill clients with co-occurring mental health and substance use disorders have shown promising results (Drake et al., 1998; Dumaine, 2003; RachBeisel, Scott, & Dixon, 1999).

In recent years practitioners and research-practitioners have come to see the utility of combining more advanced treatment efforts with traditional case management skills when working with clients who have major mental illnesses. These intervention methods include behavioral family therapy and psycho-education with families, coping skills approaches, and relapse prevention efforts for clients who have co-occurring mental health and substance abuse disorders. Although these interventions can also be used as stand-alone interventions, some case managers have been trained to use them as part of everyday case management services. This more advanced approach to case management combines the use of supportive, therapeutic coping and traditional case management skills and is called *clinical case management*. Thus, in addition to the enhancement of social and instrumental supports, advocacy, and the coordination of interventions, clinical case management includes the following (Sherrer & O'Hare, 2008):

- Comprehensive assessments and monitoring of client progress (e.g., mental status, substance use, family relationships, role functioning in the community and at work)
- Crisis intervention
- Psychoeducation and behavioral family therapy with the client and his or her family
- Stress-management skills
- Social skills training to help clients better use social supports
- Substance abuse counseling including relapse-prevention techniques
- Medication monitoring

Clinical case management interventions have great potential for enhancing treatment continuity as social workers not only coordinate much of the treatment but also are engaged in providing much of the care themselves. In this way, clinical case management is an ideal model of intervention whereby practitioners can integrate the best of supportive, therapeutic coping, and case management skills with clients who present some of the greatest psychosocial challenges in the field.

PART THREE

Applying Combinations of Essential Skills with Individuals, Couples, Children and Their Families

CHAPTER EIGHT

Adult Disorders: Schizophrenia and Mood and Anxiety Disorders

SCHIZOPHRENIA, major mood disorders, and anxiety disorders cover a broad spectrum of mental health problems from the severe to the moderately debilitating. Schizophrenia and bipolar disorder are generally considered severe mental illnesses given that they share symptoms of psychosis (i.e., thought disorders such as hallucinations and delusions). Major depression can be equally debilitating but, in general, is not considered a psychotic disorder (though some depressed clients may experience transitory psychotic symptoms). Anxiety disorders include specific phobias, panic attacks with agoraphobia, generalized anxiety disorder, and posttraumatic stress disorder, among others. These disorders often co-occur with substance abuse or dependence, and a wide range of other functional psychosocial problems-in-living often accompany them. Interventions for these disorders are well researched, and clients with these conditions who receive interventions based on evidence-based practices have a good chance of reducing symptoms and improving their overall quality of life.

Schizophrenia

Assessment

There are several subtypes of schizophrenia that share a number of common indicators: positive symptoms such as delusions and thought disorders (e.g., implausible beliefs, bizarre inferential reasoning), hallucinations (i.e., seeing, hearing, feeling, or smelling stimuli that do not exist outside of the person's perceptual field), incoherent or disorganized speech (e.g., inability to make logical sense, construction of odd and novel words), disorganized or bizarre behavior; and negative symptoms, including extreme social withdrawal and flattening of affect (i.e., difficulty with nonverbal emotional expression). Different subtypes of schizophrenia tend to emphasize some symptoms more than others. For example, people with schizophrenia who demonstrate severe paranoia are likely to have prominent delusions about being spied on by aliens or government officials. Persons with catatonia are likely to show symptoms of muscle rigidity, grimacing, and other behavioral disturbances. Most people with schizophrenia are diagnosed as disorganized or undifferentiated because they show a range of relevant symptoms. To meet the diagnostic criteria for this disorder, the client must have demonstrated a prodromal, prepsychotic period of six months that must include one month of fully active symptoms. During this time, the person, often in his or her late teens or early twenties, may have become withdrawn and demonstrated strange behaviors (e.g., muttering to him- or herself incoherently, engaging in disturbing preoccupations) but has not yet shown a full complement of symptoms to meet the diagnostic criteria. Once the client has demonstrated one month of actively psychotic symptoms, the diagnosis of schizophrenia applies (O'Hare, 2005; Sadock & Sadock, 2003).

Although the onset of the disorder often occurs in the late teens and early twenties, onset for women generally occurs a few years later than it does for men. Other symptoms and disorders may co-occur with schizophrenia. Depression and anxiety often accompany the disorder and may be treated concurrently. Many people diagnosed with schizophrenia also have other neurological disorders, such as tics or seizures, which can be treated along with the primary disorder. Another common problem associated with schizophrenia is substance abuse. One-third or more of clients in treatment for schizophrenia also abuse alcohol or other drugs, and about half of all people with severe and persistent mental illnesses will develop a substance use disorder at some time in their lives.

Schizophrenia is a chronic disorder that often has a long and deteriorating trajectory. Medications to control psychotic symptoms (e.g., hallucinations) are helpful for many clients but are often accompanied with negative side effects on the nervous system. Tardive dyskinesia, for example, is a disorder of the extrapyramidal nervous system indicated by a shuffling gait and facial grimacing. Although some progress has been made in recent years with regard to reducing the side effects of these drugs, the overall effects of antipsychotic medications on positive and negative symptoms has not improved substantially.

Because schizophrenia is a biopsychosocial disorder, an assessment should go well beyond itemizing the symptoms in DSM-IV criteria. A multidimensional-functional (MDF) assessment should examine the following:

- Overall mental status: In addition to psychotic symptoms, include an evaluation for depression, suicide risk, problems with anxiety, and substance abuse.
- Quality of current relationships: Note interactions with family, the nature and frequency of contacts, how much time the client spends alone or with others whom he or she considers close acquaintances or friends, and the nature of those relationships and whether they are prosocial and healthful connections or increase risk for the client's overall well-being.
- Quality of daily community life: Document how the client spends his or her time, where he or she goes, with whom he or she associates; note any behavior problems that come to the attention of the police or others in the community.
- Quality of daily circumstances: Examine the quality of the client's living circumstances and determine the overall suitability of housing—safety, cleanliness, and adequacy. Query about daily diet, shopping, whether he or she cooks or relies on prepared or convenience foods; ask about routine hygiene (e.g., bathing, laundering clothes); try to determine how the client budgets his or her income, and how much is spent on cigarettes, alcohol, or other drugs.
- Clients' health: Obtain a general assessment of the client's overall health and relevant medical records; note any physical disabilities and determine the kind of assistance that the client does or will receive and any benefits for which he or she is eligible.

Given that persons with schizophrenia and other severe mental illnesses often suffer from multiple problems, a comprehensive assessment is crucial, and practitioners should go beyond taking a one-time snapshot assessment to try to follow and monitor the different problem areas over time.

A variety of scales are available to enhance routine assessments and provide a foundation for monitoring clients' progress over time. Other simple indexes can be helpful as well: Have clients been taking their medication consistently? How often do they miss appointments? Have they been arrested for minor infractions in the community? How often are they admitted to the local emergency room or the regional psychiatric facility? How many days have they worked in the past month? These simple indicators can tell practitioners much about clients' overall well-being and functioning in the community.

Intervention

Treatment of the seriously mentally ill has become more humane in the past thirty years or so in response to deinstitutionalization, strengthened civil rights protection, increased advocacy, and better funding for community-based services. Although there have been some negative consequences in the wake of deinstitutionalization (e.g., increased homelessness of mentally ill persons, further criminalization of mentally ill persons, increased stigma in the community), most observers would agree that these problems pale in comparison to the virtual imprisonment that many persons with mental disorders experienced in public hospitals for much of their lives.

The use of psychosocial interventions for which there is a body of supporting outcome research has become a major focus of research and responsible treatment policy (Lehman, Steinwachs, and Co-investigators of the PORT Project, 1998; Mueser & Jeste, 2008). At the forefront has been the widespread adoption of programs for assertive community treatment (known as PACTs) and variations of it (covered in the previous chapter). These models, at their best, coordinate psychiatric care (i.e., medication) with regular contacts with case managers in the community to monitor clients' overall functioning and to bolster social and instrumental supports. Often the agencies become representative payees for the client to help with money management. Many states also have programs to provide subsidized housing and assistance in finding employment. However, other interventions that have been shown to be considerably effective have not been disseminated widely. These include cognitive-behavioral coping skills, family psychoeducation and behavioral family therapy for people who have a mentally ill family member, and social skills training to help clients become better engaged in daily community life. These interventions have been shown to be reasonably effective in controlled trials, and practitioners could readily integrate them into a well-coordinated multidisciplinary case management model.

Working with people diagnosed with schizophrenia can be both challenging and rewarding. The interventions described subsequently also apply to people with major depression and severe bipolar disorder who struggle with recurrent psychotic symptoms and have difficulties functioning in the community. Later in this chapter, interventions for nonpsychotic major depression will be discussed. Clients with severe mental illnesses, both schizophrenia and severe mood disorders, have often experienced considerable trauma in their lives, including physical abuse, sexual abuse, or neglect; also, in part as a result of the disorder, they can be very withdrawn and socially isolated. Given their difficulties in process-ing information (because of thought disorders), suspicions resulting from delusions, and difficulties relating to other people, people with schizo-phrenia may be difficult to engage in treatment. Nevertheless, research supports the view that these clients respond positively to social supports provided specifically by treatment staff. They can be engaged in treat-ment and learn to connect with others successfully.

Clients with serious mental illnesses including schizophrenia have dif-ficulties relating to and trusting others. Some of this mistrust may be due to the severity of thought disorders, the tranquilizing effects of medication, and learned responses to prior abuse and trauma. Some clients' treatment experiences may have contributed to their distrust of treatment staff, because of either negative encounters with mental health professionals or the fact that many entry-level staff members do not remain long in their jobs. Whatever the cause, the development of a working alliance with a person who suffers from schizophrenia requires unusual consistency and an incremental, patient approach. However, engagement can vary greatly from client to client, and it will vary with the same client depending on his or her mood and mental status at the time. A good working principle is to begin with problem-solving efforts that target daily stressors that clients confront at the treatment center or in the community. Over time, as clients become more comfortable with a practitioner, they may be willing to reveal some of their more disturbing thought disorders and hallucinations. Beyond that, as trust develops, clients may be willing to take on greater challenges, such as spending more time in the community, developing rela-tionships further, or taking on a part-time job. Helping a very withdrawn client become more connected to others can be a considerable challenge. For very schizoid or paranoid clients, there may always be severe limita-tions to trusting others.

Enhancing motivation can be a challenge, especially for those clients who are depressed and very withdrawn. Medication side effects and sub-stance abuse can also make it difficult to engage many clients. It is impor-tant for practitioners to start with relatively modest goals and to build on small successes over time. Careful examination of the goals that the client finds important is essential for successful engagement. Many mentally ill clients have felt powerless for some time and can benefit from being treated as collaborators in their treatment planning. Keeping goals concrete and achievable is also important. Many clients have a hard time accepting that they have a mental illness, and the more practical the goals are, the better it is for them. Practical goals include daily living skills such as doing laundry, grocery shopping, opening a checking account, showing up to appointments on time, and engaging in brief, focused conversations. Practitioners should carefully track successes and give clear and direct evaluative feedback to clients. For most clients, their actual successes best reinforce their motivation.

Clients with severe mental illnesses also appreciate being treated with authenticity. Practitioners should avoid abstract and overly intellectualized approaches to therapeutic engagement and keep their interactions with clients "real." Being "real" means that practitioners focus on clients' everyday concerns and keep their own comments and conversation focused on goals that are essential to clients' meeting their everyday needs. Clients with thought disorders and delusions may be inclined to engage practitioners in discourse such as the meaning of life, whether we have been taken over by aliens, or to what extent we are all under the control of government officials. Practitioners should try to be respectful and reassuring about these matters but to focus on concerns that are more immediate to maintaining stability in the community. Over time, clients' sharing of their daily concerns will engender a certain degree of trust, and clients may become more forthcoming about other key concerns (e.g., past trauma, substance abuse).

Various effective interventions for people with schizophrenia emphasize the use of therapeutic coping skills. These include cognitive-behavior therapy, family psychoeducation, and behavioral family therapy for people with a mentally ill family member. The intervention methods share some essential skills but are unique interventions in their own right.

Cognitive-behavior therapy uses a combination of skills to help clients challenge some of their more disturbing and dysfunctional thinking, to regulate anxiety and stress, and to improve coping behaviors in the community. Although many clients' problems are accompanied by troubling or dysfunctional beliefs, people with severe mental illnesses often struggle with beliefs that are out of the norm and may be extremely debilitating. Paranoid delusions, fears of persecution, convictions based in paranoia, and auditory hallucinations that command clients to harm themselves or others can create formidable barriers to client improvement. Although medication can control hallucinations, psychotropic medications may have a lesser effect on beliefs and convictions.

Nevertheless, recent studies in cognitive therapy with severely mentally ill people suggest that clients can derive considerable benefit from the cognitive-behavior approach (Alford & Correia, 1994; Mueser, Rosenberg, Jankowski, Hamblen, & Descamps, 2004). The first step in the approach is to help the client identify the problematic belief. This does not mean verbally convincing the client that a belief is false or unrealistic. It simply means that you both agree that the client's particular belief or conviction creates a problem in daily living. Second, the client is encouraged to keep a log or diary to further examine the belief and rate the strength of the belief daily. Third, the practitioner encourages the client to examine the false belief for content and discuss its plausibility (e.g., What evidence supports your belief?). Although this may sound like an attempt to discredit the belief, it may provide the client with an opportunity to gain some objectivity with respect to the belief and, perhaps, cause some doubts about its plausibility. The practitioner should avoid engaging in debate about the belief but simply introduce some questions that may bring the plausibility of the belief into question in the client's mind. Fourth, the practitioner encourages the client to consider and explore alternative explanations for the belief. Fifth, the client should then be encouraged to test out the beliefs and examine evidence that confirms or disconfirms them. For example, the client should engage in conversations with people whom he or she knows and try to determine whether other people share in their beliefs. It may be that a client's delusions are more pronounced as he or she becomes more withdrawn, but as the client spends more time with others, a particular bothersome belief dissipates. Practitioners should stay on task with the client and follow up to see whether the client in fact tests out (i.e., behaviorally disconfirms) his or her hypotheses. Thus, it is essential to monitor and evaluate client progress.

Cognitive-behavior methods can be fairly eclectic and should be designed to address clients' specific needs. An overall cognitive-behavior plan can include other methods, such as social skills training, the use of modeling, role-playing, and corrective feedback to help clients improve their ability to develop and maintain relationships with others. Rehearsal of conversational skills, for example, can be a safe way to help clients identify their strengths and weaknesses relating to others. With some practice, clients can use their improved social skills with increased confidence in the community.

To apply cognitive-behavior therapy (CBT) to help clients improve their social skills, practitioners should provide a sound rationale for learning the skills (e.g., making friends, getting a job). Of course, clients are likely to be anxious about initiating conversations with strangers, so the practitioner and client should first construct a hierarchy of social encounters that the client can tolerate. For example, the client may begin by making small talk with support staff (e.g., receptionists, administrative assistants, or maintenance personnel) to see whether he or she can become more comfortable having conversations with familiar people. To control anxiety, the practitioner can show the client how to calm him- or herself (e.g., deep, slow breathing) before attempting a new conversation. Next, the client might attempt a brief conversation with someone in the community whom he or she knows by sight, such as a friendly cashier in the local convenience store. In short, the hierarchy may gradually increase to initiating a conversation with someone the client does not know, again, to discuss everyday things such as the weather or news events. Over time (with monitoring and evaluation) clients can become more comfortable, confident, and skilled in conversing with others (Bellack, Mueser, Gingerich, & Agresta, 1997).

Overall, CBT with mentally ill people is versatile and can address a wide range of problems. In summary, the guiding principles are as follows: define the problem; identify troubling or dysfunctional beliefs; explain the rationale for the intervention; examine and gently question the rationale that supports the troubling or dysfunctional beliefs; set up a series of behavioral tasks to gradually test those beliefs; and provide modeling, role-playing, and rehearsal to prepare clients to practice their skills in the community. After a client has shown measurable success, depending on how far the client wants to go, the practitioner can continue to suggest more challenging goals.

The skills for working with severely mentally ill clients who have a co-occurring substance use disorder are quite similar to the general CBT methods described previously. However, the practitioner must be knowledgeable about alcohol and other drugs and the unique risks associated with co-occurring substance abuse and mental illness. Alcohol and other drugs can worsen depression, increase anxiety, interfere with therapeutic benefits of medication, and lead to impaired judgment and community-related problems. A complete MDF assessment with a mentally ill person requires a thorough substance use assessment: What substances does the client use? How much of each substance? How often? What seem to be the short- and long-term psychological, social, and physical consequences of their substance use?

Substance abuse can make the development of a good working alliance even more challenging than otherwise. However, practitioners can disarm some of the client's defensiveness regarding the self-report of substance use if the practitioner assures the client that he or she will not be penalized for being forthcoming about drug use. The social worker can further impress on the client that many of the challenges in dealing with mental illness will be only more difficult to deal with if the client uses alcohol or other drugs. Thus, a nonjudgmental attitude about substance use and a focus on the client's healthful self-interest should mark the assessment. It is also important to begin linking the client's self-reported problematic thoughts, feelings, and interpersonal difficulties with substance use. In addition, the identification of key high-risk situations and helping clients anticipate and cope with those situations (e.g., when depressed or hallucinating) are critical to long-term improvement. Thus, engaging the client in a collaborative monitoring plan to assess use of alcohol and other drugs is important. The practitioner should help clients make consistent connections between their psychosocial complaints and their substance use and enhance motivation by collaborating on mutually agreed-on treatment goals and by emphasizing the use of coping skills to target high-risk situations.

Practitioners should apply interventions for dual disorders in a staged sequence. Similar to the stages of change discussed in chapter 4 (i.e., precontemplation, contemplation, preparation, action, maintenance), a staged approach developed specifically for work with dual-disordered clients has been used with some success. The approach includes eight stages: (1) preengagement, (2) engagement, (3) early persuasion, (4) late persuasion, (5) early active treatment, (6) late active treatment, (7) relapse prevention, and (8) remission or recovery (Bellack, Bennett, & Gearon, 2007; Mueser, Noordsy, Drake & Fox, 2003). The purpose of the staged approach is to help clients set goals to their level of readiness to engage in treatment. In early stages, clients are generally not aware they have a problem or are not quite convinced. Helping them test out whether drugs affect their mood and behavior might help them see for themselves whether it is a problem. A brief period of sobriety can be illuminating for clients. In the middle stages, clients generally begin to cut down and change at-risk behaviors. In later stages, clients focus more on solidifying gains and preventing relapse.

In all stages of improvement, supportive and coping skills are applied as needed. Many at-risk situations threaten to cause clients to backslide: visiting friends and family, hanging out with unemployed acquaintances, dealing with daily stressors, and coping with symptoms of their disorders, as well as disappointment and losses. Role-playing and rehearsal can be used to prepare clients for these likely eventualities and increase their chances of getting through them without serious relapses. Anticipating at-risk situations should be a planned part of intervention. Clients can monitor their progress in coping with at-risk situations and discuss the outcomes with the practitioner, to work on improving their coping skills. In this way, the intervention is understood as a collaborative work in progress.

Having a severely mentally ill parent, son, or daughter can be extremely stressful for family members and for the client. The client's behavior may upset the family, and family reactions may unwittingly provoke or upset the client. For example, a twenty-year-old man with schizophrenia who lives at home may become extremely depressed and suicidal, discontinue his medication (without telling anyone), become psychotic, respond belligerently to hallucinations, make matters worse by using alcohol or other drugs, and become enraged when told his hygiene is poor (e.g., which may result from paranoid ideation about someone trying to poison him in the shower). Families with a mentally ill member can benefit greatly from professional care and support in the form of both psychoeducation and behavioral family therapy (Dixon et al., 2001). Both approaches have been shown to be very helpful, and elements of both can be combined in an eclectic manner depending on the specific needs of the family. Psychoeducation is a more didactic approach that can be used with single or multiple families simultaneously. Practitioners usually explain the nature of mental illness and general coping strategies in a support group format. Behavioral family therapy, though it includes a similar educational dimension, is a more formal intervention that focuses directly on enhancing family members' communication, coping, and problem-solving skills. The intervention should also be closely coordinated with psychiatric and case management services. Family psychoeducation and behavioral family therapy can vary by modality (single or multiple family groups), should ideally be conducted over longer rather than shorter periods (e.g., a year), and should be implemented flexibly to accommodate the family members who can attend. The following overview of skills assumes an eclectic psychoeducational and/or behavior family therapy approach.

In addition to completing an MDF assessment on the identified client, a thorough assessment of the family system is needed to consider family members' thoughts and feelings about the client, how they interact with the client, the impact each family member's behavior has on the client, and the effect the client's behavior has on each family member. The analysis of the interactions of family members with the client is essential. A social worker who engages families with a mentally ill member can do quite a bit to instill optimism, provide realistic yet positive expectations, and offer emotional support as a basis for establishing a sound working alliance. The social worker should also be able to make a long-term commitment to resolving crises and stabilizing the family's ability to cope with the client's illness. Psychoeducation and behavioral family therapy have been shown to provide real relief and measurably improve the overall situation.

Providing accurate and up-to-date information to families about schizophrenia is a good place to start. For many years, some practitioners promoted untested theories (e.g., the schizophrenogenic mother, double-bind theory) that, for example, the mother or dysfunctional family communication caused mental illness. As with other problems, a stressful family environment can make matters worse, but there is no evidence that the behavior of family members causes schizophrenia or bipolar disorder. Psychoeducation, provided by a knowledgeable social worker, can help families understand that (1) they did not cause the client's mental illness, (2) a mentally ill person can be hard to deal with, (3) if they learn to be calmer and more focused in their dealings with the mentally ill family member, that person is likely to respond in a calmer manner as well, (4) the client's consistent use of medication is very important, (5) the family and the mentally ill family member can learn to communicate and solve problems more effectively, and (6) the research on working with families shows that the situation can improve greatly for both the client and the mentally ill person if the family collaborates with the practitioner.

Once family members show that they understand the importance of medication compliance and turning down the emotional temperature in the household by becoming more problem focused and less reactive to the client's disturbing behaviors, the work on improving communication and problem solving can begin. The social worker should take time to identify positive and problematic interaction patterns among family members and note the effects these behaviors have on the client and family members. It is important to identify both constructive and problem interactions, as increasing good interactions can help reduce problematic ones. It is important to hear what everyone has to say and to make a special effort to encourage the client to express him- or herself.

The social worker should strive to keep the focus on present problems and avoid excavating previous problems (unless absolutely necessary to resolve a current dilemma). An example of a common difficulty is that the client stays up late at night watching television and keeps the volume high. The father, who rises early, becomes enraged and confronts the young man in an aggressive way that leads to a confrontation. This initial outburst leads to much heated argument regarding the father's disappointment in his son. The son feels provoked and explodes in anger toward his father, attacking him physically.

To prevent similar outbursts, the social worker can ask the father and son to calmly reenact the encounter in the office (or in the home in the case of a home visit). Occasionally asking them to stop and talk about what they are thinking and feeling in the moment, the practitioner can help slow down the action and help them get perspective on the situation and remain calm and open to solutions. The family can then brainstorm some solutions and consider ways to express thoughts and feelings to the client without being overly provocative. After a brief discussion, the immediate solution becomes apparent: the parents decide to buy some headphones so that the young man can watch television at night without disturbing anyone.

Conversation in the next session might focus on reasons the young man stays up so late; whether he has trouble sleeping; and whether he takes his medications, uses illicit drugs, or simply sleeps too long during the day. What is particularly important about this approach is that it serves as a vehicle to engage the family in a calm problem-solving process and provides a context for improving communication skills that include calmer and more measured expression of feelings and needs to one another.

Families should also be encouraged to look for the signs of relapse in the mentally ill family member. These might include excessive withdrawal from contact with others, signs that the family member is not taking medication, or indications of alcohol or other drug use. Early intervention by consulting the social worker can help head off a serious relapse and possible hospitalization. Social workers can encourage families to engage in stress-reducing activities, such as renting a movie and having pizza, going for walks together in the local park, or taking a day trip. Individual family members should also be encouraged to find stress-reducing activities on their own. If one family member carries a disproportionate share of the burden of looking after the client's needs, some arrangements should be made to give that person some planned relief time. When crises do erupt (e.g., a suicide attempt, the client is overcome by an apparent psychotic episode), the social worker should discuss contingency plans with the family so that they know whom to call and what actions to take. Of course, long-term planning options should be discussed as well. Although some families may choose to be the primary caretakers of a schizophrenic young adult, many families will have great difficulty sustaining that level of care and may decide to help their child make arrangements to live in the community.

In recent years, the emphasis in treatment of mental illness has gradually shifted from a reactive approach that concentrated mostly on controlling symptoms to a more proactive, holistic strategy that emphasizes client initiative, skill building, and enhancing all areas of life—in short, going beyond the "sick" role. This comprehensive approach, called illness management and recovery, uses many of the interventions discussed herein that emphasize increasing adaptive capacities and life skills. Key evidence-based interventions included in this approach are "psychoeducation about mental illness and its treatment, cognitive-behavioral approaches to medication adherence (e.g., incorporating cues for taking medication into daily routines), developing a relapse prevention plan, strengthening social support by social skills training, and coping skills training for the management of persistent symptoms" (Mueser et al., 2006, p. s33).

Taken together, there is a range of effective psychosocial interventions for use in working with people with schizophrenia. In addition to building a strong working alliance, social workers can now use evidence-based practices that have been shown to be effective: family psychoeducation and behavioral family therapy, coping skills approaches, and assertive case management.

Mood Disorders

Assessment

Millions of Americans experience moderate to severe mood disorders, conditions that can be acute, chronic, and recur from time to time. Mood disorders primarily include major depression and dysthymic disorder. Almost one-quarter of the population will develop a mood disorder (primarily a depressive disorder) at some point, and about 1 percent of the population is likely to be diagnosed with bipolar disorder, a mix of manic and depressive episodes. Women are more likely to experience clinical depression, and elderly people are likely to experience depression coupled with other medical problems, such as memory difficulties and Alzheimer's disease. Depression also co-occurs with many other disorders, including substance abuse, addiction, and anxiety disorders.

Major depression is marked by a consistently depressed mood, diminished pleasure in previously enjoyed activities, significant weight loss, substantial changes in appetite, sleep disturbances, marked changes in energy levels, feelings of worthlessness or guilt, difficulty concentrating, or recurrent thoughts of death (APA, 2000). Depression can have a major impact on other areas of the client's life, such as relationships and job productivity. Depression often coincides with primary health problems. Clients diagnosed with variations of bipolar disorder experience (in addition to periods of severe depression) periods of abnormally elevated mood, irritability, flight of ideas, pressured and rapid speech, distraction, psychomotor agitation, and sometimes an increase in pleasurable activities that might put the client at risk for negative consequences (e.g., promiscuity, unrestrained shopping). Practitioners who work with clients with major mood disorders should become familiar with differential diagnoses of these disorders, which the DSM-IV describes in more detail.

Suicide is always a cause for concern for mood-disordered clients, and practitioners should always conduct careful assessment of suicide risk. Key risk factors for suicide include serious mental disorders (e.g., schizophrenia, alcoholism, depression), a history of suicide attempts, family history of serious depression or suicide attempts, expressed suicidal intent, having a plan and access to means (e.g., owning a gun, hording medications), having communicated a sense of hopelessness, having experienced a traumatic or stressful event (e.g., sudden loss of a loved one), and having recently been diagnosed with a serious physical illness. Practitioners should conduct thorough assessments of suicidal intent in an open, calm, and straightforward manner with clients; consult with supervisors and colleagues; and clearly document the client's suicidal ideation and a plan to monitor and intervene if necessary. Psychiatric evaluations for medication are strongly recommended.

An MDF assessment should go beyond signs and symptoms and examine how mood disorders manifest across all relevant domains of well-being. In addition to key mental status and diagnostic signs and symptoms, a careful look at any history of impulsivity (e.g., previous suicide attempts) or risky behaviors (e.g., during manic episodes) is warranted, as is a detailed history of substance abuse. Unresolved losses and traumatic events are common in clients with recurrent depression and should be carefully reviewed. The quality of relationships with family members, friends, and coworkers may indicate problems that are related to depression. Problems in occupational roles and overall health are often associated with depression as well. In the functional analysis, reconstructing a two-week diary with a depressed client can also provide clues to situational factors that may exacerbate the symptoms. Depression symptoms can vary considerably over time. Clients might have good days and bad ones. Variations in depressive symptoms do not necessarily occur randomly, but they might occur as a result of work stress or periods of alcohol abuse (e.g., weekends), or as a function of recurrent relationship difficulties. Having clients self-monitor their symptoms can help them become readily engaged in the treatment process and reduce a general feeling of helplessness.

Intervention

Interventions for major mood disorders usually include psychotropic medication. Thus, practitioners should consult with attending physicians to coordinate interventions and keep apprised of the client's consistency in taking the prescribed dosage. The interventions that follow were designed and tested primarily with clients diagnosed with depressive disorders, yet they also apply in some cases to clients who have bipolar disorders but function better in the community.

Interpersonal psychotherapy and cognitive-behavioral interventions have been shown to be comparably effective for depressed clients (e.g., Butler, Chapman, Forman, & Beck, 2006; Hollon & Beck, 1994; Weissman, Markowitz, & Klerman, 2000). However, regardless of the formal intervention chosen, effective use of supportive skills and a sound working alliance are essential for helping depressed clients. Depressed clients often present with low energy, and encouraging them to express their thoughts and feelings openly can take considerable effort on the part of the practitioner. The client's concentration may be impaired to the point where he or she has difficulty following the conversation. The guilt that a depressed client experiences may be severe, and some clients feel that they deserve punishment. Clients may consider suicide a viable option to end the emotional misery. A calm and empathic exploration of the client's negative thinking is critical to understand the client's internal distress, but practitioners should keep an open mind regarding other contributing factors (e.g., depression runs in the family, a substance abuse problem, other medical conditions that may cause depression). Various therapeutic coping skills are helpful for depressed clients. Practitioners who use interpersonal psychotherapy (IPT) or CBT for depression use some common skills, but there are distinctions between the two approaches. Both are described below.

The practitioner who elects to use CBT for depression should explain the basic cognitive model to the client. The cognitive model of depression focuses on the impact of automatic negative thoughts on the mood of the client, dysfunctional thinking (e.g., I am a really bad person, I'll never accomplish much of anything in my life), and negative cognitive schemata. The practitioner initially focuses on negative thought content and dysfunctional thought processes as the primary cause of the client's depression, as discussed in chapter 6 (e.g., dichotomous thinking, hindsight bias). Next, the practitioner using CBT should help the client carefully examine the reasonableness of these thoughts, and then, most important, test these troubling beliefs out in their daily life. The steps can be summarized as follows:

- Identify negative automatic thoughts.
- Teach the client to monitor and record automatic thoughts and associated moods and situations.
- Actively engage the client in a rational exploration of the presenting problem by examining the client's automatic negative thoughts

to unearth the client's false assumptions and dysfunctional thought processes.

· Follow through in this collaborative exploration to determine whether there is evidence to support the negative and problematic thoughts.
· Encourage the client to consider alternative explanations for their belief.
· Challenge the client to identify the real implications of the belief if it were true.
· Collaboratively design "experiments" to test whether the client's dysfunctional beliefs or expectations are true.
· Encourage the client to use a journal to document the experiences, and use the data to evaluate the outcome of the experiments. It is likely that the experiments will disconfirm the client's dysfunctional beliefs.

The client's act of disconfirming dysfunctional beliefs is, presumably, at the heart of the change process in CBT. Increased self-efficacy is best advanced through behavior change, not through interpretation or explanation. As the client improves, the practitioner helps him or her solidify what has been learned through self-monitoring and repeated behavioral testing of the dysfunctional beliefs. Because depression can recur, the practitioner develops a plan to help the client anticipate a relapse of depression and initiate a plan of action.

Consider the example of a late-middle-aged man who retires and becomes depressed. After a thorough examination of his negative automatic thoughts, the practitioner and the client conclude that he places an extraordinary value on occupational achievement and the admiration of others. He now thinks, "I am worthless. I have nothing to do. People no longer admire me, and there is no hope for me in the future. I am useless. I might as well give up and end it all." After examining these beliefs, the social worker and client agree that they seem a bit extreme, but the social worker empathizes with the client's current feelings and state of mind. After a rational examination of his claims that he is worthless to everyone and has nothing else to offer, the client agrees to test out his beliefs regarding his worthlessness in his community, a place to which he recently moved after retirement.

The practitioner then poses the question in contrast to the "I am worthless" belief: given your high level of expertise in business, do you really believe there is really nothing for you to do that would help you reclaim your sense of self-worth? After some discussion, the client agrees to investigate a range of ideas: volunteer work, involvement in local politics, limited consulting work with local businesses. With careful testing of his beliefs over time, the client quickly finds that he is overwhelmed with requests for help from others in the community and that his sense of self-worth gradually returns. It also appears that making new friends and becoming socially more involved has some positive effects on his mood.

Interpersonal psychotherapy shares some similarities with CBT. This well-researched approach is also somewhat pragmatic, oriented to the here and now, goal focused, and generally short-term in duration. Also, IPT is based on a somewhat different premise from that of CBT. The main assumption in IPT is that depression has its roots in dysfunctional relationships in the present. Although past relationship problems may have contributed to the client's depression, IPT does not emphasize examination and interpretation of the past. The essential skills of IPT emphasize that the practitioner do the following:

- Develop a sound working relationship with the client
- Explore the client's thoughts and feelings relative to depression
- Encourage expression of feelings
- Conduct a thorough review of depressive symptoms
- Refer the client for a psychiatric evaluation for possible medication
- Conduct a careful analysis of the client's communication patterns and interpersonal behaviors within their relationships and identify significant problems
- Identify changes the client would like to see in their relationships
- Use the therapeutic relationship as a laboratory for assessing interpersonal behaviors, provide constructive feedback, and suggest changes
- Encourage the client to experiment with different approaches to relating to others, depending on the problem
- Monitor and evaluate client efforts to improve their relationships

In general, IPT is used to address three types of interpersonal problems related to depression: unresolved grief, interpersonal role disputes, or role transitions. With grief, the practitioner facilitates the mourning process, examines the loss and attending symptoms, and helps the client reconnect with other social supports to help alleviate the depressive symptoms associated with loss. If the focus is an interpersonal role dispute, the practitioner should identify the conflict and review problem-solving strategies to help ameliorate the conflict. For problems related to role transitions, the practitioner might assist the client in mourning the old role by examining thoughts and facilitating the expression of feelings about the loss. The practitioner can then help the client address the new role in a more positive light with an emphasis on attaining mastery and accessing relevant support systems. If the client has interpersonal deficits that impede relationship satisfaction, the practitioner should help the client reduce isolation, improve social skills, and encourage the formation of new relationships. Termination focuses on helping the client develop a plan to maintain improvements over time.

How would IPT treatment differ for the depressed retiree discussed earlier? An IPT practitioner would focus not on examining whether the client's beliefs were dysfunctional but on helping the client engage other people in his community, as his retirement has left him without his usual social supports. He might also spend some time mourning his lost role as an important leader, but he would be encouraged to rediscover and renew that role by gradually becoming more engaged in the new community. On the basis of reviews of controlled research, it is likely that either IPT or CBT would be an effective intervention in this case. Both approaches emphasize the importance of a strong working alliance and the improvement of interpersonal relationships. Perhaps they are two somewhat different roads that end at the same destination.

Emotion-focused therapy (Greenberg & Watson, 2006; for more discussion, see chap. 10, "Couples in Conflict") should also be noted here as a promising approach to depression. Three controlled studies have shown it to be comparable to other evidence-based practices. Emotion-focused therapy focuses on enhancing emotional processing, and accepting and making sense of distressing emotions.

Regardless of the method used, case management is often an essential part of interventions for depression. As with the case illustration of the retiree, coordinating psychiatric evaluation, bolstering social supports, and encouraging new occupational roles are essential skills that contribute to successful outcomes for depressed clients.

Anxiety Disorders

Assessment

Anxiety disorders include panic disorder (usually accompanied by agoraphobia), obsessive-compulsive disorder, posttraumatic stress disorder, social anxiety, generalized anxiety disorder, and specific phobias. Although there are important differences among the disorders, there are overlapping symptoms and some similarities in the skills used in effective intervention approaches. In addition, many conditions co-occur with anxiety disorders (e.g., depression, substance abuse), and clinically significant anxiety can accompany many life challenges: interpersonal problems, occupational stress, financial difficulties and stress, and other problems-in-living (APA, 2000; Bellack & Hersen, 1998; O'Hare, 2005).

People predisposed to one type of anxiety disorder are at risk to develop others at some time during their lives. Evidence suggests that some people are genetically at risk to be "nervous," and this increased anxiety is likely to manifest as one type of disorder or another. For example, a person who is very shy, has night terrors, and is terrified of small animals as a child is at greater risk for agoraphobia or obsessive-compulsive disorder as an adolescent and adult. The essential skills needed to treat anxiety disorders will be presented here with the understanding that practitioners should pursue additional instruction and supervision in the use of evidence-based approaches specifically designed for each disorder.

Panic attacks are accompanied by some combination of accelerated heart rate, sweating, trembling, shortness of breath, feelings of being smothered or choking, chest pain, nausea, feeling faint or experiencing derealization (feelings of unreality) or depersonalization (being detached from oneself). Clients experiencing a panic attack may report that they feel like they are "losing control," "losing their mind," "going crazy," or are afraid that they are dying. Some clients report paresthesia (numbness or tingling sensations), and chills or hot flashes. With panic disorder, the fear of experiencing another attack persists. If clients begin to consciously avoid places or situations in which they feel they will experience another panic attack, they may meet the criteria for agoraphobia as well. In severe cases, panic disorder with agoraphobia can leave people quite incapacitated, housebound, often depressed, and unable to perform their usual occupational and social functions.

People suffering from obsessive-compulsive disorder experience recurrent and persistent thoughts, impulses, or images that they find distressing, and then engage in a compulsive behavior or mental ritual intended to neutralize the obsession. For example, if a client experiences repeated and intrusive obsessions that she contracted a deadly parasitic disease because she touched another person, then she may engage in repeated hand washing to neutralize that thought and the possibility of contagion. For another client, an obsessive thought (e.g., anger at another person) may compel him to engage in compulsive praying to neutralize the thought so that no harm befalls the other person as a result of the obsession. Many people with obsessive-compulsive disorder firmly believe that their thoughts alone can have an actual impact on independent events (e.g., If I think the plane might crash, it will!). Although most adults realize that their thoughts do not influence external realities, they still struggle with the obsession. As with panic disorder, obsessive-compulsive disorder can become so debilitating that people cannot function in their normal social or occupational roles because they spend so much mental energy and time in compulsive rituals. However, the more clients engage in compulsive rituals to obtain temporary relief, the more they inadvertently reinforce the obsession. A person with a phobia of germs, for example, may spend hours each day washing her hands and disinfecting her home.

Most people who experience traumatic events tend to recover from the incident and go on with their lives. Although they might always recall the trauma with some accompanying anxiety, anger, or sadness, most people who have experienced extreme stressors do not continue to suffer from acute and chronic symptoms of anxiety and depression as a result. Posttraumatic stress disorder afflicts people who have experienced extreme stressors or trauma in their lives but have not recovered from the impact of the events even after a few months have passed. Posttraumatic stress disorder is associated with a range of traumatic events, including near-death experiences such as a severe car accident, the witnessing of killings in combat or criminal acts, or sexual assault or physical abuse. The person who develops posttraumatic stress disorder in response to trauma generally develops three categories of symptoms: physiological hyperarousal (e.g., startle, hypervigilance), avoidance (e.g., not thinking about things that remind the person of the experience, avoiding places or doing things that invoke images of the events), and reexperiencing of symptoms (e.g., flashbacks, nightmares). Depression and substance abuse often co-occur with posttraumatic stress disorder.

People suffering from generalized anxiety disorder engage in excessive worry for extended periods of time; often feel restless or have difficulty concentrating; and are often fatigued, irritable, and have trouble sleeping. People with social phobia experience intense worry and anxiety symptoms in social situations such that it interferes significantly with their social and occupational functioning. Specific phobias are fears of certain objects, animals, or situations. When confronted by them, a person with a phobia experiences extreme distress and makes every effort to get away from the situation and avoid it in the future. Some might tolerate it only with great discomfort. Common phobias include insects, dogs and other small animals, flying in commercial airliners, closed spaces, bodies of water, and heights.

In addition to recognizing key signs and symptoms of anxiety disorder, an MDF assessment requires that the practitioner gauge the effects of these disorders across all key domains: overall mental status; emotional well-being, including other forms of emotional distress (e.g., depression); how the disorder affects close relationships with family members; and how the anxiety interferes with social and occupational functioning. Key points in a functional analysis should include the identification of antecedents (e.g., situations, thoughts, specific people, drug use) that appear to coincide with a worsening of anxiety symptoms. Assessment of anxiety disorder requires the establishment of a hierarchy of fears so that the intervention can proceed from a moderately fearful situation to the most fearful. Each target fear also requires a hierarchical breakdown of objectives so that clients can approach the anxiety-inducing situation one step at a time in order to experience anxiety reduction at each successive level and, as a result, reinforce their conviction so they can successfully proceed to the next. The focused functional assessment is a routine prelude to the exposure therapies explained subsequently.

Intervention

Interventions with anxiety disorders require a common set of skills that are tailored to each client's needs and preferences. The skills include psychoeducation, cognitive restructuring, self-regulation of physiological anxiety symptoms, imaginal (covert) exposure and, most important, prolonged in vivo exposure to the feared situation whenever feasible. Cognitive-behavioral interventions are well-established evidence-based interventions for serious anxiety disorders, including obsessive-compulsive disorders (e.g., Abramowitz, Brigidi, & Roche, 2001; Steketee, 1993), agoraphobia and panic attacks (e.g., Antony & Swinson, 2000; Butler et al., 2006), posttraumatic stress disorder (e.g., Butler et al., 2006; Rothbaum, Meadows, Resick, & Foy, 2000), as well as other anxiety disorders described previously.

Clients with anxiety disorders can benefit considerably from empathic understanding and the practitioner's motivational support. Most people can relate to the experience of anxiety and fear on some level, and have probably experienced intense fear or worry at least one time in their life. Clients may also be embarrassed or ashamed of their fear, despite that fear is common. By way of support and enhancing motivation, social workers can confidently reassure most clients that if they commit to an evidence-based approach, conquering their anxiety problems is well within their grasp.

Practitioners must first become knowledgeable about anxiety disorders, carefully conduct a full MDF assessment to determine whether there are co-occurring problems that may cause or worsen the anxiety, and examine the effects of the anxiety disorder on other areas of the client's life. Psychoeducation regarding the nature of the disorder is essential and may provide considerable relief to the client.

As part of an extended functional assessment, the practitioner should engage the client in a collaborative effort to monitor anxiety symptoms and use a log, chart, or diary to keep track of the specific patterning of thoughts, anxiety symptoms, behaviors, and situational factors associated with anxiety. Typical questions, depending on the disorder, might include the following: How often do these panic attacks occur? Do they occur at certain times or in some situations more than others? Are your obsessions worse at some times of the day or certain days of the week more than others? How much time do you spend engaged in rituals to counter the obsession? Self-monitoring for a few weeks can be therapeutic for many clients by helping them feel that they are taking action, collaborating in treatment, and gaining some objective understanding of the problem, and helping them feel some beginning sense of mastery and control over their distress.

Dysfunctional thinking associated with anxiety disorders is not necessarily distorted or irrational. Although most adult clients are well aware that their anxiety may be a somewhat exaggerated or even irrational response to a feared situation (e.g., germs, going into a grocery store), this is not always the case. With posttraumatic stress disorder, for example, the client's response to memories of war or sexual assault are based on real and frightening events, and recollections might continue to evoke acute emotional distress. However, the client knows that the feelings and fears have endured well beyond the situation (i.e., the threat) and now negatively affect his or her life and the well-being of those around them. For people who suffer from severe anxiety, the challenge is not to dispel the reasons for anxiety as unrealistic but to accept what has occurred in the past, manage anxiety and associated symptoms successfully, and emphasize coping with life in the present. Cognitive reappraisal (i.e., cognitive restructuring) involves four main steps: (1) teach the client to identify the anxiety-producing belief, (2) generate alternative explanations, predictions, or beliefs, (3) challenge the logic of the original belief and examine the respective evidence for it, and (4) consider a more realistic alternative belief and commit to a more realistic interpretation or prediction.

Before covert or real-life exposure can begin, however, clients need to learn a critical skill: to manage their physiological symptoms by learning breath control, progressive muscle relaxation, and meditation. Anxiety symptoms are self-perpetuating in the sense that physical symptoms of anxiety (e.g., nervousness, quickening heart rate, butterflies in the stomach) provoke frightening images in the mind and increase avoidance behavior (which alleviates anxiety only in the short run). Taking several deep breaths (slowly exhaling) is an easy and relatively quick way to quell the intensity of some anxiety symptoms. Progressive muscle relaxation involves gradually tensing each muscle group, holding the tension for ten seconds, then releasing the tension and feeling the subsequent relaxation. Practitioners typically guide the client to begin with their toes and work their way up each muscle group to their forehead. Meditation is a practiced discipline of clearing the mind, focusing on something neutral, and relaxing the body. Deep breathing may initially accompany meditation as well. There are many variations on these helpful, well-established methods. Many excellent books, tapes, and videos are available to help practitioners learn these techniques for their own health and well-being and for teaching clients about these valuable tools. The approach selected should be the one that the client feels most comfortable with. If nothing else, a client with anxiety should learn to think calming thoughts and to take long, slow, deep breaths to reduce feelings of anxiety. Learning how to reduce physical symptoms of anxiety will help facilitate the effective use of exposure methods.

Covert (i.e., imaginal) exposure can be used to reduce anxiety related to the object of the client's fears. In covert exposure, the client uses his or her imagination or mind's eye to gradually confront his or fear in a step-by-step manner while guided by the practitioner. As with most effective exposure interventions, the practitioner and the client must first build a hierarchy of fears (i.e., list the thoughts or situations from the least to the most frightening). Second, depending on the specific nature of any one fear, the practitioner and client may list a step-by-step approach to gradually confront each fear in turn. Third, the client should learn how to use the subjective units of distress scale (SUDS, also known as systematic desensitization; see chap. 6) to indicate to the practitioner how much anxiety he or she experiences at various points.

Let's consider two case illustrations. For example, a socially phobic woman needs to become a more "public" person to advance her career. After a detailed assessment, she may list the following social situations, from that which evokes the least anxiety to the one that causes the most anxiety: making a presentation to a small group of familiar colleagues, making a presentation to a small group of unfamiliar colleagues, hosting an informal business cocktail party for mixed familiar and unfamiliar people, making a presentation to a large group of familiar colleagues, and making a presentation to a large group of unfamiliar colleagues. For a person diagnosed with obsessive-compulsive disorder who obsesses about germs and needs to compulsively wash dozens of times per day, the hierarchy of fears (again, from least fear producing to most) might be as follows: inadvertently touching another person's clothes, touching an exterior doorknob or handrail on the stairs at work, touching the doorknob in a public bathroom, touching the sink in a public bathroom, touching the wastebasket, and touching the toilet. In both cases, the practitioner would teach the client to use breath control and muscle relaxation, and then the practitioner would introduce these scenarios into the client's mind beginning with the least fearful (i.e., touching another person's clothes). As the client considers each step, he is asked to hold the particular image in his imagination for a while and maintain breath control until he feels that the anxiety has been reduced to a minimum. On occasion, the practitioner will ask the client how much anxiety he is experiencing. Clients can be initially instructed to raise a finger if they are too anxious or to simply report their level of anxiety when prompted. An agreed-on level of say thirty on the SUDS, which ranges from zero to one hundred, can be used for this purpose. At that point, the client and practitioner may either increase the intensity of that particular image (e.g., You are touching the doorknob now for ten, twenty, or thirty seconds) or, if the client feels that his anxiety about this situation is under better control, he might move on to the next step in the hierarchy (e.g., touching the sink).

Although covert exposure can be helpful for many clients, there is little substitute in the long run for a real-life approach to the feared situation. Eventually, clients will have to do this to conquer their fear. For some anxiety disorders, covert desensitization is simply not robust enough to resolve the problem, though it may provide an excellent warm-up exercise to prepare the client for exposure. The woman with social phobia would have to prepare presentations for small groups repeatedly until she feels she can take on a larger group, and so forth. For the man with obsessive-compulsive disorder, the exposure intervention will take on a slightly different form. He will have to not only touch surfaces with germs (i.e., the exposure) but also refrain from washing his hands right away (i.e., response prevention), and when he does, wash them only once for a minute or so. The approach of exposure with response prevention is by far the most successful psychosocial intervention for dealing with this often-disabling condition.

Other anxiety disorders, such as generalized anxiety or specific phobias, can be addressed with all or some of the therapeutic coping skills. For generalized anxiety, learning and practicing relaxation skills (e.g., meditation, breath control), taking time out three times per week to exercise, and having someone to talk to about one's worries may be sufficient. For specific phobias, graduated exposure is often sufficient. However, anxiety can be a tenacious problem, and it has a way of insinuating itself into other areas of life. It can cause irritability and sleep problems, somatic difficulties (e.g., headaches, nausea), and interpersonal and family problems. Anxiety problems often co-occur with depression and substance use disorders. Lifestyle changes can greatly reduce anxiety and prevent its recurrence. These changes may include regular vigorous exercise, reduced use of alcohol or other drugs, and reduced overall stress (e.g., changing jobs, resolving financial difficulties and relationship conflict). For people with seriously debilitating anxiety disorders, case management may be necessary to coordinate multiple services (e.g., psychiatry for medication, primary care for a physical examination, treatment for a co-occurring substance abuse problem, and referral to a mutual help group for people with anxiety disorders).

Summary

Schizophrenia mood disorders, and anxiety disorders collectively account for a large percentage of clients who receive mental health services. Social workers need to be knowledgeable about these conditions to conduct thorough and accurate MDF assessments. In addition, manualized interventions (i.e., intervention guidelines based on research) are now readily available to help practitioners learn evidence-based practices and plan effective interventions. Nevertheless, practitioners first need to hone discrete supportive, therapeutic coping and case management skills to tailor evidence-based practices to each client.

Case Study: José

José García is a seventy-one-year-old man who recently lost his wife to a battle with cancer. He has lived with his son, Hector, and his son's wife, Juanita, for about two years. José and his late wife, Esmeralda, had moved in with Hector after it was discovered that she had a potentially terminal illness. The younger couple has two children, Javier and Jesus. Javier is usually away at college; Jesus is in high school and lives at home. After his wife passed away, José became profoundly depressed. Although it appeared to be a severe grief reaction, which is understandable after fifty-one years of committed marriage, his depression showed few signs of abating even one year after her death. Hector and Juanita became increasingly concerned and began to inquire about help for José, first from their parish priest, then from a physician who referred José and his family to a social worker at the local community health center.

The Comprehensive Service Plan (Assessment, Intervention, Evaluation)

Use all available information from the client and significant others, your observations, and input from other professionals to conduct both quantitative and qualitative aspects of this MDF assessment.

Client identification data: (gender, age, marital status, sexual orientation; family composition; employment; racial, ethnic, cultural, religious/spiritual affiliation and identity)

José García is a seventy-one-year-old male, recently widowed. He lives with his son and daughter-in-law (Hector and Juanita), and has been retired for several years from his job of ten years as an apartment building supervisor and maintenance person. Prior to that job, he had worked for the city supervising building maintenance and had engaged in similar work for about thirty years. He is a devout Roman Catholic, attends church regularly, and defines his cultural background as such: "I came here from Puerto Rico when I was a boy, and I'm proud of being Puerto Rican, but I am, first and foremost, an American. I served my country." Mr. G. speaks Spanish fluently, reads a popular local Hispanic newspaper, and enjoys participating in the local Hispanic festivities during holidays.

The presenting problem
Description of problem (client's view)

Mr. G., when asked why he believes he has been referred to this clinic, said the following: "I lost my wife. I don't care whether I live or die. Sometimes I see her. I talk with her. I think she is suffering without me. I want to die so I can be with her and comfort her."

Description of problem (practitioner's view)

Mr. G. is apparently suffering from a profound grief reaction. However, his depressive symptoms have not abated for almost a year since his wife died. It appears that he has reported other signs and symptoms of severe depression. He also appears to be very anxious, wrings his hands constantly, and has a hard time sitting still. He appears to be quite agitated at times, especially when he reported that he "talks with his wife, and feels that she is suffering" in the afterlife.

Psychosocial history with an emphasis on problem trajectory

Mr. G. was born and raised in Puerto Rico. He came to this country with his parents when he was six years old. He grew up in New York City, joined the army after high school, and moved to this area after he was honorably discharged. As the U.S. was not at war at that time, he did not engage in combat. He grew up locally, worked for the park's department and other city maintenance jobs, and worked his way up to become a supervisor. He and his wife, Esmeralda, were married in their early twenties (after Mr. G. was discharged from the army), and they had two children, Hector and his sister, Margarita, who is married and moved to the Midwest a few years ago. He reports having always been on good terms with both his children.

Mr. G. recalls drinking alcohol heavily in his youth, and although he drank during his years in the service, he reports that he moderated his alcohol use after he married. He says he stopped drinking for a while because he had recalled his father's heavy drinking when growing up and remembers some physical fighting between his parents. When his wife became pregnant with Hector, he resolved not to let the same thing happen. He recalls his father as often absent and wonders aloud if he was depressed. He also recalls becoming depressed off and on over the years, and once spent three weeks in a psychiatric facility after having tried to hang himself. He reports now that he felt discouraged in the early days about not being able to make a living and support his wife and children adequately. At that time, Mr. G.'s father was still alive, and would often criticize his son's ability to "be a man and make something of himself." Mr. G. reported that, after that incident, his wife took him to see the local priest and made him promise that if he ever became depressed again, that he would not try to hurt himself. The priest impressed on Mr. G. that he would not be admitted into heaven if he died by suicide and could not be buried in a Catholic service. Since then, Mr. G. recalled that he had fewer problems with depression, especially as his children got older and his life became more financially stable, but he always suffered from chronic worries. His wife was able to take in sewing work in addition to outside jobs to help with the bills, and he reported that he and his wife felt a great sense of pride as they gradually became better able to maintain good standing in their neighborhood.

However, about ten years ago, Mr. G. had another episode of serious depression after he retired from the city. He reports that he did see a mental health counselor at that time with his wife and began to feel better after he took on a part-time job as an apartment building maintenance man, a job that later became a full-time job. Since then, Mr. G. reports that he has felt fine. And although he was concerned during his wife's illness, he did not experience a return of serious depressive symptoms until she became seriously ill and, even more so, after she passed away.

Attempts to resolve the problems, previous treatment and relevant outcomes

Over the past year, Mr. G. has become almost incapacitated by his depression. His son and daughter-in-law have been very supportive, but Mr. G. has shown little sign of rebounding. Although previous interventions for depression were noted earlier, no efforts to provide treatment for this latest recurrence have been attempted. The family has assumed that this response was a normal grief reaction, and has hoped that he would come around on his own. The couple became particularly alarmed when he said he no longer wanted to attend mass, and that he no longer had faith in God. They felt that he was feeling hopeless. They are also concerned because he has been talking to himself loudly at night, and recently has seemed very forgetful. They became nervous as, more than once, he forgot to turn off the stove, and one cold night wandered outside on his own. When they found him sitting under a tree in the nearby park in only his shirt and pants, he was talking aloud and did not seem to know where he was.

The individual assessment

Mental status, cognitive disturbances: Describe the client's level of hallucinations, delusions, disorientation, bizarre behavior or speech, memory problems, serious confusion, or other symptoms of serious cognitive impairment. Include other troubling or dysfunctional beliefs or convictions.

Beyond the normative indicators of a grief reaction, Mr. G. appears to be severely depressed, a problem he has had off and on during his adult life. He also expresses clear suicidal ideation. In addition, although details are limited at this time, he appears to be showing signs of memory problems. He also speaks with conviction about seeing his dead wife and talking with her (she, apparently, converses with him). Whether these experiences are the result of extreme grief reactions, indicate delusions associated with severe depression, or are related to some other cognitive disturbance or tinged with cultural/religious beliefs is not determined at this time. Mr. G. also seems to be very restless, often agitated, and his son and daughter-in-law seem concerned about his excessive worry, wringing of his hands, talking to himself at night, and wandering the house at all hours. They are worried about his leaving the house unannounced again, and are concerned for his safety. The existence of an anxiety disorder should be examined further.

How would you rate the client's overall mental status during the past month?

POOR [0]   IMPAIRED [1]   MARGINAL [2]   GOOD [3]   EXCELLENT [4]

Mental status, emotional distress: Describe the client's level of depression, anxiety, and overall ability to regulate emotions.

Mr. G.'s depression appears profound; he suffers from feelings of hopelessness, helplessness, despair; he reports somatic distress, trouble sleeping, and loss of appetite. There have never been signs of mania or hypomania. His anxiety may also account for some appetite and sleep problems, and his constant hand wringing is accompanied by an acute worry that his wife continues to suffer in the afterlife. He seems inconsolable that he can't be with her to comfort her.

How would you rate your client's emotional well-being over the past 30 days?

POOR [0]   IMPAIRED [1]   MARGINAL [2]   GOOD [3]   EXCELLENT [4]

Behavioral problems: Describe the client's overall ability to regulate behavior. Consider things such as ability to express oneself effectively; ability to work at things patiently; and tendencies to verbally or physically lash out at others, run away, harm oneself, or to engage in impulsive, criminal, or substance-abusing behavior. How would you describe the client's overall impulse control?

Mr. G. has demonstrated some troublesome and unpredictable behaviors. He has walked out of the house unannounced; otherwise he is generally inactive, and he has shown little interest in his usual sources of pleasure— working around the house or in the yard, doing minor repairs, seeing some of his acquaintances in the local park. He has attempted to kill himself in the past, although he has made no suicide gestures in recent years despite his expressed desire to die. His risk of suicide should be considered moderate at this time.

How would you rate your client's behavioral control generally over the past 30 days?

POOR [0]   IMPAIRED [1]   MARGINAL [2]   GOOD [3]   EXCELLENT [4]

Adaptive strengths and coping abilities. Describe the client's ability to cope with problems and everyday stressors. How would you describe the client's ability to assess problem situations, deal with triggers, cope with stress, solve problems, and perhaps reach out to others for help to deal effectively with difficulties?

Until this past year, Mr. G. was very active, and outgoing in a number of ways. As noted above, he was active around the home. He has friends in town, mostly retired men his age, and he would spend time with them playing cards or just visiting. He took an active interest in his grandchildren and seemed to be on good relations with them. His coping abilities and usual adaptive strengths are quite impaired at this time.

How would you rate your client's overall adaptive strengths and coping abilities over the past 30 days?

POOR [0]   IMPAIRED [1]   MARGINAL [2]   GOOD [3]   EXCELLENT [4]

Health problems: Describe the client's overall health. Aside from normal, transient illnesses, think about the client's general health habits (e.g., smoking, heavy drinking, exercise, weight), chronic primary health disorders, the client's opinion of his or her own health, ability to engage in usual activities relatively free from discomfort, overall energy level, hospitalizations, and treatments for illness other than psychiatric ones. Consider the client's documented medical history and any ongoing treatments.

Mr. G. is in very good physical health, has not been taking medication in recent months, although he does suffer from arthritis in his knees. Occasionally he has been known to take some analgesics for the pain.

How would you rate your client's health over the past 30 days?

POOR [0]   **IMPAIRED** [1]   **MARGINAL** [2]   **GOOD** [3]   **EXCELLENT** [4]

Use of alcohol and other drugs: Describe the client's use of alcohol, illicit substances (e.g., cocaine, heroin, marijuana, hallucinogens) and abuse of prescription medication. How often does the client use them, in what quantity, and how serious are the psychological, physical, or social consequences associated with use?

Although he reported a history of alcohol abuse when he was young, Mr. G. reports no problems with alcohol and has never used illicit substances or abused prescription medication. He drinks sherry now and then, but usually confines his consumption to a glass or two according to his son's report.

How would you rate the client's functioning in the past month with regard to substance use?

POOR [0]   **IMPAIRED** [1]   **MARGINAL** [2]   **GOOD** [3]   **EXCELLENT** [4]

Recreational activities: Consider what the client does for fun (alone or with others), hobbies, relaxation (reading, watching television, playing video games or cards) and physical exercise (e.g., walking, jogging, biking). How would you describe the client's overall involvement in positive recreational activities?

Although active physically and socially in recent years, Mr. G.'s recreational outlets have been seriously limited over the past year (noted earlier).

How would you rate the adequacy of the client's participation in healthy recreational activities over the past 30 days?

POOR [0]   **IMPAIRED** [1]   **MARGINAL** [2]   **GOOD** [3]   **EXCELLENT** [4]

Material resources: Describe your client's current or (if institutionalized) most recent living situation overall. Consider such things as adequacy of food, clothing, shelter, and safety.

Mr. G. is well cared for. He contributes to his son and daughter's household with his retirement income and all his physical needs are adequately met.

How would you rate the overall adequacy of the client's material resources over the past month?

POOR [0]   IMPAIRED [1]   MARGINAL [2]   GOOD [3]   EXCELLENT [4]

Independent living/self-care: Describe how well the client manages the household; takes care of personal hygiene; and eats, sleeps, and otherwise cares for his or her own basic needs.

Although his physical needs are met, Mr. G. would not currently be able to care for himself since he has been suffering from this acute grief reaction/recurrent depression. Sometimes he needs encouragement to take care of daily hygienic needs, and his son and grandson have assisted him in this manner. He would also go without eating on occasion without some coaxing.

How would you rate the client's ability to live independently and take care of their basic needs over the past 30 days?

POOR [0]   IMPAIRED [1]   MARGINAL [2]   GOOD [3]   EXCELLENT [4]

Work (role) satisfaction: Describe the client's current work-related or other important role-related activities (e.g., work, student, home, volunteer, retired, disabled). Describe the activities and responsibilities that occupy the client in a productive manner.

Although retired, Mr. G. remained active before his wife became seriously ill and died, helping neighbors, keeping up maintenance on his son's house, and visiting friends and neighbors whom he thought needed company. Generally, those activities have fallen by the wayside.

> How would you rate the client's work or role satisfaction over the past 30 days?
>
> POOR [0]   **IMPAIRED [1]**   MARGINAL [2]   GOOD [3]   EXCELLENT [4]

Legal problems: Describe any legal problems the client has had or continues to have. These include minor infractions (e.g., public drunkenness, shoplifting, minor traffic violations, public disturbances) and more serious crimes (e.g., assault and battery, rape, burglary, driving under the influence). Consider the client's status (e.g., probation, awaiting imprisonment, parole). Also, consider any civil suits leveled at the client or pending financial judgments. Overall, how would you describe the client's current legal situation?

Mr. G. has never had any legal difficulties of note.

> How would you rate the client's legal situation over the past 30 days?
>
> POOR [0]   IMPAIRED [1]   MARGINAL [2]   GOOD [3]   **EXCELLENT [4]**

DSM-IV Diagnosis

Axis I   Major depressive disorder, recurrent, 296.3
          Generalized anxiety disorder, 300.02
          Bereavement v62.82

Axis II   No diagnosis

Family and social assessment

Family relations: Describe the client's current family structure including authority, hierarchy, alliances, roles, rules, boundaries, subsystems (e.g., couple, siblings, parent-child alliances), and patterns of interactions and quality of communications. Describe specific problems in the family; describe specific adaptive strengths in the family. How does the family describe their own racial, ethnic, cultural, and religious identities?

Mr. G., according to his report and that of his son and daughter-in-law, has always been close to them, and they have consistently provided support to him and their mother over the years. After moving into Hector and Juanita's home, there was a period during the first year or so of tension and some verbal conflict. Mr. G., as reported by Hector and Juanita, often "intruded" on the parents' efforts to counsel and, occasionally, discipline their son Javier, who was sometimes in trouble during his high school years. The couple was making efforts to resolve this dispute with Mr. G. when Hector's mother took a turn for the worse, and Mr. G. became more preoccupied with his wife's difficulties. In addition, with Javier out of the home much of the time, there is no occasion to provoke these disputes. The couple reports no problems with Jesus, who appears to be doing well in school and reports a good network of friends. The parents report no problems with him at home. Overall, this appears to be a supportive household of three generations.

How would you rate the quality of the client's immediate family relationships over the past 30 days?

POOR [0]   **IMPAIRED** [1]   **MARGINAL** [2]   **GOOD** [3]   **EXCELLENT** [4]

Immediate social relationships (close friends and acquaintances): Describe the quality of the client's relationships with friends and acquaintances. Over the past month, how would you describe the quality of the interaction overall between the client and others with respect to closeness, intimacy, general interpersonal satisfaction, effective communications, degree of conflict, level of hostility, aggression, and evidence of any emotional or physical abuse?

As for Mr. G., his relationships with friends and acquaintances have suffered a lot since his wife died and his depression has set in. Although some of his friends have called or stopped by to see him, he has told Hector and Juanita that he does not want to see anyone or have any company. He continues to isolate himself from those who seem to care about him.

How would you rate the quality of the client's immediate social relationships over the past 30 days?

POOR [0]   **IMPAIRED** [1]   **MARGINAL** [2]   **GOOD** [3]   **EXCELLENT** [4]

Extended social relationships: Describe the type and quality of relationships between the client and others in the client's community (other than close friends and family). These people might include other families, law enforcement, human service agencies, school personnel, coworkers, and others from whom the client receives support or with whom the client is having serious conflict.

According to Hector, Mr. G. is well respected and liked in his community. As noted earlier, he is on good relations with his neighbors, is known by local law enforcement for his work on the community watch committee, and has been active for years on committees that organize local Puerto Rican festivities. Even local school personnel are acquainted with him through these efforts. Since his wife's illness and death, however, he has been noticeably absent from these activities.

How would you rate the quality of the client's social relationships over the past 30 days?

POOR [0]   **IMPAIRED [1]**   MARGINAL [2]   GOOD [3]   EXCELLENT [4]

A concise summary of the MDF assessment: Highlight the client's areas of distress and adaptive strengths. Emphasize those areas that are most likely to be emphasized in the intervention plan.

Mr. G. appears to be suffering from an acute grief reaction and a concurrent recurrence of a major depressive disorder. In addition, he may be experiencing an exacerbation of a preexisting anxiety disorder. Mr. G. should be considered a suicide risk as well. His depressive symptoms include hopelessness, sleep and appetite disturbance, loss of pleasure in daily activities, social isolation, and lowered activity and energy level. Of additional concern are Mr. G.'s unusual behavior, apparent memory problems, and reports of having conversations with his deceased wife. Although the nature of these reports is not clear, further examination for cognitive disorder should be pursued. Mr. G.'s symptoms appear to be affecting most domains of well-being, and on a functional level, he has been quite debilitated since his wife's death. Nevertheless, he is being well supported by an attentive son and daughter-in-law, who are in a good position to monitor his behavior and provide emotional support.

Recommendations for further focused assessment: Note recommended referrals to consultants or additional instruments to be used.

Referral to psychiatric evaluation is strongly recommended.

THE COMPREHENSIVE SERVICE PLAN SUMMARY

Problems: Briefly describe key problems to be addressed	Goals: State desired outcome for each problem.	Objectives: Describe specific stepping stones toward each goal; update as client progresses.	Interventions: Describe intervention approaches to be used.	Assessment and evaluation: Describe indexes and scales used to track progress.
Acute grief reaction/recurrent depressive symptoms including hopelessness, suicidal ideation, poor sleep and appetite, lowered energy and activity level, social isolation/withdrawal	Resolve grief and alleviate all symptoms of depression	Initial objectives: help client acknowledge wife's death and begin verbalizing his feelings of despair, loneliness	*Supportive skills:* Develop a working relationship with Mr. G., and join with his closest support system—his son and daughter-in-law—as collaborators	Monitor Mr. G.'s suicidal ideation closely; coach Hector and Juanita regarding signs of increased suicidal risk
	Reduce frequency and intensity of suicidal thoughts	Discuss any specifics regarding plans to hurt himself if he is feeling suicidal	*Therapeutic coping skills:* Examine Mr. G.'s beliefs carefully regarding his concerns about his wife's well-being in the afterlife, his sense of hopelessness, and feeling that his life cannot go on	Have H. and J. keep a chart regarding Mr. G.'s sleeping and eating habits
Chronic anxiety	Improve appetite and sleep	Begin developing a more consistent routine around sleeping and eating habits; monitor changes		Monitor frequency of visitors and how long they stay
	Increase activity level and return client to socialization level prior to wife's death	Plan at least one brief home visit from a close friend within the next week or two	Conduct a review of his life with Esmeralda and explore his openness to reviewing pictures, other memorabilia, and perhaps creating some kind of memorial to her in his garden or in some other way	Later, note increases in Mr. G.'s activity level around the house and any increases in social activities
Memory problems; question of delusional beliefs?	Reduce/alleviate stress and anxiety level	Reduce stress with supervised walks, moderate exercise		
	Further assess apparent cognitive dysfunction			

Encourage his expression of feelings about his grief and fears about his wife's well-being

As he slowly improves, increase social contacts in his home

Case management skills: Later, bolster social supports by encouraging visitors and gradually returning client to former level of social activity

Consider referring him for spiritual counseling when he seems open to discussing his wife and his anger at God

Refer client for psychiatric services for specialized mental status exam and consideration of medication for his depression

CHAPTER NINE

Adult Disorders: Substance Use and Personality Disorders

Substance Abuse

Assessment

TENS OF MILLIONS OF AMERICANS meet the criteria for abuse of and dependence on alcohol, illicit drugs, and prescription drugs. Substance abuse and addiction costs the country hundreds of billions of dollars annually in health-care costs, addiction treatment, lost productivity, criminal activity and adjudication, and other related social problems. Substance abuse is diagnosed when excessive use leads to a person's failure to fulfill major role obligations (e.g., work, school, home), recurrent use in hazardous situations (e.g., driving under the influence), recurrent legal problems, and continued use despite persistent or recurrent social, psychological, or interpersonal problems USDHHS, 2000). Substance dependence is diagnosed when three or more of the following conditions have been met: tolerance; withdrawal symptoms; using more of the substance than intended; difficulty cutting down use; frequent drug-seeking behavior; impairment of social, occupational, or recreational activities; and continued use despite persistent or recurrent psychological or physical problems. Although physiological tolerance often accompanies dependence, a diagnosis of dependence need not include tolerance as a prerequisite (APA, 2000).

Scientific research strongly suggests that various interacting biopsychosocial factors cause substance use and addictions: genetic predisposition, family learning history, cultural influences, and social-environmental influences. Substance abuse and addiction also co-occur with a range of other psychiatric and psychosocial disorders: schizophrenia, mood disorders, anxiety disorders, eating disorders, personality disorders, domestic violence, and child abuse and neglect. Regardless of the field of practice, social workers will encounter many clients who abuse and are addicted to substances. It is of utmost importance that all social workers have a working knowledge of the pharmacological properties of the most common drugs of abuse (e.g., alcohol, narcotics, amphetamines, tranquilizers) and, at a minimum, know how to conduct screening and assessment of substance abuse problems and to refer clients for subsequent intervention. Ideally, all social workers should be trained to provide some level of intervention for substance abuse and addiction given its high co-occurrence rate with other disorders and psychosocial conditions.

There is a wide range of instruments available to assist in an MDF assessment of substance abuse and addiction (USDHHS, 2003b). However, scales should be used in the context of a multidimensional qualitative assessment whereby the practitioner explores these core essential questions: What substances does the client use? How much of each substance does the client use? How often does the client use the substance(s)? Under what circumstances does the client use? What are the short- and long-term consequences of drug use with regard to psychological, emotional, behavioral, interpersonal, and community functioning? (O'Hare, 2005).

Will clients who abuse substances answer such questions accurately or truthfully? The answer is: it depends on the circumstances. Many clients are quite forthcoming about their use and abuse of alcohol, illegal drugs, and prescription medication. Other clients withhold more because of the stigma associated with substance abuse and addiction, and because they are understandably concerned about discussing illegal behavior. However, some clients may minimize their use or deny the importance of consequences of use largely because they do not believe that they have a problem. Sorting out use patterns, severity of the consequences, and the extent to which the client's concerns are congruent with the actual magnitude of the problem can be quite challenging.

With experience, practitioners can become adept at facilitating client disclosure of substance use and abuse. Linking together psychological, behavioral, legal, and medical indicators of substance abuse in a straightforward, nonjudgmental way can often help clients be more forthcoming. Using information from multiple sources and confronting contradictory information in a straightforward manner can be illuminating. However, recent thinking in the emerging practice of motivational interviewing (Miller & Rollnick, 2002) suggests that arguing with clients does little good and simply invites resistance. Collaborating with clients to sort through the pros and cons of substance abuse is less coercive and places the responsibility on clients to decide whether they want to do something about the problem. Focusing on careful listening, rolling with resistance, and respecting clients' personal autonomy will encourage clients to engage in treatment.

Functional analysis is critical to a complete substance abuse assessment. Most clients follow a pattern in their abuse of alcohol and other drugs. A two-week monitoring period can be helpful for clients ready to engage in treatment. Having clients keep a log to document which substances they used, how much, how often, and under what circumstances can be productive and help practitioners to identify key cognitive, emotional, or situational factors that increase the likelihood of using substances. This analysis is particularly valuable for setting goals and implementing therapeutic coping skills targeting at-risk situations.

Intervention

Variations of cognitive-behavioral coping skills interventions, behavioral couples therapy, and behaviorally based contingency management strategies have been ranked among the most effective approaches for substance abuse and dependence (e.g., Carroll & Onken, 2005; Higgins et al., 2003; Miller, Meyers, & Hiller-Sturmhofel, 1999; Monti & Rohsenow, 1999; O'Farrell & Falls-Stewart, 2003). These approaches use an array of therapeutic coping skills, including motivational interviewing, cognitive appraisal of the pros and cons of substance abuse, coping with emotional distress that can trigger relapse, improving social skills, skills to refuse drugs and alcohol, seeking out sober social supports, and reducing risks associated with use (i.e., harm reduction) to support sobriety, reduce relapse, and prevent recidivism. These strategies are well researched (though more needs to be done) and have been increasingly incorporated into traditional approaches to addictions treatment. In addition to outpatient settings, behavioral methods are often used in inpatient treatment, halfway houses, therapeutic communities, and traditional recovery services. Practitioners help the client conduct an accurate functional analysis of their own behavior regarding substance use by recognizing how specific thoughts, feelings, behaviors, and situations can put them at risk to relapse. Once the client becomes skilled at recognizing antecedents (i.e., "triggers"), he or she can use an array of standard cognitive behavioral self-regulatory skills to moderate or abstain from use and possible relapse.

Many clients seek help from mutual support groups during or after formal treatments have ended. These include Alcoholics Anonymous (AA), Narcotics Anonymous (NA), and other groups. Although studies of mutual help groups for substance abuse have shown mixed results, there is reason to believe that clients who stick with them have a better chance of achieving and maintaining sobriety. Coping skills have also been shown to facilitate client participation in traditional twelve-step approaches (e.g., Humphreys, 1999; USDHHS, 2000).

Clients with substance abuse problems arrive in treatment for many reasons and at many levels of readiness to change. However, many clients who seek social work services, despite having a substance abuse problem, do not present it as their primary reason for seeking help. Voluntary clients are more likely to present mental health concerns (e.g., depression, anxiety), family problems (e.g., couples conflict, parent-child problems), health-related concerns, or legal problems (e.g., court-ordered domestic violence) as their presenting complaint. Depending on the client's referral circumstances and readiness to change, practitioners should be flexible in how they initially approach the matter of substance abuse and be ready for a range of responses from the client.

Evidence has demonstrated that the therapeutic alliance is as important to clients with substance abuse problems as it is with other clients. Substance abuse still carries a degree of stigma, and it is important to emphasize a nonjudgmental approach. Despite that many prescription drugs that are abused are pharmacologically more dangerous than some street drugs, society tends to view those who use illicit substances in a more negative light. Providing effective care for the client requires a solid working alliance that communicates that you are there not to judge but to help the client recognize the personal psychosocial and health costs associated with abuse and addiction, motivate him or her to take action, and improve his or her overall quality of life.

Engaging clients with a substance abuse problem initially depends on where they are in the change process. Prochaska, DiClemente, and Norcross's (1992) stages of change model (described in chapter 6) is a helpful descriptive rubric for determining a client's readiness to engage in the change process. In general, clients who are in the precontemplation stage do not think that they have a substance use problem. These clients are often court-ordered or otherwise involuntary clients and are not interested in treatment. Clients in the contemplation stage may admit that they have a problem sometimes and tend to be more willing to explore the possibility that they do have a problem. Clients in the preparation stage have decided that they have a problem and are on the verge of doing something to deal with it. Those in the action stage have accepted that they have a substance use problem and are fully engaged in treatment. Clients in the maintenance stage have been through a period of treatment and are now trying to solidify their gains and prevent relapse. To successfully engage clients and increase their chances of committing to substance abuse treatment, it is essential to meet clients where they are.

Research on motivational interviewing (Miller & Rollnick, 2002) has also demonstrated that when clients are treated respectfully, allowed to formulate the problem on their own, and given a choice of treatment goals in a spirit of collaboration, they are more likely to engage in treatment. Flexibility in setting initial treatment goals is important so that clients feel that the practitioner's agenda is not coercing them. Practitioners should "roll" with the client's resistance. Many clients attempt to cut down or eliminate the use of one drug or another. This approach may work for some people, and at a later date, they may be more willing to consider abstinence if they failed to moderate intake. A pattern of two steps forward and one step back is not uncommon when working with clients who abuse or are dependent on substances. Practitioners should avoid ideological approaches to substance abuse treatment based on personal or anecdotal experience (e.g., always insisting on abstinence despite the client's age or problem severity) and focus on the use of well-researched methods that allow for partial successes early in treatment and a range of intervention goals (e.g., harm reduction, moderation, abstinence).

Clients experiencing substance abuse and addiction have developed patterns of alcohol and drug use in response to an array of psychological, emotional, behavioral, and situational vulnerabilities and risk factors. Some clients are more likely to drink as a result of depression or anxiety, others as a way to cope with social situations or loneliness, and others as an attempt to neutralize withdrawal symptoms. The use of substances to cope with psychosocial or physical cues does, in fact, provide some temporary relief but often at a high cost. Over time, the negative effects of substance abuse may offset the positive effects, but because of the habit-forming nature of substances, changing one's usage patterns through situational adjustments (e.g., not drinking before driving), cutting down, or abstaining can become difficult. When the costs of use override the benefits, people who abuse alcohol or other drugs are more likely to seek help, often under pressure from others (e.g., family members, doctors, courts).

There is a range of therapeutic coping skills that, alone or in combination, have been shown to be moderately effective with people who abuse alcohol or other drugs. Psychoeducation is certainly an important part of an overall approach but alone is typically not sufficient to cause lasting change. In brief treatment, practitioners might tailor a psychoeducational approach to provide individualized feedback to a client after having conducted a full assessment, possibly with collaborative input from a physician. After having examined the type and amount of substances used over time, and having made some estimates about the impact on the client's psychological, social, and physical well-being, a social worker may summarize the assessment about negative consequences and make treatment recommendations. Many clients, particularly those who abuse substances but are not dependent (e.g., youthful experimentation, excessive social drinking) often respond positively to this feedback and make efforts to cut down and moderate their consumption. It is also important that practitioners help clients link reduced substance use with other improvements in their life, such as feeling more energetic, being more productive at work, improving important relationships, and improving overall health.

This initial progress can also serve as an extended assessment (in the form of clients' self-monitoring) to determine whether clients have an abuse problem or are dependent on alcohol or other drugs. It also provides an opportunity to examine other co-occurring problems (e.g., depression, anxiety) to determine whether there is any change in these areas and to further assess potentially co-occurring disorders. Extended self-monitoring can be a powerful therapeutic tool that engages clients to fully participate in determining for themselves how serious their substance use difficulties are. The practitioner can facilitate an analysis of the pros and cons of clients' substance use and help clients determine the seriousness of the problem on their own. They can then collaborate in determining which goals seem realistic and feasible. In this way, the practitioner does not impose judgment about the seriousness of the problem on the client; the client determines that on his or her own with the support and informed guidance of the practitioner.

Self-monitoring thoughts, emotional states, behaviors, and situations that precipitate alcohol or drug use might be the most important survival skill for people struggling to control abuse or overcome dependence. Distorted or negative thoughts (e.g., I'll never get another good job; My kids will never want to see me again; I'll never feel better physically) can be discouraging and make a good excuse to say, "Oh, heck with it" and yield to the urge. Alcohol and other drugs are also an effective short-term way to anesthetize oneself against anxiety, depression, grief, anger, disappointment, and other negative feelings. Clients who learn to identify negative mood states as a potential antecedent to substance use can prepare for those situations and have alternatives available: calling a friend who does not abuse, calling an AA or NA sponsor, going for a walk or partaking in other healthful distraction. Early in the recovery process, cravings may have a strong physiological component; later on, psychological cues can be just as compelling—just ask a former cigarette smoker about situational cravings even ten years after quitting. Clients' routine behaviors and circumstances associated with substance use can also be powerful triggers. A middle-aged man in early recovery who for years met his friends at the local tavern four or five times per week will have a hard time abstaining if he just stops by the tavern to say hello to his buddies. Over time, engaging in self-monitoring provides a client with a cognitive map that helps him or her anticipate where the trouble spots will be on the road to recovery and how to avoid them or deal with them when they cannot be avoided.

An examination of dysfunctional thinking regarding substance use may be an important part of the initial treatment stage. Over time, people who abuse alcohol and other drugs develop rather specific but erroneous beliefs, known as "expectancies," about the effects that substances provide them with. Examples include expectancies of increased social assertiveness, reduced tension, and enhanced sexuality, among others. Although alcohol does provide some of these positive effects in the short run, negative consequences tend to overtake positive effects after years of abuse. Despite the negative consequences of abuse, clients often continue to deny, minimize, or rationalize substance abuse regardless of the negative consequences (e.g., arrests for drunk driving, job loss, divorce, health problems). Respectfully presenting the evidence to the client and having him or her consider the discrepancies between expectancies and external evidence can help reduce denial and minimization.

Other cognitive distortions regarding substance abuse may occur as well. As a result of depression (secondary to heavy chronic drinking), clients may think that they are hopeless, they will never be able to stop their use of alcohol or other drugs, and their lives will never get better. Practitioners can offer evidence that many people feel despondent initially and that their thinking may be distorted by feelings of hopelessness caused by substance-related depression. Practitioners can help clients focus on incremental gains, one day at a time, to stimulate some initial reinforcing progress, to increase feelings of self-efficacy, and to boost optimism about further progress. Behavioral successes can debunk clients' dysfunctional belief that they are hopeless and encourage them to achieve incremental successes.

Many clients with addictions have had serious relationship difficulties, sometimes as a result of their substance abuse. Some of these problems may also have been related to inadequate social skills, worsened by the effects of intoxication. Modeling, role-playing, and rehearsing assertiveness and better communication skills can be of great assistance for clients, so they can have better control when they encounter interpersonal emotional triggers. For example, a woman engaged in substance abuse treatment after a divorce may have to deal with a formerly abusive husband with whom she shares child-care arrangements. These situations trigger raw and difficult emotions about problems not yet resolved and may put the client seriously at risk for relapse. Role-playing such a scenario can be a good way to prepare for such an encounter. Rehearsing how the client may feel in such a circumstance and helping her plan to cope with those feelings can help her get through the encounter without resorting to drinking. (Forewarned is forearmed.) Success experiences in situations that are likely to provoke relapse can build self-confidence and help her maintain sobriety.

The same stress-management skills described for dealing with anxiety problems (see chapter 8) can also help clients maintain moderation or sobriety. When overly stressed, a client in recovery can stop, take a deep breath, think, endure, and learn to accept passing emotional upsets without resorting to the desire to drink or use other drugs. It also gives the client time to initiate a previously discussed action plan (e.g., go home, call a friend, take a long walk, wait for the feeling to pass). In the long run, many people struggling with abuse or addictions turn to exercise to reduce anxiety and depression, and the emotional distress that often precedes relapse. Before suggesting any exercise regimen, however, practitioners should encourage clients to get a physical exam.

Despite deciding to cut down or stop drinking and eliminate illegal drug use, clients are still likely to find themselves in social circumstances where others are drinking or using drugs. Role-playing and rehearsing and practicing refusal skills can benefit clients who may be uncomfortable in the early stages of recovery. Practicing easy-to-remember phrases such as, "No thanks," "I'm all set," "I've got my drink," "I'm taking medication," or "I'm not feeling well today" can be just enough to ward off the temptation to say, "OK, why not?"

Therapeutic coping skills for helping substance-abusing or dependent clients are currently at the forefront for early intervention, treatment, and recovery. Practitioners who learn these approaches can help clients cope with cognitive and emotional triggers and prepare them to cope successfully with situations that put themselves at risk for relapse. However, clients often need more than improved coping skills. Successful interventions for substance abuse and dependence often require the cooperation of two or more service providers as well as improvements in social and instrumental supports.

A case management framework is often used to augment some of the more effective intervention programs for people with addictions. These are multifaceted approaches for working with seriously dependent individuals that emphasize coordinating treatment efforts among various agencies, facilitating access to other social and health services, and following through with the provision of social and concrete supports. Community reinforcement and contingency management approaches have been shown to be among the most effective interventions for seriously addicted clients (Abbott, Weller, Delaney, & Moore, 1998; Azrin, Sisson, Meyers, & Godley, 1982; Carroll & Onken, 2005; Higgins et al., 1993). A community reinforcement (CR) approach is a multifaceted strategy designed to help seriously addicted people by using multiple layers of social and instrumental supports to stay clean and sober. Supports are likely to include some combination of job or housing assistance, financial benefits, mutual help groups, and substance abuse counseling. For many clients who have been court ordered to continue treatment, contingency management (CM) may be added to CR to balance rewards with possible sanctions if the client is caught using illegal drugs again. The emphasis in CM is on the if-then condition: if the client remains abstinent from drugs (e.g., clean urine screens) and does not otherwise violate probation, then he or she can continue to receive treatment and other forms of assistance in the community; if the client uses drugs or commits a violation, then he or she might have to return to prison (depending on the specifics of the contract or court-ordered conditions). The CR and CM programs vary from state to state, and their implementation depends largely on the levels of coordination between the criminal justice system and mental health and substance abuse treatment agencies. These programs are very promising, but they require more research and closely supervised and coordinated implementation.

Case management skills are often essential in providing substance abuse interventions. Coordinating medical referrals; linking clients to social supports such as twelve-step and other mutual help groups; and communicating with employers, probation officers, and the courts are essential skills for implementing complex and effective substance abuse services for seriously substance-dependent clients.

Personality Disorders

A personality disorder is defined as "an enduring pattern of inner experience and behavior that deviates markedly from the expectations of the individual's culture, is pervasive and inflexible, has an onset in adolescence or early adulthood, is stable over time, and leads to distress or impairment" (APA, 2000, p. 685). This section addresses two of the more commonly diagnosed personality disorders: antisocial and borderline personality disorders.

Assessment of Antisocial Personality Disorder

People diagnosed with antisocial personality disorder (APD) often demonstrate a pervasive pattern of disregard and violation of the rights and safety of others (e.g., criminality, deceitfulness, violence, impulsivity); a record of irresponsibility with regard to relationships, work, or financial commitments; and a lack of remorse regarding the violation of others' rights. This last quality is often associated with psychopathy, a quality manifested in a subset of people with APD. Although many people, mostly male, engage in criminal acts in their youth (e.g., stealing, selling small amounts of drugs), many mature out of these activities and grow into responsible adults. The antisocial person who demonstrates psychopathic personality traits, however, tends to be a more chronic and inflexible person who shows little remorse for behavior and seems to lack an awareness of others' feelings and needs altogether (Hare, Harpur, Hakstian, Forth, & Hart, 1990). Many antisocial and psychopathic people also have substance use disorders and are at high risk of perpetrating domestic violence against their partners and any children living with them.

In addition to a complete mental status exam, an MDF assessment with antisocial personalities should carefully examine interpersonal and occupational history, substance abuse, and other impulsive high-risk behaviors. Functional assessment should examine patterns of impulsive substance abusing or other socially offending behaviors for significant patterns and high-risk situations. Access to relevant medical and legal records as well as previous mental health and substance abuse treatment information is important. Antisocial clients can be engaging and charming, and they often are very good at hiding important information. Assessment should also include expert consultation for a violence risk assessment and standardized testing for psychopathy.

Intervention

Antisocial and particularly psychopathic people are potentially dangerous and difficult to treat. Occasionally, there are reports of social workers having been seriously harmed or killed by APD clients, which serves as a stark reminder that practitioners should work as part of an expert team with comprehensive assessments (including risk for violence) and close supervision. Despite the best of intentions, traditional psychotherapeutic interventions (e.g., insight oriented) have been shown to be ineffective with APD clients. Only external contingencies (e.g., balancing rewards and sanctions) and close, structured supervision (e.g., collaboration with probation or parole officials) stand a reasonable chance of keeping some clients' behaviors in check and improving overall psychosocial functioning. Thus, working with antisocial and psychopathic persons is best done as a collaborative effort that includes some combination of mental health and substance abuse services in collaboration with court-ordered supervision. In addition, because many APD clients are prone to violence, practitioners must weigh the likely effectiveness of psychosocial interventions against the danger some clients pose to the community at large. Criminal justice and mental health collaborations have yet to arrive at reliable criteria for when to treat versus when to incarcerate. Thus, much work remains to be done in advancing more coordinated interventions efforts, particularly for criminally involved clients.

However, several structured cognitive-behavioral interventions have been shown to be effective with clients diagnosed with APD, many of whom are court ordered to treatment for substance abuse (Gendreau, 1996; McGuire & Hatcher, 2001). These approaches often include the CR and CM approaches. In the most effective programs, cognitive-behavioral interventions start while clients are in prison and continue when they are released into the community. Such treatments may include a halfway house or a therapeutic community or other supervised arrangement (often including the services of a parole officer). Because of the high rate of co-occurring substance use disorders, prevention of drug relapse after release is also a major component of multifaceted programs. Currently, the policy debate regarding what to "do" with people with APD has moved beyond the dichotomy of prison versus treatment. A third way, therapeutic jurisprudence, suggests an integration of law enforcement efforts and psychosocial services.

Working with APD clients (let's assume for the sake of simplicity that some, but not all, are also psychopathic) is often challenging. To increase the chances of good outcomes, practitioners must make an effort to cultivate a respectful, sensitive relationship with each client. Because APD clients can be charming, well spoken, humorous, and engaging, like any other client, they can also be manipulative, seductive, and exploitive if given the opportunity. Inexperienced social workers often begin with rather idealized expectations about working with APD clients. Before long, some practitioners become disillusioned when they realize that, despite the client's apparent sincerity, they were being conned. With close supervision and experience, however, practitioners can learn to detect when a client is candid and when a client is manipulating for some other gain (e.g., lighter sentencing, early release).

There are ways to enhance engagement with APD clients, including being realistic with clients about meeting court requirements, being clear about the limits of informed consent and confidentiality (e.g., practitioners must report on treatment progress, lack of compliance with treatment contract, illegal behaviors), reviewing a treatment contract with unambiguous guidelines regarding clients' responsibilities (e.g., showing up on time, following through on tasks), giving clients some flexibility in treatment goals, assessing readiness to change, and advocating for clients' rights when necessary (Rooney & Bibus, 2001). Despite the justified caution, some involuntary APD clients genuinely do want to change and improve their lives (O'Hare, 1996), and practitioners should accord these clients every opportunity to demonstrate their commitment to change.

Clients with APD often have a particularly negative and dysfunctional view of their relationships with others (e.g., the whole world is a battlefield; it's dog eat dog; you've got to take what you can get, any way you can get it). Given the abuse histories of many of these clients (as victims), it may be understandable that they view interpersonal relations in exploitive terms. But even the most hardened criminals know that not everyone is out to harm other people; these characteristics may simply describe the kind of people they are used to spending time with. Practitioners can, at a minimum, challenge these beliefs respectfully to help clients at least consider that there are trustworthy people in the world, that not everyone in the world is out to harm others, and that they may be able to develop more worthwhile, less exploitive relationships in the future.

It may also be helpful for practitioners to associate this distorted thinking and negative view of the world with an increased likelihood of recidivism. Some clients may not be able to imagine positive alternatives. Nevertheless, it is worth trying to help APD clients at least consider positive outcomes while also being realistic about their willingness to make positive changes and engage in more prosocial behaviors.

For court-ordered clients who seem to engage in treatment, self-monitoring can be a useful and concrete way to identify at-risk situations in daily life. "At risk" means situations that increase the likelihood of reoffending, such as reestablishing relationships with old friends, drinking or using illegal drugs, committing a crime, and engaging in violence, among other offenses. For these clients to change, they must become more adept at using foresight to see the at-risk situations ahead of time. Helping APD and impulsive clients see such situations through self-monitoring may forestall relapse in recovery or the committing of another crime.

This deficit in foresight on the part of many APD clients is often accompanied by an unwillingness to accept responsibility for their behavior. For example, a client might say, "I had no intention of using drugs, but they put it right in front of my face. How could I resist? It wasn't my fault." Whereas, with a little planning, the client might have surmised that going to a party with former friends would expose the client to alcohol, drug use, and gambling. Otherwise-impulsive clients can learn self-monitoring, but it takes considerable practice and rehearsal with the social worker, who should focus not only on the potential positive outcomes of avoiding high-risk situations but also on the likelihood of punishment if the client slips. Relapse and reincarceration rates among criminally involved APD clients underscore the challenges social workers face.

But what does the client do if he or she, in fact, encounters a high-risk situation? Having engaged in self-monitoring and identified high-risk circumstances, practitioners can help clients improve their coping skills. For example, social workers can role-play and rehearse with clients some ready excuses for removing themselves from high-risk situations (e.g., I have to go to work; I'm on my way to see my probation officer and I'm late; I've got a doctor's appointment). As clients make more progress, they might reach the point where they can tell the truth (e.g., I'm not staying; I don't feel like going back to prison; I don't drink anymore; I don't use drugs).

Other coping skills that may be of help include stress management and brief meditation to help impulsive clients pause before acting on sudden urges that may put them or other people in jeopardy. Learning not to give in to snap decisions can be especially difficult for APD clients. The use of imagery during meditation can be helpful, such as contrasting images of staying on the outside and avoiding a return to prison.

Antisocial clients are also likely to demonstrate deficits in interpersonal skills. Role-playing and rehearsing how to engage a prospective employer or how to communicate constructively with a potential friend or romantic partner can be challenging. But clients should practice these skills in real-life situations when possible. Including the spouses or family members of people with APD should be considered when possible. Social workers can incorporate skills for working with couples and families as needed. Communication training, problem solving, and enhancing social supports can go a long way to help APD clients establish a behavioral repertoire that goes beyond avoiding high-risk situations to make their lives more rewarding on multiple levels.

However, it is unlikely that therapeutic coping skills methods alone will be sufficient to keep APD clients from relapsing. More comprehensive approaches require the coordinated efforts of a professional team: social workers, psychiatrists, and probation officers all working within a well-run, court-mandated program. The CR and CM approaches are best implemented in the context of a case management model. Implementation of these programs usually involves networking and coordination with mental health, substance abuse, and health and criminal justice professionals, as well as arranging and facilitating the provision of social and instrumental supports.

Because of the difficult and sometimes intractable nature of antisocial, criminal, and psychopathic behavior, programs that include a sound working alliance, coping skills, and CR and CM methods require long-term commitment to be successful. Although controlled trials of such programs have shown promising results for nonviolent drug offenders, well-organized programs are not yet widespread in this country. Case management services are essential to ensure coordination and clear communication among various services, maintenance of benefits to which clients may be entitled, and consistent follow-through by clients enrolled in these programs.

Assessment of Borderline Personality Disorder

People diagnosed with borderline personality disorder (BPD) demonstrate a combination of characteristic behaviors that often include severe mood swings, short-lived psychotic episodes, unpredictable and often impulsive behaviors, suicidal or pseudosuicidal gestures, and other high-risk or dangerous behaviors. Often these problems are worked out in the context of tumultuous relationships in which clients seem to vacillate between emotional extremes of idealizing their partners to demonizing them. Clients diagnosed with BPD are often depressed, and substance abuse should also be considered a co-occurring condition that may exacerbate many cognitive, affective, and behavioral difficulties. Helping people diagnosed with BPD is a challenge given the clients' highly disordered thinking, emotional outbursts, and impulsive and sometimes dangerous behaviors. Although researchers have debated the reliability of the disorder (i.e., the consistency with which trained diagnosticians identify it), interventions that focus on problems related to deficits in regulating extreme emotional outbursts and impulsive behaviors have been shown to be effective.

A thorough MDF assessment is likely to show problems across most domains of psychosocial well-being. Mental status symptoms are likely to include distorted thinking, depression, suicidal thoughts, and anxiety problems, among other difficulties. Impulsivity is often a risk and includes harmful acts directed at oneself or at others. Interpersonal conflict is often evident in both close relationships and problems in the community. Substance abuse frequently co-occurs with BPD, and very depressed clients often show serious deficits in basic self-care. Practitioners should review health problems and refer clients for medical exams, given the higher risk for transmittable diseases associated with unprotected sex and drug abuse, high-risk behaviors that are common among people diagnosed with BPD.

Functional assessment is crucial with clients who manifest symptoms of BPD. Often these clients will go through periods of relative calm, but tracking behavior over time (especially if clients are willing to cooperate by keeping a log or diary early on in treatment) reveals important data on interpersonal or situational antecedents associated with impulsive outbursts, self-mutilation, substance use, or bouts of depression. As with many clients, self-monitoring is a good way to help clients become collaborators in the intervention and intellectualize their problems, a step that might help clients better cope with intense surges of emotion.

Intervention

Cognitive-behavior therapy (CBT), including the variation dialectical behavior therapy (DBT), is currently the psychosocial treatment of choice for BPD (e.g., Davidson et al., 2006; Giesen-Bloo et al., 2006; Linehan, 1993; Linehan et al., 2006; Simpson et al., 1998). The effectiveness of CBT/DBT extends to co-occurring disorders as well. Clients diagnosed with BPD are likely to respond positively to practitioners who provide a mature, nonexploitive, reliable, and empathic working relationship. The relationship can serve as a laboratory to help clients learn to identify dysfunctional thinking, better regulate emotional distress, and learn to engage in more adaptive problem solving. Successful incorporation of coping skills can also lead to a greater ability to regulate intense emotions, control impulsive behaviors, cultivate less conflicted relationships, and lead to a more satisfying life in general.

Practitioners who employ DBT use a range of modified CBT skills to help clients develop more effective ways to deal with dysfunctional thinking, intense feelings, and impulsive behaviors. In that respect, DBT is like other cognitive-behavioral treatments, but the skills are often tested to the extreme when dealing with these troubled and often unpredictable clients. Practitioners who use DBT are also flexible in that they use a flexible range of modalities, sometimes in combination, including individual therapy,

supportive and skills-based group therapies, and sometimes brief hospitalization. Because of the high probability of BPD co-occurring with other
disorders, such as substance abuse or depression, practitioners may use
concurrent interventions (e.g., detoxification, substance abuse counseling,
antidepressant medication). In addition, clients diagnosed with BPD often
find themselves in high-risk circumstances, such as involvement in criminal activities (e.g., dealing drugs) or victimization (e.g., physical or sexual
assault). High-risk and sometimes traumatic events precede clients'
involvement in treatment and often occur during the intervention. Thus,
flexibility and resourcefulness are required of the practitioner who takes
on the challenge of working with BPD clients. Although flexibility may be
the watchword, there are essential skills that have, as a treatment package,
been shown to help people diagnosed with BPD. A brief description of
these skills follows.

Practitioners who choose to work with clients who manifest symptoms
of BPD require considerable confidence in their skills, inner calm when
dealing with clients who express extreme emotions, a clear focus on guiding the intervention plan, well-defined personal boundaries regarding their
responsibility to clients, and a high tolerance for clients who engage in
high-risk behaviors. Clients with BPD have been known to threaten suicide;
to cut, burn, or otherwise mutilate themselves privately or in the presence
of others (including in front of their practitioners on occasion); to engage
in dramatic and attention-seeking behavior that puts them at considerable
risk; and to vacillate between extremes of false self-confidence and protracted periods of self-described helplessness, worthlessness, and depen-
dency. Clients with BPD may go through periods of being hospitalized for
suicide attempts, engaging in illegal behaviors, or making multiple and
frequent phone calls demanding a practitioner's undivided attention. Episodes of screaming rage and childlike crying may occur in the same hour-
long session.

Practitioners should strive to maintain a balance between empathic
attunement to clients' pain and maintaining a matter-of-fact, problem-
oriented approach to helping clients articulate their emotions and improve
daily coping skills. Practitioners should avoid an inclination to be too nurturing. Although generalizations should be made with caution, clients who
present themselves as chronically unable to cope with their emotions or
take responsibility for their day-to-day behavior are likely to become less
functional when practitioners reinforce their sense of helplessness or feeling that they are out of control. However, if clients express strong suicidal
ideation, practitioners should err on the side of caution and intervene as

needed despite that such ideation is often a false alarm and is not followed up by genuine suicide attempts.

Cognitive-behavior therapy (CBT) skills have been shown to adapt readily to the struggles of clients diagnosed with BPD and can be used to address the often extreme distress such clients experience in their thinking, dealing with emotions, and problem behaviors. However, Linehan and colleagues (Linehan, 1993; Linehan et al., 2006) have adapted CBT skills specifically for BPD clients. Clients diagnosed with BPD need help identifying dysfunctional thinking, challenging such thoughts, and understanding how the thoughts are linked to extreme emotions and emotionally upsetting situations. Such clients often have highly distorted thinking that provokes or is activated in response to extreme emotions. Extreme and distorted kinds of thinking can range widely: "I am worthless and deserve to die," "I want to kill my boyfriend," "I am evil and need to be punished severely," to "I am a genius, so I can't learn anything from therapists," "No one can possibly understand me," "I am clairvoyant," and so on. Although some distortions of the BPD client might sound delusional, the beliefs are often ephemeral and come and go in response to external stresses or perceived threats to self-worth. True delusions, as in clients diagnosed with severe mental illnesses, tend to be more consistent and accompanied by other serious symptoms (e.g., hallucinations, social withdrawal).

Clients dealing with dysfunctional thoughts initially require some standard Socratic questioning, as when using CBT with a depressed client. If a client diagnosed with BPD reports that she feels overwhelmed with shame and rage and can barely control her behavior when she sees a former abusive boyfriend at work, a close examination of automatic negative thoughts might identify a core problem. For example, if the client says: "When I see him, I get really embarrassed. I know he's been talking about me to everyone, telling them lies. I wish I could kill him. I'd like to see him burned alive for what he did to me." Of course, after establishing that the client is just feeling this way and has no intention of actually harming him (or having someone else do it for her), these thoughts need to be isolated, identified, and explored to determine their level of reasonableness. Helping the client cognitively examine the situation can help her identify those feelings, bring them into some perspective, and help her gain some inner sense of calm and control.

The practitioner might empathize with the client about how difficult it must be to feel this intensely when she sees her ex-boyfriend at work but suggest: "Let's see if we can work together to help you learn how to cope with these upsetting feelings so you are not feeling so overwhelmed." The practitioner might guide the client in analyzing the details of what she experiences and feels when she sees her ex-boyfriend. Consider the following illustration:

PRACTITIONER: What is the first thought that comes to mind when you see him walk through your work area at the office?

CLIENT: I feel humiliated, and I want to run away.

PRACTITIONER: It must be terrible to feel that kind of embarrassment, but I really want you to tell me what you are thinking when you see him. What is going through your mind?

CLIENT: Well, I guess what I am thinking when I see him is that he's probably telling everyone about our sex life, and how we did drugs together. I know he wouldn't be saying nice things about me. He hates me. I think people are laughing at me behind my back. It's so humiliating.

PRACTITIONER: So you are concerned that he is presenting you in a bad light to other people and discussing personal things, stuff you may not feel too good about?

CLIENT: Yeah, that's about it, I guess.

PRACTITIONER: So, what is the worst thing that he might say about you?

CLIENT: You know, what guys say, that I'm a slut, a crack whore.

PRACTITIONER: It sounds to me that you think everyone will believe him. I thought you told me he had been suspended for being drunk on the job a couple of months back. What makes you think everyone will believe him if he says awful things about you?

CLIENT: I guess I just assume that people will believe him, that they will think the worst of me.

The ensuing conversation then stimulates a broader discussion about why she has such a low opinion of herself and how her lack of self-confidence and self-worth affects her behavior in relationships. By identifying and discussing her automatic negative thoughts about herself, the client might also begin to challenge her extreme negative self-statements. It may also help her to understand and cope with the intense feelings that are provoked by similar situations.

However, disconfirming the client's low opinion of herself will take more time. Clients struggling to control more extreme emotions need coping skills to help deal with those feelings in the present, regardless of whether they can change negative thinking in the short run. Borrowing from Zen philosophy, Linehan and colleagues teach core mindfulness skills to help clients reduce overreactions to emotionally provocative situations.

Core mindfulness skills focus on helping clients "take perspective," that is, step back and observe themselves in the moment with some psychological distance, reflect on the provocative situation calmly, and fully experience the here and now of events. The practitioner might suggest, "When you see your ex-boyfriend, you feel intense shame and rage, and have a hard time keeping your cool. Next time you see him at work, I want you to try this: pretend that you are in a play; I want you to watch what is happening to yourself. Take notes after the incident. Write down what you were think-ing, feeling, doing, and, generally, what is going on around you. In this way, you can see yourself in the situation, and not let the situation control you. Do you think you can try that?"

No doubt, for clients having a tough time keeping a grip on intense feelings, such a task would be a challenge. Practitioners might suggest rehearsing the scenario in the session. After having clients share some details about similar situations that have happened, role-playing the scene with clients can be a helpful way to prepare them to deal with similar circumstances. As troubling thoughts and feelings (and possibly behaviors) emerge during role-playing, practitioners can ask clients to note them, stop role-playing, and explore exactly what is going on cognitively and emotion-ally. In this way, role-playing can prepare clients to stay calm during the next encounter. Being able to "survive" the next encounter without suc-cumbing to an emotional meltdown can boost the sense of self-confidence of the client in the example and yield a feeling that she can control her feelings instead of having them control her.

Practicing and achieving core mindfulness can be hard work. Clients diagnosed with BPD often engage in dysfunctional or even self-destructive behaviors (e.g., cutting, drug abuse) to avoid having to deal with distressful emotions. The DBT practitioner teaches distress tolerance skills to help clients learn how to accept emotional distress as a part of life. Emotion regulation skills help clients be more in command of their emotions. These skills include accurately identifying feelings and determining what pur-pose a particular emotion serves. Practitioners can help clients reduce their vulnerability to what Linehan refers to as the emotion mind through prob-lem solving, taking action to increase positive emotional events, taking a paradoxical stance by acting in ways that are contrary to an emotion evoked in a situation (e.g., being polite and civil to someone who is sarcas-tic at your expense), and increasing awareness and acceptance of one's emotions. Clients diagnosed with BPD (or any client trying to better regu-late emotional distress) need to learn that experiencing strong emotions is not a calamity, but simply an uncomfortable experience that can be reme-died through calm reflection, taking action to ameliorate the situation, and engaging in activities (e.g., talking to a friend, going for a walk) that provide comfort and relief from the slings and arrows of everyday life. Clients are encouraged to stop overreacting, to not make the situation worse, to take a deep breath, to experience the intense feelings but let them pass, to seek solace and relief in concrete ways, and to keep focusing on long-term solutions.

Many problems experienced by clients diagnosed with BPD concern the distress they experience within the context of relationships—with parents, siblings, children, friends, lovers, coworkers, and neighbors. Thus, to help clients learn to clarify their thinking and better regulate their emotional reactions, they must develop behavioral skills to diffuse and prevent small incidents from turning into major conflagrations. This can be achieved through modeling, role-playing, rehearsing, and practicing interpersonal effectiveness skills. Learning to cope better in interpersonal and other social situations requires learning better communication skills and assertiveness skills. Essential components of these approaches include teaching clients how (1) to actually listen to what another person is saying, (2) to communicate thoughts and feelings clearly and calmly to the other party, (3) to take action as needed, and (4) to follow through on their intentions.

There may be no better way for practitioners to teach good listening skills than to model them for clients. Good listening is a cultivated and practiced skill. Even experienced practitioners get distracted and lose focus now and then while a client is speaking. Practitioners can also role-play an upsetting scenario with a client and instruct the client to pay attention to what is being said and to not allow emotional distress to distract him or her from careful listening. After the brief interchange, practitioners can ask, "What was it that I was trying to say to you? Were you really listening to me, or were you thinking about something else, like, what to say next?" Role-playing in this way can help clients prepare for an upsetting encounter or emotionally evocative situation. Practitioners can suggest that clients write down their reflections in a diary after the actual encounter to integrate their practice of core mindfulness. Through success experiences in everyday life, clients' self-confidence will increase along with their long-term ability to achieve self-control over emotional and behavioral responses.

Self-regulation skills include improving problem-solving skills (i.e., brainstorming, coming up with solutions, experimenting, evaluating), using self-reinforcement methods (e.g., rewarding oneself for achieving goals), and learning to cope with minor setbacks and relapses without becoming overly despondent (e.g., a mistake is not the end of the world).

Reminding clients to avoid "catastrophizing" and to view problems as temporary setbacks can be reassuring for clients who tend to see things in extremes of success versus failure rather than their efforts as a work in progress.

Over time, as clients diagnosed with BPD begin to feel more confident as a result of some successes, practitioners can help them formulate an overall long-term plan to maintain their gains. Good health habits, maintaining positive relationships, moderating or abstaining from alcohol and other drugs, and maintaining financial stability can help avoid crises and maintain long-term satisfaction in life. Practitioners should also reassure clients that seeking help in the future during times of stress is a sign of strength and good judgment, not weakness or failure.

The coordinated efforts of case management can also help clients diagnosed with BPD or those who demonstrate similar problems. Given the nature of these clients' difficulties with emotional regulation and impulse control, crises do occur, and many clients exhibit co-occurring problems and disorders. Practitioners should be prepared to access and coordinate a range of services as needed, including psychiatric emergency rooms, detoxification facilities, and other treatment services. Clients with BPD who also struggle to maintain stability in the community may also need help with additional social and instrumental supports.

Summary of Essential Skills for Substance Abuse and Personality Disorders

There is a range of common essential supportive, coping, and case management skills that, when offered in optimal combinations, can provide effective care for clients with substance use and personality disorders, conditions that often co-occur. Although many clients are also considered resistant or difficult to treat, they provide a potentially gratifying challenge for the practitioner who has strong personal boundaries, a deep reservoir of empathy, and a strong commitment to help people lead more useful and satisfying lives. Variations of cognitive-behavioral coping skills implemented in a well-coordinated case management framework have been shown to be the most promising approaches for many clients.

Case Study: Nikki

Nikki is a nineteen-year-old white woman recently referred to an outpatient mental health clinic after having been admitted involuntarily (via the hospital's emergency room) to an inpatient psychiatric facility for two weeks.

She had been found unconscious on the street by police responding to an anonymous phone call. They found her on the sidewalk in front of an abandoned building in the industrial end of the city. Apparently, Nikki was highly intoxicated on alcohol and had other drugs, including hallucinogens, amphetamines, and marijuana, in her bloodstream. After a few days of detoxification in the inpatient unit, she became forthcoming about her difficulties over the past few years.

The Comprehensive Service Plan
(Assessment, Intervention, Evaluation)

Use all available information from the client and significant others, your observations, and input from other professionals to conduct both quantitative and qualitative aspects of this multidimensional-functional assessment.

Client identification data: (gender, age, marital status, sexual orientation; family composition; employment; racial, ethnic, cultural, religious/spiritual affiliation and identity)

Nikki is a nineteen-year-old white single female. Aside from occasional contact with her estranged mother, she has no other family. She has never obtained regular employment, and she claims to be a member of a satanic group (she maintains that it is not a cult). She was not raised in any formal religious denomination, and is of mixed Northern European ancestry.

The presenting problem
Description of problem (client's view)

Nikki maintains that, aside from being down once in a while, she doesn't really have any problems. She feels that she was "having a bad day" when the police found her, and that she does not need psychological or psychiatric care. She feels that she needs to recommit to her satanic beliefs and perhaps be more careful about the amount of drugs she uses.

Description of problem (practitioner's view)

This practitioner believes that Nikki has had a long-standing problem with depression, very poor self-esteem, has engaged in much self-loathing, and appears to engage in many high-risk behaviors, including self-mutilation, high-risk sexual behaviors, and uncontrolled drug abuse. The social network with which she associates is, to different degrees, engaged in criminal behavior, and she has been sexually assaulted on numerous occasions. She also appears to maintain a range of implausible beliefs—notwithstanding the fact that she claims they are religious in nature, she also claims to be able to foretell the future, read people's minds, and sometimes control other's behavior through the intercession of Satan. Thus, Nikki maintains a number of implausible and dysfunctional beliefs, has extreme difficulties maintaining her mood and regulating her emotions, engages in a number of high-risk behaviors that are potentially harmful to her (in addition to direct self-mutilation), and has very poor interpersonal relationships, often with people who are clearly exploiting her. She has no employment history, educational deficits, and no social supports.

Psychosocial history with an emphasis on problem trajectory

Nikki reports that since she dropped out of her junior year of high school, she had been living on the street with a "group of people like me." Apparently, the group is reported to be a self-styled group of satanists who practice black masses and similar rituals. Their "meetings" usually involve getting together in known abandoned buildings on the outskirts of the city, using large amounts of alcohol, drugs, and "anything else we feel like using," engaging in various anti-God rituals, and having indiscriminate sex. On describing these events, it soon became apparent that some of the sexual encounters amounted to sexual assault. Nikki reports that the members often pool their money to survive, and members engage in a variety of part-time occupations, some legal and some not. Illegal activities include sales of drugs, prostitution, and doing errands for local criminal gangs. Nikki claims that she attempted suicide because she felt that she no longer wanted to belong to this group, and there did not seem to be any other option for escaping.

Nikki was raised by both of her parents until she was about twelve years old. The parents considered themselves members of a group of self-described "pagan witches." Her father worked odd jobs, was a heavy drinker, used drugs, and was often verbally abusive to Nikki. He and her mother, who claimed to be a pagan faith healer and expert in reading Tarot, would often have sex in the home without making any effort to be private in the encounters. Often, other friends and associates of theirs would participate in group sexual encounters. Nikki often witnessed these, and when she was eleven, she was raped by one of the male participants, an acquaintance of her father. This act was, apparently, beyond the mother's tolerance, and she told her husband, Ted, to leave or she would call the police and report the rape. He left and has not been heard from since.

Nikki and her mother continued in a rather tumultuous relationship. Nikki reported having little or no limits. Her mother continued to have friends and lovers in the house, though she was more discrete about her relationships and sexual activities after Ted was gone. Nikki began using alcohol and marijuana at age twelve, began missing school, and somehow remained enrolled in classes until she was sixteen. She dropped out of school after the first week of her junior year.

After dropping out of school, her mother told her she could no longer live with her, and Nikki joined a group of acquaintances who lived primarily on the streets of the nearby city. Homeless youths in that locale have been caught sleeping in some of the local abandoned buildings and are suspected of being responsible for a number of crimes. Youth workers have identified a number of them as heavy drug users, peripherally involved with some criminal gangs, and are known to be at a higher risk of contracting sexually transmitted diseases. Nikki was diagnosed with a sexually transmitted disease but tested negative for the AIDS virus.

Although she has had various tattoos for three years now and has adorned herself with metal objects (pierced tongue, ears, eyebrows, and other body parts), over the past year she has taken to using an arts-and-crafts razor to carve satanic designs in her skin. She claims that one particular design has to be recarved weekly to "keep it fresh for Satan, my lover." She believes that through this bodily portal, she receives his strength. Thus, the place where she maintains the design is particularly mutilated. She claims that when the police found her, she had slit her wrist, not really meaning to do it, but felt hopeless and that even Satan had abandoned her.

Attempts to resolve the problems, previous treatment and relevant outcomes

Nikki, despite her problems, has managed to survive for three years on the street, occasionally in homeless shelters, has contacted the homeless youth workers, has managed somehow to obtain temporary, legal work (usually off the books), and is (despite her high-risk behaviors) in good health overall. She has never had formal treatment to quell her high-risk behaviors, possible mood disorder, or substance abuse.

The individual assessment

Mental status, cognitive disturbances: Describe the client's level of hallucinations, delusions, disorientation, bizarre behavior or speech, memory problems, serious confusion, or other symptoms of serious cognitive impairment. Include other troubling or dysfunctional beliefs or convictions.

Although the client manifests no clear thought disorders on the level of hallucinations, at a minimum, she may entertain some delusional beliefs about her abilities to predict the future, read people's minds, and effect their behaviors through mind control (with the "devil's help"). However, since people of various other religions claim as much, a conservative view would suggest that the client maintains some odd or implausible beliefs. Despite these, apparently, grandiose ideas, she does seem to have a very low opinion of herself and routinely puts herself in circumstances where she is likely to encounter risk of harm. She expresses some degree of hopelessness about her situation and is not particularly oriented toward the future (e.g., she does not discuss plans beyond daily survival).

How would you rate the client's overall mental status during the past month?

POOR [0]   IMPAIRED [1]   MARGINAL [2]   GOOD [3]   EXCELLENT [4]

Mental status, emotional distress: Describe the client's level of depression, anxiety, and overall ability to regulate emotions.

Client appears to be extremely depressed, although Nikki maintains that she is usually OK. Her affect is almost flat; she expresses extreme pessimism about herself, the world, her own future; and she reports little pleasure in life aside from drug-related experiences. It is hard, because of her lifestyle, to get a baseline on her sleep and eating habits since they are so irregular anyway. She does report angry outbursts, occasional physical fights, and she expresses an enormous amount of rage toward her parents, other people she keeps company with on the street, and society in general. Her mood swings are likely to be related to her drug use, but it is hard to determine at this point what her moods are generally like since she has had only two weeks of sobriety since detoxification.

How would you rate your client's emotional well-being over the past 30 days?

POOR [0]   IMPAIRED [1]   MARGINAL [2]   GOOD [3]   EXCELLENT [4]

Behavioral problems: Describe the client's overall ability to regulate behavior. Consider things such as ability to express oneself effectively; ability to work at things patiently; and tendencies to verbally or physically lash out at others, run away, harm oneself, or to engage in impulsive, criminal, or substance-abusing behavior. How would you describe the client's overall impulse control?

Nikki's high-risk behaviors and impulsivity in general are a major concern. She appears to manifest little judgment or concern about the risks associated with the people with whom she consorts, sexual behaviors, and her drug use. Her emotional outbursts have often been associated with fighting, though she tends to describe these incidents as primarily justified by self-defense.

How would you rate your client's behavioral control generally over the past 30 days?

POOR [0]   IMPAIRED [1]   MARGINAL [2]   GOOD [3]   EXCELLENT [4]

Adaptive strengths and coping abilities. Describe the client's ability to cope with problems and everyday stressors. How would you describe the client's ability to assess problem situations, deal with triggers, cope with stress, solve problems, and perhaps reach out to others for help to deal effectively with difficulties?

As noted earlier, Nikki does demonstrate quite a bit of resourcefulness and street smarts. She has survived on the streets with little external financial support for about three years. She is articulate and has written some interesting poetry, although the subject matter is disturbing. She has published two pieces in the local newspaper published for and by homeless people.

How would you rate your client's overall adaptive strengths and coping abilities over the past 30 days?

POOR [0]   IMPAIRED [1]   MARGINAL [2]   GOOD [3]   EXCELLENT [4]

Health problems: Describe the client's overall health. Aside from normal, transient illnesses, think about the client's general health habits (e.g., smoking, heavy drinking, exercise, weight), chronic primary health disorders, the client's opinion of his or her own health, ability to engage in usual

activities relatively free from discomfort, overall energy level, hospitalizations, and treatments for illness other than psychiatric ones. Consider the
client's documented medical history and any ongoing treatments.

Aside from her diagnosed STD (now being treated), her being somewhat
malnourished, and some superficial wounds, the client is in relatively good
health. Long-term concerns include that she may continue to use illicit
substances and that she has smoked cigarettes since she was fifteen years
old.

How would you rate your client's health over the past 30 days?

POOR [0]   **IMPAIRED** [1]   **MARGINAL** [2]   **GOOD** [3]   **EXCELLENT** [4]

Use of alcohol and other drugs: Describe the client's use of alcohol, illicit
substances (e.g., cocaine, heroin, marijuana, hallucinogens) and abuse of
prescription medication. How often does the client use them, in what quantity, and how serious are the psychological, physical, or social consequences associated with use?

As best as can be determined, at this point, the client has been a regular
user of alcohol since she was thirteen years old and began using marijuana
about that time as well. In more recent years she has also used hallucinogenic drugs including psilocybin, mescaline, and a variety of MDMA-type
drugs, which also typically include amphetamines. Although she has also
used crack cocaine in the past year or so, she has never injected drugs, has
never used narcotics (e.g., heroin), and has never abused pharmaceuticals
claiming that the drug companies are not to be trusted in any way. Much
of the use of hallucinogens appears to be associated with the "satanic"
rituals she engages with her associates, but her usual (often daily) drugs of
abuse seem to be alcohol (inexpensive vodka or wine) and marijuana.
When the police found her unconscious, she was intoxicated, primarily by
alcohol and marijuana. When she was detoxified during hospitalization
there was no evidence of delirium tremens, and she was not sedated during
that time.

How would you rate the client's functioning in the past month with regard
to substance use?

POOR [0]   **IMPAIRED** [1]   **MARGINAL** [2]   **GOOD** [3]   **EXCELLENT** [4]

Recreational activities: Consider what the client does for fun (alone or with others), hobbies, relaxation (reading, watching television, playing video games or cards) and physical exercise (e.g., walking, jogging, biking). How would you describe the client's overall involvement in positive recreational activities?

Other than occasional television watching, the client reports few recreational activities. Although she has occasionally written and published poems as noted earlier, she spends most of her daily activities procuring small amounts of money and looking for supplies of food, alcohol, and places to spend the night.

How would you rate the adequacy of the client's participation in healthy recreational activities over the past 30 days?

POOR [0]   **IMPAIRED [1]**   **MARGINAL [2]**   **GOOD [3]**   **EXCELLENT [4]**

Material resources: Describe your client's current or (if institutionalized) most recent living situation overall. Consider such things as adequacy of food, clothing, shelter, and safety.

Although the client has managed to survive on the streets, in a conventional sense, her access to material resources is quite impaired.

How would you rate the overall adequacy of the client's material resources over the past month?

POOR [0]   **IMPAIRED [1]**   **MARGINAL [2]**   **GOOD [3]**   **EXCELLENT [4]**

Independent living/self-care: Describe how well the client manages the household; takes care of personal hygiene; and eats, sleeps, and otherwise cares for his or her own basic needs.

Similar to previous comment—client is surviving minimally.

How would you rate the client's ability to live independently and take care of their basic needs over the past 30 days?

POOR [0]   **IMPAIRED [1]**   **MARGINAL [2]**   **GOOD [3]**   **EXCELLENT [4]**

Work (role) satisfaction: Describe the client's current work-related or other important role-related activities (e.g., work, student, home, volunteer, retired, disabled). Describe the activities and responsibilities that occupy the client in a productive manner.

Other than surviving, the client has serious educational deficits and has little record of employment. Other than surviving on the streets, she has embraced little by way of a productive role.

How would you rate the client's work or role satisfaction over the past 30 days?

POOR [0]   IMPAIRED [1]   MARGINAL [2]   GOOD [3]   EXCELLENT [4]

Legal problems: Describe any legal problems the client has had or continues to have. These include minor infractions (e.g., public drunkenness, shoplifting, minor traffic violations, public disturbances) and more serious crimes (e.g., assault and battery, rape, burglary, driving under the influence). Consider the client's status (e.g., probation, awaiting imprisonment, parole). Also, consider any civil suits leveled at the client or pending financial judgments. Overall, how would you describe the client's current legal situation?

Despite her activities, the client has no outstanding legal charges or judgments against her. She has never been charged with a crime. Although confronted by the police on a number of occasions, they have only referred her to the homeless shelters and encouraged her to seek mental health or substance abuse treatment.

How would you rate the client's legal situation over the past 30 days?

POOR [0]   IMPAIRED [1]   MARGINAL [2]   GOOD [3]   EXCELLENT [4]

DSM-IV Diagnosis

Axis I   304.80 Poly-substance related Disorder
           300.4 Dysthymic Disorder

Axis II   301.83 Borderline Personality Disorder

Family and social assessment

Family relations: Describe the client's current family structure including authority, hierarchy, alliances, roles, rules, boundaries, subsystems (e.g., couple, siblings, parent-child alliances), and patterns of interactions and quality of communications. Describe specific problems in the family; describe specific adaptive strengths in the family. How does the family describe their own racial, ethnic, cultural, and religious identities?

Although she has had occasional phone conversations with her mother, Nikki has seen little of her over the past two years. Her mother did visit her in the hospital during the two weeks she was an inpatient. They tentatively agreed to meet, perhaps during outpatient sessions. Other than this connection, Nikki has no family relations to speak of.

> How would you rate the quality of the client's immediate family relationships over the past 30 days?
>
> **POOR [0]   IMPAIRED [1]   MARGINAL [2]   GOOD [3]   EXCELLENT [4]**

Immediate social relationships (close friends and acquaintances): Describe the quality of the client's relationships with friends and acquaintances. Over the past month, how would you describe the quality of the interaction overall between the client and others with respect to closeness, intimacy, general interpersonal satisfaction, effective communications, degree of conflict, level of hostility, aggression, and evidence of any emotional or physical abuse?

Despite the risky and dysfunctional nature of her peer group, they are the only social supports that she has, and they do provide some level of companionship and material support. Although these would not generally be considered "healthy" associations, in light of the lack of any other supports, they do assist her in daily survival.

> How would you rate the quality of the client's immediate social relationships over the past 30 days?
>
> **POOR [0]   IMPAIRED [1]   MARGINAL [2]   GOOD [3]   EXCELLENT [4]**

Extended social relationships: Describe the type and quality of relationships between the client and others in the client's community (other than close friends and family). These people might include other families, law enforcement, human service agencies, school personnel, coworkers, and others from whom the client receives support or with whom the client is having serious conflict.

The police, workers in the homeless shelters, members of voluntary organizations, and a variety of other informal contacts in the community (some store owners, restaurant workers) have provided a tangible level of social and material support for Nikki. She seems to know a lot of people and they appear to be motivated by goodwill.

How would you rate the quality of the client's social relationships over the past 30 days?

POOR [0]　　IMPAIRED [1]　　MARGINAL [2]　　GOOD [3]　　EXCELLENT [4]

A concise summary of the MDF assessment: Highlight the client's areas of distress and adaptive strengths. Emphasize those areas that are most likely to be emphasized in the intervention plan.

Nikki is a homeless, drug-dependent, depressed, and otherwise interpersonally impoverished young woman who engages in a range of behaviors that carry a high risk of self-harm. Her views of herself, others, and the future are quite negative and pessimistic. She appears to be chronically depressed and chronically abuses drugs, engages in self-mutilation, and has maintained only marginal relationships with people also addicted to drugs. She maintains some unusual beliefs associated with an unconventional type of religion but otherwise demonstrates no clear mental illness. Her lack of long-term family nurturance, healthful role modeling, and normative disciplining appear to have left her interpersonally and emotionally impoverished. Although she has developed some impressive survival skills, she is likely to deteriorate on the streets in coming years without psychological interventions and long-term social and material rehabilitative supports.

Recommendations for further focused assessment: Note recommended referrals to consultants or additional instruments to be used.

More intensive substance use assessment and psychiatric assessment for possible medication.

THE COMPREHENSIVE SERVICE PLAN SUMMARY

Assessment/Problems	Goals	Objectives	Interventions	Evaluation plan
(Briefly describe key problems to be addressed.)	(State desired outcome for each problem.)	(Describe specific stepping-stones toward each goal. Update as client progresses.)	(Describe specific interventions to be used.)	(Describe indexes to be used for tracking progress.)
Severe, chronic depression and suicidal ideation	Reduce depression and suicidal ideation to minimal levels	Begin examining cognitions regarding sense of hopelessness about herself and her situation; have her self-monitor weekly	*Supportive skills:* Develop collaborative working relationship with client and focus on initial motivation; acknowledge initial distrust, suspicion	Monitor and report level of hopelessness weekly: 0 = "hopeless" to 10 = "very optimistic."
Hopelessness, negative appraisal of self/others	Improve self-image			Have her note any occasion of self-mutilation and her cognitions, mood, and circumstances prior to it
Difficulties regulating emotions, impulsivity, self-mutilation, and other impulsive behaviors	Develop better controls over emotional regulation and impulsive behaviors	Begin to identify emotional responses and link to negative thoughts and problem behaviors; monitor as above	*Therapeutic coping skills:* Examine and review client's negative beliefs about self; explore nature of relationships with others (including effects of family upbringing); later, explore and challenge unusual religious convictions and beliefs in paranormal powers	Have her self-report type, frequency, and quantity of drug abuse and antecedent mood or events
Drug abuse	Reduce/eliminate abuse of alcohol and other drugs	Identify triggers that potentiate relapse		
Lack of meaningful interpersonal relationships, including estrangement from her mother (only available family member)	Examine potential for more satisfying relationships/ explore potential for reconciliation with mother	Examine nature of relationships; identify best recent mutually supportive relationship; consider scheduling a meeting with her mother at a future date to discuss tentative relationship	Help client identify disturbing thoughts and upsetting feelings; help client learn to accept and tolerate distress without responding impulsively	
Educational and employment deficits and related lack of instrumental supports	Assess employment potential and completing high school equivalency	Consider residence in halfway house for at least six months; participate in skills review for possible part-time employment	(including both self-harming behaviors and responding by using alcohol and other drugs)	
			Teach basic stress management (e.g., breathing, meditation) to cope with stress, emotional distress, and upset	

THE COMPREHENSIVE SERVICE PLAN SUMMARY (Continued)

Assessment/Problems	Goals	Objectives	Interventions	Evaluation plan
(Briefly describe key problems to be addressed.)	(State desired outcome for each problem.)	(Describe specific stepping-stones toward each goal. Update as client progresses.)	(Describe specific interventions to be used.)	(Describe indexes to be used for tracking progress.)
			Role model and practice drug-refusal skills	
			Coach in conversational and other interpersonal skills that she may practice during her stay in halfway house residence	
			Coach conversations in sessions with mother (later in treatment) focused on potential reconciliation	
			Case management skills: Facilitate psychiatric referral and follow-up as needed	
			Review social supports and link client to mutual help groups	
			Review potential instrumental supports and other available financial benefits	
			Explore opportunities to complete high school degree equivalency, and/or obtain skills training or supported employment	

CHAPTER TEN

Couples in Conflict

ONE WOULD BE HARD PRESSED to find a committed couple that does not experience some degree of conflict and relationship distress. Partners who are very much in love will disagree about matters covering a wide range of topics: how to raise their children, how to spend their money, how to balance domestic responsibilities, what types of relationships each partner can have outside the marriage, how to best cope with in-laws and other relatives, where to go on vacation, and so on. The difference between marriages that fail and marriages that thrive is reflected in the research findings on good marriages: partners who maintain long-standing and loving relationships treat each other with respect, are willing to compromise, and are effective communicators and problem solvers; that is, they reconcile differences constructively and without harming each other. All couples have problems, but those who stay together happily cope with them more effectively.

Social workers should be mindful of the fact that much of what is now considered a "good" marriage in modern America is tied somewhat to the idea of the egalitarian relationship. Although many heterosexual and same-sex couples willingly embrace the idea of equality and power sharing in marriage and relationships, couples from some religious and cultural traditions may adhere to more circumscribed roles. Thus, before applying the essential skills of assessment and intervention with a couple, the social worker should first ask the couple about their beliefs and expectations of a "good" marriage. In addition, most families in the United States do not have two adult parents or guardians in the home. The conventional nuclear family is now a statistical minority (Collins, Jordan, & Coleman, 2007). Social workers should be open to a broader definition of what constitutes the family unit and work with available adults, whether partners living together, relatives from different generations, other family members, and so forth. Family assessments based on conventional views of the family are less relevant than they were a few decades ago.

Couples' conflicts are sometimes associated with a wide range of problems, many of them potentially quite serious. These problems include domestic violence, child abuse and neglect, substance abuse, isolation from the wider community (e.g., neighbors, schools), and other co-occurring disorders, such as anxiety, depression, and other forms of mental illness. Couples' conflicts can have short- and long-term effects on children: poor modeling for conflict resolution; feelings of shame, anger, or guilt; and a negative outlook on developing committed relationships. Thus, assessment and intervention with couples can provide a solid foundation for additional work with children and their families. Chapters 11 and 12 address interventions applied in the context of family therapy.

Assessment

It is helpful to conceptualize couples' problems in terms of both content and process. Clearly identifying what couples are conflicted about and how they attempt to cope (e.g., communication patterns) provides two important avenues for completing the assessment and developing the intervention plan. As with an individual assessment, it is important to assess couples across multiple domains. The social worker should begin by simply asking the couple to take turns describing what each person believes is the problem from his or her point of view. However, relying exclusively on what each partner presents in an unstructured narrative will result in an inadequate assessment for at least these three reasons: (1) the couple may not be aware of how one problem in their relationship affects another (e.g., problems causing emotional or behavioral problems in their children; effects of depression or substance abuse on the other partner), (2) they may not be aware of how problems with their children may strain the marriage as well (e.g., differences in child-rearing practices rooted in personal history or cultural differences), and (3) they may have reason to lie to cover up embarrassing or even criminal behavior (e.g., child abuse, illicit drug use). Thus, a multidimensional assessment of both the couple and each individual client is necessary.

As noted earlier, couples tend to engage in conflict for several common concerns: relationship commitment and sex, personal finances, child rearing, relationships with extended families, and sharing household responsibilities. Certainly there are others. It is important to allow each partner to explain, from his or her point of view, the problem. Listening carefully, patiently, and respectfully provides effective modeling for the other partner (who should be discouraged from interrupting). It demonstrates to each partner, in turn, how to listen attentively, to acknowledge that the message is understood, and to accept what his or her partner is saying (even in disagreement) in both content and feeling. The other partner does the same to hear the other person's explanation and view of the problem. The act of each partner saying what he or she feels as the other person listens can be a compelling experience for both—and it may be the first time in weeks or months that the couple has respectfully listened to each other. Such an experience can set a new tone, a feeling of starting fresh, for further discussion.

After both partners have had a chance to explain their side, the practitioner should explore the experience further: "Frank, what were you thinking and feeling as you listened to Sharon tell her side of the story?" And, then, offer the other person the same opportunity. Again, this experience provides the couple with another chance to engage in active listening as each partner responds. At this point, the partner who is listening may interrupt since the other partner is reacting, perhaps emotionally, to what is being said. Again, the practitioner should gently discourage the partner from reacting and ask him or her to listen quietly. Orchestrating an experience in which couples have to contain their emotional responses while listening to a partner can be a rewarding experience—one that reinforces the belief that they can discuss emotionally upsetting things with each other without the discussion erupting into a destructive quarrel. Planned exchanges during the office visit must be planned for and repeated at home during the week at mutually convenient and relaxing times. The couple should agree to a particular topic they want to discuss with the practitioner, preferably starting from the bottom of the problem hierarchy (i.e., easy problems first, then gradual work toward the tougher ones). But the couple must commit to respectful listening without interruption, and accept that, even if they cannot resolve the issue at hand, they can agree to disagree for the time being. This process might take a few weeks of practice, but it lays the foundation for a successful intervention with a couple.

Although this listening exercise might sound more like an active part of an intervention, it is an essential part of the assessment as well. The practitioner has the opportunity to observe closely how each partner acts in the presence of the other: what each person says and how, facial expressions, body language, and other behaviors. These behaviors can indicate how the couple behaves at home and, especially, how they treat each other.

This process analysis is often at least as important as the actual content of the complaints that the couple presents.

Once the partners are able to speak and listen to each other successfully without interruption, the assessment can continue. Practitioners should explore the details of their complaints in depth, again, giving each partner the chance to explain his or her side without interruption. An exhaustive list of problems and questions would fill a large volume, but following are a few examples:

- *Intimacy and commitment*: Do you spend time together? What do you like to do with each other? Do you both enjoy those activities together? Do you actively make plans to spend time together? Do you avoid spending time together? Are you affectionate with each other? How do you express your affection for each other? What kind of personal friendships or other relationships do you maintain outside your marriage? Are any of them exclusive to one of you or the other? Are you both OK with those relationships? Do you share any friends in common?
- *Extended family:* Whose family do you see around the holidays? How did you come to that arrangement? How do you get along with each other's family members? Do any family members visit your home? How long do they usually stay? Are there any financial ties or obligations with any extended family members? Are there any conflicts with each other's family that cause either of you distress?
- *Work and home finances*: Do you both work outside the home? How many hours per week do you work, including your commuting time? Are your jobs stressful? How does your work affect your mood when you are at home? Who pays the bills? Do you share responsibilities for paying the bills? Do you have separate checkbooks or credit cards? Do you maintain separate budgets? How is that working out? Do you fight about money? Are you having financial problems, such as excessive debt? Have you ever declared bankruptcy or had collection agencies come after you for unpaid obligations? Have you ever worked on a budget together? Do you discuss major purchases together?
- *Parenting*: Do you have a shared parenting philosophy, or do you often disagree about how you reward or discipline your children? What day-to-day expectations do you have of your children regarding their behavior and responsibilities in the home, school performance, social activities? What do you do when your children do not

meet those expectations or disobey you? How much fun time do you spend with your kids playing, reading, watching movies, and so forth? Do you do this together as parents or do you take turns depending on your schedule? What activities do your kids enjoy the most with you? Do these occasions often end in conflict? How does that come about usually?

- *Household obligations:* What routine chores need to be done around the house? Do you share in some or all of these activities or delegate different jobs to each other? Do either of you feel that the distribution of domestic duties is unfair, given the amount that you work outside the home? Do your children participate in routine household duties? How does that work out?

Questions such as these make good openers for matter-of-fact discussions about the mundane aspects of everyday life. Asking only one or two questions can often reveal conflict in other areas as well. Again, discussing the content of these problems is important to understand the type and severity of the couple's difficulties, but it is equally important to observe their communication style, emotion, and body language as they discuss these matters. The level of affect (e.g., anger, distress, anxiety, sadness) and body language expressed during the discussions can often re-create the couple's distressing experiences quite realistically. With minimal coaching (and occasional refereeing) practitioners can obtain a relatively accurate re-creation of how the couple is struggling—their thoughts, feelings, and behaviors, and the situations that precipitate conflict. The content of the couple's problems and strengths (both as individuals and as a couple) should cover all domains of psychosocial well-being, and an analysis of how the couple relates to each other will likely provide a firm foundation for detailed functional assessment.

Although most sessions should include both partners, there are two reasons to interview each partner alone at least one time: (1) one person may have problems that do not result from the couple's conflict but may contribute to them, and (2) one or both partners may want to discuss something in private without the other partner. The purpose of conducting an individual assessment (in the presence of the other partner, if both agree to it) is to determine whether anyone has any significant problems that may affect the relationship (for more on conducting individual assessment, see chapter 4). These problems can be relatively common: depression, anxiety, stress, substance abuse, criminal behavior. History taking on these matters can certainly help determine, to some degree, the age of onset and trajectory of the problems and to what extent the couple's problems exacerbate these matters or strain the relationship. Long-standing disorders that precede the relationship, such as substance abuse, may require individual intervention or referral (e.g., outpatient detoxification, medication) before the couple's work with the social worker can resume. With respect to interviewing each partner alone, it is helpful for practitioners to know whether one partner has kept any problems secret in the relationship (e.g., a partner is having an affair, has huge gambling debts, or has a drug problem about which the partner is unaware). If someone does have a secret, the practitioner needs to discuss with that person whether he or she will reveal the secret at some point and, if so, what the consequences might be. If the client chooses not to reveal the secret, the practitioner needs to discuss with that individual whether couples' work can realistically continue. These problems are sometimes difficult to resolve, and there are no solid guidelines for these types of dilemmas.

In addition to focusing on multiple problem domains (e.g., psychological, social, health, substance abuse) with each partner and as a couple, practitioners should complete a detailed functional assessment that builds on the initial analysis of the couple's communication style. How does the couple interact when things are going well and when they are in conflict? What is the couple's typical week like? What situations or problems seem to trigger animosity or outright conflict? How does the couple fight? Do they simply avoid each other and not talk about it or do they fight openly? How long does the conflict and animosity last? What attempts do they make to short-circuit the conflict or reconcile afterward? What additional problems seem to be related to the conflict? What factors (e.g., external stressors at work, substance abuse, money problems) seem to precipitate conflict? Are these problems also the results of conflict?

Having the couple work together on a self-monitoring diary can be a helpful way to carry out a functional assessment of their life together, to engage them more as participants in treatment, and to give them an opportunity to collaborate as a couple on an important task. Practitioners can instruct the couple to construct the diary over two weeks. The partners should keep the task simple by having each person take brief notes about his or her daily schedule, key behaviors, important events, activities, and feelings about what was happening. By working closely with the couple to re-create a typical weekly scenario, the practitioner can obtain a relatively accurate and intimate view of each person's daily life. Re-creating the details of daily life is an excellent way to illuminate when and why things go either well or poorly for the couple. When I was a young and inexperienced practitioner, I had a difficult time sorting out why a couple was routinely arguing, until I had them conduct a similar exercise and realized that they fought intensely only on Friday nights: after the husband came home from the local tavern having spent a good portion of his weekly pay. This oversight underscores a key point about conducting a thorough MDF assessment: if the practitioner does not ask, the client may not tell! Knowing which risk factors are associated with the clients' problems and knowing how their thoughts, feelings, behaviors, and situations interact over time provides an invaluable assessment template for understanding the couple's strengths and vulnerabilities. The practitioner can then collaborate to set intervention priorities.

Intervention

A fair amount of controlled research has been conducted on interventions for couples' problems. In addition, other research has shown that couples' therapy can be helpful for clients when one partner has a disorder such as depression, anxiety, or substance abuse (Shadish & Baldwin, 2005). Couples' interventions that have garnered the most evidence for effectiveness include emotion-focused therapy (EFT; Johnson & Greenberg, 1995; Snyder, Castellani, & Whisman, 2006) and behavioral couples' therapy (BCT; Jacobson & Addis, 1993; Jacobson & Margolin, 1979; Lebow, 2000; O'Farrell & Fals-Stewart, 2003; Shadish & Baldwin, 2005; Snyder et al., 2006; Thomas & Corcoran, 2001). Although these are distinct approaches, the essential skills of both models are presented here in an eclectic framework that highlights what seem to be their complementary aspects: the importance of both partners learning to communicate empathically to better understand the sources of each other's emotional distress and engaging in mutually reinforcing behaviors.

Accurate listening and empathic responses are central to the helping relationship regardless of the presenting problem, and working with couples provides the practitioner with the opportunity to model these skills. As each partner in turn addresses the practitioner at various points, the other partner has the opportunity to watch closely as the practitioner listens, subtly encourages further expression, and then responds in a way that helps the speaking partner feel respected and understood. This experience can be invaluable for the couple and provides a template for them to reference when they practice these critical skills at home. The practitioner teaches skills through modeling. The practitioner demonstrates that listening requires giving the other person undivided attention and respecting and accepting what is said, even when the other partner is communicating emotionally charged material that may be critical of the listener.

Supportive skills also facilitate the setting of intervention goals. Helping couples build a problem hierarchy can help them feel less hopeless or out of control. In this way, supportive skills also help bolster the couple's morale. Many couples are quite pessimistic when they begin couples' work, having been demoralized after months or years of conflict. In addition, one or both partners may not be ready to make any changes or may be at a different stage of readiness to change. Supportive skills can encourage clients to weigh the pros and cons of change, even after having been in a troubled relationship for many years.

Supportive skills lay the groundwork for implementing the key skills of EFT. A cornerstone of EFT is to help (through modeling, rehearsal, and practice) each partner attend to the other's emotional responses. This approach involves the use of basic supportive skills, including the attentive, empathic, and active listening discussed earlier, as well as demonstration through clear, empathic communication that each partner really understands what the other feels. The recognition and mutual understanding of each other's emotional responses is central to maintaining feelings of trust and intimacy. It also lays the groundwork for helping partners recognize the cycle of dysfunctional relationship patterns that may have been learned from family or previous relationships.

Of course, getting to the point at which partners can communicate empathically with each other and demonstrate a willingness to communicate on a deep emotional level often requires wading through some emotional conflict. As common sense suggests, relationships do not develop independently from the effects of each person's interpersonal history. Everyone has a relationship history of some kind, usually beginning with parents. The effects and consequences of relationships over the years cumulatively influence both the strengths and deficits we bring to an intimate relationship and our selection of partners. For some, being in an intimate relationship is easy, exciting, and relatively conflict free; for others, intimacy is anxiety provoking, disappointing, and fraught with frustration, anger, and conflict. Some people have had close, caring relationships with their parents and siblings as children, and these lessons may carry over to the formation of close friendships and close, intimate romantic relationships. Others who grew up with chronic conflict with adults who provided poor modeling in respectful communication and effective problem solving may have more difficulty maintaining satisfying intimate relationships. Regardless of history, however, adults who successfully cultivate deep intimacy, the ability to communicate feelings accurately, and the willingness to attend to the feelings of a partner in an authentic way are more likely to maintain satisfying, long-term relationships. With EFT, practitioners attempt to impart these skills to troubled couples.

The core skills of EFT can help conflicted and emotionally troubled couples cultivate emotional attunement if the practitioner provides sufficient support and helps each person gradually open up to his or her partner. For individuals who have suffered emotional rejection, harsh criticism, trauma, or other forms of emotional and physical abuse by important people in their lives, the process of opening up to a partner can be difficult. Practitioners need to establish a hierarchy of topics or problems to address and, on the basis of the clients' emotional responses, start with the problems that evoke moderate emotions before moving to matters that evoke more intense feelings. Gradual exposure to highly affect-laden material works better than does diving right in, an approach that is likely to cause some clients to close up or even discontinue therapy.

Although learning to listen and empathize with one's partner is the foundation for better communication and increased intimacy, improvements might not be sufficient to resolve serious problems and maintain a healthy relationship over time. Learning to recognize and deal with emotional conflict is a coping skill, a skill that practitioners can facilitate and have partners practice with each other. Once each partner acknowledges and expresses underlying feelings, the practitioner can help them link their feelings to past experiences. How did they come to feel this way? What prior experiences might account for their feelings? Are the feelings the result of a prior relationship in one's family or a previous romantic relationship, or are they the result of harm in the current relationship?

Practitioners who employ EFT endeavor to help couples reenact the core emotional conflicts in the here and now, to bring the past into the present by discussing themes of conflict that seem to echo from prior relationships. Once such a conflict presents itself, practitioners and clients can name it and attempt to understand how it affects the current relationship. This interpretation or explanation that links previous and current conflicts can be instructive for partners, help them better understand each other, engender mutual empathy, and help them resolve their own conflicts in a more realistic way. With improved understanding, partners may be more accepting of each other and address their mutual needs in a more realistic light.

It is also widely recognized that interpretation and improved understanding of why we do what we do, though sometimes helpful, is not sufficient to bring about lasting change. For partners to improve and maintain an intimate, stable relationship over time, each person must improve his or her behavior toward the other person consistently. Insight means little if partners better understand why they have problems but fail to change the way they communicate, problem solve, and treat each other. Behavioral couples' therapy has been shown to be effective because it emphasizes helping partners take responsibility for their own behavior, and improve their behavior toward one another so that it becomes a more sustained and mutually rewarding experience over time.

There are two major areas in which partners can improve: better communication and more successful problem solving, two areas that are the main focus of BCT. If the couple increases their empathic understanding with EFT (as described earlier), then improved communication skills can help them sustain that and improve their understanding over time. As mutual goodwill builds up, communication becomes easier, partners become more tolerant of minor infractions, and both are better prepared to take on problem solving in areas of more serious conflict. Again, practitioners must take the lead in modeling good communication skills. Careful and respectful listening, reflecting what one thinks one has heard, and allowing the other person to respond to verify that he or she accurately understood the message are essential skills that a couple needs to practice throughout the course of couples' therapy. Couples should repeat the process of listening, reflecting, and responding until both partners feel that they have gotten their messages across and have been adequately understood. Although the practitioner takes the initiative in modeling this process, clients should practice their skills in the presence of the practitioner and at home.

In addition to empathic listening and taking turns in the communication process, the practitioner can also help clients apply basic cognitive skills to help them avoid some of the communication pitfalls that often provoke conflict. These are the same critical-thinking skills that were discussed in chapter 2. During emotional encounters, partners may lapse into dysfunctional ways of making their points, such as exaggeration (i.e., catastrophizing), all-or-nothing thinking (dichotomizing), engaging in hindsight bias (sometimes called "Monday-morning quarterbacking"), and overgeneralizing. Other unhelpful and provocative habits can destroy goodwill, including name-calling, cursing, deliberately not listening to the other person, interrupting the other person while he or she is speaking, turning away and leaving the room in a fit of pique, or running out of the house or leaving in a huff. Of course, these behaviors, while not conducive to effective communication and problem solving, at least stop short of more extreme problems such as shoving, spitting, kicking, hitting, and other more dangerous forms of aggression often associated with domestic violence. Nevertheless, learning to keep the temperature down by using effective communication skills and not resorting to more emotionally provocative methods can reduce the likelihood of verbal arguments escalating into physical violence, a problem for which younger couples are at greater risk.

If the couple can begin mastering effective communication skills, they will then be prepared to tackle some of the content problems: money matters, parenting, extended family conflict, collaborating on household tasks, and so on. Problem-solving skills involve identifying the problem, expressing views clearly and calmly, brainstorming a hierarchy of solutions together, putting the plan in motion, and honestly evaluating the results. If, for example, a couple disagrees on how to handle an adolescent son's disobedience, the couple can consider a hierarchy of potential solutions, such as having the family discuss house rules, initiating mild sanctions (e.g., on television or video games), revoking other privileges, or restricting freedoms (e.g., grounding). The couple may disagree about how to proceed. One partner may want to be more lenient, and the other may want to consider a more aggressive approach. The practitioner can help them come to a consensus, such as beginning with lighter restrictions first and moving up the hierarchy to more restrictive methods as needed. If the couple sticks together on the plan and evaluates each step honestly, they will either succeed or have to resort to more assertive methods. The fact that they work collaboratively on the project might, in itself, have positive effects on their son's behavior. Children and adolescents often feel a profound sense of disappointment and anger when their parents engage in conflict over parenting practices and cannot cooperate with each other.

Behavioral couples' therapy works on the assumption that the quality of a relationship depends on the couple's ability to engage in mutually pleasing (i.e., reciprocally and positively reinforcing) behavior. Although it would be ideal if couples could enact a sense of mutual caring through empathic listening alone, actions often speak louder than words, and behavior changes more readily increase a sense of mutual goodwill. To get things started, the practitioner needs to carefully interview the partners in each other's presence to find out which behaviors each finds pleasing and rewarding. This discussion alone can be an epiphany for some couples, especially those that have engaged in years of trying to read each other's minds rather than ask what the other likes. This phenomenon can cover a host of areas, from preferences for food, entertainment, sexual activity, and social engagements, to housework, vacation plans, getting together with extended family, and money matters. After taking a thorough inventory of preferences, the couple can then develop a hierarchy of intervention goals. Assuming that there are no emerging crises to address, gradually moving up the hierarchy from easier challenges (e.g., sharing housework) to more difficult ones (e.g., having extended family members as house-guests) is recommended.

Adapting Couples' Work for Specific Problems: A Substance Use Disorder

Most clinical research on couples' work with substance use disorders has been conducted with behavioral couples' therapy (e.g., Epstein et al., 2007; O'Farrell & Fals-Stewart, 2003). Substance use disorders are difficult to treat, and special considerations need to be met before couples undertake an intervention for this problem. As indicated in chapter 9, practitioners must have a thorough understanding of how to conduct an assessment of a substance use disorder, an understanding of drug effects, and a recognition of the psychosocial and health consequences of substance abuse and addiction. It is also important for practitioners to keep in mind that substance abuse problems can be highly variable, often do not follow the predictable trajectory of stage theories, and can be addressed with a variety of agreed-on goals: reduced use, reduced types of substances used, changed context of use (i.e., reduced harm), and abstinence. Partial successes toward any of these goals should be rewarded, and constant monitoring and evaluation is required over long periods of time. Often, one partner initially seeks treatment and the other joins later. However, practitioners should be prepared to engage in couples' work with only one partner (unilateral therapy), which is addressed briefly at the end of this section.

Practitioners should be prepared, especially early on in treatment, to intervene in crises as needed. Binge drinking, drug overdoses, domestic violence, child welfare interventions, hospitalizations, police interventions, and so forth are all potential occurrences in work with substance-abusing clients. Medical consultation is also likely, especially for prescription psychiatric medications (e.g., antidepressants, antianxiety drugs) and medications that may help some clients stay clean and sober (e.g., naltrexone, disulfiram). In BCT, the nonaddicted partner participates in the medication regimen by monitoring the addicted client's cooperation in taking medication. After a period of initial stability, BCT practitioners emphasize implementing homework assignments and rehearsing behaviors. These may include practicing basic communication and problem-solving skills for smaller problems and gradually taking on the more difficult ones as successful experiences accumulate. It is important early in treatment to increase a sense of goodwill through improved empathic communication to take on the difficult work of helping the substance-abusing partner remain clean and sober or continue cutting down. Helping the abusing partner deal with urges to drink by finding alternative behaviors (e.g., taking walks together, going to the movies) or reducing other at-risk situations (e.g., planning grocery shopping together rather than stopping off at the bar, skipping what was cocktail hour at home) are structural changes that can help the substance-abusing partner stretch out that important period of initial sobriety. Couples can also plan special days when they devote much of their time to something that they both like, such as taking a short trip together, going for a hike, working in the garden, or taking in a ball game. These activities should be opportunities to engage in events without alcohol that both can enjoy. After a period of sobriety and after goodwill has improved, the couple can apply the same skills to other problems as well. Moreover, one partner can facilitate other coping skills, such as those discussed in chapter 9, and rehearse them in couples' work. The couple can practice stress management, improved social skills, and drink-refusal skills together at home.

The initial period of sobriety can be difficult for the couple. But if the partner successfully avoids a serious relapse, couples can move to the next step of improving their relationship, a step that can also be challenging if they have long-standing mutual problems. But if they succeed, the improved relationship quality can provide a bulwark of support for the addicted partner, helping him or her reduce the chances of relapse. However, couples and practitioners should be prepared to continue working on relapse-prevention strategies. Identifying potential triggers of drinking and drug use, having ready alternatives, knowing what to do if there is a slip, and having a contingency plan to recover quickly should continue for as long as necessary.

Should the substance-abusing partner refuse to engage in treatment, couples' work can continue with the non-substance-abusing spouse. Although there are variations of this approach, they use common skills. Practitioners should conduct an extensive assessment of the substance user's history (based on the attending partner's report) and of the couple's current difficulties. Non-substance-abusing partners often unwittingly engage in behaviors that indirectly reinforce a partner's substance abuse (e.g., nagging, calling into work sick for the abuser, drinking with the abuser, making threats and ultimatums). The non-substance-abusing spouse requires coaching to better understand the nature of his or her partner's addiction, to avoid taking responsibility for the abuser's behaviors, and to learn ways to enhance the relationship during times when the drinking partner is sober. An intervention may be useful at some point if the non-substance-abusing partner can recruit influential friends and family members to confront the substance-abusing partner. Although this approach carries risks, it can sometimes motivate an addicted person to seek help. The non-substance-abusing partner may also benefit from counseling on the effects of substance abuse on children or the risks of domestic violence. At some point, however, treatment should focus on helping the non-substance-abusing spouse learn to cope with the problem or ultimately leave the relationship.

Couples who experience severe or multiple problems are also likely to benefit from case management skills. Partner violence, child abuse or neglect, substance abuse, other co-occurring mental illnesses or other difficulties may require the coordination of services with law enforcement, courts, child welfare, or primary health and mental health agencies. Practitioners may also refer clients to mutual help and similar support groups, such as Alcoholics Anonymous, Narcotics Anonymous, anger management groups, depression support groups, and so on. Keeping in close contact with physicians after the client goes through detoxification is also an important way to link psychosocial and health-related intervention goals. Other case management activities may include providing support and counseling during a job search, advocating for full access to benefits, and making referrals for further assessment for psychiatric disorders, which may become evident after a month or two of sobriety.

Summary of Essential Skills for Couples' Work

Work with couples can be equally challenging and satisfying. Balancing the needs of both partners, maintaining a neutral posture, and facilitating improvements in empathic listening and effective problem solving often yield good results. Couples' work also lays down a solid foundation for effective work with children and adolescents through family interventions.

Case Study: Anita and Bashir

The Comprehensive Service Plan (Assessment, Intervention, Evaluation)

Use all available information from the client and significant others, your observations, and input from other professionals to conduct both quantitative and qualitative aspects of this MDF assessment.

Client identification data: (gender, age, marital status, sexual orientation; family composition; employment; racial, ethnic, cultural, religious/spiritual affiliation and identity)

Anita is a twenty-one-year-old married woman of mixed Iranian and Italian background. Her parents live about one hour away, and she has a brother in high school. She works as a waitress but wants to enroll in the local community college to pursue studies in human services. She was born and grew up in the United States. Her father, an engineer, had moved to the United States in the late 1970s before the Iranian revolution and met Anita's mother at work. Her mother became a full-time homemaker after they wed.

Anita is married to Bashir, a twenty-four-year-old man who emigrated as a teenager with his parents from Lebanon in the late 1990s. He is an only child. His parents run a bakery, and Bashir drives the delivery truck for their large and growing business. Neither Anita nor Bashir are devout in their religious beliefs (she identifies herself as Christian; he identifies himself as a nonpracticing Muslim), but they are both proud of their cultural heritage and celebrate all relevant holidays together and with extended family.

Anita and Bashir have been married for three years, and they have a three-year-old at home (Anita was pregnant with Habib at the time they were married).

The presenting problem
Description of problem (client's view)

The couple has been fighting off and on since they were married, and things escalated soon after the birth of Habib. Bashir complains that he works very hard and that Anita expects too much from him around the house. Anita complains that she is too homebound, and that she wants to pursue her education so she can pursue a career in human services and increase their income in the future. She complains that Bashir is too authoritarian, does not listen to her, and spends too much time away from the home when he is not working. Bashir complains that he expected his wife to show more commitment to their home and raising his son, wants more children in the future, and she should put off her education for now. He says he can make enough money to meet their needs.

Description of problem (practitioner's view)

The couple appears to have fundamental differences about their respective roles and expectations for their future life together. Anita made reference to the fact that her mother was a full-time homemaker, had given up a good job at the request of her father, and has always resented that decision to some degree. Anita feels strongly that she does not want to make the same mistake and feels that with more education, she could contribute financially as an equal in the relationship. To achieve this, she wants Bashir to assume more domestic duties. Bashir, on the other hand, feels that they had an implicit arrangement when Habib was born—Anita would raise his son, and he would be the full-time provider. Bashir claims that he has the support of both his parents and his father-in-law, and that she has little support, aside from her mother, from both families regarding her desire to pursue a human services career. Thus, there is some tension between Anita and Bashir regarding extended family alliances. As for communication, the couple appears to be committed to each other but tend to shout a lot and interrupt often. They feel very strongly about their respective positions, and there seems to be little room for compromise at this point. There does not appear to be any history of physical violence, and they both adore their son, Habib.

Psychosocial history with an emphasis on problem trajectory

Bashir grew up in Lebanon and moved to the United States with his parents. He reports a generally uneventful childhood, though he was well aware of political tensions and violence in his own country. His father had relatives in the United States who helped him immigrate and set up a bakery business. Bashir admires both of his parents very much. After completing high school, he went to work full-time for his father, driving a delivery truck. The business was growing, and Bashir believes that he will take over the business someday as his father decides to slow down and retire. Bashir reports no history of mental health or substance abuse problems, but he feels that he has been under a lot of stress in the past few years. He has no regrets about the unplanned pregnancy and birth of Habib, but he feels that it has placed a great strain on him financially and has caused a lot of tension with Anita.

Anita grew up in a middle-class neighborhood and considered her father very "Old World" and somewhat strict. Her mother stayed at home but was somewhat resentful of not having pursued her career. Nevertheless, she and Anita's father seemed to have a solid marriage. Anita recalls that her father particularly set very strict limits regarding her dress; makeup; where, when, and with whom she could socialize, and so on, and felt a bit "out of it" socially compared with her friends, whose parents seem to be more permissive. Although she does not outwardly resent her father for his strictness, she seems to bristle at Bashir's injunctions that she "commit herself to motherhood."

Anita claims to have "rebelled" somewhat in high school and started smoking cigarettes, drinking alcohol, and smoking marijuana. When her father found out, she recalls that she was restricted to the home for three months during her junior year in high school, a time that disrupted her social life with long-lasting effects. She had been seeing a young man whom she felt, at the time, in love with, and she resented her father for disrupting that relationship. It ended soon after Anita's "confinement." Although she stopped using alcohol and marijuana when she found out she was pregnant (Bashir also disapproved of her drug use, though he occasionally smoked marijuana as well), Anita continues to smoke cigarettes when Bashir is not around (she revealed this as a "secret" during the individual assessment interview).

The couple was married in a civil ceremony, and since then have been mainly preoccupied with the daily stresses and strains of raising their young son, paying their mounting bills, and surviving financially. Anita is becoming bored, resents being housebound, and wants some freedom to socialize with friends and pursue her education. Bashir is resisting.

Attempts to resolve the problems, previous treatment and relevant outcomes

Both have only discussed their concerns with their own parents, a strategy that only made Anita resentful. Both Bashir's father and father-in-law are more sympathetic to his case, disapproving of Anita's, but Anita's mother provides her with some support. These discussions were causing some tension between the families, so the couple decided not to discuss the matter with them anymore for the sake of keeping the peace. Neither partner has any mental health or substance abuse treatment history.

The individual assessment[1]

Mental status, cognitive disturbances: Describe the client's level of hallucinations, delusions, disorientation, bizarre behavior or speech, memory problems, serious confusion, or other symptoms of serious cognitive impairment. Include other troubling or dysfunctional beliefs or convictions.

---

[1] For illustration purposes, both individual assessments are combined here. Under usual circumstances, individual assessments would be documented separately.

Anita: No indications of cognitive disturbances; some indications of guilt regarding her desire to pursue her education further.

> How would you rate the client's overall mental status during the past month?
>
> POOR [0]   IMPAIRED [1]   MARGINAL [2]   <u>GOOD [3]</u>   EXCELLENT [4]

Bashir: No serious indications of cognitive disturbance; expresses some resentment regarding Anita's desire to pursue a profession.

> How would you rate the client's overall mental status during the past month?
>
> POOR [0]   IMPAIRED [1]   MARGINAL [2]   <u>GOOD [3]</u>   EXCELLENT [4]

Mental status, emotional distress: Describe the client's level of depression, anxiety, and overall ability to regulate emotions.

Anita appears to be somewhat depressed, expresses some guilt about her unplanned pregnancy, the circumstances of her marriage, and feeling that she is letting down Bashir and her father by not obtaining their full approval. She does report some difficulties sleeping and has been smoking more (she blows the smoke out the apartment window), which she also feels guilty about, since she is carefully hiding this behavior from Bashir, who she knows would be very angry about it. She feels sometimes, "I am just dragging myself throughout the day." It is possible she suffered from postpartum depression, but she was not treated, and her symptoms do not appear to be severe. When asked, she reports no suicidal ideation at this time or recently.

> How would you rate your client's emotional well-being over the past 30 days?
>
> POOR [0]   <u>IMPAIRED [1]</u>   MARGINAL [2]   GOOD [3]   EXCELLENT [4]

Bashir reports a fair amount of stress. Although his presentation is generally upbeat and he shows no signs of depression or related somatic complaints, he does talk about losing his temper often. He reported an incident recently in which he almost got into an altercation during a traffic jam. Another driver accused him of cutting in at a tollbooth and yelled a racial epithet at him. Bashir jumped out of the truck but was dissuaded from taking further action when a state trooper emerged from a patrol car parked on the nearby median. Bashir just smiled and waved, glared at the other driver, and got back in the truck. But he was upset with himself for almost going too far and fuming over the incident for the next couple of hours. "I wouldn't normally let an ignorant fool like that bother me, but I've been pretty on edge lately. I really need some time to relax, but things are pretty tight right now at home, and my dad depends on me. The holy days are coming up too, so orders are off the charts, which is good for business but not my blood pressure." He also reports trouble sleeping and regrets occasionally losing his temper at home, yelling at Anita and pounding his fist on the kitchen table.

How would you rate your client's emotional well-being over the past 30 days?

POOR [0]   IMPAIRED [1]   MARGINAL [2]   GOOD [3]   EXCELLENT [4]

Behavioral problems: Describe the client's overall ability to regulate behavior. Consider things such as ability to express oneself effectively; ability to work at things patiently; and tendencies to verbally or physically lash out at others, run away, harm oneself, or to engage in impulsive, criminal, or substance-abusing behavior. How would you describe the client's overall impulse control?

Anita: As suggested earlier, Anita's energy level appears to be down, and although three-year-old Habib keeps her busy, she feels that she no longer has time or wants to do some of the things she used to enjoy, reading particularly.

How would you rate your client's behavioral control generally over the past 30 days?

POOR [0]   IMPAIRED [1]   MARGINAL [2]   GOOD [3]   EXCELLENT [4]

Bashir: Considerable amount of stress, losing his temper, difficulty relaxing and feeling at ease.

How would you rate your client's behavioral control generally over the past 30 days?

POOR [0]   IMPAIRED [1]   <u>MARGINAL [2]</u>   GOOD [3]   EXCELLENT [4]

Adaptive strengths and coping abilities. Describe the client's ability to cope with problems and everyday stressors. How would you describe the client's ability to assess problem situations, deal with triggers, cope with stress, solve problems, and perhaps reach out to others for help to deal effectively with difficulties?

Anita: Despite her mild to moderate depression, Anita is holding up well. She reports being quite active with her child, spends a lot of time playing with him, cuddling, and otherwise caring for him. She clearly enjoys being a mother but seems exhausted much of the time, possibly as a result of the depression.

How would you rate your client's overall adaptive strengths and coping abilities over the past 30 days?

POOR [0]   IMPAIRED [1]   MARGINAL [2]   <u>GOOD [3]</u>   EXCELLENT [4]

Bashir: Is also doing well. A hard worker, responsible and determined to make things work out at work and at home.

How would you rate your client's overall adaptive strengths and coping abilities over the past 30 days?

POOR [0]   IMPAIRED [1]   MARGINAL [2]   <u>GOOD [3]</u>   EXCELLENT [4]

Health problems: Describe the client's overall health. Aside from normal, transient illnesses, think about the client's general health habits (e.g., smoking, heavy drinking, exercise, weight), chronic primary health disorders, the client's opinion of his or her own health, ability to engage in usual activities relatively free from discomfort, overall energy level, hospitalizations, and treatments for illness other than psychiatric ones. Consider the client's documented medical history and any ongoing treatments.

Anita: Aside from some depressive symptoms, she reports being in very good health. Smoking is a concern that she acknowledges.

How would you rate your client's health over the past 30 days?

POOR [0]   IMPAIRED [1]   MARGINAL [2]   GOOD [3]   EXCELLENT [4]

Bashir: Also in good health, but he, as does his father, has high blood pressure. He does not take medication but is aware of the need to relax, reduce stress, and exercise.

How would you rate your client's health over the past 30 days?

POOR [0]   IMPAIRED [1]   MARGINAL [2]   GOOD [3]   EXCELLENT [4]

Use of alcohol and other drugs: Describe the client's use of alcohol, illicit substances (e.g., cocaine, heroin, marijuana, hallucinogens) and abuse of prescription medication. How often does the client use them, in what quantity, and how serious are the psychological, physical, or social consequences associated with use?

Anita: Has reported occasional marijuana smoking on the few occasions when she has been able to "get away" and visit her female friends. Otherwise, she is not drinking or using other drugs.

How would you rate the client's functioning in the past month with regard to substance use?

POOR [0]   IMPAIRED [1]   MARGINAL [2]   GOOD [3]   EXCELLENT [4]

Bashir: Reports occasionally drinking beer or wine with his male friends. Other than occasional intoxication, he reports no problems with alcohol and does not use illicit drugs or any nonprescribed pharmaceuticals.

> How would you rate the client's functioning in the past month with regard to substance use?
>
> POOR [0]   IMPAIRED [1]   MARGINAL [2]   <u>GOOD [3]</u>   EXCELLENT [4]

Recreational activities: Consider what the client does for fun (alone or with others), hobbies, relaxation (reading, watching television, playing video games or cards) and physical exercise (e.g., walking, jogging, biking). How would you describe the client's overall involvement in positive recreational activities?

Anita: In the last couple of years she reports very little by way of enjoyable recreational activities. Bemoans feeling "overweight and out of shape." She used to be more active, jogged, and enjoyed other activities such as reading, noted earlier. Reports she has not been out to a movie in two years.

> How would you rate the adequacy of the client's participation in healthy recreational activities over the past 30 days?
>
> POOR [0]   <u>IMPAIRED [1]</u>   MARGINAL [2]   GOOD [3]   EXCELLENT [4]

Bashir: Also reports less time "for fun" but goes out once a week with his male friends (most are friends of Middle Eastern descent who met through business dealings). They sometimes play cards or backgammon, have a few drinks, tell stories. He also looks forward to this time each week; he complains about lack of exercise, though says, "I'm on and off the truck all day. It can be a workout, just not much fun."

> How would you rate the adequacy of the client's participation in healthy recreational activities over the past 30 days?
>
> POOR [0]   IMPAIRED [1]   <u>MARGINAL [2]</u>   GOOD [3]   EXCELLENT [4]

Material resources: Describe your client's current or (if institutionalized) most recent living situation overall. Consider such things as adequacy of food, clothing, shelter, and safety.

Material resources for both Anita and Bashir are good. Although they are struggling financially, their basic needs are adequately met.

Anita:

> How would you rate the overall adequacy of the client's material resources over the past month?
>
> POOR [0]   IMPAIRED [1]   MARGINAL [2]   GOOD [3]   EXCELLENT [4]

Bashir:

> How would you rate the overall adequacy of the client's material resources over the past month?
>
> POOR [0]   IMPAIRED [1]   MARGINAL [2]   GOOD [3]   EXCELLENT [4]

Independent living/self-care: Describe how well the client manages the household; takes care of personal hygiene; and eats, sleeps, and otherwise cares for his or her own basic needs.

Both care for themselves adequately, although Anita has been somewhat neglectful of daily self-care possibly as a result of depression.

Anita:

> How would you rate the client's ability to live independently and take care of their basic needs over the past 30 days?
>
> POOR [0]   IMPAIRED [1]   MARGINAL [2]   GOOD [3]   EXCELLENT [4]

Bashir:

> How would you rate the client's ability to live independently and take care of their basic needs over the past 30 days?
>
> POOR [0]   IMPAIRED [1]   MARGINAL [2]   GOOD [3]   EXCELLENT [4]

Work (role) satisfaction: Describe the client's current work-related or other important role-related activities (e.g., work, student, home, volunteer, retired, disabled). Describe the activities and responsibilities that occupy the client in a productive manner.

Anita: Although Anita more than adequately fills her current role as mother and full-time homemaker, she is despondent and frustrated over her perceived lack of opportunity to pursue her education.

> How would you rate the client's work or role satisfaction over the past 30 days?
>
> **POOR** [0]   **IMPAIRED** [1]   **MARGINAL** [2]   **GOOD** [3]   **EXCELLENT** [4]

Bashir: Seems satisfied with his role as primary breadwinner and likes his role in the family business despite daily stress and strain.

> How would you rate the client's work or role satisfaction over the past 30 days?
>
> **POOR** [0]   **IMPAIRED** [1]   **MARGINAL** [2]   **GOOD** [3]   **EXCELLENT** [4]

Legal problems: Describe any legal problems the client has had or continues to have. These include minor infractions (e.g., public drunkenness, shoplifting, minor traffic violations, public disturbances) and more serious crimes (e.g., assault and battery, rape, burglary, driving under the influence). Consider the client's status (e.g., probation, awaiting imprisonment, parole). Also, consider any civil suits leveled at the client or pending financial judgments. Overall, how would you describe the client's current legal situation?

Neither partner has any legal problems to report.

Anita:

> How would you rate the client's legal situation over the past 30 days?
>
> **POOR** [0]   **IMPAIRED** [1]   **MARGINAL** [2]   **GOOD** [3]   **EXCELLENT** [4]

Bashir:

> How would you rate the client's legal situation over the past 30 days?
>
> POOR [0]   IMPAIRED [1]   MARGINAL [2]   GOOD [3]   <u>EXCELLENT [4]</u>

Anita:

DSM-IV Diagnosis

Axis I   v61.10 Adjustment Disorder with Depressed Mood, chronic
          Consider 300.4, Dysthymic Disorder
          v61.10 Partner Relational Problem

Axis II   No diagnosis

Bashir:

DSM-IV Diagnosis

Axis I   v61.10 Partner Relational Problem

Axis II   No diagnosis

Family and social assessment

Family relations: Describe the client's current family structure including authority, hierarchy, alliances, roles, rules, boundaries, subsystems (e.g., couple, siblings, parent-child alliances), and patterns of interactions and quality of communications. Describe specific problems in the family; describe specific adaptive strengths in the family. How does the family describe their own racial, ethnic, cultural, and religious identities?

As indicated, there is some tension between the partners that is inadvertently provoked by their parents. Although the couple's parents have not interfered, with the exception of Anita's mother, they have let their feelings known that they think Anita should stay home and give up her plans to return to school. This has provided Bashir with some degree of support for his views but has increased tension between him and Anita. Other than that, there has been no overt conflict among family members.

> How would you rate the quality of the client's immediate family relationships over the past 30 days?
>
> POOR [0]   IMPAIRED [1]   MARGINAL [2]   <u>GOOD [3]</u>   EXCELLENT [4]

Immediate social relationships (close friends and acquaintances): Describe the quality of the client's relationships with friends and acquaintances. Over the past month, how would you describe the quality of the interaction overall between the client and others with respect to closeness, intimacy, general interpersonal satisfaction, effective communications, degree of conflict, level of hostility, aggression, and evidence of any emotional or physical abuse?

As a couple, Anita and Bashir have no friends in common. They both have separate friends, and Bashir sees his friends more frequently than Anita sees hers. The couple married soon after Anita discovered she was pregnant and have had little time or opportunity to meet other young couples with children.

> How would you rate the quality of the client's immediate social relationships over the past 30 days?
>
> POOR [0]   IMPAIRED [1]   <u>MARGINAL [2]</u>   GOOD [3]   EXCELLENT [4]

Extended social relationships: Describe the type and quality of relationships between the client and others in the client's community (other than close friends and family). These people might include other families, law enforcement, human service agencies, school personnel, coworkers, and others from whom the client receives support or with whom the client is having serious conflict.

The couple has little involvement in the community. Outside of work, Bashir has a few friends but the couple is somewhat cut off from the community, not involved with the school as of yet, and have no other ties with community organizations. They appear to be somewhat isolated.

> How would you rate the quality of the client's social relationships over the past 30 days?
>
> POOR [0]   IMPAIRED [1]   <u>MARGINAL [2]</u>   GOOD [3]   EXCELLENT [4]

A concise summary of the MDF assessment: Highlight the client's areas of distress and adaptive strengths. Emphasize those areas that are most likely to be emphasized in the intervention plan.

Anita and Bashir are a young couple who genuinely care for each other and are attentive parents to their young son, Habib. As with many young couples, they are under considerable financial stress, have some tension over extended family relations, do not have a mutual support group of friends or acquaintances, and are somewhat cut off from the community in general. Bashir shows signs of stress and can be angry and argumentative during discussions at home; Anita is frustrated with him and her stay-at-home status, and she appears moderately depressed. Attempts to discuss their concerns often end in heated arguments, usually without any resolution.

Recommendations for further focused assessment: Note recommended referrals to consultants or additional instruments to be used.

Continue to monitor Anita's symptoms of depression. Refer if they do not abate after a few couple sessions.

The Comprehensive Service Plan Summary

Assessment/problems	Goals	Objectives	Interventions	Evaluation plan
(Briefly describe key problems to be addressed.)	(State desired outcome for each problem.)	(Describe specific stepping stones toward each goal. Update as client progresses.)	(Describe specific interventions to be used.)	(Describe indexes to be used for tracking progress.)
Inability to communicate about disagreements regarding each other's respective roles	Come to a mutually satisfactory resolution about short- and long-term roles for both partners in marriage	Identify those areas regarding roles that are open for discussion by either partner and those that both are willing to discuss; list in a hierarchy from least difficult (e.g., child care) to most difficult (e.g., Anita returning to school)	*Supportive skills:* Focus on joining the couple and modeling empathic listening skills *Therapeutic coping skills:* Teach and coach emotion-focused communication skills (e.g., empathic listening to emotional content without interrupting); demonstrate mutual understanding verbally and nonverbally	Develop self-anchored scale for each partner to rate how well each felt that the other listened and demonstrated understanding (e.g., 0 = "not at all," 1 = "a little," 2 = "somewhat," 3 = "a good amount," and 4 = "very well"). Report results weekly.
Mild to moderate depression and stress symptoms in Anita and Bashir, respectively	Reduce symptoms of depression and stress; enhance opportunities for healthy relaxation	Identify and list potential opportunities for physical and social recreation for each partner	Have couple practice in the office and (initially) twice weekly at home after Habib is asleep; start with easier items on the objectives list	Use same scaling device to have each partner rate how well the other made efforts to help or sooth during the week. Have both report weekly and provide specific examples.
Social isolation; lack of mutual friends and similar social supports	Expand social supports; reduce isolation	Identify local community organizations of mutual interest	Have couple review perceptions of their own parents' marriages; consider what they believe worked for them and what did not; examine how goals for their life together may be similar/different	

Identify mutually reinforcing activities that each partner can do for the other at home; these may include household and child-care duties; also include activities that are mutually soothing to reduce depression and stress; emphasize mutual gain over competition

Demonstrate basic stress management to Bashir; have him practice as needed and report results weekly

Case management skills: Plan exploratory participation in local Muslim American organizations, particularly those geared toward younger couples; these may include mosque-related activities; enlist in-laws to provide once-weekly baby-sitting

Explore Anita's return to school (part-time, initially) within six months as mutual social supports become available

Consider referring Anita for medication evaluation if depression worsens

CHAPTER ELEVEN

Internalizing Disorders of Childhood and Adolescence

EMOTIONAL OR INTERNALIZING DISORDERS, the focus of this chapter, refer primarily to depression and anxiety disorders in children and adolescents. For the sake of simplicity, the term *children* in chapters 11 and 12 generally refers to both children and adolescents. When emphasizing a specific age group, I will refer to younger children, older children, or adolescents as the case may be. Although sadness, disappointment, and a variety of fears are common during childhood, internalizing disorders are more chronic and generally more severe than transitory mood problems that may be a function of family problems, general distress, or problems in school. Internalizing disorders refer to depression and a range of anxiety disorders, including school phobia (e.g., refusing to go to school), specific phobias (e.g., bugs, dogs), obsessive-compulsive disorders, post-traumatic stress disorder, and social phobia (i.e., extreme shyness) among others.

The biopsychosocial framework provides a sound underpinning for understanding children's internalizing disorders. Many children inherit a predisposition to anxiety or depression (or both), and real stressors in their lives may exacerbate this tendency. Often these stressors have their origins in the child's family: domestic violence, abuse, neglect, high conflict, unemployment, substance abuse, divorce, and so forth. Children often have good reasons to be sad and anxious. Nevertheless, depression and anxiety can be debilitating and portend a lifetime of struggle with mood disorders and associated behavioral problems.

There is good reason, however, to be hopeful in working with children, given that there are effective interventions available. If the family is relatively intact and supportive, child-focused interventions can be readily implemented. If the family is highly conflicted or exhibits evidence of child neglect or abuse, the focus must first be on the family as a whole, with emphasis on stabilizing the parent or couple subsystem or intervening with a single parent. Without the cooperation of the parents or guardians, interventions with younger children, in particular, are less likely to be successful. Thus, the current trend in the outcome research is to implement interventions for children and adolescents in the context of a family therapy model when possible.

Externalizing disorders, the focus of chapter 12, are childhood and adolescent problems marked primarily by behavior disorders, including oppositional defiant disorder, conduct disorders, and to some extent, attention deficit disorders. Anxiety and depression sometimes co-occur with externalizing disorders. In adolescents, for example, depression often co-occurs with conduct disorder.

It can be helpful to think of interventions with children and their families as a kind of transfer of learning across several levels. First, the social worker might conduct an assessment with the child alone and with a parent or both parents present. In this way, the practitioner obtains his or her own perspective on the child, can observe the parents' behavior with the child, and can provide modeling for the parents regarding how to connect with and relate to the child more effectively. Parents frustrated with their child's behavior may inadvertently overwhelm or shame a child in efforts to motivate him or her to be less fearful, to do better in school, or to change some other behavior. Should assessment proceed to intervention, the skills the practitioner demonstrates with the child in the presence of the parents can provide effective modeling to improve parenting skills (e.g., empathic listening, nurturing, positive disciplining), improve communications among family members, and demonstrate a calm and rational approach to problem solving. Thus, through modeling, the practitioner is transferring skills in relating and intervening with the child to the parents, an essential goal for long-term maintenance of gains for the child.

Last, the practitioner cannot overlook the importance of connecting with community resources outside the family: teachers and school administration, law enforcement, medical professionals, coaches, and so on, depending on the problems the child or adolescent is experiencing. These important participants in the child's life can serve as responsible monitors and reporters of the child or adolescent's progress, and they are in key positions to help reinforce important changes. If, for example, a child is severely phobic in social situations, it makes little sense to focus on the child's well-being exclusively in the context of the family. Although there may be dynamics in the family that discourage the child from becoming more involved socially (e.g., the child's mother suffers from agoraphobia; there is domestic violence or child abuse in the home), it would be helpful for the child if the practitioner coordinated services with some interested party (e.g., a teacher, a sports coach) outside the home to monitor progress. In keeping with the generic social work ecosystem assessment model, monitoring the problem and intervening on several levels is, again, the hallmark of effective social work practice with children and adolescents. Working with a child alone in a consulting room, insulated from the input of family, teachers, and other collaborators, is no longer considered competent practice with children and adolescents.

Assessment

The term *internalizing disorders* is somewhat of a misnomer, as some problems associated with anxiety and depression are observable. Very anxious children may suffer from debilitating shyness, compulsive rituals to ward off anxiety from frightening or disturbing obsessions, or traumatic distress associated with child physical or sexual abuse. Depressed children may generally appear socially withdrawn, chronically angry, or despondent.

In general, assessment with children should be conducted on several levels: (1) alone with the child to observe behavior and to get a feel for how the child relates to the practitioner without family members present, (2) in the presence of the family to observe how the child reacts to family members and how they relate to the child, (3) through consultation with people outside the family, such as teachers or coaches—in short, anyone (with consent of the parent or guardian) who is in a strategic position to observe the child in another social context.

An MDF assessment for internalizing disorders should include an analysis of how the child's difficulties developed over time, how the problem has varied in intensity in the context of family and other social contexts, and how the problem currently manifests itself across various domains, including mental status, family and social well-being, recreational activities, and school performance (Beidel & Turner, 2005; Chorpita & Southam-Gerow, 2006; O'Hare, 2005; Stark et al., 2006). Children suffering from anxiety and depression may have vague notions about what is bothering them or may be very specific about why they are sad or afraid. Social workers should carefully listen to their reasons. Depending on the child's age and abilities, practitioners can employ various methods to help children discuss the potential sources of sadness or fears: drawing, playing games, using dolls or other figures, using storybooks that depict other children dealing with fears or sadness, or other creative outlets. Children, depending on their age, may have difficulty articulating what troubles them with ordinary interviewing methods. There is also the possibility that a child does not want to reveal certain things because he or she feels threatened by a parent, guardian, or other person or because the child is worried about the consequences of reporting certain events. The causes of these concerns may involve problems at school, child abuse, domestic violence, drug use, or other potentially criminal behavior. Children learn at a young age to censor themselves if they have been taught not to talk about their problems with strangers or outsiders.

Other children may reveal their troubles indirectly. A child who fears going to school might talk about a child abduction he saw on a television show. A depressed child may focus on unhappy themes such as the loneliness, loss, or disappointment that characters in a storybook express. Accepting a child's reasons for fears or sadness at face value, initially, can help the child to express feelings and expound on the specific theme. But it may take some sleuthing and more in-depth analysis of family interactions and reports from others to identify the actual sources of fears or sadness. There is also the possibility that the child may have very supportive parents and an otherwise supportive social environment and may struggle with emotional difficulties for which there is a family history and no obvious environmental cause. Nevertheless, it is important to try to rule out possible environmental factors that may contribute to the child's distress.

Keeping in mind that the causes of depression and anxiety disorders in children, adolescents, and adults can have multiple biopsychosocial sources, practitioners should maintain a balanced approach and avoid drawing premature conclusions during an assessment. In some cases, there may be one prominent factor that seems to overwhelmingly account for a child's emotional distress: practitioners should consider the impact of sexual or physical abuse, traumatic losses, or witnessing deadly violence. However, most cases will not yield to simple explanations. One way to avoid premature formulations is to examine the changes in a child's life over time, that is, to develop a detailed trajectory of when the child began to demonstrate difficulties (e.g., the family moved, the child started school, a sudden loss in the family) and follow that trajectory to the present. Examining changes in the family, particularly in the parents, over time can help provide a cause-effect analysis that will yield useful clues as to what social or environmental factors may negatively affect the child.

Depression and anxiety are problems that often run in families because of both genetic and generational family behavioral problems (e.g., alcoholism, criminality). Taking a careful family history can be helpful in this regard. Many young children are shy and fearful at times but most mature out of this phase; some do not. An analysis of family interactions sometimes suggests reasons why children are afraid or depressed. Other times, however, children who are well cared for and loved at home experience most of their difficulties outside the family system. Children and younger adolescents may have problems with anxiety and depression related to engaging in school or other broader social activities. When a child appears well nurtured in the home, yet has emotional difficulties in other social venues, assessment from objective observers in those situations can be revealing.

Anxiety and depression can also be associated with more severe forms of child psychopathology, such as serious mental illnesses, developmental disabilities, or neurological problems. Referral to specialists who can provide testing and diagnosis for such disorders is necessary. Should the more serious causes be ruled out, practitioners should consider how the child's emotional distress manifests itself in other areas of the child's life: How does the distress affect other family members, including the parents? Are the child's difficulties affecting his or her ability to relate to peers at school or inhibiting social development? Is the child's emotional distress interfering with school performance? How does the teacher respond to the child who is fidgety, anxious, or listless in the classroom? One should also consider the possibility of substance abuse, especially as children approach middle-school age. The use of alcohol, marijuana, inhalants, or other drugs is a real possibility and would readily contribute to symptoms of internalizing disorders including social withdrawal and depression.

Practitioners should also be attuned to the cultural context and level of assimilation to American child-rearing norms and expectations when assessing internalizing disorders in children. Although one should avoid overgeneralizations about any ethnic, racial, or religious group, asking parents for help in understanding how their cultural traditions influence their child-rearing practices (e.g., rewards, discipline, social expectations) is important. In cases where parenting practices diverge somewhat from the practitioner's cultural expectations, practitioners should strive to find common ground or explain in a nonjudgmental way how the family's norms may be somewhat different from those of other families, the school, or broader community. Children will often use other parents' behavior as a benchmark to challenge their own parents, particularly as the children get older. The child's parents should at least be aware of what other parents consider ordinary so that they can better judge their own estimations of what is too strict or too permissive in parenting practices. Above all, parents need to agree on norms so that they can set limits with a unified voice.

There may also be occasions when the parent's ideas of acceptable behavior or reasonable discipline may be too far from the norm. For example, in some religions, corporal punishment is acceptable and even considered a positive, virtuous form of punishment. Of course, the term *corporal punishment* can mean a lot of things, and the practitioner (in keeping with his or her own beliefs and local laws and customs) has to decide where to draw the line (e.g., three whacks on the behind with an open hand versus hitting a child with a paddle, belt, or kitchen utensil). The practitioner should also be transparent with his or her beliefs and communicate them to the parents. However, if a social worker considers that a parent's disciplining practices go over the line and constitute neglect or abuse, the practitioner then has to report the incident to the local child welfare authorities. This may sever any working relationship with a family, but that is a risk the social worker is obligated to take.

The functional assessment is critical for determining factors that may cause or exacerbate the child's depression or anxieties. Tracking the details of a child's behavior over the course of a typical week at home, school, and elsewhere can be very telling in terms of sequencing those factors that affect the child's well-being over time. When is the child doing well? Under which circumstances? When and where does the child manifest problems and emotional distress? How frequent and severe are the problems? Do the problems vary a lot in terms of frequency and severity? Do they vary as a function of specific circumstances? How do the parents, siblings, teachers, friends, acquaintances, coaches, and anyone else in the child's life respond to the child's fears or withdrawal behaviors? How do these responses affect the child? What responses seem to improve the child's mood or help him or her become more involved socially?

Once the social worker has a solid grasp of the patterns and sequencing of factors that affect the child's mood and behavior, working with the family to create a hierarchy of problems is the next step. In general, starting with a moderately difficult problem and working toward more challenging problems is a sound way to proceed. For example, for a very shy child, setting up a playdate for an hour with one child whom he or she likes would be a safe start. A likely winning strategy is to gradually increase the amount of time and add another playmate or two over time. At the same time, if the child's parents have serious marital problems (possibly a source of anxiety for the child), couples' work should be initiated concurrently. It will be of limited help for a child to become more adventurous socially if he or she is in constant fear of returning home to face screaming matches or even violence between parents. Consulting with key school personnel is also helpful, especially if teachers and playground monitors are recruited to help the child engage socially rather than withdraw.

Detailing the day-to-day life of children struggling with depression or anxiety generally reveals the key psychosocial factors that contribute to their difficulties. Practitioners should also note situations in which the child appears to function better or to be more comfortable. A balanced assessment that highlights the child's vulnerabilities and strengths provides a good working template for planning an intervention, particularly setting goals and objectives.

Intervention

A large and growing body of research supports a range of cognitive-behavior therapies for internalizing childhood and adolescent disorders (e.g., Beidel & Turner, 2005; Chorpita & Southam-Gerow, 2006; Compton, Burns, Egger, & Robertson, 2002; Kazdin & Weisz, 1998; Ollendick & King, 1998; Silverman & Berman, 2001; Stark et al., 2006). Although these approaches are often applied in individual and group modalities, cognitive-behavioral approaches for childhood and adolescent disorders are increasingly implemented in the context of behaviorally oriented family therapies (e.g., Compton et al., 2002; Northey, Wells, Silverman, & Bailey, 2003). Although many essential skills for working with children are fairly easy to learn and implement, practitioners demonstrate the real art of applying evidence-based practices with children when they apply skills concurrently on several levels: with the child, with the parents and family as a whole, and often in conjunction with other key people in the child's life. Last, although there are some differences in approach when intervening with depressed or anxious children, essential skills for both of these disorders overlap and interventions should be tailored to the child's specific needs.

General considerations regarding the application of supportive skills with children and adolescents certainly apply when dealing with anxious or depressed children. However, depressed or anxious children or adolescents may require a slower pace and more patience to draw them out, help them to talk about what troubles them, and motivate them to try new ways of dealing with problems. Children, particularly younger children (age six and younger) may have a hard time articulating what is troubling them, and the practitioner may have to work with the child's own metaphors and with adults who know the child to understand what is going on in the child's daily life. As noted previously, play, drawing, storytelling, and the use of dolls or other figures can facilitate communication with children. However, the goal of such exploration should be to verify one's clinical hunches. Developing a rapport with a child on a one-on-one basis is important, but it should not be the exclusive form of engagement. Seeing the child alone and with his or her family will result in a more accurate assessment of the child's psychological, emotional, and behavioral well-being.

Developing trust with depressed or anxious children or adolescents will depend, in part, on how adults (primarily parents) have treated them. It stands to reason that young people come with predisposed expectations about their social worker based on past experiences with other adults. The working relationship with a child provides an ideal opportunity to determine what those expectations are (e.g., adults are trustworthy, adults are scary, adults want to hurt me, adults make me feel bad about myself). Again, rather than guess at interpretations based on the child's self-report, body language, or symbolic communications during play, practitioners should test out their clinical hypotheses through data gathering of multiple types of information from multiple sources, including observations of the child during the one-on-one interview.

Younger anxious or depressed children might be difficult to motivate. When working with children alone and in family sessions, it is important to find out what they enjoy, what makes them feel good about themselves, and what helps them feel safe. Younger children are less likely to respond to explanations, psychoeducation, or interpretations, so it is important for interventions to be more action oriented early on to help them achieve small but significant successes and to reduce their feelings of helplessness and despair. Planning helpful tasks (e.g., organizing or decorating his or her bedroom with the help of a parent) early on can be beneficial for the child and provides an opportunity to see how committed to the intervention the other family members are. Observations of family members along with their self-reports can help answer ongoing questions: Does the child suffer from emotional neglect? Is there psychological or physical abuse going on? Asking the family to try new things may help bring out some of these matters into the open. Keeping a close eye on family interactions also provides many clues about the family's overall level of care, cooperation, and emotional well-being. Developing a relationship with the other family members is as important as developing a rapport with the child. After all, the long-term goal is usually to help the family function better and to learn coping skills that will sustain the child's psychological and physical well-being over time.

Younger adolescent clients present a somewhat different situation with regard to developing a working relationship. They have had more experience with adults in their life, and they can truly benefit from the one-on-one relationship they develop with a practitioner, even if their parents are only marginally supportive. Again, how they relate to a social worker may reveal a fair amount about the relationships they have had with other adults in their lives. Are they withdrawn from the practitioner, showing little interest in engaging in treatment? Are they hostile, cynical, and generally negative in their initial dealings with the social worker? Careful listening and gentle reflection can help remove some of these barriers. It can be illuminating for practitioners to simply ask young clients to tell them about the people in their lives (e.g., parents, friends, teachers). Unlike younger children, older children and younger adolescents often are better able to articulate what troubles them. Being authentic and showing genuine concern for clients' distress (without being too maternal or paternal) can help younger adolescents feel that they have an ally in whom they can confide.

Finally, joining the family (i.e., developing a working alliance) is critical to maintain the family's cooperation in helping the child or adolescent client. This often involves a balancing act, particularly when there is evidence of emotional or physical abuse. Maintaining the alliance can be a challenge if the parents or guardians feel that they are being blamed for the child's emotional difficulties. It is important to identify both strengths and areas that require improvement when working with families, but emphasis should be not on laying blame but on solving problems and maintaining improvements over time. Including all family members when possible can help forge a feeling that helping the child requires everyone's contribution. Practitioners should also extend the working alliance to other important adults in the child's life such as teachers, coaches, and others who can contribute to supporting and maintaining the child's well-being over time.

Educating children about how their thoughts, feelings, and behaviors work together in different situations can be especially helpful for them. Although younger children may have difficulty dealing with such abstract concepts, older children and adolescents can benefit from some help in identifying and articulating thoughts and beliefs that affect their moods positively or negatively. Depressed or anxious children may secretly harbor dysfunctional ideas about themselves, other people, and the world around them. These beliefs, expectations, and attributions may be closely associated with despair, feelings of hopelessness, vague anxiety about life, outright fears of specific things, current situations, or the future. Anxious children may be worried about their parents (e.g., Will they leave me? What if they get sick or die?), other children at school (e.g., Why don't they like me or want to play with me? I'm afraid of getting hurt by other kids), or circumstances in the neighborhood (e.g., Some bad people live on my street; I know a kid who got shot and died). Children's fears range from imaginary monsters, bugs, and dogs to the other end of the spectrum: children who have experienced horrific trauma (e.g., repeated physical abuse, sexual assault) or violence in everyday life. Many children have suffered losses early in their lives and may suffer from feelings of despair that they may not understand or be able to articulate. Other children may simply have inherited an anxious temperament or proneness to depression that colors their everyday life. Identifying the troubling thoughts and stating them in the open can help children open a door to better understanding what their fears or sadness are all about. Often, parents may not know what is troubling their children or may be too preoccupied themselves with serious daily stressors to give the children's troubles any priority. In other circumstances, the parents may be a primary cause of their child's emotional distress, and thus may be even less likely to recognize and validate the child's experience.

Practitioners can teach children to evaluate their own thinking processes and feelings by educating them about their own emotional processes. These skills include helping children identify, differentiate, and understand their feelings; identify frightening thoughts; and develop a keener awareness of how physical sensations (e.g., upset stomach) can provoke anxiety. Children can learn to assess and gauge their own anxiety level and track their progress over time. One common way to help children identify their feelings is by using picture books that illustrate different emotional expressions, and helping them accurately identify the feelings and think about times they have felt that way. Linking children's anxiety to specific circumstances can help them better anticipate problems and understand the effects of anxiety in everyday life. This helps prepare them for learning ways to reduce anxiety and develop problem-solving skills to cope better with their fears.

Practitioners can help children follow through on self-monitoring their thoughts, feelings, and behaviors by teaching them to recognize and evaluate their own covert (inner) self-talk (i.e., quietly talking to themselves) and discover ways to cope with depressive and frightening thoughts. When children feel anxious or sad, encourage them to talk to themselves in an analytical way about what they are feeling at the moment so that they can examine emotionally charged thoughts in a realistic light and gain perspective. Children need to realistically assess thoughts that provoke anxiety or depression before the practitioner can consider coping strategies. For example, a child who is fearful of a bully in school can say to himself: "I know that Billy is mean and likes to frighten people, but I can ignore him and stay close to my friends. There's nothing wrong with being afraid of someone who likes to hurt other people. The school social worker also told me that it's not wrong if I tell the teacher or playground monitor, because it would help others who might be afraid of Billy too." A child who is depressed may think that her parents do not really love her, because if they did, they would do everything possible to stay together as a family. The practitioner might help her engage in a different kind of self-talk: "I know a lot of kids whose parents got divorced. They don't say their parents don't love them. They say they have two parents and two homes to go to. I guess that just because my parents got divorced and don't want to live with each other doesn't mean that they don't love me." Although many problems cannot be resolved merely by helping children identify the thought and consider a different way of looking at the problem, helping children link thoughts and feelings together can help them understand that they are not merely at the mercy of their own negative feelings. Identifying, monitoring, and engaging in some cognitive coping can provide a solid foundation for behavior change methods and improve the ability to cope with depression and anxiety in the long run.

Practitioners can use behavioral coping skills for children and adolescents in a variety of combinations, including teaching relaxation training skills, using imagery, rehearsing new behaviors, role-playing, modeling, and practicing. Teaching children problem-solving and self-regulating skills (e.g., self-assessment, evaluation, reinforcement) can help them maintain their gains over time. Practitioners can apply these skills in treating both depression and anxiety.

Ideally, therapeutic coping skills should be implemented in a graduated sequence: (1) cognitive coping exercises (as described previously), (2) relaxation techniques (e.g., simple breathing exercises) to help the child gain some control over anxiety, (3) preparing the child to take action by using imaginal change techniques to rehearse changes in their mind's eye, (4) rehearsal of the planned changes through role-play and practice, and (5) implementation of actual changes in the child's everyday life. A key point in the change process is to make changes gradually by working up the hierarchy from moderately challenging situations to more difficult ones.

Although this sequence may be the ideal approach for planning and implementing change, there is a place for initially taking more active steps early on with older children and adolescents. Young people who are depressed, for example, often benefit from being coaxed into action with relatively straightforward tasks that help motivate them and provide a sense of accomplishment. If young people are poorly motivated because of their depression, have become inactive, and avoid situations and people because of fears and anxieties, the development of a step-by-step plan to increase their activity level can initially be very helpful and serve as a catalyst for further change. Identifying activities that they used to enjoy or ones that they would like to try can take some discussion, but once the activities are identified, a plan should be implemented that starts with short-term goals and leads up to a significant accomplishment, such as writing a story for a school contest, starting a small garden, or starting a part-time job (for older adolescents). For children or adolescents who are more socially withdrawn or even socially phobic, joining a club, structured group activity, or community project can be helpful because the activities are planned out and interactive. These more action-oriented approaches can reduce isolation and provide a sense of accomplishment and self-worth. However, with very anxious clients, practitioners should not move too quickly. Encouraging young clients to take more active steps initially should be decided on a case-by-case basis. Overall, a good rule of thumb is to have clients consider doing just a little more than they think they are capable of accomplishing.

Taking some initial action steps can help many young clients readily engage in the change process and provide them with an initial feeling of success and optimism. However, lasting change, especially for clients with more serious depression or anxiety disorders, depends in large part on achieving incremental success while working up a hierarchy of increasingly challenging objectives.

Teaching a phobic child to control symptoms of anxiety is a key step before moving toward a more action-oriented phase of the intervention. The initial action phase referred to earlier should be considered a preliminary step to help mobilize the child or adolescent and his or her family members. However, before engaging in a more focused and sustained effort toward behavior change, the child or adolescent must also develop some mastery over his or her anxiety symptoms. Relaxation skills for children and young adults can be readily taught and easily learned by children and adolescents alike. They should be kept relatively simple. By now, the child should have learned that what they think, how they feel, and what they are doing are all interconnected. Anxious thoughts create anxious feelings, and what the child does next after having such a thought can either worsen or lessen the anxiety he or she feels. Practitioners who have successfully taught a client how to identify when and why he or she feels anxious can introduce relaxation training by teaching the young client to simply take a few moments for a few slow deep breaths, hold each one for a few moments, and exhale slowly. As with watching a suspenseful movie, people will almost stop breathing when they are anxious, as they are afraid and waiting to see what happens next. Practitioners should model and instruct the young client to tell him- or herself, "I can cope with this situation." When children are overanxious, they tend to lose focus and are less likely to cope successfully with an anxiety-provoking situation, a setback that tends to makes matters worse and can leave them feeling less confident, more anxious, and more discouraged than before. Other forms of relaxation exercises include progressive muscle relaxation and guided imagery (i.e., helping a child or adolescent imagine calming, happy situations in his or her mind's eye). Meditation may be more appealing to older adolescents, and it involves a bit more learning and practice. It has become a core skill for many people who have learned to cope with daily stress, anxiety disorders, and depression.

Once children have learned to calm themselves and control anxiety somewhat, they can incorporate the next essential therapeutic coping skill: covertly rehearsing what they want to accomplish next. This approach appeals to children and adolescents. Children know how to daydream, and the practitioner can put that ability to good use. Through the use of imagery, young clients can begin to master fears or overcome depression by practicing what they want to achieve, step-by-step, in their imaginations. Systematic desensitization, described in chapter 6, is essentially the same technique. The use of the SUDS scale can be a big help during these exercises, because it provides young people with a tool to measure how anxious they feel during the imaginal exposure exercise and can reinforce them when they employ it as a form of self-evaluation.

For example, a child is afraid to leave home and go to school, and appears to be depressed because of isolation from his peers. The practitioner completes an MDF assessment, but results reveal no compelling family problems that account for the distress. A good starting point is to help the client imagine confronting difficulties a little bit at a time. The practitioner can help a younger child imagine himself leaving the house with a new backpack, getting on the school bus with the other kids in the neighborhood, riding to school, sitting in the classroom engaged in his studies, having lunch in the cafeteria, making new friends on the playground, and coming home at the end of the day—all of which may initially be scary thoughts. The practitioner can begin by having the child do some simple breathing exercises and then proceed through this sequence of events in his imagination. The practitioner should closely observe the child's body language (e.g., tension, squirming in his seat, not breathing deeply) should he begin to become anxious. As the client proceeds from one step to the next, the practitioner can help the child remain calm by reminding him to breathe fully and maintain the image in his mind until he feels comfortable with it. Then, he can move on to the next step in the hierarchy.

If the child is not comfortable with this type of exercise, the practitioner can use other activities, such as play figures and blocks (e.g., to build a model of the school, to invent and play out scenarios with other children) or a blank coloring book, to create images at each step of the hierarchy (e.g., the school bus, sitting at the lunch table). Over time, the child is likely to become calmer discussing each scene in the hierarchy.

Covert exposure and the use of coping skills in the relative safety of the practitioner's office is a good start but is usually not sufficient to help the child master fear or overcome depression. Children and adolescents (and adults, for that matter) generally do not achieve intervention goals until they successfully use their new skills in everyday life. Planning the first action steps is critical to ensure success. Assuming that a supportive parent is in the picture, planning that first day of school for the phobic child should make the day as positive as possible. For the first few days, it might be helpful for a parent to accompany the child to school, spend a few minutes with the child before the school day begins, and gradually reduce the amount of time to a quick hug and good-bye as the child more readily engages with other students. Perhaps taking the bus is the next challenge, and the child (having had some initial success) may take to this goal more readily. Graduated exposure may take a few days or a few weeks, but most anxious children will readily engage once they attain some mastery over their anticipation of anxiety and make it through the first few days of school.

The next step in using therapeutic coping skills is to help the client begin engaging in graduated exposure, that is, practicing the behavior a little at a time while gradually increasing the challenge. For a socially anxious child, the practitioner and parents might arrange an opportunity for the child to practice a presentation in front of people the child knows— friends from an after-school program or neighborhood children. Although making a presentation to a friendly audience might not be as compelling as the real classroom experience, it might be enough of a confidence booster to help the client feel more able to take on the real experience. Whatever the source of fear (as long as it presents no real danger), graduated exposure treatments are the most effective form of intervention for anxiety disorders in children.

Kendall (1992, 1994) developed and tested a sixteen-week program of teaching children how to better cope with emotional disorders. The program incorporates, in a more formal way, the skills discussed herein and is quite similar to a range of other cognitive behavior therapy models, including those that target depression in children and adolescents. The approach also combines psychoeducation, emotional regulation, problem solving, social skills, and efforts to increase activity in social contexts (Stark et al., 2006). A brief summary of these essential skills follows:

- Session 1: The practitioner develops a rapport with the child, creates a no-pressured environment to put the child at ease, assesses the child's understanding of the problem, and gauges readiness for treatment.
- Sessions 2 and 3: The practitioner helps the child accurately identify and better understand his or her own feelings and emotional responses. Methods often include looking at pictures of others and identifying what the person might be feeling, or role-playing scenarios to demonstrate how a person might act when sad, anxious, or angry. The practitioner moves at the child's pace.
- Session 4: When the child has learned to identify anxiety accurately, the practitioner helps him or her use tension as a cue for relaxation skills (e.g., muscle relaxation, breathing exercises).
- Session 5: The practitioner helps the child identify and articulate the content of his or her cognitive processes through self-talk, covert challenging of these cognitions, and replacement with coping self-talk to reduce anxiety.
- Session 6: The child then learns and starts using problem-solving strategies. The method focuses on helping the child identify distressing situations, feelings, and thoughts, and then exploring coping and problem-solving responses to ameliorate the situation.
- Session 7: The child learns to engage in self-evaluation of his or her own performance without self-judging. This includes self-reinforcement for good efforts and partial successes.
- Session 8: The child reviews his or her progress, summarizes what has been learned, and records coping skills for future reference.
- Sessions 9–16: The child builds on his or her self-assessment and coping skills by implementing them with real anxiety-provoking problems—covertly and in real life—in a graduated manner using the anxiety self-rating scale (0–100).
- The termination process emphasizes evaluation, reward for successes, anticipation of future challenges, and the child's and family's requests for occasional booster sessions as needed. Parents need to take over at this point and help keep the child on track with encouragement, reminders, and reinforcement.

When working with children, case management skills are often a key part of the intervention plan and may include any and all of the following:

- Making referrals for psychological testing, medical examinations, or other specialized assessments (e.g., childhood sexual abuse)
- Interviewing key informants in the child's life (e.g., teachers, coaches, other significant adults)
- Coordinating services with other providers (e.g., school social worker, juvenile justice officer, big brother or sister)

Depending on the service mission of the agency they work in, social workers should think well beyond the consulting room (having obtained informed consent) and work with the larger community system, those key people who can observe, influence, and reward psychosocial improvements in their young clients' lives.

Incorporating Essential Coping Skills into Family Therapy for Depressed and Anxious Children

There are three major reasons to use family therapy in the context of helping depressed or anxious children and adolescents: (1) to resolve other problems in the family that appear to have a negative impact on the client (e.g., mental disorders, couples' conflict, domestic violence, child abuse and neglect, substance abuse, behavioral problems in parents or siblings), (2) to have at least one parent and possibly other family members participate in helping the child or adolescent learn new coping skills and reinforce their use, (3) to improve communication and problem-solving skills in the family for the benefit of the client and to improve family functioning as a whole. Most practitioners and researchers agree on this point: interventions with children or adolescents are hampered considerably if problems in the family that contribute to that child's problems are not addressed in a constructive manner. Children and adolescents are more likely to succeed if other family problems are addressed concurrently and if other family members support their efforts to improve. Chapter 4 discusses the essential skills of assessing family functioning, and chapter 5 discusses skills for intervention.

Summary

Multiple factors contribute to the cause and maintenance of childhood and adolescent anxiety and depressive disorders. If a family is relatively intact and functions well, children and adolescents might respond well to a combination of individual and family interventions, with other family members serving as important allies in helping them overcome their difficulties. If an MDF assessment strongly suggests that a child's emotional difficulties are, at least in part, a result of family dysfunction, then improvements in the child or adolescent's condition are likely to require direct intervention through family therapy to improve family communications and resolve specific problems that may pull the child or adolescent into parental conflicts and harm him or her directly (e.g., substance abuse, domestic violence, psychopathology). Contemporary evidence-based approaches to help children and adolescents with emotional disorders flexibly combine individual interventions that focus on the child, with family therapy to reinforce the child's progress and resolve family problems that are likely to act as obstacles to the child's long-term gains. Case management approaches are often necessary to recruit other collaborators in the community to help a child or adolescent generalize progress to other settings such as school. Case management efforts are also necessary to coordinate care with other providers, such as school psychologists, child psychiatrists, and other professionals.

Case Study: Lyla
The Comprehensive Service Plan
(Assessment, Intervention, Evaluation)

Use all available information from the client and significant others, your observations, and input from other professionals to conduct both quantitative and qualitative aspects of this multidimensional-functional assessment.

Client identification data: (gender, age, marital status, sexual orientation; family composition; employment; racial, ethnic, cultural, religious/spiritual affiliation and identity)

Lyla is a seven-year-old African American girl who lives with her mother, Philippa, who is twenty-seven years old and works as a nurse's aid in a local general hospital. Her father, Antwon, is thirty-four. Philippa and Antwon are not married and do not live together, but in the past two years, Antwon has visited Philippa and his daughter at least once weekly. Antwon works during the day as a manager of a small grocery store in town and works three nights per week as a security guard. For the past three years, he has also been a secular deacon in his church. Philippa and Antwon both trace their heritage to the rural southern United States.

The presenting problem
Description of problem (client's view)

In response to the practitioner's query as to why she came with her mom, Lyla responds (while hiding behind the chair in which her mother is sitting), "I don't know." Her mother reports that Lyla "has a lot of fears," that she "does everything she can to stay away from school," and that she "wakes up screaming sometimes at night." She adds that when she is in school, she tends to keep to herself, does her work, and likes to color a lot. She sometimes plays with one other girl in her class.

Description of problem (practitioner's view)

In addition to Philippa's description, it also appears (from a private interview with Philippa) that there has been a lot of conflict since Lyla's dad came back on the scene. The heated encounters apparently are very upsetting for Lyla, and she tends to have more night terrors after the incidents. This increased anxiety may also contribute to Lyla's school phobias and clinging to her mother.

Psychosocial history with an emphasis on problem trajectory

Philippa reports that Lyla was a difficult child from the beginning, that she was very difficult to soothe, cried excessively, and "always seemed to be really sensitive." Early on, she was diagnosed with a congenital immune deficiency, for which she has been treated on and off for many years. Lyla has had a series of serious infections and has spent a lot of time in the hospital for such a young person—often weeks or months at a time. She missed a fair amount of school, was never in day-care or preschool programs, and is a bit behind in her education. Despite being almost eight years old, she is just starting the first grade. Philippa, with the urging of a friend who is an elementary school teacher, did a fair amount of remedial work with Lyla, especially with regard to teaching her how to read. Lyla reads at a fourth-grade level but needs to catch up in other areas.

During the early years, Antwon was actively in the picture but was struggling with a drug problem, according to Philippa. She finally insisted that he not come around anymore because his presence was too upsetting for Philippa and possibly for Lyla as well. There was some evidence of physical abuse directed at Philippa, although she characterized it as "not that bad. I could handle him OK."

Philippa grew up with both parents, two sisters, and a brother in a working-class home. Her dad worked on the local commuter railroad and her mother, who stayed at home when the children were young, would later take part-time work cleaning offices downtown after business hours. During that time, the children would be on their own to do their homework and take care of some of the domestic duties. Philippa recalls her own trouble with anxiety as she became a teenager and had (what she later found out by reading a popular woman's magazine) a "panic attack." Despite the attack, Philippa pressed on, told no one about it, and over time, found that she was able to "work through it." Eventually she "got over it." She still occasionally feels a "little panicky" but has learned to slow down, breathe deeply, and "let it pass." She also reports that she finds prayer to be helpful in times of stress.

After Lyla was born, Philippa was supported, in part, by her own mother and father, who helped her out financially for a time while she was finishing her associate's degree and training as a nurse's aid. Once working, she was able to afford her own apartment and moved out of her parents' home. She has been working steadily since then, enjoys being a mom, and has good friends whom she can reach out to in times of need. Antwon, having been out of touch for a while, returned a couple of years ago and wanted to "reconnect." Although Philippa does not want to marry him (and he hasn't broached the subject), she feels that it is important for her daughter to know her dad. Despite some heated arguments over parenting and other personal matters, Philippa continues to let Antwon visit. When they are not arguing, Lyla seems to enjoy her father's company. Antwon entered drug rehab about four years ago and joined a local church congregation. Over the past year, he was appointed a deacon and participates in various church activities.

Attempts to resolve the problems, previous treatment and relevant outcomes

Because Lyla spent so much time away from formal classes, it has only been recently that Philippa sought help to cope with Lyla's clingy behavior, her refusal to go to school, and her disturbing night terrors. She was hoping Lyla would "grow out of these problems" as things became more stable at home.

The individual assessment

Mental status, cognitive disturbances: Describe the client's level of hallucinations, delusions, disorientation, bizarre behavior or speech, memory problems, serious confusion, or other symptoms of serious cognitive impairment. Include other troubling or dysfunctional beliefs or convictions.

Lyla reports being afraid of the other kids in school; she says they can be loud and tease her sometimes. She talks about being afraid that her mom won't come and pick her up after school (her mom, conveniently, works the seven-to-three shift), or that something will happen to her mom while she's away. She has also drawn colored pictures of some of the images she recalls from her night terrors: images of witches carrying her away from home to some dark, faraway place. She says she sleeps with her mom most of the time and is afraid that the witches will come into the house and take her away. The fears and anxieties, from both her mom's observational reports and those of Lyla's, seem very intense and quite debilitating. These are more than transitory childhood fears.

> How would you rate the client's overall mental status during the past month?
>
> **POOR [0]   IMPAIRED [1]   MARGINAL [2]   GOOD [3]   EXCELLENT [4]**

Mental status, emotional distress: Describe the client's level of depression, anxiety, and overall ability to regulate emotions.

In addition to her reported fears, Lyla appears to be depressed, does not smile, and seems to be under a fair amount of emotional distress. Her mother reports that when she wakes up from night terrors, she sometimes cries uncontrollably.

> How would you rate your client's emotional well-being over the past 30 days?
>
> **POOR [0]   IMPAIRED [1]   MARGINAL [2]   GOOD [3]   EXCELLENT [4]**

Behavioral problems: Describe the client's overall ability to regulate behavior. Consider things such as ability to express oneself effectively; ability to work at things patiently; and tendencies to verbally or physically lash out at others, run away, harm oneself, or to engage in impulsive, criminal, or substance-abusing behavior. How would you describe the client's overall impulse control?

Aside from her refusal to go to school, Lyla is very obedient and compliant. She will do most of what her mother asks her to do. Philippa reports that she seems to be so cooperative so that Philippa will not get angry at her for any particular reason. She is able to play by herself when she knows her mother is nearby and will color or read for hours at a time.

How would you rate your client's behavioral control generally over the past 30 days?

POOR [0]   **IMPAIRED** [1]   **MARGINAL** [2]   <u>**GOOD** [3]</u>   **EXCELLENT** [4]

Adaptive strengths and coping abilities: Describe the client's ability to cope with problems and everyday stressors. How would you describe the client's ability to assess problem situations, deal with triggers, cope with stress, solve problems, and perhaps reach out to others for help to deal effectively with difficulties?

Aside from her fears and depression, Lyla appears to be a very intelligent and well-behaved girl. She shows potential to do very well in school once she becomes more comfortable there and less socially isolated. At this point, however, she is not coping well with the normal transition from home to school.

How would you rate your client's overall adaptive strengths and coping abilities over the past 30 days?

POOR [0]   **IMPAIRED** [1]   <u>**MARGINAL** [2]</u>   **GOOD** [3]   **EXCELLENT** [4]

Health problems: Describe the client's overall health. Aside from normal, transient illnesses, think about the client's general health habits (e.g., smoking, heavy drinking, exercise, weight), chronic primary health disorders, the client's opinion of his or her own health, ability to engage in usual activities relatively free from discomfort, overall energy level, hospitalizations, and treatments for illness other than psychiatric ones. Consider the client's documented medical history and any ongoing treatments.

Lyla's chronic immune system disorder appears to be improving. She is not taking antibiotic treatments at the time, although doctors are monitoring her condition regularly. Other than this condition, she is in good health.

How would you rate your client's health over the past 30 days?

POOR [0]   IMPAIRED [1]   MARGINAL [2]   GOOD [3]   EXCELLENT [4]

Use of alcohol and other drugs: Describe the client's use of alcohol, illicit substances (e.g., cocaine, heroin, marijuana, hallucinogens) and abuse of prescription medication. How often does the client use them, in what quantity, and how serious are the psychological, physical, or social consequences associated with use?

There is no current evidence of the abuse of alcohol or other drugs by the client or her parents.

How would you rate the client's functioning in the past month with regard to substance use?

POOR [0]   IMPAIRED [1]   MARGINAL [2]   GOOD [3]   EXCELLENT [4]

Recreational activities: Consider what the client does for fun (alone or with others), hobbies, relaxation (reading, watching television, playing video games or cards) and physical exercise (e.g., walking, jogging, biking). How would you describe the client's overall involvement in positive recreational activities?

Aside from her interests in coloring and reading, Lyla's recreational outlets are very circumscribed. She gets little exercise and is used to staying indoors, perhaps as a consequence of past long convalescences.

How would you rate the adequacy of the client's participation in healthy recreational activities over the past 30 days?

POOR [0]   IMPAIRED [1]   MARGINAL [2]   GOOD [3]   EXCELLENT [4]

Material resources: Describe your client's current or (if institutionalized) most recent living situation overall. Consider such things as adequacy of food, clothing, shelter, and safety.

Lyla's material needs are well cared for.

> How would you rate the overall adequacy of the client's material resources over the past month?
>
> **POOR** [0]   **IMPAIRED** [1]   **MARGINAL** [2]   **GOOD** [3]   **EXCELLENT** [4]

Independent living/self-care: Describe how well the client manages the household; takes care of personal hygiene; and eats, sleeps, and otherwise cares for his or her own basic needs.

Not applicable to Lyla. Mother's abilities as homemaker and parent are exceptional.

> How would you rate the client's ability to live independently and take care of their basic needs over the past 30 days?
>
> **POOR** [0]   **IMPAIRED** [1]   **MARGINAL** [2]   **GOOD** [3]   **EXCELLENT** [4]

Work (role) satisfaction: Describe the client's current work-related or other important role-related activities (e.g., work, student, home, volunteer, retired, disabled). Describe the activities and responsibilities that occupy the client in a productive manner.

Lyla's role as a student is somewhat limited at this time. When she is in school, she works well independently, but she is socially isolated because of her fears and anxieties.

> How would you rate the client's work or role satisfaction over the past 30 days?
>
> **POOR** [0]   **IMPAIRED** [1]   **MARGINAL** [2]   **GOOD** [3]   **EXCELLENT** [4]

Legal problems: Describe any legal problems the client has had or continues to have. These include minor infractions (e.g., public drunkenness, shoplifting, minor traffic violations, public disturbances) and more serious crimes (e.g., assault and battery, rape, burglary, driving under the influence). Consider the client's status (e.g., probation, awaiting imprisonment, parole). Also, consider any civil suits leveled at the client or pending financial judgments. Overall, how would you describe the client's current legal situation?

The client and her parents have no legal problems at this time.

> How would you rate the client's legal situation over the past 30 days?
>
> **POOR** [0]   **IMPAIRED** [1]   **MARGINAL** [2]   **GOOD** [3]   <u>**EXCELLENT** [4]</u>

DSM-IV Diagnosis

Axis I   Separation anxiety disorder 309.21

Axis II   No diagnosis

Family & social assessment

Family relations: Describe the client's current family structure including authority, hierarchy, alliances, roles, rules, boundaries, subsystems (e.g., couple, siblings, parent-child alliances), and patterns of interactions and quality of communications. Describe specific problems in the family; describe specific adaptive strengths in the family. How does the family describe their own racial, ethnic, cultural, and religious identities?

Current conflict between Philippa and Antwon, though not the main cause of the child's fears, certainly do not help the situation. The conflicts they have are long-standing, although in the past year or so they have made progress agreeing on when Antwon can visit and in talking about their own tenuous relationship together. At this point, Philippa's parents express concern about Antwon but have become more accepting of his return to the picture, as his standing in the community has improved as a result of his steady appearance as a deacon in a local church. Their future together is currently uncertain. Philippa continues to feel a strong bond of support from her parents. Antwon's parents are both deceased.

> How would you rate the quality of the client's immediate family relationships over the past 30 days?
>
> **POOR** [0]   **IMPAIRED** [1]   **MARGINAL** [2]   <u>**GOOD** [3]</u>   **EXCELLENT** [4]

Immediate social relationships (close friends and acquaintances): Describe the quality of the client's relationships with friends and acquaintances. Over the past month, how would you describe the quality of the interaction overall between the client and others with respect to closeness, intimacy, general interpersonal satisfaction, effective communications, degree of conflict, level of hostility, aggression, and evidence of any emotional or physical abuse?

Lyla's social adjustment is somewhat limited for her age. Whereas most children in her age group are actively working, playing, and seeking out company in groups, she keeps to herself, and only interacts with other adults or children when encouraged.

How would you rate the quality of the client's immediate social relationships over the past 30 days?

POOR [0]   **IMPAIRED [1]**   **MARGINAL** [2]   **GOOD** [3]   **EXCELLENT** [4]

Extended social relationships: Describe the type and quality of relationships between the client and others in the client's community (other than close friends and family). These people might include other families, law enforcement, human service agencies, school personnel, coworkers, and others from whom the client receives support or with whom the client is having serious conflict.

When considering Lyla and her mother as a family unit, they are not well integrated into the community. Although Philippa has friends at work, she has been somewhat isolated herself over the past couple of years given that most of her time when not at work is spent caring for Lyla and taking care of related responsibilities. Philippa has been somewhat cut off from former friends, her church attendance, and other social connections.

How would you rate the quality of the client's social relationships over the past 30 days?

POOR [0]   **IMPAIRED** [1]   **MARGINAL [2]**   **GOOD** [3]   **EXCELLENT** [4]

A concise summary of the MDF assessment: Highlight the client's areas of distress and adaptive strengths. Emphasize those areas that are most likely to be emphasized in the intervention plan.

Lyla's anxiety problems are likely the consequence of a number of contributing factors: an inherited anxious temperament (her mom struggled with anxiety problems for years), early and prolonged separations because of medical problems, and disruption in family life with accompanying conflict. Although her mother has provided a comfortable, nurturing, and enriching upbringing for Lyla, she has been working as a single mom and has often lacked the supports she needed to help Lyla spend more time away from her, both at school and other activities, such as after-school events, weekend day-camp activities sponsored by the church, and similar opportunities for Lyla to socialize and engage more with other children away from her mother.

Recommendations for further focused assessment: Note recommended referrals to consultants or additional instruments to be used.

None at this time.

THE COMPREHENSIVE SERVICE PLAN SUMMARY

Problems: Briefly describe key problems to be addressed	Goals: State desired outcome for each problem.	Objectives: Describe specific stepping stones toward each goal; update as client progresses.	Interventions: Describe intervention approaches to be used.	Assessment and evaluation: Describe indexes and scales used to track progress.
Fears and night terrors Lyla's separation anxiety and school refusal Need for more social networking and supports for mom	Reduce anxieties and night terrors Have child attend school regularly; increase other social activities Increase social activities for mother without Lyla	Develop an evening ritual with fun stories; set up schedule for gradually having Lyla sleep in her own bed Develop a clear morning ritual and schedule for getting ready for school; discuss reward system with her mom to facilitate this plan	*Supportive skills:* Develop a working relationship with her mom; include her dad when it seems necessary to quell couple's tensions; develop a fun and relaxed rapport with the child, first with her mom, then alone. *Therapeutic coping skills:* Help Lyla identify her feelings and fears, learn what anxiety is, and help her understand how it affects the way she thinks and behaves; use drawings, pictures, and other fun media to help her better understand that her fears can't harm her or her mom. Role-play some of the situations at school that she might find scary; help her learn to breathe deeply, exhale, and quell her anxiety when she feels scared.	Develop a chart so Lyla can record how many hours per night she sleeps in her own bed (from mom's observations). Use a similar chart to record how much time it takes Lyla to get ready for school; set reasonable goals for a special weekend reward.

Help Lyla practice self-talk to covertly challenge her fears when her mom drops her off at school and reassure herself that her mom will be there every day to pick her up.

Develop an exposure hierarchy with her mom; start by planning time together at the school a few minutes early (before school begins); during this time she and her mom can read part of a story about brave princesses and daring little girls. This time should be gradually reduced by a minute a week, and Lyla encouraged to play with other children before class begins.

THE COMPREHENSIVE SERVICE PLAN SUMMARY (Continued)

Problems: Briefly describe key problems to be addressed	Goals: State desired outcome for each problem.	Objectives: Describe specific stepping stones toward each goal; update as client progresses.	Interventions: Describe intervention approaches to be used.	Assessment and evaluation: Describe indexes and scales used to track progress.
			Improve communication and problem solving between Philippa and Antwon to make visits more fun for Lyla and less anxiety provoking; visits should be extended so Antwon can spend more time with Lyla without her mom present. Broaden Philippa's social network and supports so she spends at least one weekly event without her daughter. Participate in more parent-teacher and similar school and church activities where children are supervised in activities separate from parents.	

CHAPTER TWELVE

Behavioral Externalizing Disorders of Childhood and Adolescence

EXTERNALIZING DISORDERS are observable behavioral problems, including oppositional defiant disorder (e.g., chronic disruptions, disobedience) and conduct disorder (e.g., fire setting, theft, animal cruelty, sexual promiscuity, interpersonal aggression, drug use). Oppositional defiant disorder (ODD) is usually associated with younger children, whereas conduct disorder (CD) tends to be identified with adolescents. Externalizing disorders have been shown to be associated with family risk factors that include substance abuse and criminality (particularly in fathers), other forms of mental illness in the family, highly disruptive family conflict, domestic violence, and child abuse and neglect. Conduct disorder may also be an antecedent for joining gangs or developing an antisocial personality as an adult. Adolescents who show a pronounced lack of concern for others' welfare and a virtual absence of remorse or guilt concerning the harmful consequences of their behaviors are more likely to meet criteria for psychopathy as adults. Practitioners should be prepared to assess for attention deficit/ hyperactivity disorder (ADHD), a problem that often co-occurs with CD. This assessment may require the assistance of a professional trained in specific diagnostic testing for ADHD and associated learning disabilities (e.g., in reading or math).

Assessment

The DSM-IV-TR criteria for ODD and CD reflect the basic description herein, and practitioners should review them in detail (APA, 2000). However, assessment should go beyond a basic description, and practitioners should conduct a thorough MDF assessment that at least examines how the child's or adolescent's disruptive behavior is associated with key mental status indicators (e.g., thought disorders), emotional well-being (e.g., depression), level of impulsivity (e.g., aggression), interpersonal relations at home and in the community, school performance, substance abuse, and overall health. Any and all of these problems can exacerbate behavioral problems, and CD can aggravate other psychosocial difficulties (McMahon, Wells, & Kotler, 2006; O'Hare, 2005; Smith, Barkley, & Shapiro, 2006). For example, practitioners should carefully review mental status and mood to identify more serious problems, such as delusional thinking or the possibility of major mood disorder or onset of schizophrenia in older adolescents. Practitioners should carefully examine impulsive behaviors including violence and substance abuse to identify more immediate dangers of harming others, becoming involved in criminal activity (e.g., drug dealing, gang affiliation), or putting oneself in harm's way. Practitioners should carefully assess family relationships to determine whether the child or adolescent is being physically abused and the competence of parental supervision. Older adolescents may also be putting others in the home in danger (e.g., physically or sexually abusing a sibling, threatening adults for drug money). Moreover, practitioners should explore the client's associations in the community with gang members, street criminals, and drug dealers. Some effort to determine the client's general health should be made, especially for risks of contracting sexually transmitted diseases or intravenous drug use.

A functional assessment of a child's or adolescent's behavior over time is essential. Disruptive behavior in children and more serious conduct-disordered behavior in adolescents does not happen at random but in patterns that highlight important antecedents of such behaviors. Is violent behavior, for example, more likely to occur at home or in the community? Where, with whom, and how often is the abuse of alcohol or other drugs occurring? Does the adolescent associate with anyone who appears to have a more prosocial effect on his or her behavior (e.g., older adults who act as unofficial mentors)? How structured is the child's or adolescent's behavior during the week? Does he or she leave home and return at regular hours? Does he or she attend school regularly, if at all? What other strengths and positive adaptive abilities does the adolescent have? Is he or she using them to full potential? At what times during the week does the adolescent seem more likely to get into trouble? How often does he or she have encounters with law enforcement or school administration?

Given the nature of some of these behaviors, it is unlikely that adolescent clients will provide a fully transparent picture of their daily routines, particularly those activities that they do not want the practitioner to know about. Interviewing adults in the family is essential whenever possible. It is also important to acquire informed consent from parents and guardians to talk with juvenile officers, teachers, coaches, and others who may have regular opportunities to observe the client. When the practitioner lays down the expectation early that he or she wants all adults in the client's world to be in contact, that sends a clear signal that the practitioner cannot help unless he or she knows what is really going on in the client's life. Relying solely on the client's self-report or on that of his or her parents is likely to lead to a skewed or incomplete representation of the facts.

For obvious reasons, the social worker should expect that parents or guardians might not be forthcoming in their support for the child or adolescent. In the case of younger children, they may be either more defensive about the child's behavior or more willing to blame the child exclusively, especially if there has been abuse in the home. If the practitioner suspects that abuse is a contributing factor to the client's disruptive behavior, he or she will have to conduct a more thorough abuse assessment. If the client and his or her family cooperate more readily, the practitioner will have an easier time identifying the antecedents to the behavioral difficulties. As a result, the practitioner will be better able to help the parents improve their nurturing and disciplining skills. For more troubled adolescents, there may be a longer history of domestic conflict or ineffective parenting, which results in greater difficulty for the parents to employ effective disciplinary measures. For older adolescents who are getting involved in criminal activities, the emphasis may have to shift to engaging external authorities to rein in the client's behavior. Only after having completed a thorough MDF assessment based on multiple informants can the practitioner design an intervention plan at the proper level of care. Can this problem be managed within the family unit alone? Should school personnel become involved? Is it necessary to coordinate efforts with the criminal justice system? In more serious cases, practitioners should be prepared to intervene at all levels.

Co-occurring ADHD

Many behaviorally disordered children also struggle with signs and symptoms of ADHD, such as not paying attention to academic and other tasks, becoming easily frustrated and bored, being easily distracted, tending to be disorganized and forgetful, being fidgety, and reacting impulsively to frustration. Many of these symptoms overlap considerably with the conduct-disordered child or adolescent, and the casual observer will not be able to distinguish the causes of their impulsivity or difficulty following directions or staying on task. These behaviors, frustrating for teachers, parents, and other adults, tend to disrupt the daily routines of others. Sorting out ADHD from other behavioral disorders can be difficult, but one can determine if the signs of ADHD are situational or not. Some children may do well in the relatively quiet structure of a well-run classroom but not at home. For other children, home life may be conducive to completing their work, but they may have difficulty functioning well in school. When such contextual disparities become apparent, practitioners should consider the possibility of situational problems before applying a diagnosis of ADHD.

Intervention

A large and growing body of research supports a range of cognitive behavior and contingency management therapies for externalizing childhood and adolescent disorders (e.g., Alexander, Waldron, Newberry, & Liddle, 1988; Farmer, Compton, Burns, & Robertson, 2002; Foster, 1994; Kazdin & Weisz, 1998; McMahon & Forehand, 1984; McMahon, Wells, & Kotler, 2006; Ollendick & King, 1998; Silverman & Berman; 2001; Smith, Barkley, & Shapiro, 2006; Thyer, 1995; Webster-Stratton & Herbert, 1994). Cognitive-behavioral approaches for children's disorders are increasingly implemented in the context of behaviorally oriented family therapies (e.g., Compton, Burns, Egger, & Robertson, 2002; Northey, Wells, Silverman, & Bailey, 2003) and are often incorporated into ecological and multisystemic frameworks to deal with complex and serious behavior problems such as youthful delinquency (e.g., Henggeler, Shoenwald, Borduin, Rowland, & Cunningham, 1998). Treatment for co-occurring ADHD is likely to include stimulant medications. Although serious debate continues with regard to overprescribing medications, more than one hundred controlled trials attest to their effectiveness in improving concentration, enhancing school performance, and reducing disruptive behaviors. These medications have been shown to work particularly well when combined with well-run contingency management programs in the classroom and at home (Farmer et al., 2002; Smith et al., 2006).

Developing and maintaining a supportive, collaborative, and empathic relationship with behaviorally disordered children, adolescents, and their families can be challenging. Children with internalizing disorders (e.g., depression, anxiety) tend to be a bit quieter and more compliant, and perhaps evoke greater sympathy. They tend to suffer in silence and incur less social disapproval from the adults around them. Parents, teachers, school officials, community juvenile officers, and social workers, however, are more likely to have their attention drawn to behaviorally disordered children and adolescents, and they become increasingly frustrated in attempting to deal with them. Often, overly punitive measures or, conversely, the lack of constructive disciplinary measures further reinforce much of this "bad" behavior.

To maintain an empathic link with conduct-disordered children and adolescents, it is important for practitioners to keep in mind that the clients are generally not happy with their circumstances. Their goal in life is not to incur the wrath of adults around them, though the opposite may seem to be the case. Impulsivity, learning difficulties, trouble regulating emotional responses, and failure to get along with others reveals a picture of young people who are quite distressed. Their frustrations are palpable, and their readiness to disobey or associate themselves primarily with others who are often in trouble seems, at times, almost beyond their control.

Developing a working relationship with behaviorally disordered children, adolescents, and their families is a challenge. Often, both parents are not in the picture, so practitioners should be prepared to deal with a single parent, often one who is overwhelmed. Complaints from the school and others in the community only increase the parent's frustration, which often leads to ineffective punishments, hollow threats, and sometimes contempt and despair about having a "normal" family life.

Practitioners must connect with the identified child or adolescent as well as the parents/guardians in a way that does not communicate blame. Although taking history and conducting a thorough analysis of the problem over time is essential, practitioners must take pains to be empathic and emphasize a forward-looking, problem-solving approach. Depending on the severity of the problem, practitioners should communicate optimism that many behavior disorders in children and adolescents can be brought under control, but that everyone involved will have to consider making adjustments. Communicating the sense that everyone is "in this together" is helpful and positive.

The practitioner should listen carefully to each family member. When everyone feels that their concerns, frustrations, and desires have been heard, practitioners can then underscore the common ground they all share: everyone has expectations, and everyone has to give something to get what they want and live together as a family. Unless there is outright abuse and criminality (e.g., sexual or physical abuse, domestic violence), practitioners should avoid the victim-villain characterization that many troubled families bring into the consulting room. If there is abuse or violence, social workers then have to confront the challenge of balancing their being a mandated reporter (i.e., obligated by law to report abuse to child welfare authorities) and maintaining a viable working alliance. If that is not feasible, then therapeutic work may have to be continued by another practitioner if the case has been adjudicated.

Often, with seriously behaviorally disordered children or adolescents, the child or adolescent and his or her family are often very discouraged and feel that there is little likelihood for improvement. It is important to do two things to help bolster the family's morale: (1) help motivate them by focusing on problems that they can improve, and (2) set reasonable goals. Although it may be temporarily heartening to tell parents and the child you know that matters can improve, this will do little to convince your clients in the long run. For them to feel "in their guts" that things can get better, they must experience some initial successes. These immediate goals can be any one of the following examples: a time-out from fighting; a temporary truce or contract to abide by certain house rules; elimination of yelling, name-calling, and other behaviors that are unnecessarily provocative and create a contentious atmosphere; an agreement on the part of the parents not to make any decisions regarding how to parent or discipline their child or adolescent until they agree on a basic policy (this is an important step because much dysfunctional parenting results from a lack of parental consistency and cooperation); an agreement on the part of the child or adolescent that he or she shares in some part of the solution, so cooperation is important. If a family can honor these basic guidelines for even a week or two, it can create an atmosphere more conducive to making progress in more long-term challenges.

If there are two parents or adult authorities, it is important that the practitioner meet with them alone for a session or two to help them agree on setting limits with the child or adolescent. This step is critical. The parents must be able and willing to use their authority, and they must cooperate to help a conduct-disordered child. As is often the case, they will likely reveal other differences and sources of conflict that are not directly related to the child's or adolescent's problem. The child or adolescent may be triangulated; that is, he or she may become a target to which parents attribute their difficulties as a couple. Couples' problems must be assessed thoroughly (see chapter 10) and differentiated from problems the couple are having in their role as parents. For example, if there is infidelity in the relationship, and one partner is angry and will not cooperate with the other on any other matters (e.g., money, parenting), then this problem must be addressed separately from their difficulties as parents. Parents will often agree in principle that it makes little sense to take it out on the kids, even though they often, unwittingly perhaps, engage in scapegoating, sabotage (e.g., deliberately or unwittingly thwarting progress in an attempt to further disrupt the marriage), or other forms of triangulation. Substance abuse in one or both parents is often a problem in behaviorally disordered families. Without addressing it, there is little the family is likely to accomplish by focusing on the child's or adolescent's difficulties exclusively. Once parents agree to temporarily set aside their own difficulties and cooperate for the welfare of the child, the work can proceed. Once the child or adolescent is stabilized, matters unique to the couple can be revisited. Sometimes, a successful experience in parenting can reduce hopelessness, reduce tension in the household, and increase both goodwill and the feeling that the couple may be better able to resolve some of their own difficulties.

The goals set for the young client during this early period should also be achievable, and parents should be willing to reward partial successes. Of course, the goals depend on the type of problem and severity, as well as the age of the child. But small successes are important, and parents have to cooperate in helping their child achieve these. Optimism and the use of positive reinforcement are overwhelmingly more productive than are sanctions and punitive measures, which should be used only as a last resort.

Coping skills for behaviorally disordered children and adolescents were developed partly on the premise that such young people have deficits in the way they perceive and understand interpersonal relationships, difficulties understanding and regulating their own emotions, and a lack of problem-solving skills. Many children and adolescents, for reasons that include temperament, family history, and social circumstances, tend to see other people's behavior as potentially exploitive, harmful, or threatening. Young people's own difficulties in coping with frustration, managing their own anger, and tending to lash out verbally or physically when they feel threatened or challenged exacerbates this distortion in understanding how relationships work. For some young people, the reality of everyday violence and exploitation in their community (e.g., drug dealing, violence, gang activities, a culture steeped in violence) further aggravates their expectations and tendencies. Even the most even-tempered, well-loved child can face serious challenges in dealing with a daily reality in which force and threats of violence occur frequently.

When working with children or adolescents, it is important to engage in focused conversations about their daily encounters with others and to pursue nonjudgmental questioning about their relationships. What do they think the other person expects of them? What does the young client offer that person? How would another person, perhaps, deal with the same situation? For example, the child reports that someone knocked over her lunch tray in the cafeteria in school. How did that happen? What was her reaction? What did the other person say? Then what happened? Carefully examining such thoughts, feelings, and behaviors in real-life, daily scenarios will provide a blueprint (a cognitive schema) for the way they tend to interpret and deal with interpersonal relations.

Other questions should explore different types of relationships: Do you have any close friends? Who is your best friend? Why is that person your best friend? What do you have in common? Does that person think that you are his or her best friend? Examining the client's priorities in that relationship, what he or she expects from the other person, what the client brings to the relationship, and his or her level of trust can go a long way toward understanding how the client relates to others and how the client sees him- or herself in a relationship.

Gradually, a picture of the client's relationships will emerge. Since the client already will have been identified as behaviorally disordered, the practitioner should be prepared for a variety of responses: on one extreme, the client is able to form a prosocial and nonexploitive relationship with at least one other person; at the other extreme, the client tends to see all relationships as threatening and potentially harmful. Some antisocial children may be able to engage in healthful prosocial relationships, but because of the circumstances, such relationships are limited in scope or opportunity. For example, if a child has witnessed or personally experienced much abuse at home, or has encountered a lot of violence in his or her immediate community, the child may keep any trusting relationships rather circumscribed. Adolescents in similar circumstances may show little ability to engage in relationships unless there is some mutually agreed-on contract that binds them to each other (e.g., cooperating in criminal behaviors under pain of retaliation),which are relationships that are not generally considered healthful.

If children or adolescents seem to be able to relate to others on a more functional and empathic level, and want to get along with others and reduce conflict in their life, there is much that practitioners can do. Cognitive-behavioral efforts that focus on social skills can help them more accurately read and interpret the behavior and feelings of others in social situations, and respond in ways that promote healthful relationships. Practitioners should discuss some of the client's actual daily encounters in school and elsewhere, help the client assess those interactions and social situations, examine the possibility that the client negatively distorts others' intent, and suggest the possibility of trying out more prosocial cognitions. As with the lunch-tray incident mentioned previously, the practitioner should help the client carefully examine the situation: What were your immediate thoughts and feelings about what happened? How did the other person respond? Did you think he or she was laughing at you? Could it be that he or she was just nervous? Did the person say say, "Excuse me" or "I'm sorry"? Do you think the person did it on purpose? Of course, there are several possibilities. Perhaps the class bully did do it on purpose. What then? The practitioner might examine the client's options: So, you thought of attacking him. What do you think that would have accomplished? What do you think the resulting consequences might have been? What if someone got seriously hurt? What if that person were you?

Perhaps the adolescent was actually targeted in a incident, but perhaps not. In either case, it is critically important to help young people stop, think about what happened, identify their feelings, and consider the potential consequences of their behaviors before acting. Children and adolescents who are categorized as oppositional, conduct-disordered, or antisocial tend to act impulsively before they think, and they often do not allow for time to process their feelings and determine what really happened. Their negative blueprint of the world being so difficult readies them to lash out and defend themselves rather than stop, think, feel, and decide calmly what a balanced response might be. In some cases, peer expectations demand an immediate, and often aggressive, response.

Once practitioners examine a problem in detail with clients, they can help impulsive clients rehearse the "stop, think, feel, act" routine by modeling the cognitive process. Practitioners can guide them by modeling prosocial self-statements (i.e., self-talk) aloud in the presence of the child or adolescent, help the client rehearse these skills by prompting them with cues to practice the self-statements, track the problem over time, and reward him- or herself for showing self-control. The steps to follow should include (1) identifying the event (e.g., client was called a name, pushed, or threatened by another), (2) stopping to accurately appraise the situation, (3) identifying one's feelings, and (4) considering the response that will best lead to a positive outcome for the client (preferably, a nonviolent resolution). Helping adolescents identify and control their anger and other related responses, and use constructive responses to avert aggressive encounters (e.g., calmly joking about it, changing the subject) can go a long way toward helping them avoid negative, and sometime tragic, violent encounters.

Using guided meditation and other visualization techniques for covert practice often appeals to adolescents and can be a low-anxiety approach to helping them walk through the "stop, think, feel, act" routine before practicing it in real life. This exercise can help young people relax and visualize themselves identifying, processing, and responding to a potentially problematic situation in a prosocial manner (the technique is similar to that described in general in chapter 6). After having practiced the stop, think, feel, act process in the mind's eye, the practitioner can use role-playing to act out scenarios that are likely to provoke the client, try variations of it, and gradually make the scenario more challenging for the adolescent to respond in a constructive way. Interjecting humor now and then may help put the young person in a constructive frame of mind and get some perspective on the problem. Although role-playing is helpful, there is no substitute for practicing in the real world, and it is likely that the client will have more than sufficient opportunities to try out his or her new skills in everyday life. Although it is not practical to plan such events, the client should be ready to use his or her new skills when the opportunity naturally arises, and to write down a few notes to evaluate how he or she handled the situation. Helping adolescents monitor and evaluate their own reactions is essential for them to make progress and maintain gains over time. If the practitioner is working with a child or adolescent in a situation of family therapy, and parents support the child's efforts, then parents should be included in this part of the intervention as therapeutic collaborators to offer encouragement and reinforcement for the child's progress.

Improving Parenting Skills

Family therapy can greatly enhance cognitive-behavioral interventions with conduct-disordered children. Family sessions can be used to improve communication, to work on problem solving, and to improve interpersonal behaviors among family members. But a core aspect of effective family therapy for behaviorally troubled children and adolescents is the improvement of parenting skills. Parents have the responsibility to use their authority both to nurture their children and to provide consistent, positive disciplining. Single parents at times face even greater challenges in caring for a behaviorally disordered child. Much of this section describes the essentials of effective parenting in general, but the principles apply to younger children with emerging behavioral disorders and to conduct-disordered adolescents.

When a young person's behavior requires an intervention, it is often the case that parents have not consistently had good parenting skills. If parents lose control over an adolescent who has become potentially dangerous, the juvenile justice system may intervene as surrogate parent to determine court-ordered supervision, family therapy, and institutionalization in psychiatric care facilities or juvenile detention centers, depending on the severity of the disordered behavior.

In principle, effective parenting is not complicated: providing consistent, genuine caring and nurturance; providing for the child's psychosocial and physical well-being; showing an interest in the child's ideas, thoughts, feelings, and experiences; being vigilant about the child's activities and companions inside and outside the home; and having clear policies about which behaviors deserve reward and which deserve sanction. In actual practice, however, being an effective parent with a conduct-disordered child is a challenge. For various reasons, some parents are more skilled than others. Often, ineffective parents lack assertiveness, are uncomfortable using authority, are immature or inexperienced, were subjected to ineffective parenting when they were children, were victims of abuse or neglect, had parents who had mental illnesses or substance abuse problems, or had parents who were simply overwhelmed by money problems and other life circumstances. Although such factors can affect anyone's parenting skills, there is good reason to believe that most parents can learn to be more effective.

Practitioners should be clear and focused about identifying both the strengths and the deficits that a parent brings to treatment when trying to cope with a behaviorally disordered child. As discussed earlier, if a parent has serious problems of his or her own, then he or she may need to address these before improving parenting skills. For example, drug-using parents are not likely to be vigilant and attentive to young adolescents who are testing their parent's limits. If a mother is sleeping off her heavy drinking every day when her daughter comes home, then she has lost an opportunity to engage her daughter and discuss her day, deal with problems, give her support, and monitor her homework. When such problems occur consistently, children and adolescents often begin to feel that their parents do not care what they are doing during or after school.

Assuming that an individual's or a couple's problems in the family are mitigated to the point at which parents can focus on improving parenting skills, there is much that a practitioner can do to help them make some positive adjustments. For starters, the social worker can demonstrate nurturance (e.g., emotional and physical caring and playing). This approach may be more helpful with parents who have young children and are anxious or overly concerned that their children are on their best behavior at all times. Sitting with the family and playing a game that includes the child can be a great way to develop a sense of family fun. The parents may see that, with a little investment in the nurturing side of family life, their efforts to enforce ordinary levels of discipline come with less effort.

Some parents become very anxious as their children approach adolescence. Perhaps they recall some of their own risky behaviors (which they probably kept from their own parents) or are afraid of unwanted pregnancy, getting into trouble, drinking alcohol and using other drugs, the dangers of driving, and so forth. However, rather than respond to the onset of adolescence with a sense of fun and engage older children in adult conversations about high-risk behaviors, some parents allow their anxiety to transform them into rigid disciplinarians. As a result, their adolescent children express resentment about being treated like children and are likely to rebel. Although reasonable limits are important and needed during this time, what is also needed is a lot more conversation about the matters that parents lie awake at night worrying about. More conversation, more interest in what the adolescent is doing, and less arbitrary rule enforcement can reduce tensions and markedly improve parent-teen relationships. Many parents are unwilling to engage adolescent children as young adults; as a result, tensions, conflicts, and behavior problems remain unresolved.

Practitioners can help parents engage their adolescent sons and daughters by modeling this kind of "adult" conversation in front of the parents, and then inviting the parents to join in. Many parents recall their adolescent years as a time when their parents were always yelling at them and threatening them with sanctions of one kind or another. Practitioners can help parents relax a bit by discussing the high-risk concerns associated with adolescence and by helping them engage their sons and daughters in frank discussions about sex, drugs, and other high-risk behaviors. Modeling and in-session practice can get things started, but parents need to continue these conversations at home.

There are occasions, however, especially with conduct-disordered children and adolescents, when talking is not enough. Nurturance and understanding is no guarantee that children and adolescents will not engage in serious problem behaviors. Parents must be willing to use their authority in a constructive but definitive manner. Parents should negotiate the use of graduated sanctions that fit the crime, so to speak. If both parents are available, they must implement disciplinary (i.e., limit setting) measures in concert and without ambivalence. Single parents need to be reasonably consistent with their directives. Brief time-outs or loss of television privileges work well. If cooperation with reasonable tasks (e.g., picking up toys, doing homework) is not forthcoming, parents can increase sanctions. For older children or adolescents, sanctions need to be commensurate with the infraction.

Practitioners can help parents understand that they should not discipline in a way that communicates disrespect or contempt for a child or adolescent. Parents should discipline calmly, with simple, clear communications. It is also important for parents to give a clear reason why they are disciplining the child, and to frame that reason in a way that focuses on long-term outcomes. Parents who say, "I don't have to give you a reason" are modeling authoritarian and unreasonable behavior. It is important that practitioners help parents understand that arbitrary use of their authority only inspires frustration and contempt on the part of the child and overlooks the opportunity to communicate purposeful concern about the child's long-term well-being.

The following are specific ways to teach parents more effective parenting techniques. They should be adjusted to the specific problems and ages of children and adolescents:

- Explain the rationale for an approach (e.g., efforts to increase prosocial behavior or reduce negative behavior) to parents.
- Demonstrate skills through role-play.
- Have parents explain the desired behavior to the child until the child demonstrates that he or she understands it.
- Have the child role-play to demonstrate the behavior with the parent.
- Direct the parent to demonstrate the approach with the child while the practitioner observes and coaches.
- Allow parents to practice during the session without direct coaching.
- Assign parents the task of practicing the new skills at home.
- Review parents' performance in the following session.
- Teach parents to pinpoint problem behaviors (e.g., by recording compliance and noncompliance) and monitor them at home.
- Explain how to shape the child's behavior by stringing together rewards and sanctions to increase the child's constructive and prosocial behaviors.
- Teach parents to monitor their children at all times, even when they are away from home. This involves parents knowing where their children are, what they are doing, who they are with, and when they will return. Children must be held accountable for such things.
- Demonstrate to parents how to be somewhat flexible, particularly with older children, and practice problem-solving and negotiating strategies. Help them understand that being an effective parent does not mean winning every battle decisively.

- Assign the parents with specific tasks to practice at home as the child's progress dictates.
- Direct parenting techniques toward improving the child's behavior and performance at school if needed.
- Arrange for regular communication between parents and teachers to compare notes on behaviors and school performance.
- Help parents design achievable, specific goals for their children.
- Encourage adults (e.g., parents, teachers) involved in the treatment to give praise and tangible rewards for prosocial behaviors.

Behavioral Family Therapy Skills

Parenting skills are best taught and practiced within the context of behavioral and other similar family therapies (e.g., structural and strategic approaches):

- Identify problem behaviors between family members, negotiate solutions, and improve positive interactions (particularly by reducing coercive interactions).
- Demonstrate communication and problem-solving skills for all family members, and continually monitor and evaluate improvements.
- Provide interventions for couples to improve communication and problem solving (on issues other than parenting differences as well).
- Facilitate the style, direction, and intensity of communications so they become increasingly constructive (e.g., one person speaks at a time, no interruptions, specificity in what parents say, no accusations or name-calling).
- Negotiate straightforward contingency contracts to facilitate either the couple's relationship or parenting skills.

As discussed in chapter 4, practitioners should continue to monitor communication patterns, alliances in the family, the parents' use of authority, and the overall emotional tone of the family's communications. Practitioners need to work at all levels—with the individual client, with the parent or parents as a couple, and with the whole family—to improve and maintain the cooperation and consistency necessary to help behaviorally disordered children or adolescents.

Case Management Skills: Engaging the Broader System and Contingency Management

Even the most skilled efforts with children and adolescents and their families may not be sufficient to improve behavior and overall family functioning. Often, when working with seriously conduct-disordered adolescents, social workers must coordinate the intervention with other agencies: schools, criminal justice, primary health services, and other community resources. The principles for working with the broader system in a case management framework include the need for professional initiative on the part of the social worker to enhance the coordination of services, to keep all parties on the same page with a clearly communicated and negotiated intervention plan, and to bolster social and instrumental supports as needed. Intervention plans are likely to include contingencies for prosocial behavior (rewards) and antisocial behavior (sanctions). The specific skills practitioners need are summarized as follows:

- Engage in assertive case management with social systems (e.g., schools, law enforcement, criminal justice) as needed and arrange for other instrumental social supports.
- Actively include teachers and other school personnel in the treatment plan to generalize and maintain prosocial behavioral improvements.
- Encourage all parties to work from the same intervention plan, and particularly to use a contingency management strategy, by listing the behaviors that are expected of the adolescent and the clear consequences for positive and negative behaviors. All participants in the intervention must stick to the contingency management plan so responses of parents and other involved adults can be swift, fair, and consistent.
- Arrange for long-term follow-up, booster sessions, and other needed services.

For clients with co-occurring ADHD, interventions might also include:

- Using psychoeducation to teach parents about the causes, developmental course, and prognosis for ADHD; recommending books and videos to parents so they can research the problem on their own time, and teaching parents to understand that the behavior of all family members can either help or hinder a child's difficulties.
- Teaching parents to reduce stress in the household through calm and clear communication skills, sound discipline practices, and

enjoyable activities to reduce overall stress. Such changes can create a quieter atmosphere that is more conducive to relaxation and improved concentration for the child with ADHD.

- Reviewing basic problem solving (i.e., define the problem, develop a plan, anticipate obstacles, implement and evaluate the plan) to approach daily problems in a more organized, focused, and systematic manner.
- Discussing environmental management in the home (e.g., organized, uncluttered, a place to work privately) to reduce distractions, facilitate self-control, increase concentration, and improve problem solving.
- Demonstrating for parents how to reduce the child's negative behaviors and increase task-focused behaviors, including positive reinforcement to the child for productive behaviors and ignoring negative or distracting behaviors.
- Showing parents how to attend to their child's noncompliance by breaking down complex tasks, reducing distractions, and giving simple, direct commands while providing immediate reinforcement for prompt compliance.
- Discussing how to develop a token home economy with the child by negotiating rewards for prompt compliance and sanctions or withheld rewards for noncompliance or negative behaviors.
- Showing parents how to implement time-out procedures for noncompliance and encouraging parents to issue a command to the child, wait a few seconds, and issue it again. If the child does not comply, parents direct him or her to stay in time-out (e.g., a few minutes for young children, more time for older children). Parents can lengthen time-out if the child continues to be oppositional or disruptive.
- Encouraging cooperation between parents and teachers to improve school behavior and academic performance; instructing parents and teachers to use a common scorecard and to implement rewards and sanctions based on daily school reports.
- Consulting with teachers on classroom contingency management plans; teachers who see that the child's work is broken down into increments and that the child is on task implement the plan by providing consistent rewards; in contrast, teachers sanction disruptive behaviors with time-out or temporary loss of privileges.
- Reviewing and evaluating the results of the plan with the parents, anticipating events that could lead to occasional setbacks, and planning for possible booster sessions.

Summary

Behaviorally disordered children and adolescents, including those with co-occurring ADHD, often require that social workers use their full complement of skills: supportive skills to maintain an often fragile working alliance with a difficult adolescent or conflict-ridden family, coping skills to help parents deal directly with disruptive behaviors in the home, and case management skills to increase social and instrumental supports, coordinate multiple services, and maintain consistent implementation of the intervention plan. By working directly with individual children or adolescents, improving parents' coping skills and family functioning, and providing a more coherent set of contingencies in children's lives across multiple systems, practitioners can make real progress in helping oppositional or conduct-disordered children and adolescents and their families.

Case Study: Chi

The Comprehensive Service Plan (Assessment, Intervention, Evaluation)

Use all available information from the client and significant others, your observations, and input from other professionals to conduct both quantitative and qualitative aspects of this multidimensional-functional assessment.

Client identification data: (gender, age, marital status, sexual orientation; family composition; employment; racial, ethnic, cultural, religious/spiritual affiliation and identity)

Chi is a fifteen-year-old male from a Vietnamese family. He lives with his father, Quan, and his mother, Hue. His sister, Binh, is in her freshman year at college, and lives in a dormitory. Quan and Hue left Vietnam (separately) for the United States in the mid-1970s, after the fall of Saigon. Quan was an officer in the South Vietnamese army; after arriving in the United States, he worked a variety of jobs. For the past ten years, he has worked steadily managing an electronics store. His wife, Hue, had been a full-time homemaker, but in recent years she has begun to work part-time in local Vietnamese and other Asian restaurants as a waitress and hostess. They identify themselves as Roman Catholic. Hue attends church. Quan and the children do not. They identify with Vietnamese and Chinese culture and heritage, and celebrate both American and Vietnamese heritage during the holidays.

The presenting problem

Description of problem (client's view)

Chi states that he does not know why he was arrested or sent to a mental health center. He claims that he was arrested for no reason, just because the "police like to hassle me."

Description of problem (practitioner's view)

Chi was recently arrested after having beat another teenager severely with a piece of steel pipe because the other boy failed to pay him money, presumably in exchange for marijuana. The police report that witnesses identified him as a rising young drug dealer with a penchant for violent retribution against those who don't pay on time. Since this was his first arrest, the judge remanded him to a juvenile diversionary program where he is to receive family counseling and substance abuse treatment. His diversionary status is contingent on his cooperation, lack of further arrests, school attendance, and progress reports from the social worker.

Psychosocial history with an emphasis on problem trajectory

After three interviews with Chi and his parents (i.e., an individual interview with Chi, a couple's interview, and an interview with Chi and his parents together), the following facts have been determined. Quan and Hue met in the early 1980s at a church supper in a rural town in the northern United States. They soon became engaged. Hue became pregnant, but lost her first child soon after birth. Hue was depressed for some time after that. During that time, Quan also become somewhat distant, and (according to Hue) was also very depressed at times, drank a lot of alcohol, and had frequent violent outbursts of anger, smashing furniture or other objects, often after he had been drinking. He would often get up in the middle of the night, have a few drinks while sitting alone talking to himself, and return to bed. He would find it difficult to return to work the following day. After a time, the outbursts subsided somewhat, and he was able to moderate his drinking. He said that talking with other Vietnamese immigrants he worked with sometimes was upsetting but sometimes helped. He was clearly suffering from having witnessed many combat situations and related atrocities.

After conferring with a physician a few years after the death of their first child, Hue became pregnant with Chi. The parents report that Chi was somewhat oppositional early on and during grade school. Quan became increasingly strict with his son, insisting on certain rules of decorum regarding mealtime behaviors, cleaning and ordering his room, and strict obedience in every other way. As Chi entered adolescence, Quan became somewhat physical in response to Chi's verbal rebelliousness. Quan admitted having hit Chi on a fairly regular basis—always using on open hand but nevertheless hitting him hard enough to knock him down on several occasions. Chi responded by becoming increasingly aggressive and began hitting back. When things escalated about a year ago, Chi began missing school, spending days at a time living on the street, and keeping company with alleged gang members in the neighborhood. He did not complete his second year of high school, and two months ago was arrested and referred to the clinic.

Attempts to resolve the problems, previous treatment and relevant outcomes

Quan and Hue did try to get help for Chi. They attended pastoral counseling in their local church for a few visits, but Quan became angry when the counselor accused him of battering his son. Quan felt blamed and guilty and decided not to return. Otherwise, they have sought out no other treatments. Quan mentioned that an elderly physician he saw when he was drinking heavily told him to get psychiatric help for combat fatigue, but Quan never followed up on that suggestion and would not take the medication that the doctor recommended (he does not recall what it was).

The individual assessment

Mental status, cognitive disturbances: Describe the client's level of hallucinations, delusions, disorientation, bizarre behavior or speech, memory problems, serious confusion, or other symptoms of serious cognitive impairment. Include other troubling or dysfunctional beliefs or convictions.

Chi is clearly an angry, depressed, and suspicious young man. He sees the world as a very dangerous place, and feels that he has to prove himself in his community and that, if he does not demonstrate that he is fearless of others, that they will "defeat" him. He refuses to even look at his father during the interview, but he softens a bit when his mother addresses him. He sees no need to return to school and feels that he can make his own way without going to college like his sister. He feels very pessimistic about his own future. He says he prefers to live on the street and feels that the local gang is his "real family."

> How would you rate the client's overall mental status during the past month?
>
> POOR [0]　　IMPAIRED [1]　　MARGINAL [2]　　GOOD [3]　　EXCELLENT [4]

Mental states, emotional distress: Describe the client's level of depression, anxiety, and overall ability to regulate emotions.

Chi is a very angry young man, but he also appears to be very depressed. Although he does not report the usual classic signs of major depression (e.g., sleep, appetite, low energy), it is hard to sort out these signs and symptoms because it appears that he chronically uses marijuana. He does not report any overt signs of suicidal ideation but claims that he can be fearless in his dealings with other gang members because he is not afraid to die. He stated: "Once you decide that you don't care if you die, you are capable of anything. That is why others fear me."

> How would you rate your client's emotional well-being over the past 30 days?
>
> POOR [0]　　IMPAIRED [1]　　MARGINAL [2]　　GOOD [3]　　EXCELLENT [4]

Behavioral problems: Describe the client's overall ability to regulate behavior. Consider things such as ability to express oneself effectively; ability to work at things patiently; and tendencies to verbally or physically lash out at others, run away, harm oneself, or to engage in impulsive, criminal, or substance-abusing behavior. How would you describe the client's overall impulse control?

Chi has long had difficulties in school. Although he gives every impression of being highly intelligent, he has difficulty completing his work, he becomes impatient quite readily, and his frustration quickly leads to anger and taking some kind of physical action. He has trouble sitting still and prefers to "do things with my hands—I hate school. I can't sit there all day doing reading or listening to people. It makes me crazy." He says the only thing he likes about school is his shop class, and he reports liking his shop teacher, Mike. "Mike is cool. He shows you how to do stuff, and he's nice, but he doesn't take any sh— from you either." Chi has been reported to have simply left school in the middle of class and wander the streets. When he was arrested recently, it was during school hours. He has also run away from home but usually returns after two or three days. He clearly is ready to fight, and though he claims to not carry weapons, he was found with a short utility-type blade in his pocket. From his report, he seems to be quite ready to settle disputes or perceived slights with his fists. Chi appears to be an angry young man who sees the world as his personal battlefield, is easily offended by perceived slights, and is ready and willing to risk his life even when he is clearly outmatched and the odds are against him. He is also engaged in a criminal enterprise: selling marijuana. Although he was fortunate to be remanded to this diversionary program, he could easily transition in the next few years to selling narcotics and other drugs, and become more involved with more violent and dangerous felons.

How would you rate your client's behavioral control generally over the past 30 days?

POOR [0]   IMPAIRED [1]   MARGINAL [2]   GOOD [3]   EXCELLENT [4]

Adaptive strengths and coping abilities. Describe the client's ability to cope with problems and everyday stressors. How would you describe the client's ability to assess problem situations, deal with triggers, cope with stress, solve problems, and perhaps reach out to others for help to deal effectively with difficulties?

Chi is quite resourceful, albeit in a way that is not really adaptive. He is, in a sense, brave, and is willing to take on big challenges. His ability to channel that energy and initiative, however, is currently directed at the wrong things. If he were able to focus on some of his educational challenges or had the opportunity to focus on some technical training, these qualities might serve him better. Currently, he is not adapting well.

How would you rate your client's overall adaptive strengths and coping abilities over the past 30 days?

POOR [0]   IMPAIRED [1]   MARGINAL [2]   GOOD [3]   EXCELLENT [4]

Health problems: Describe the client's overall health. Aside from normal, transient illnesses, think about the client's general health habits (e.g., smoking, heavy drinking, exercise, weight), chronic primary health disorders, the client's opinion of his or her own health, ability to engage in usual activities relatively free from discomfort, overall energy level, hospitalizations, and treatments for illness other than psychiatric ones. Consider the client's documented medical history and any ongoing treatments.

He reports no health problems. Results of a recent physical reveal that he is in perfect health.

How would you rate your client's health over the past 30 days?

POOR [0]   IMPAIRED [1]   MARGINAL [2]   GOOD [3]   EXCELLENT [4]

Use of alcohol and other drugs: Describe the client's use of alcohol, illicit substances (e.g., cocaine, heroin, marijuana, hallucinogens) and abuse of prescription medication. How often does the client use them, in what quantity, and how serious are the psychological, physical, or social consequences associated with use?

Chi admits to chronic marijuana use but no other drugs. His blood tests revealed no other drugs in his system, though enough time had elapsed after his arrest and confinement at home that this means little. He also claims that he has an occasional beer, though he does not really like it much. He reports that he does not use any illicit pharmaceuticals such as synthetic narcotics or barbiturates.

How would you rate the client's functioning in the past month with regard to substance use?

POOR [0]   IMPAIRED [1]   MARGINAL [2]   GOOD [3]   EXCELLENT [4]

Recreational activities: Consider what the client does for fun (alone or with others), hobbies, relaxation (reading, watching television, playing video games or cards) and physical exercise (e.g., walking, jogging, biking). How would you describe the client's overall involvement in positive recreational activities?

Chi has been known to hang out at the local arcade. Many of his "customers" are there as well (he mostly sells pot to other teenagers). He likes video games, particularly those that act out military-type shooting adventures.

He claims to have the highest score on one popular military shooting game. He finds this activity relaxing. Other than this activity and occasionally watching television, he reports no other recreational outlets.

> How would you rate the adequacy of the client's participation in healthy recreational activities over the past 30 days?
>
> POOR [0]   IMPAIRED [1]   MARGINAL [2]   GOOD [3]   EXCELLENT [4]

Material resources: Describe your client's current or (if institutionalized) most recent living situation overall. Consider such things as adequacy of food, clothing, shelter, and safety.

Chi is well provided for. If he goes without food or adequate clothing, it is the result of a kind of ascetic self-denial as a self-styled "soldier."

> How would you rate the overall adequacy of the client's material resources over the past month?
>
> POOR [0]   IMPAIRED [1]   MARGINAL [2]   GOOD [3]   EXCELLENT [4]

Independent living/self-care: Describe how well the client manages the household; takes care of personal hygiene; and eats, sleeps, and otherwise cares for his or her own basic needs.

As noted, Chi is cared for by his parents. Chi is resourceful, but I question whether he could really take care of himself independently.

> How would you rate the client's ability to live independently and take care of their basic needs over the past 30 days?
>
> POOR [0]   IMPAIRED [1]   MARGINAL [2]   GOOD [3]   EXCELLENT [4]

Work (role) satisfaction: Describe the client's current work-related or other important role-related activities (e.g., work, student, home, volunteer, retired, disabled). Describe the activities and responsibilities that occupy the client in a productive manner.

At fifteen years old, Chi's predominant role is to obtain his education, and he is having extraordinary trouble doing that. As suggested earlier, he will probably have to do remedial work to complete enough credits to finish his second year in high school.

How would you rate the client's work or role satisfaction over the past 30 days?

POOR [0]   IMPAIRED [1]   MARGINAL [2]   GOOD [3]   EXCELLENT [4]

Legal problems: Describe any legal problems the client has had or continues to have. These include minor infractions (e.g., public drunkenness, shoplifting, minor traffic violations, public disturbances) and more serious crimes (e.g., assault and battery, rape, burglary, driving under the influence). Consider the client's status (e.g., probation, awaiting imprisonment, parole). Also, consider any civil suits leveled at the client or pending financial judgments. Overall, how would you describe the client's current legal situation?

Chi is in serious trouble. If he fails to keep to the terms of this diversionary program, the judge assured him that he could be incarcerated in the juvenile detention facility until he is eighteen years old.

How would you rate the client's legal situation over the past 30 days?

POOR [0]   IMPAIRED [1]   MARGINAL [2]   GOOD [3]   EXCELLENT [4]

DSM-IV Diagnosis

Axis I   Conduct disorder, adolescent-onset 312.82
Cannabis abuse 305.20
Consider attention deficit/hyperactivity disorder 314.01
Dysthymic disorder 300.40

Axis II   No diagnosis

Family and social assessment

Family relations: Describe the client's current family structure including authority, hierarchy, alliances, roles, rules, boundaries, subsystems (e.g., couple, siblings, parent-child alliances), and patterns of interactions and quality of communications. Describe specific problems in the family; describe specific adaptive strengths in the family. How does the family describe their own racial, ethnic, cultural, and religious identities?

Chi's relationship with his father has clearly contributed to his current situation. Quan admits, "Maybe I've been pretty rough on him, at times." Hue tactfully suggested that Quan has always been "angry, upset and sad" about the war and has never left it behind. The hostility, anger, and violence that grew over the years between Chi and his father must clearly be resolved for both Chi's sake as well as for his father. Hue has played the role of quiet intermediary but can do little more than try to comfort them both. However, Quan and Hue have remained close over the years, and Chi does respond, somewhat, to his mother's interventions. Chi has expressed regret that he makes his mother worry about him. Chi is also fond of his sister, Binh, and admits missing her since she left for college.

How would you rate the quality of the client's immediate family relationships over the past 30 days?

POOR [0]   IMPAIRED [1]   MARGINAL [2]   GOOD [3]   EXCELLENT [4]

Immediate social relationships (close friends and acquaintances): Describe the quality of the client's relationships with friends and acquaintances. Over the past month, how would you describe the quality of the interaction overall between the client and others with respect to closeness, intimacy, general interpersonal satisfaction, effective communications, degree of conflict, level of hostility, aggression, and evidence of any emotional or physical abuse?

Chi's acquaintances are mostly younger teens who he refers to as "gang-banger wannabees," more mischief makers than criminals—at least not yet. Chi avoids the older male gang members, except in dealings as an intermediary to sell marijuana. Chi reports that some of his friends are "cool," and he seems to enjoy their company, but he does not bring them home because he feels that they would not be welcome or that his father would hassle them all the time. Thus, his parents have little idea about whom he associates with since they never meet their son's friends and acquaintances.

How would you rate the quality of the client's immediate social relationships over the past 30 days?

POOR [0]   IMPAIRED [1]   <u>MARGINAL [2]</u>   GOOD [3]   EXCELLENT [4]

Extended social relationships: Describe the type and quality of relationships between the client and others in the client's community (other than close friends and family). These people might include other families, law enforcement, human service agencies, school personnel, coworkers, and others from whom the client receives support or with whom the client is having serious conflict.

Chi's relations with local law enforcement, school personnel, and others in the community (e.g., shop owners) are somewhat contentious. Although he is seen as troubled and somewhat disruptive to those around him, consultation with the juvenile officer and his teachers reveals that he appears to be very intelligent and can be engaging and personable as well.

How would you rate the quality of the client's social relationships over the past 30 days?

POOR [0]   <u>IMPAIRED [1]</u>   MARGINAL [2]   GOOD [3]   EXCELLENT [4]

A concise summary of the MDF assessment: Highlight the client's areas of distress and adaptive strengths. Emphasize those areas that are most likely to be emphasized in the intervention plan.

Chi is a troubled fifteen-year-old who appears to demonstrate many signs of a growing conduct disorder and a chronic problem with marijuana abuse. He and his father have had a long-standing conflicted and often physically violent relationship. Chi has been emotionally and physically abused by Quan. Chi appears to be depressed (which may be exacerbated by marijuana abuse), is quite hostile at times, shows poor impulse control, and sees many in the world as his enemy, but he does appear able to develop some genuinely caring relationships. He expresses some sense of remorse regarding the difficulty his behavior has caused his mother and feels badly that he has disappointed his sister as well. He looks up to her and misses her. He clearly has trouble concentrating in school and should be tested by the school psychologist for ADHD and other specific learning disorders.

Recommendations for further focused assessment: Note recommended referrals to consultants or additional instruments to be used.

Refer to psychologist for additional assessment of ADHD and learning disabilities. Discuss the possibility of Quan participating in individual or couple sessions (as he prefers) to assess angry outbursts and depression; consider possibility of unresolved posttraumatic stress disorder symptoms.

THE COMPREHENSIVE SERVICE PLAN SUMMARY

Problems: Briefly describe key problems to be addressed	Goals: State desired outcome for each problem.	Objectives: Describe specific stepping stones toward each goal; update as client progresses.	Interventions: Describe intervention approaches to be used.	Assessment and evaluation: Describe indexes and scales used to track progress.
Behavioral impulsivity, aggression, fighting, running away, consequent legal problems	Reduce/eliminate aggressive behavior and associating with gang members and their acquaintances	Focus on one interaction per week in school; describe feelings of provocation, assessment, and reactions	*Supportive skills:* Develop a working relationship with Chi individually; focus on basic trust and identify some incentive for his participation (e.g., initially, to stay out of juvenile detention) and use a motivational posture to help engage him.	Have Chi keep a chart and indicate the following per week: •Number of fights with others outside home •Number of angry encounters or fights with his dad •Number of times he used marijuana
Chi's interpersonal skill deficits	Develop nonviolent ways of resolving disputes	Identify and monitor negative thinking about himself and others; offer counter interpretation	Join with Quan and Hue; avoid blaming Quan for causing Chi's behavior problems; focus on improving the situation as a family. Plan to include Binh during semester break.	Rate his overall mood: 0 = "very bad," 1 = "bad," 2 = "neither good nor bad," 3 = "good," 4 = "great."
Depression, marijuana abuse	Improve overall mood; reduce or eliminate marijuana use	Monitor and report any marijuana use, how much and what preceded his decision to use	*Therapeutic coping skills:* Individually, explore Chi's negative and hostile distortions regarding others; his readiness to overreact aggressively to perceived slights; review his history with his dad, make connections, and see if there is a chance for reconciliation.	Have family rate their view of Chi's cooperativeness, respect: 0 = "very bad," 1 = "bad," 2 = "neither good nor bad," 3 = "good," 4 = "great."
Conflicts at home, ineffective parenting	Develop more effective parenting skills, eliminate physical abuse, use positive contingencies in concert with court mandates	Have two family discussions per week for twenty minutes; focus initially on one another's daily activities; monitor level of respect, awareness of careful listening, not interrupting; note indications of conflict and what occurred		Summarize school reports and reports from juvenile officer.
Educational/learning difficulties	Improve school attendance and performance	Achieve one full week of perfect attendance; 90 percent for a month Complete 90 percent of school-work each week for a month		Collate all data and share with Chi and his family weekly.

Role-play potentially problematic scenarios, and model how to stop, think, breathe, and evaluate the situation before reacting; emphasize negative consequences of not staying calm; practice more effective communication skills.

Apply similar coping skills to identifying triggers (e.g., frustration) to reduce and eventually eliminate marijuana use.

Family sessions should focus on a fresh start and calm, respectful communications in all directions; focus particularly on Chi and Quan's interactions, talking things out; encourage apologies, forgiveness, and mutual respect in the future; model effective communications, calm expression of feelings; practice at home and report in session; develop a few new rules around Chi's behavior while living at home; emphasize cooperation with some reasonable flexibility (e.g., homework, curfew).

The Comprehensive Service Plan Summary (Continued)

Problems: Briefly describe key problems to be addressed	Goals: State desired outcome for each problem.	Objectives: Describe specific stepping stones toward each goal; update as client progresses.	Interventions: Describe intervention approaches to be used.	Assessment and evaluation: Describe indexes and scales used to track progress.
			Case management skills: Coordinate intervention plan with juvenile court, juvenile officer, school personnel. Have Chi report to Officer Callahan weekly in person; return school reports of attendance and completed work to parents and social worker. Refer for psychological evaluation, medical evaluation for potential ADHD meds; consider individual therapy for Quan (PTSD?) or mutual help group in his community.	

CHAPTER THIRTEEN

From Essential Skills to Evidence-Based Practices

As discussed in Chapter 1, basic interventions are generally used with people experiencing problems that tend to be mild to moderate in severity and relatively uncomplicated. These constitute the stressors and strains of everyday life: mild depression, relationship problems, stress and anxiety, and other transitory problems. People with such difficulties often respond well to basic counseling skills, including empathic listening, problem solving, and perhaps basic case management, such as a referral to a support group. More advanced interventions are those strategies that have been shown to be effective with problems that are more complex and accompanied by a greater degree of psychosocial dysfunction. Social work intervention with these problems requires greater knowledge of human behavior, the use of more advanced assessment methods, and the ability to carry out more complex strategies. Providing assessment, intervention, and evaluation with major mental illnesses (e.g, schizophrenia, bipolar disorder, major depression), addictions, disabling anxiety disorders, child abuse and neglect, childhood emotional and behavioral disorders, and eating disorders, among other problems, can be very challenging even for seasoned practitioners.

As a result of decades of efforts of practitioners and practitioner-researchers who share a commitment to practice research and evaluation, social workers now have many effective intervention options from which to choose. Evidence-based practices (EBPs) are interventions that have been shown repeatedly to be effective in controlled trials. Although the term *evidence-based* with regard to psychosocial interventions has been coined relatively recently, *evidence-based medicine* came into vogue in the early 1990s and has since been applied to the broader arena of psychosocial interventions—hence, the more generic term *evidence-based practice.*

However, the movement toward empirically supported practice has been around since at least the early 1960s. The term *empirically supported practice* is a bit more ambiguous and applies to two related aspects of evidence-based practice: (1) the use of controlled research (i.e., experimental designs) to test psychosocial interventions and to determine how the approaches compare to no intervention or alternative intervention methods, and (2) the evaluation of how well social work interventions are implemented in everyday treatment settings. These evaluation efforts are typically naturalistic; that is, they are not conducted under controlled circumstances or compared to alternative interventions.

Most academic, professional, and governmental agencies that have a vested interest in advancing evidence-based practices use the first criteria to define evidence-based practices: psychosocial interventions that have been tested repeatedly in controlled trials and repeatedly shown to be effective with clients experiencing serious psychosocial problems. These studies tend to be methodologically rigorous and include the following design criteria: the clients recruited to participate in studies must be "real" clients (as opposed to, for example, graduate students playing the role of clients); the participants are usually randomly assigned to the experimental intervention group or comparison group (to rule out treatment expectancy bias); the practitioners who provide the interventions are trained specifically to provide the experimental or comparison approach; and multiple scales and related measures are used to determine that the two groups are generally equal (in terms of problem severity and other characteristics) at baseline (the beginning of the study) and to determine whether one group gains more benefit from treatment than does the other group. After a few studies demonstrating that a particular approach is reasonably effective when compared to no treatment (i.e., delayed treatment) or some alternative approach, the intervention method is then published as a "manualized intervention" and practitioners can become acquainted with the basic guidelines and learn how to implement the approach. There are a host of evidence-based practices available for working with clients who have severe mental illnesses, major affective disorders, anxiety disorders, substance use disorders, eating disorders, and childhood emotional and behavioral disorders, among other problems.

However, the second rubric of evidence-based practices is also important. Just because a practitioner claims to be using an EBP, it does not necessarily follow that the practitioner is implementing it well or that the client will improve as a result of the intervention. To ensure that EBPs are well used, it is important that practitioners evaluate their own practice. Evaluating one's own practice means defining and measuring the client's presenting difficulties, defining the intervention to be used (e.g., an EBP), and monitoring the client's progress over the course of the intervention (which includes repeatedly using the instruments used at baseline to determine whether the client is improving on key indicators). This approach, as described in chapter 4, is referred to as naturalistic single-subject evaluation. On a practical level, this is the only single-subject evaluation method that practitioners can use routinely in everyday practice. Other approaches that include planned changes to the intervention (to determine whether a change in the intervention will yield more benefit for the client) constitute a kind of controlled clinical research that requires special approval from an institutional review board before implementation.

Evaluative research is somewhat different from naturalistic evaluation. In evaluative research, practitioners test hypotheses about the use of a novel intervention approach. Thus, the purpose is primarily knowledge building, not intervention for client benefit. The easiest way to distinguish naturalistic evaluation from evaluative research is to answer the following question: does the evaluation procedure I am about to implement alter the way services would otherwise be provided to the client under current agency treatment procedures? If the answer is yes, then the client should be made aware of that modification and be given the opportunity to voluntarily participate (i.e., give informed consent). However, if collecting qualitative and quantitative data at baseline, at specified intervals during the intervention and at termination is part of routine service (to which clients are given the opportunity to approve voluntarily on admission to the agency), then the activity is considered routine (i.e., naturalistic) evaluation and no additional special permissions are required.

In summary, EBPs are currently defined as a consensus of findings from controlled outcome research, and evaluation of one's own practice shows whether the approaches are implemented well (e.g., Gibbs & Gambrill, 2002; O'Hare, 1991, 2005; Proctor, 2003; Rosen, 2003; Thyer, 2004). Although selection of an EBP does not guarantee a good outcome for clients, evaluation of the EBP's implementation can help fine-tune the approach by considering ongoing evaluative feedback from clients and other collaborators (e.g., family members, teachers). Thus, rather than simply implement EBPs by adhering strictly to the manual (which practitioners who are unfamiliar with a practice may be tempted to do), practitioners should make modifications based on clinical judgment informed by evaluative feedback (from the client and others) to implement approaches with a reasonable balance of flexibility and fidelity (i.e., congruence) to the ideal model. In principle, the basic elements of EBPs are commensurate with the most recent Council on Social Work Education guidelines for social work education (see www.CSWE.org). The guidelines call for teaching "empirically based theories and knowledge" in human behavior courses, "empirically based interventions" in practice courses, and preparing students to "evaluate their own practice." The guidelines are, in a nutshell, the driving rationale for this introductory practice text. Without a body of scientific knowledge to guide assessments and the initial selection of intervention strategies, social workers would have to resort to tradition, argument by authority, intuition, and a lot of guesswork. These criteria can no longer support professional, ethical, and accountable social work practice.

Evidence-based social work practice (EBSWP) is the planned use of empirically supported assessment and intervention methods combined with the judicious use of monitoring and evaluation strategies for the purpose of improving the psychosocial well-being of clients (O'Hare, 2005).

The primary characteristics of EBSWP are

- The conducting of a qualitative assessment informed by current human behavior research and accompanied by the use of reliable and valid quantitative assessment instruments (e.g., scales, indexes), which also provide a baseline for further monitoring and evaluation.
- The selection and implementation of interventions that have been shown to be effective in controlled outcome research. Reasonable flexibility in implementing evidence-based practices is necessary to accommodate client needs and situational factors.
- The implementation of evaluation methods as part of practice at the individual and program level.

Testing Combinations of Essential Skills: The Role of Controlled Outcome Research

The main thrust of this text has been twofold: to articulate the essential skills of social work practice and to describe how those basic skills can be combined to form more advanced effective practices. So, how do we know what combinations of essential skills have been shown to be effective with moderate to severe psychosocial conditions? That is where the role of clinical practice theory and research come in. Many practitioners and practitioner-researchers, using both theoretical and pragmatic (i.e., experiential trial and error) guidelines, developed what they believed would best constitute effective intervention methods. However, because the quest to develop such approaches was scientific, they insisted on using the methodological guidelines of the controlled trial to test new approaches. Controlled experimental studies of clinical interventions are the gold standard for demonstrating the efficacy of psychosocial interventions. Using controlled experimental designs to test psychosocial interventions came into its own in the 1960s, and this type of research has grown in quality and quantity to the present day. Early efforts tended to focus on mild to moderate psychosocial problems typical of outpatient therapy practices. For these problems, research showed several different approaches to have comparable results, which led some to erroneously conclude that anything works. However, as practitioner-researchers began to examine the effects of specific interventions on more specific and more challenging problems, differences began to emerge. Traditional insight-oriented psychotherapies, which dominated the helping professions through the 1970s, came to be seen as theoretically interesting but often no more effective than basic counseling. For more serious problems, including major depression, schizophrenia, serious anxiety disorders (including posttraumatic stress disorder), borderline personality disorder, addictions, eating disorders, couple and family problems, and serious childhood and adolescent disorders, cognitive-behavioral interventions have been shown repeatedly to result in better and more cost-effective outcomes, and they often have longer-lasting effects. Interpersonal psychotherapies based on a more here-and-now, pragmatic focus on role conflicts, losses, and interpersonal difficulties, have also been shown to demonstrate substantially positive results when applied to depression, couples' problems, and eating disorders. Emotion-focused therapy has accumulated significant findings to support its use with depressed clients and conflicted couples. Family therapies that emphasize the application of behavioral skills to work with mentally ill family members, conduct-disordered and substance-abusing adolescents, and children with emotional disorders are now considered the most effective of family therapies. Case management skills are often included as part of therapeutic interventions but have also been packaged as comprehensive strategies to intervene with serious psychosocial disorders where coordination of complex cases is required, such as with people with mental illness or conduct disordered clients with co-occurring substance use disorders. In short, effective practices for social workers are now eclectic combinations of supportive skills to engender a solid and compassionate working relationship, therapeutic coping skills to enhance existing strengths and learn new ways of effective coping, and case management skills to reduce social and environmental barriers and coordinate complex interventions.

Objections to Evidence-Based Practices

Practitioners who prefer more intuitive or creative approaches to selecting interventions often object strenuously to the assertion that controlled research is the best strategy for determining intervention efficacy. Objections raised include the following: (1) cause and effect (e.g., If my client improves, why can't I conclude that my intervention was effective? Don't my clients just know when a treatment has worked?), (2) experience (e.g., After thirty years of practice experience, I know which interventions are effective), (3) personal preference (e.g., Why can't I just use the interventions that I like best? Why can't I be creative with my clients?), and (4) uniformity (Don't evidence-based practice manuals make practice too technical and robotic?).

Response to Objection No. 1

Simply observing that a client has improved does not rule out the possibility that the client would have improved without treatment or for other reasons. The same is true if the client reports improvement and attributes the change to the intervention. Clients will certainly, under most circumstances, know whether they feel better, whether their problems have improved, and whether they are coping better. However, the client or practitioner may not be in a position to determine whether improvement resulted from the intervention or some other factor. It is simply not an easy thing to know. If the client likes the practitioner, he or she may attribute improvement to the intervention, but that is not the same as knowing that improvement resulted from the intervention.

Many clients' problems are transitory, and clients sometimes improve with the passage of time for various personal or circumstantial reasons. The practitioner also does not know whether the client would have improved even more with the use of some other intervention. Positive outcomes in an individual case prove little about the general effectiveness of any intervention. As an experienced practitioner, I was always very happy when a client improved, but I rarely assumed that it was necessarily the result of my efforts. Conversely, if clients do not improve, we should not be too quick to conclude that we have done a poor job. As in medicine, the practitioner can apply the intervention with considerable skill, but the outcome might still be a poor one. How is this so? There is much that we still do not know about psychosocial problems and how to intervene with them successfully. In addition, some problems may simply be beyond our ability to help.

Response to Objection No. 2

As for the experience argument, there is good reason to believe that, because of generally loose standards in social work education and in the mental health and social services fields, practitioners can continue for years providing substandard work as long as such work does not attract the attention of state health authorities or practice negligence does not come to light in a civil suit. Only the most egregious examples of malpractice tend to reach the public eye: for example, when a client dies as a result of poorly trained practitioners employing a fad therapy they learned in a weekend workshop, or when a practitioner attempts to nurture or "re-parent" a client through sexual intercourse, or when a practitioner continues to work with a client for many years without any ostensible results despite that other more effective interventions were available. Practice experience is certainly important, but it does not, by itself, guarantee expertise. Experience is an important vehicle of learning, but without the guidance of an empirical knowledge base, it is simply that, experience. It does not tell us whether those years of experience have resulted in more effective interventions. Expertise is experience that is guided by a body of research findings. As Eileen Gambrill (2001), a leading social work scholar has opined, social workers often use argument-by-authority to justify their choice of theories and practices rather than critical thinking informed by an empirical knowledge base. As most competent professionals are aware, the selection of theories and practices must now be based on sound research evidence, not claims to tradition or experiential authority.

Response to Objection No. 3

As for the argument that social work practitioners should simply use the interventions they like best, students should be reminded that social work is professional practice guided by laws and state health regulations, licensing, certifications, and ethical guidelines. Human behavior knowledge and interventions are informed by scientific methods. Practitioners will purchase liability insurance annually to protect themselves from the costs of potential civil lawsuits and criminal charges. Although a career in social work can be personally enriching, social work is not a personal enrichment hobby or a form of performance art. Working with clients does not give practitioners unlimited prerogative to exercise what they consider their own creativity. Practicing social workers put themselves and their clients at considerable risk by trusting in their own intuition or applying their own judgment without the benefit of a professional knowledge base.

Fortunately, guidelines for what constitutes evidence-based practices are improving all the time. Social workers have a large, well-codified body of knowledge regarding human behavior problems and effective practices to help guide assessment and intervention methods. That process of using the best available evidence to support practice is an essential quality of a competent and ethical professional social worker. Simply following one's own personal convictions without reference to a representative body of scientific research evidence to support a practice approach is no longer considered ethical practice, and doing so certainly increases liability risk.

Response to Objection No. 4

One of the arguments of proponents of unsubstantiated (and in many cases, nontestable) theories and practices is that engaging in assessment and intervention informed by a knowledge base is somehow robotic, technical, or inhuman. Actually, it is quite easy to argue the opposite: practitioners who simply use an approach that they find personally appealing and attempt to justify that approach with humanistic platitudes rather than a verifiable knowledge base engage in a form of self-indulgent and possibly negligent practice. As with medicine, psychology, and other mature professions, social workers, at their best, bring their humanity to their work, give the utmost priority to engaging their clients on a personal but real level, and dedicate themselves to keeping abreast of the current knowledge base in their field so they can do their best work for the sake of clients. Applying assessment and intervention guidelines with flexibility and informed practice judgment is a given. Few would dispute that practice is often fraught with ambiguity. But philosophical aphorisms, self-indulgent claims to wisdom, and claims of being naturally compassionate are no substitute for caring, knowledgeable, and skilled practice.

EBSWP in a Broader Service Delivery Context

Despite some ambivalence, support is growing for the adoption of EBPs in social work and the allied professions. A wide range of influential professional and governmental bodies are promoting EBPs, and thus the evolution and implementation of EBPs in behavioral health and social services is well on its way. Refinement and integration of policy, academic research, practice, and evaluation will continue into the foreseeable future, resulting from interdisciplinary efforts across the helping professions, not the efforts of an ideologically parochial few.

Figure 10 illustrates a working model of the interrelationships among policy and administration, research and education, practice and evaluation, and consumer expectations. The arrows suggest influence from one sphere to another. In brief, the working model suggests, first, that practice scholars in research and academia are primarily responsible for knowledge development and dissemination of evidence-based practices. Practice scholars can directly influence policy makers and administrators and help guide them in developing optimal programming. Second, policy makers and administrators are responsible for service delivery and evaluation. They must respond directly to the needs of consumers, funding sources, accreditation bodies, and regulatory agencies. However, administrators and policy makers also have valuable insights into the complexities of program implementation and must work closely with practice scholars to refine the real-world application of evidence-based practices. Third, with the support of social work educators and agency supervisors, practitioners become the linchpin for the implementation of EBPs. Without proper training and support through continuing education and supervision, EBPs will not be implemented effectively at the individual client level. This task can be facilitated by the judicious use of fidelity and outcome measures to see that EBPs are implemented with an acceptable degree of fidelity and effectiveness. Practitioners, in concert with clients, also generate special insights from the ground up into the finer points of implementing EBPs, and they must work with practitioner-researchers and evaluators to develop more effective interventions. Thus, the process of knowledge building becomes a collaborative effort that cycles continuously through practice, theory, research, evaluation, and policy implementation and refinement. These processes are complex, and the evolution of EBP models will be accompanied by debate for some time (Gambrill, 2006; Johnson & Austin, 2006; O'Hare, 1991, 2005).

Policy, Administration, and Research

Although the use of scientific knowledge to guide practice is not new in principle, the medical profession formalized the term *evidence-based* in the early 1990s by promulgating its use in daily delivery of medical care (Evidence-Based Medicine Working Group, 1992; Sackett, Straus, Richardson, Rosenberg, & Haynes, 2000). Since that time, the literature on evidence-based medicine and EBPs in mental health and related fields has grown exponentially. To date, more than forty professional organizations have offered practice guidelines for mental health and substance abuse interventions for adults and children (Stuart, Rush, & Morris, 2002). A few

FIGURE 10. A MODEL FOR IMPLEMENTING EVIDENCE-BASED SOCIAL WORK PRACTICES

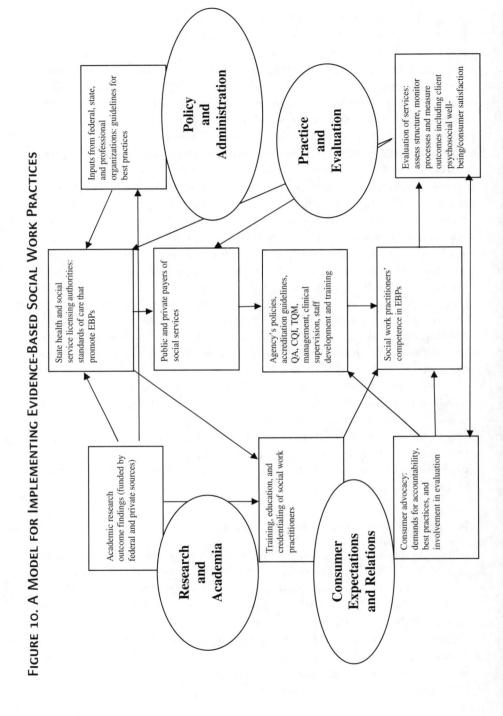

of the more prominent organizations include the American Psychological Association, the American Psychiatric Association, the American Academy of Child and Adolescent Psychiatry, the American College of Mental Health Administrators, the Campbell Collaboration, various branches of the National Institutes of Health, and the Agency for Healthcare Research and Quality, to name just a few. Although these and many other academic, governmental, and private sector organizations actively play a variety of roles (e.g., funding relevant research, compiling research and distributing other relevant resources, engaging in evaluation), all, in principle, support the use of practices that are supported by controlled research. However, members of these agencies and supporters of EBPs in general are likely to continue debating what constitutes adequate methodological standards for determining evidence-based practice. Although there are a range of opinions regarding what constitutes EBPs and how to implement them (Gambrill, 2006), the choices that lie ahead in this regard should emphasize methodological standards for determining good program outcomes rather than tangential ideological debates that are likely to result in vague treatment guidelines that defy evaluation in the real world of social work service delivery.

Goldman et al. (2001) have made several important points regarding the implementation of EBPs: (1) EBP is now a driving force for improving intervention quality and service accountability, (2) EBPs are underused, (3) because there are gaps in best-practices research for some problem areas and more complex co-occurring problems, there remains plenty of room for informed clinical judgment when implementing EBPs in the field, and (4) research on the development, dissemination, and implementation of EBPs must and will continue. To date, there are few empirical guidelines for implementing EBPs in human services agencies. Nevertheless, there is a growing expectation that implementing EBPs in community practice settings will require a flexible synthesis of science and consensus building that results in high-quality programming that is amenable to continuous monitoring, evaluation, troubleshooting, and incremental refinement (O'Hare, 2005; Wandersman, 2003). Although observers of the EBP scene like to opine that local values, clinical judgment, and other nonspecific factors will undoubtedly be part of the decision-making process regarding how to adopt and implement EPBs, there is little research at this point on how these factors influence implementation and client outcomes.

Evidence-based guidelines are now increasingly tied to accreditation standards promoted by organizations such as the National Committee on Quality Assurance (NCQA), the Joint Commission on the Accreditation of

Healthcare Organizations (JCAHO), and the Commission on the Accreditation of Rehabilitation Facilities (CARF). Although these organizations
emphasize a range of process and performance indicators, they are increasingly emphasizing the use of EBPs.

Consumer Expectations and Relations

The direct and indirect influences of consumers will be increasingly felt as
EBPs evolve and are disseminated. Client advocacy groups such as the
National Alliance for the Mentally Ill are becoming more educated about
EBPs and involved in advocacy efforts to deliver best practices (Bond, Salyers, Rollins, Rapp, & Zipple, 2004). Consumer groups will enhance their
influence by seeking the assistance of academic researchers and other
informed advocates who can help consumer representatives keep abreast
of current developments in evidence-based interventions. As a result of the
proliferation of EBPs, informed-consent guidelines relevant to services in
adult and child mental health, substance abuse, gerontology, and other
fields will have to be improved to more explicitly educate everyday consumers about the availability of evidence-based intervention methods. Consumers have a right to know what the medical and social science
communities know about best practices (Meyers & Thyer, 1997). Because
many practitioners have not been trained in EBPs or reject them outright
on personal or ideological grounds, many clients continue to receive substandard care. In the future, agencies that fail to provide informed consent
to clients regarding EBPs are likely to incur greater liability risk. Companies that sell malpractice insurance may take a forward position by requiring that their service providers be trained in EBPs to be eligible for
malpractice insurance.

Practice and Evaluation

It should be apparent at this point that many social workers at the BSW,
MSW, and postgraduate level will require additional education and training in EBPs if they have not already obtained it. This task will fall both to
schools and to agencies, which will carry some of the obligation to provide
staff development. Additional training in EBPs will have to be tied to continuing education for social work credentials. And those who accredit training events and seminars may have to use evidence-based standards to
judge the relative value of training experiences. Nevertheless, becoming
more knowledgeable about EBPs is one thing; consistent and effective
implementation is quite another. To implement EBPs effectively, practice

at the agency level must be accompanied by integrated evaluation processes whereby evaluation processes implemented at assessment, clinical review, termination, and follow-up provide data for both individual client and program evaluation. Naturalistic evaluation methods employing multidimensional measures of client well-being and consumer satisfaction can augment current clinical documentation requirements that many accreditation agencies, as well as federal and state regulators and private insurers, mandate. Some degree of standardization (e.g., statewide or federal common assessment/evaluation instrument package) will be required. Consultants from schools of social work can serve an invaluable role by providing requisite training, evaluation, and statistical skills to enhance quality assurance programs in human service agencies.

Social Work Education and Research

The fundamental role of full-time social work faculty is to teach and to develop and disseminate knowledge regarding human behavior, assessment, intervention, and evaluation methods. Traditionally, the helping professions, including social work, have maintained that they can create and enforce their own practice standards; as a result, practitioners have often felt entitled to exercise a high degree of professional autonomy. Nevertheless, there are considerable challenges ahead with regard to teaching, implementation, and evaluation of social workers' use of EBPs.

How will social work academia respond to these challenges? There is considerable debate among social work educators regarding the nature of evidence, the types of methodologies employed in testing and evaluating interventions, and the proportionate role of practice wisdom in actual practice. Writing from the practice perspective of social services in Great Britain, Webb (2002) acknowledges these struggles but characterizes the adoption of EBPs as policy is a foregone conclusion. He goes on to provide a reasonable framework for decision making that incorporates the use of EBP guidelines but fully appreciates the significant level of indeterminacy in day-to-day practice. His model includes the use of evidence-based protocols, or clinical decision-making and feedback mechanisms based on clinical judgment to refine ongoing practice. Webb's views are commensurate with those of others (e.g., Randall, 2002) who acknowledge that the implementation of EBPs will have to come about as a reciprocal exchange between researchers and practitioners. At this point in social work's evolution, the debate hinges no longer on whether EBPs will be adopted but on how they will be implemented.

To advance EBPs, social work educators will need to

- Upgrade current human behavior curricula to critically reflect contemporary multivariate behavioral and social science theory and research
- Teach students how to judge the relative validity of such theories by critically analyzing the methodological quality of theory-driven research
- Teach evidence-based qualitative and quantitative assessment methods
- Teach evidence-based basic skills (e.g., relationship building, cognitive-behavioral coping skills, case management skills) for clients with mild to moderate psychosocial distress
- Teach and give priority in curricula to advanced EBPs (i.e., optimal combinations of basic skills) for working with moderate to severe psychosocial problems across all major fields of practice
- Teach students how to critically analyze the methodological components of outcome and evaluation research so that they can better judge the efficacy and effectiveness of published practice research
- Teach students how to use an array of research and evaluation designs, to critically understand their relative strengths and weaknesses (e.g., threats to internal and external validity), and to use the design that best addresses the right question under suitable circumstances
- Teach students to identify gaps in the current practice knowledge base
- Teach students to implement EBPs and maintain the integrity of the intervention but apply EBPs with reasonable flexibility by considering clients' needs, co-occurring problems, problem complexity, and special circumstances
- Teach self-evaluation methods that practitioners can use routinely in everyday practice environments (e.g., qualitative case analysis, nonexperimental single-subject designs, naturalistic monitoring and evaluation of programs)
- Emphasize informed consent regarding the use of both the intervention and evaluation methods
- Model critical thinking for students and respect for the cumulative hard-wrought efforts of practitioner-research scholars, demonstrate a willingness to change one's mind when compelling evidence disconfirms favorite theories or practices, and downplay the relevance of personalities in the field who emphasize marketing their theories and practices over verifying their methods
- Expand academic-agency links to promote training, evaluation, and

research on EBPs (e.g., institutes for evidence-based social work practice)

- Improve standards for accrediting and licensing social workers to reflect current knowledge of human behavior theory, empirically based assessment protocol, and EBPs
- Provide training opportunities for field instructors and supervisors who need to upgrade their knowledge and skills with respect to EBPs

Given the necessity of employing methodological rigor in human behavior research and in testing psychosocial practices, EBSWP is less likely to go the way of other ideological and theoretical fads. For social workers to maintain important roles in mental health, substance abuse, gerontology, child welfare, and other fields, employing rigorous methodological standards to develop and select psychosocial practices is no longer an option but a necessity.

References

Abbott, P. J., Weller, S. B., Delaney, H. D., & Moore, B. A. (1998). Community reinforcement approach in the treatment of opiate addicts. *American Journal of Drug and Alcohol Abuse, 24*, 17–30.

Abramowitz, J. S., Brigidi, B. D., & Roche, K. R. (2001). Cognitive-behavioral therapy for obsessive compulsive disorder. *Research on Social Work Practice, 11*, 357–372.

Alexander, J. F., Waldron, H. B., Newberry, A. M., & Liddle, N. (1988). *Family approaches to treating delinquents.* Newbury Park, CA: Sage.

Alford, B. A., & Correia, C. J. (1994). Cognitive therapy of schizophrenia: Theory and empirical status. *Behavior Therapy, 25*, 17–33.

American Psychiatric Association (2000). *Diagnostic and statistical manual of mental disorders* (4th ed.). Washington, DC: Author.

Antony, M. M., & Swinson, R. P. (2000). *Phobic disorders and panic in adults: A guide to assessment and treatment.* Washington, DC: American Psychological Association.

Appelbaum, P. S. (1996). Law and psychiatry: *Jaffee vs. Redmond*: Psychotherapist-patient privilege in the federal courts. *Psychiatric Services, 47*, 1033–1052.

Azrin, N. H., Sisson, R. W., Meyers, R., & Godley, M. (1982). Alcoholism treatment by disulfiram and community reinforcement therapy. *Journal of Behavior Therapy and Experimental Psychiatry, 13*, 105–112.

Bagley, C., & Mallick, K. (2000). Prediction of sexual, emotional, and physical maltreatment and mental health outcomes in a longitudinal cohort of 290 adolescent women. *Child Maltreatment, 5*(3), 218–226.

Bandura, A. (1986). *Social foundations of thought and action: A social cognitive theory.* Englewood Cliffs, NJ: Prentice-Hall.

Bandura, A. (1999). A sociocognitive analysis of substance abuse: An agentic perspective. *Psychological Science, 10*, 214–217.

Beck, A. T. (1976). *Cognitive therapy and the emotional disorders.* New York: New American Library.

Beck, A. T. (1996). Beyond belief: A theory of modes, personality and psychopathology. In P. M. Salkovskis (Ed.), *Frontiers of cognitive therapy* (pp. 1–25). New York: Guilford Press.

Becvar, D. S., & Becvar, R. J. (1996). *Family therapy: A systemic integration* (3rd ed.). Needham Heights, MA: Allyn & Bacon.

Bedell, J. R., & Lennox, S. S. (1997). *Handbook for communication and problem-solving skills training: A cognitive-behavioral approach.* New York: John Wiley.

Beidel, D. C., & Turner, S. M. (2005). *Childhood anxiety disorders: A guide to research and treatment.* New York: Routledge.

Bellack, A. S., Bennett, M. E., & Gearon, J. S. (2007). *Behavioral treatment for substance abuse in people with serious and persistent mental illness.* New York: Routledge.

Bellack, A. S., & Hersen, M. (Eds.). (1998). *Behavioral assessment: A practical handbook* (4th ed.). Boston: Allyn & Bacon.

Bellack, A. S., Mueser, K. T., Gingerich, S., & Agresta, J. (1997). *Social skills training for schizophrenia: A step-by-step guide.* New York: Guilford Press.

Berg, I. K. (1999). Constructivist therapies: Solution-focused and narrative. In J. O. Prochaska & J. C. Norcross (Eds.), *Systems of psychotherapy: A transtheoretical analysis* (4th ed., pp. 437–456). Pacific Grove, CA: Brooks/Cole.

Beutler, L. E., Clarkin, J. F., & Bongar, B. (2000). *Guidelines for the systematic treatment of the depressed patient.* New York: Oxford University Press.

Bieling, P. J., McCabe, R. E., & Antony, M. (2006). *Cognitive-behavioral therapy in groups.* New York: Guilford Press.

Birchler, G. R., & Spinks, S. H. (1980). Behavioral-systems marital and family therapy: Integration and clinical application. *American Journal of Family Therapy, 8*, 6–28.

Bjorklund, D. F. (2000). *Children's thinking: Developmental function and individual differences* (3rd ed.). Belmont, CA: Wadsworth/Thomson Learning.

Bloom, M., Fischer, J., & Orme, J. G. (2006). *Evaluating practice: Guidelines for the accountable professional* (5th ed.) Boston: Allyn & Bacon.

Bond, G. R., Becker, D. R., Drake, R. E., Rapp, C. A., Meisler, N., Lehman,

A. F., et al. (2001). Implementing supported employment as an evidence-based practice. *Psychiatric Services, 52*, 313–322.

Bond, G. R., Salyers, M. P., Rollins, A. L., Rapp, C. A., & Zipple, A. M. (2004). How evidence-based practices contribute to community integration. *Community Mental Health Journal, 40*, 569–588.

Bowlby, J. (1980). *Attachment and loss*. New York: Basic Books.

Browne, G., & Courtney, M. (2007). Schizophrenia housing and supportive relationships. *International Journal of Mental Health Nursing, 16*, 73–80.

Butler, A. C., Chapman, J. E., Forman, E. M., & Beck, A. T. (2006). The empirical status of cognitive-behavioral therapy: A review of meta-analyses. *Clinical Psychology Review, 26*, 17–31.

Caplan, A. (2006). Ethical issues surrounding forced, mandated, or coerced treatment. *Journal of Substance Abuse Treatment, 31*, 117–120.

Carroll, K. M., & Onken, L. S. (2005). Behavioral therapies for drug abuse. *American Journal of Psychiatry, 162*, 1452–1460.

Chorpita, B. F., & Southam-Gerow, M. A. (2006). Fears and anxieties. In E. J. Mash & R. A. Barkley (Eds.), *Treatment of childhood disorders* (3rd ed., pp. 271–335). New York: Guilford Press.

Clark, D. A., & Beck, A. T. (with Alford, B. A.). (1999). *Scientific foundations of cognitive theory and therapy of depression*. New York: John Wiley.

Coffey, D. (2003). Connection and autonomy in the case management relationship. *Psychiatric Rehabilitation Journal, 26*, 404–412.

Collins, D., Jordan, C., & Coleman, H. (2007). *An introduction to family social work* (2nd ed.). Belmont, CA: Thomson Higher Education.

Compton, S. N., Burns, B. J., Egger, H. L., & Robertson, E. (2002). Review of the evidence base for treatment of childhood psychopathology: Internalizing disorders. *Journal of Consulting and Clinical Psychology, 70*, 1240–1266.

Compton, B. R., & Galaway, B. (1999). *Social work processes* (6th ed.). Pacific Grove, CA: Brooks/Cole.

Craighead, L. W., Craighead, W. E., Kazdin, A. P., & Mahoney, M. J. (Eds.). (1994). *Cognitive and behavioral interventions: An empirical approach to mental health problems*. Boston: Allyn & Bacon.

Davidson, K., Tyrer, P., Gumley, A., Tata, P., Norrie, J., Palmer, S., et al. (2006). A randomized controlled trial of cognitive-behavior therapy for borderline personality disorder: Rationale for trial, method, and description of sample. *Journal of Personality Disorders, 20*(5), 431–449.

Dixon, L., Adams, C., & Lucksted, A. (2000). Update on family psychoeducation for schizophrenia. *Schizophrenia Bulletin, 26*, 5–20.

Dixon, L. B., McFarlane, W. R., Lefley, H., Lucksted, A., Cohen, M., Falloon, I., et al. (2001). Evidence-based practices for services to families of people with psychiatric disabilities. *Psychiatric Services, 52*, 903–910.

Dobson, K. S., & Craig, K. D. (Eds.). (1996). *Advances in cognitive-behavioral therapy.* Thousand Oaks, CA: Sage.

Dohrenwend, B. P. (1998). Overview of evidence for the importance of adverse environmental conditions in causing psychiatric disorders. In B. P. Dohrenwend (Ed.), *Adversity, stress and psychopathology* (pp. 523–538). New York: Oxford University Press.

Dolgoff, R., Loewenberg, F. M., & Harrington, D. (2005). *Ethical decisions for social work practice* (7th ed.). Toronto: Thomson/Brooks Cole.

Drake, R. E. (1998). Brief history, current status, and future place of assertive community treatment. *American Journal of Orthopsychiatry, 68,* 172–175.

Drake, R. E., McHugo, G. J., Clark, R. E., Teague, G. B., Xie, H., Miles, K., & Ackerson, T. H. (1998). Assertive community treatment for patients with co-occurring severe mental illness and substance use disorder: A clinical trial. *American Journal of Orthopsychiatry, 68,* 201–215.

Dumaine, M. L. (2003). Meta-analysis of interventions with co-occurring disorders of severe mental illness and substance abuse: Implications for social work practice. *Research on Social Work Practice, 13*(2), 142–165.

Duncan, B. L., & Parks, M. B. (1988). Integrating individual and systems approaches: Strategic-behavioral therapy. *Journal of Marital and Family Therapy, 14,* 151–161.

D'Zurilla, T. J., & Goldfried, M. R. (1971). Problem solving and behavior modification. *Journal of Abnormal Psychology, 78,* 107–126.

Epstein, E. E., McCrady, B. S., Morgan, T. J., Cook, S. M., Kugler, G., & Ziedonis, D. (2007). Couples treatment for drug-dependent males: Preliminary efficacy of a stand alone outpatient model. *Addictive Disorders & Their Treatment, 6,* 21–37.

Evidence-Based Medicine Working Group (1992). Evidence-based medicine: A new approach to teaching the practice of medicine. *JAMA, 268,* 2420–2425.

Farmer, E. M. Z., Compton, S. N., Burns, B. J., & Robertson, E. (2002). Review of the evidence base for treatment of childhood psychopathology externalizing disorders. *Journal of Consulting and Clinical Psychology, 70,* 1267–1302.

Fisher, W. H., Packer, I. K., Grisso, T., McDermeit, M., & Brown, J. K. (2000). From case management to court clinic: Examining forensic system involvement of persons with severe mental illness. *Mental Health Services Research, 2,* 41–49.

Foster, S. L. (1994). Assessing and treating parent-adolescent conflict. In M. Hersen, R. Eisler, & P. Miller (Eds.), *Progress in behavior modification* (Vol. 29, pp. 53–72). New York: Academic Press.

Frankl, V. (1963). *Man's search for meaning: An introduction to logotherapy.* New York: Pocket Books.

Franklin, C., & Jordan, C. (2003). An integrative skills assessment approach. In C. Jordan & C. Franklin (Eds.), *Clinical assessment for social workers: Quantitative and qualitative methods* (2nd ed., pp. 1–52). Chicago: Lyceum Books.

Freud, S. (1938). *The basic writings of Sigmund Freud.* New York: Random House.

Gambrill, E. (1990). *Critical thinking in clinical practice.* San Francisco: Jossey-Bass.

Gambrill, E. (2001) Social work: An authority-based profession. *Research on Social Work Practice, 11,* 166–175.

Gambrill, E. (2006). Evidence-based practices and policy: Choices ahead. *Research on Social Work Practice, 16,* 338–357.

Geisen-Bloo, J., van Dyck, R., Spinhoven, P., van Tilberg, W., Dirksen, C., van Asselt, T., et al. (2006). Outpatient psychotherapy for borderline personality disorder: Randomized trial of schema-focused therapy vs. transference-focused psychotherapy. *Archives of General Psychiatry, 63,* 649–658.

Gendreau, P. (1996). The principles of effective intervention with offenders. In A. T. Harland (Ed.), *Choosing correctional options that work: Defining demand and evaluating the supply* (pp. 117–130). Thousand Oaks, CA: Sage.

Gibbs, L. E., & Gambrill, E. (2002). Evidence-based practice: Counterarguments to objections. *Research on Social Work Practice, 12,* 452–476.

Gold, P. B., Meisler, N., Santos, A. B., Carnemolla, M. A., Williams, O. H., & Keleher, J. (2006). Randomized trial of supported employment integrated with assertive community treatment for rural adults with severe mental illness. *Schizophrenia Bulletin, 32,* 378–395.

Goldman, H. H., Ganju, V., Drake, R. E., Gorman, P., Hogan, M., Hyde, P. S., et al. (2001). Policy implications for implementing evidence-based practices. *Psychiatric Services, 52,* 1591–1597.

Goldstein, H. (1986). A cognitive-humanistic approach to the court-ordered vs. voluntary hard-to-reach client. *Social Casework, 67,* 27–36.

Goodheart, C. D., Kazdin, A. E., & Sternberg, R. J. (2006). *Evidence-based psychotherapy: Where practice and research meet.* Washington, DC: American Psychological Association.

Goodman, C. C., Potts, M. K., & Pasztor, E. M. (2007). Caregiving grandmothers with vs. without child welfare system involvement: Effects of expressed need, formal services, and informal social support on caregiver burden. *Children and Youth Services Review, 29,* 428–441.

Greenberg, L. S., & Watson, J. C. (2006). *Emotion-focused therapy for depression.* Washington, DC: American Psychological Association.

Hare, R. D., Harpur, T. J., Hakstian, A. R., Forth, A. E., & Hart, S. D. (1990). The psychopathy checklist: Reliability and factor structure. *Psychological Assessment: A Journal of Consulting and Clinical Psychology, 2,* 338–341.

Hargreaves, W. A., Shumway, M., Hu, T.-W., & Cuffel, B. (1998). *Cost-outcome methods for mental health.* San Diego: Academic Press.

Henggeler, S. W., Schoenwald, S. K., Borduin, C. M., Rowland, M. D., & Cunningham, P. B. (1998). *Multisystemic treatment of antisocial behavior in children and adolescents.* New York: Guilford Press.

Herman, D. B., Susser, E. S., & Struening, E. L. (1998). Homelessness, stress and psychopathology. In B. P. Dohrenwend (Ed.), *Adversity and psychopathology* (pp. 132–141). New York: Oxford University Press.

Higgins, S. T., Budney, A. J., Bickel, W. K., Hughes, J. R., Foerg, F., & Badger, G. (1993). Achieving cocaine abstinence with a behavioral approach. *American Journal of Psychiatry, 150,* 5, 763–769.

Higgins, S., Sigmon, S., Wong, C., Heil, S., Badger, G., Donham, R., et al. (2003). Community reinforcement for cocaine-dependent outpatients. *Archives of General Psychiatry, 60,* 1043–1052.

Hill, C. E., Nutt, E. A., & Jackson, S. (1994). Trends in psychotherapy process research: Samples, measures, researchers, and classic publications. *Journal of Counseling Psychology, 4,* 364–377.

Hill, C. E., & O'Brien, K. M. (2004). *Helping skills: Facilitating exploration, insight, and action.* Washington, DC: American Psychological Association.

Holahan, C. J., & Moos, R. H. (1994). Life stressors and mental health: Advances in conceptualizing stress resistance. In W. R. Avison & I. H. Gotlib (Eds.), *Stress and mental health: Contemporary issues and prospects for the future* (pp. 213–238). New York: Plenum Press.

Hollon, S. D., & Beck, A. T. (1994). Cognitive and cognitive-behavioral therapies. In A. E. Bergin & S. L. Garfield (Eds.), *The handbook of psychotherapy and behavior change* (4th ed., pp. 428–466). New York: John Wiley.

Hopkins, M., & Ramsundar, N. (2006). Which factors predict case management services and how do these services relate to client outcomes? *Psychiatric Rehabilitation Journal, 29,* 219–222.

Horvath, A. O., & Greenberg, L. S. (1989). Development and validation of the working alliance inventory. *Journal of Counseling Psychology, 36,* 223–233.

Houston-Vega, M. K., & Nuehring, E. M. (1997). *Prudent practice: A guide for managing malpractice risk.* Washington, DC: National Association of Social Workers Press.

Howard, M. O., & Jenson, J. M. (1999). Clinical practice guidelines: Should social work develop them? *Research on Social Work Practice, 9,* 283–301.

Humphreys, K. (1999). Professional interventions that facilitate 12-step self-help group involvement. *Alcohol Research and Health, 23,* 93–98.

Jacobson, N. S., & Addis, M. E. (1993). Research on couples and couple therapy: What do we know? Where are we going? *Journal of Consulting and Clinical Psychology, 61,* 85–93.

Jacobson, N. S., & Margolin, G. (1979). *Marital therapy: Strategies based on social learning and behaviour exchange principles.* New York: Guilford Press.

Johnson, M., & Austin, M. J. (2006). Evidence-based practice in the social services: Implications for organizational change. *Administration in Social Work, 30,* 75–104.

Johnson, S. M., & Greenberg, L. S. (1995). The emotionally focused approach to problems in adult attachment. In N. S. Jacobson & A. S. Gurman (Eds.), *Clinical handbook of couple therapy* (pp. 121–141). New York: Guilford Press.

Kazdin, A. E. (1978). Methodological and interpretive problems of single-case experimental designs. *Journal of Consulting and Clinical Psychology, 46,* 629–642.

Kazdin, A. E. (1998). *Research design in clinical psychology* (3rd ed.). Boston: Allyn & Bacon.

Kazdin, A. E., & Weisz, J. R. (1998). Identifying and developing empirically supported child and adolescent treatments. *Journal of Consulting and Clinical Psychology, 66,* 19–36.

Kendall, P. C. (1992). *Anxiety disorders in youth: Cognitive behavioral interventions.* Boston: Allyn & Bacon.

Kendall, P. C. (1994). Treating anxiety disorders in children: Results of a randomized clinical trial. *Journal of Consulting and Clinical Psychology, 62,* 100–110.

Kernberg, O. F. (1976). *Object relations theory and clinical psychoanalysis.* New York: Jason Aronson.

Kohut, H. (1971). *The analysis of the self: A systematic approach to the psychoanalytic treatment of narcissistic personality disorders.* New York: International Universities Press.

Kuno, E., Rothbard, A. B., Averyt, J., & Culhane, D. (2000). Homelessness among persons with serious mental illness in an enhanced community-based mental health system. *Psychiatric Services, 51,* 1012–1016.

Lamb, H. R., & Weinberger, L. E. (1998). Persons with severe mental illness in jails and prisons: A review. *Psychiatric Services, 49,* 483–492.

Lambert, M. J., & Bergin, A. E. (1994). The effectiveness of psychotherapy. In A. E. Bergin & S. L. Garfield (Eds.), *The handbook of psychotherapy and behavior change* (4th ed., pp. 143–189).New York: John Wiley.

Lazarus, R. S. (1999). *Stress and emotion.* New York: Springer.

Lazarus, R. S., & Folkman, S. (1984). *Stress, appraisal and coping.* New York: Springer.

Lebow, J. (2000). What does the research tell us about couples and family therapies? *Psychotherapy in Practice, 56,* 1083–1094.

Lehman, A. F., Steinwachs, D. M., & the Co-Investigators of the PORT Project (1998). At issue: Translating research into practice: The Schizophrenia Patient Outcomes Research Team (PORT) recommendations. *Schizophrenia Bulletin, 24,* 1–10.

Leschied, A. W., Chiodo, D., Whitehead, P. C., & Hurley, D. (2006). The association of poverty with child welfare service and child and family clinical outcomes. *Community, Work and Family, 9,* 29–46.

Linehan, M. M. (1993). *Cognitive-behavioral treatment of borderline personality disorder.* New York: Guilford Press.

Linehan, M. M., Comtois, K. A., Murray, A. M., Brown, M. Z., Gallop, R. J., Heard, H. L., et al. (2006). Two-year randomized controlled trial and follow-up of dialectical behavior therapy vs. therapy by experts for suicidal behaviors and borderline personality disorder. *Archives of General Psychiatry, 63*(7), 757–766.

Lum, D. (2007). *Culturally competent practice: A framework for understanding diverse groups and justice issues* (3rd ed.). Belmont, CA: Thomson/Brooks/Cole

Lutzker, J. R., Bigelow, K. M., Doctor, R. M., Gershater, R. M., & Greene, B. F. (1998). An ecobehavioral model for the prevention and treatment of child abuse and neglect: History and applications. In J. R. Lutzker (Ed.), *Handbook of child abuse research and treatment* (pp. 239–266). New York: Plenum Press.

Lyons, S. J., Henly, J. R., & Schuerman, J. R. (2005). Informal support in maltreating families: Its effect on parenting practices. *Children and Youth Services Review, 27*, 21–38.

Mahler, M. S., Pine, F., & Bergman, A. (1975). *The psychological birth of the human infant: Symbiosis and individuation*. New York: Basic Books.

May, R. (1969). *Love and will*. New York: Norton.

McGuire, J., & Hatcher, R. (2001). Offense-focused problem solving: Preliminary evaluation of a cognitive skills program. *Criminal Justice and Behavior, 28*, 564–587.

McMahon, R. J., & Forehand, R. (1984). Parent training for the non-compliant child: Treatment outcome, generalization, and adjunctive therapy procedures. In R. F. Dangel & R. A. Polster (Eds.), *Parent training: Foundations of research and practice* (pp. 298–328). New York:Guilford Press.

McMahon, R. J., Wells, K. C., & Kotler, J. S. (2006). Conduct problems. In E. J. Mash & R. A. Barkley (Eds.), *Treatment of childhood disorders* (3rd ed., pp. 137–268). New York: Guilford Press.

Mechanic, D. (1996). Emerging issues in international mental health services research. *Psychiatric Services, 47*, 371–375.

Meichenbaum, D. (1974). *Cognitive behavior modification*. Morristown, NJ: General Learning.

Meyers, L. L., & Thyer, B. A. (1997). Should social work clients have the right to effective treatment? *Social Work, 42*, 288–298.

Miller, W. R., Meyers, R. J., & Hiller-Sturmhofel, S. (1999). The community-reinforcement approach. *Alcohol Research and Health, 23*, 116–120.

Miller, W., & Rollnick, S. (2002). *Motivational interviewing: Preparing people to change addictive behavior* (2nd ed.). New York: Guilford Press.

Minuchin, S. (1974). *Families and family therapy*. Cambridge, MA: Harvard University Press.

Monti, P. M., & Rohsenow, D. J. (1999). Coping-skills training and cue-exposure therapy in the treatment of alcoholism. *Alcohol Research and Health, 23*, 107–115.

Morrison, J., & Anders, T. F. (1999). *Interviewing children and adolescents: Skills and strategies for effective DSM-IV diagnosis*. New York: Guilford Press.

Mueser, K. T., Bond, G. R., Drake, R. E., & Resnick, S. G. (1998). Models of community care for severe mental illness: A review of research on case management. *Schizophrenia Bulletin, 24*, 37–74.

Mueser, K. T., Drake, R. E., & Bond, G. R. (1997). Recent advances in psychiatric rehabilitation for patients with severe mental illness. *Harvard Review of Psychiatry, 5*, 123–137.

Mueser, K. T., & Glynn, S. M. (1999). *Behavioral family therapy for psychiatric disorders* (2nd ed.). Oakland, CA: New Harbinger.

Mueser, K. T., & Jeste, D. V. (Eds.). (2008). *Clinical handbook of schizophrenia.* New York: Guilford Press.

Mueser, K. T., Meyer, P. S., Penn, D. L., Cancy, R., Clancy, D. M., & Salyers, M. P. (2006). The illness management and recovery program: Rationale, development, and preliminary findings. *Schizophrenia Bulletin, 32*, s32–s43.

Mueser, K. T., Noordsy, D. L., Drake, R. E., & Fox, L. (2003). *Integrated treatment for dual disorders: A guide to effective practice.* New York: Guilford Press.

Mueser, K. T., Rosenberg, S. D., Goodman, L. A., & Trumbetta, S. L. (2002). Trauma, PTSD, and the course of severe mental illness: An interactive model. *Schizophrenia Research, 53*, 123–143.

Mueser, K. T., Rosenberg, S. D., Jankowski, M. K., Hamblen, J. L., & Descamps, M. (2004). A cognitive-behavioral treatment program for posttraumatic stress disorder in persons with severe mental illness. *American Journal of Psychiatric Rehabilitation, 7*, 107–146.

Nathan, P. E., & Gorman, J. M. (Eds.). (2007). *A guide to treatments that work.* New York: Oxford University Press.

National Association of Social Workers (2007). Code of ethics. http://www.nasw.org.

Nichols, M. P., & Schwartz, R. C. (2006). *Family therapy: Concepts and methods.* Boston: Pearson/Allyn & Bacon.

Nisbett, R. E., & Ross, L. (1980). *Human inference: Strategies and shortcomings of social judgment.* Englewood Cliffs, NJ: Prentice-Hall.

Northey, W. F., Wells, K. C., Silverman, W. K., & Bailey, C. E. (2003). Childhood behavioral and emotional disorders. *Journal of Marital and Family Therapy, 29*, 523–545.

Nygaard, R. L. (2000). The dawn of therapeutic justice. In D. H. Fishbein (Ed.), *The science, treatment, and prevention of antisocial behaviors: Application to the criminal justice system* (pp. 23–1 to 23–18). Kingston, NJ: Civic Research Institute.

O'Farrell, T., & Fals-Stewart, W. (2003). Alcohol abuse. *Journal of Marital and Family Therapy, 29*, 121–146.

O'Hanlon, W. H., & Weiner-Davis, M. (1989). *In search of solutions: A new direction in psychotherapy.* New York: Norton.

O'Hare, T. (1991). Integrating research and practice: A framework for implementation. *Social Work, 36*(3), 220–223.

O'Hare, T. (1996). Court-ordered vs. voluntary clients: Problem differences and readiness for change. *Social Work, 41*, 417–422.

O'Hare, T. (2005). *Evidence-based practices for social workers: An interdisciplinary approach.* Chicago: Lyceum.

O'Hare, T., & Collins, P. (1997). Development and validation of a scale for measuring social work practice skills. *Research on Social Work Practice, 7*(2), 228–238.

O'Hare, T., Sherrer, M. V., Cutler, J., McCall, T., Dominique, K., & Garlick, K. (2002). Validating the psychosocial well being scale among mentally ill clients with substance abuse problems. *Social Work in Mental Health, 1,* 15–30.

O'Hare, T., Sherrer, M. V., Connery, H., Thornton, J., LaButti, A., & Emrick, K. (2003). Further validation of the Psycho-Social Wellbeing Scale. *Community Mental Health Journal, 39,* 115–129.

O'Hare, T., Tran, T. V., & Collins, P. (2002). Validating the practice skills inventory: A confirmatory factor analysis. *Research on Social Work Practice, 12,* 653–668.

Ollendick, T. H., & King, N. J. (1998). Empirically supported treatments for children with phobic and anxiety disorders: Current status. *Journal of Child Psychology, 27,* 156–167.

Orlinsky, D. E., Grawe, K., & Parks, B. K. (1994). Process and outcome in psychotherapy–Noch Einmal. In A. E. Bergin & S. L. Garfield (Eds.), *The handbook of psychotherapy and behavior change* (4th ed., pp. 270–376). New York: John Wiley.

Orlinsky, D. E., & Howard, K. I. (1986). Process and outcome in psychotherapy. In S. L. Garfield & A. E. Bergin (Eds.), *The handbook of psychotherapy and behavior change* (pp. 311–384). New York: John Wiley.

Pecora, P. J., Whittaker, J. K., Maluccio, A. N., & Barth, R. P. (2000). *The child welfare challenge: Policy, practice, and research* (2nd ed.). New York: Aldine de Gruyter.

Perlman, H. H. (1957). *Social case work: A problem-solving process.* Chicago: University of Chicago Press.

Prochaska, J. O., & DiClemente, C. C. (1984). *The transtheoretical approach: Crossing the traditional boundaries of therapy.* Homewood, IL: Dow Jones/Irwin.

Prochaska, J. O., DiClemente, C. C., & Norcross, J. C. (1992). In search of how people change: Applications to addictive behaviors. *American Psychologist, 47,* 1102–1114.

Proctor, E. (2003). Research to inform the development of social work interventions. *Social Work Research, 27,* 3–5.

Putnam, F. W. (2003). Ten-year research update review: Child sexual abuse. *Journal of the American Academy of Child and Adolescent Psychiatry, 42,* 269–278.

RachBeisel, J., Scott, J., & Dixon, L. (1999). Co-occurring severe mental illness and substance use disorders: A review of recent research. *Psychiatric Services, 50,* 1427–1434.

Randall, J. (2002). The practice-research relationship: A case of ambivalent attachment? *Journal of Social Work, 2,* 105–122.

Randolph, F. L., Ridgway, P., & Carling, P. J. (1991). Residential programs for persons with severe mental illness: A nationwide survey of state-affiliated agencies. *Hospital and Community Psychiatry, 42,* 1111–1115.

Raskin, N. J., & Rogers, C. (1995). Person-centered therapy. In R. J. Corsini & D. Wedding (Eds.), *Current psychotherapies* (5th ed., pp. 128–161). Itasca, IL: Peacock Publishers.

Reamer, F. (1995). Malpractice claims against social workers: First facts. *Social Work, 40,* 595–601.

Reamer, F. G. (1998). *Ethical standards in social work: A critical review of the NASW Code of Ethics.* Washington, DC: NASW Press.

Reamer, F. G. (2001). *The social work ethics audit: A risk management tool.* Washington, DC: NASW Press.

Reamer, F. G. (2003). *Social work malpractice and liability* (2nd ed.). New York: Columbia University Press.

Reamer, F. G. (2006). *Social work values and ethics* (3rd ed.). New York: Columbia University Press.

Richmond, M. (1918). *Social diagnosis.* New York: Russell Sage Foundation.

Rogers, C. R. (1951). *Client-centered therapy.* Boston: Houghton Mifflin.

Rooney, R. H., & Bibus, A. A. (2001). Clinical practice with involuntary clients in community settings. In H. E. Briggs & K. Corcoran (Eds.), *Social work practice: Treating common client problems* (pp. 391–406). Chicago: Lyceum.

Rosen, A. (2003). Evidence-based social work practice: Challenges and promise. *Social Work Research, 27,* 197–208.

Rossi, P. H., & Freeman, H. E. (1993). *Evaluation: A systematic approach.* Thousand Oaks, CA: Sage.

Rothbaum, B. O., Meadows, E. A., Resick, P., & Foy, D. W. (2000). Cognitive-behavioral therapy. In E. B. Foa, T. M. Keane, & M. J. Friedman (Eds.), *Effective treatments for PTSD: Practice guidelines from the international society for traumatic stress studies* (pp. 60–83). New York: Guilford Press.

Ryan, C. S., Sherman, P. S., & Judd, C. M. (1994). Accounting for case manager effects in the evaluation of mental health services. *Journal of Consulting and Clinical Psychology, 62,* 965–974.

Sackett, D. L., Straus, S. E., Richardson, W. S., Rosenberg, W., & Haynes, R. B. (2000). *Evidence-based medicine: How to practice and teach EBM*. New York: Churchill Livingstone.

Sadock, B. J., & Sadock, V. A. (2003). *Kaplan and Sadock's synopsis of psychiatry: Behavioral sciences/clinical psychiatry* (9th ed.). Baltimore: Lippincott, Williams and Wilkins.

Saleeby, D. (1996). Strengths perspective in social work practice: Extensions and cautions. *Social Work, 41*, 296–305.

Scott, J. E., & Dixon, L. B. (1995). Assertive community treatment and case management for schizophrenia. *Schizophrenia Bulletin, 21*, 657–668.

Shadish, W. R., & Baldwin, S. A. (2005). Effects of behavioral marital therapy: A meta-analysis of randomized controlled trials. *Journal of Consulting and Clinical Psychology, 73*, 6–14.

Sherrer, M. V., & O'Hare, T. (2008). Clinical case management. In K. Mueser & D. Jeste (Eds.), *Clinical handbook of schizophrenia* (pp. 309–318). New York: Guilford Press.

Shiraev, E., & Levy, D. (2007). *Cross cultural psychology: Critical thinking and contemporary applications* (3rd ed.). Boston: Pearson/Allyn and Bacon.

Shulman, L. (1999). *The skills of helping individuals, families, groups, and communities* (4th ed.). Itasca, IL: Peacock.

Siegel, D. (1984). Defining empirically based practice. *Social Work, 29*, 325–331.

Silverman, W. K., & Berman, S. L. (2001). Psychosocial interventions for anxiety disorders in children: Status and future directions. In W. K. Silverman & P.D.A. Treffers (Eds.), *Anxiety disorders in children and adolescents: Research, assessment and intervention* (pp. 313–334). New York: Cambridge University Press.

Silverman, W. K., & Treffers, P. D. A. (Eds.). *Anxiety disorders in children and adolescents: Research, assessment and intervention*. New York: Cambridge University Press.

Simpson, E. B., Pistorello, J., Begin, A., Costello, E., Levinson, J., Mulberry, S., et al. (1998). Use of dialectical behavior therapy in a partial hospital program for women with borderline personality disorder. *Psychiatric Services, 49*, 669–673.

Smith, B. H., Barkley, R. A., & Shapiro, C. J. (2006). Attention-deficit/hyperactivity disorder. In E. J. Mash & R. A. Barkley (Eds.), *Treatment of childhood disorders* (3rd ed., pp. 65–136). New York: Guilford Press.

Smith, D. W., Witte, T. H., & Fricker-Elhai, A. E., (2006). Service outcomes in physical and sexual abuse cases: A comparison of child advocacy center–based and standard services. *Child Maltreatment, 11*(4), 354–360.

Smokowski, P. R., & Wodarski, J. S. (1996). The effectiveness of child welfare services for poor, neglected children: A review of the empirical evidence. *Research on Social Work Practice, 6*, 504–523.

Snyder, D. K., Castellani, A. M., & Whisman, M. A. (2006). Current status and future directions in couple therapy. *Annual Review of Psychology, 57*, 317–344.

Sommers-Flannagan, J., & Sommers-Flannagan, R. (2003). *Clinical interviewing.* Hoboken, NJ: John Wiley.

Stanton, M. D., & Shadish, W. R. (1997). Outcome, attrition, and family-couples treatment for drug abuse: A meta-analysis and review of the controlled, comparative studies. *Psychological Bulletin, 122*, 170–191.

Stark, K., Sander, J., Hauser, M., Simpson, J., Schnoebelen, S., Glenn, R., et al. (2006). Depressive disorders during childhood and adolescence. In E. J. Mash & R. A. Barkley (Eds.), *Treatment of childhood disorders* (3rd ed., pp. 336–407). New York: Guilford Press.

Stein, L. I., & Test, M. A. (1980). Alternative to mental hospital treatment. I: Conceptual model, treatment program, and clinical evaluation. *Archives of General Psychiatry, 37*, 392–397.

Steketee, G. S. (1993). *Treatment of obsessive compulsive disorder.* New York: Guilford Press.

Strom-Gottfried, K. (2007). *Straight talk about professional ethics.* Chicago: Lyceum.

Stout, E. S., & Hayes, R. A. (2005). *The evidence-based practice: Methods, models and tools for mental health professionals.* Hoboken, NJ: John Wiley.

Stuart, G. W., Rush, A. J., & Morris, J. A. (2002). Practice guidelines in mental health and addiction services: Contributions from the American College of Mental Health Administration. *Administration and Policy in Mental Health, 30*, 21–33.

Sue, D. (2007). *Multicultural social work practice.* New York: John Wiley.

Sue, D. W., & Sue, D. (1999). *Counseling the culturally different* (3rd ed.). New York: John Wiley.

Swartz, M. S., Swanson, J. W., Hiday, V. A., Borum, R., Wagner, H. R., & Burns, B. J. (1998). Violence and severe mental illness: The effects of substance abuse and nonadherence to medication. *American Journal of Psychiatry, 155*, 226–231.

Tarasoff v. Board of Regents of the University of California et al., 17 Cal 3rd 425, 131 Cal Rptr 14, 551 P2d 334 (Cal 1976).

Tehrani, J. A., Brennan, P. A., Hodgins, S., & Mednick, S. A. (1998). Mental illness and criminal violence. *Social Psychiatry and Psychiatric Epidemiology, 33,* s81–s85.

Thomas, C., & Corcoran, J. (2001). Empirically-based marital and family interventions for alcohol abuse: A review. *Research on Social Work Practice, 11,* 549–575.

Thyer, B. A. (1995). Effective psychosocial treatments for children: A selected review. *Early Child Development and Care, 106,* 137–147.

Thyer, B. A. (2004). Science and evidence-based social work practice. In H. E. Briggs & T. L. Rzepnicki (Eds.), *Using evidence in social work practice: Behavioral perspectives* (pp. 74–89). Chicago: Lyceum.

Truax, C. B., & Carkhuff, R. R. (1967). *Toward effective counseling and psychotherapy.* Chicago: Aldine.

Tversky, A., & Kahneman, D. (1974). Judgment under uncertainty: Heuristics and biases. *Science, 183,* 1124–1131.

Uba, L. (1994). *Asian Americans: Personality, patterns, identity and mental health.* New York: Guilford Press.

U. S. Department of Health and Human Services (2000). *Tenth special report to Congress on alcohol and health.* Washington, DC: Government Printing Office.

U. S. Department of Health and Human Services (2003a). *The AFCARS report.* Washington, DC: Children's Bureau, Administration on Children, Youth and Families.

U. S. Department of Health and Human Services (2003b). *Assessing alcohol problems: A guide for clinicians and researchers* (2nd ed.). Washington, DC: National Institute on Alcohol Abuse and Alcoholism.

Van Dorn, R. A., Elbogen, E. B., Redlich, A. D., Swanson, J. W., Swartz, M. S., & Mustillo, S. (2006). The relationship between mandated community treatment and perceived barriers to care in persons with severe mental illness. *International Journal of Law and Psychiatry, 29,* 495–506.

Wakefield, J. C. (1996). Does social work need the eco-systems perspective? *Social Service Review, 70,* 1–32.

Wandersman, A. (2003). Community science: Bridging the gap between science and practice with community-centered models. *American Journal of Community Psychology, 31,* 227–243.

Webb, S. (2002). Evidence-based practice and decision analysis in social work. *Journal of Social Work, 2,* 45–63.

Webster-Stratton, C., & Herbert, M. (1994). *Troubled families—problem children. Working with parents: A collaborative process.* New York: John Wiley.

Wells, K. (2006). Child protection and welfare reform. *Child Abuse and Neglect, 30*, 1175–1179.

Weiss, J. (1995). Empirical studies of the psychoanalytic process. In T. Shapiro and R. N. Emde (Eds.), *Research in psychoanalysis: Process, development, outcome* (pp. 7–30). Madison, CT: International Universities Press.

Weissman, M. M., Markowitz, J. C., & Klerman, G. L. (2000). *Comprehensive guide to interpersonal psychotherapy.* New York: Basic Books.

Wexler, D. B. (1991). Inducing therapeutic compliance through the criminal law. In D. B. Wexler & B. J. Winick (Eds.), *Essays in therapeutic jurisprudence* (pp. 187–218). Durham, NC: Carolina Academic Press.

Whaley, A. L., & Davis, K. E. (2007). Cultural competence and evidence-based practice in mental health services. *American Psychologist, 62,* 563–574.

Wilson, C., & Powell, M. (2001). *A guide to interviewing children: Essential skills for counselors, police, lawyers, and social workers.* London: Routledge.

Wolfe, D. A., & Wekerle, C. (1993). Treatment strategies for child physical abuse and neglect: A critical progress report. *Clinical Psychology Review, 13,* 473–500.

Woods, M. E., & Hollis, F. (1990). *Casework: A psychosocial therapy.* New York: McGraw-Hill.

Wynn, R. (2006). Coercion in psychiatric care: Clinical, legal, and ethical controversies. *International Journal of Psychiatry in Clinical Practice, 10,* 247–251.

Yalom, I. (2005). *The theory and practice of group psychotherapy* (5th ed.). New York: Basic Books.

Psychosocial Intervention Scale

Client ID _____ *Date* ___/___/___/

Please check each of the skills below that you used during the most recently completed client visit.

Supportive Skills

1. Provided emotional support for my client (e.g., careful listening, empathy, positive regard). _____

2. Made efforts to enhance the client's self-confidence, bolster morale (e.g., highlight strengths, emphasize opportunities for improvement and likely benefits of participating in the intervention). _____

3. Listened carefully and showed that I understood the client's view of the problem clearly. _____

4. Cultivated a collaborative working relationship with client to enhance participation in treatment (e.g., collaborate on goals, weigh pros and cons of changing, clarify respective roles in treatment). _____

5. Actively motivated the client to increase his or her readiness to

engage in treatment (e.g,, reduce substance use, improve social skills, seek employment, adhere to medication schedules). _____

6. Actively tried to retain the client in treatment by, for example, reaching out, using motivational methods, contacting collaborators (e.g., law enforcement, health-care providers, significant others). _____

7. Helped client develop realistic goals for recovery at the client's own pace, avoided arguing with client about goals, and rolled with the client's resistance. _____

8. Used motivational strategies to help instill optimism and helped the client see how knowledge about the illness and improved coping skills could help the client achieve recovery goals. _____

Therapeutic-Coping Skills

1. Helped client identify, examine, and challenge troubling or dysfunctional thoughts, cognitions, and beliefs (e.g., hallucinations and delusions as well as other common distortions, such as "My life is hopeless," "I'll never be able to stop using drugs," "Everyone is out to get me," "Nobody likes me," "Nothing good will ever happen for me," and other fears and worries). _____

2. Examined past experiences to help client learn from previous attempts to cope with problems. _____

3. Helped client put past experiences in a more positive light. _____

4. Explored past relationships to see how they affect client's current problems. _____

5. Provided psychoeducation for my client about the problems he or she is experiencing (e.g., psychosis, depression, anxiety disorder, substance abuse, parenting skills) by presenting information and then checking and reviewing it to ensure that the client understood it. _____

6. Provided family psychoeducation and support so the family could cope more effectively with stress and emotional upsets. _____

7. Taught strategies to help client take psychiatric medication according to prescription. _____

8. Taught and helped client enhance coping skills to deal more effectively with symptoms of mental illness and/or other related problems. _____

9. Helped the client identify, express, and cope with troubling feelings/emotions (e.g., problematic anger, depression, fears and anxieties, envy, jealousy). _____

10. Taught stress/anxiety coping strategies for emotional distress (e.g., brief meditation, breathing, muscle relaxation). _____

11. Taught client to identify, assess, monitor, and regulate problem behaviors (i.e., identify triggers, attempt solutions, evaluate the results). _____

12. Taught client a specific problem-solving or coping skill to deal with a particular problem (e.g., used rehearsal, role-play, or modeling to help client learn and practice the new skill at home, work, or other situation). Specific examples include assertiveness training, communication or other interpersonal coping skills, confronting an anxiety-provoking situation, saying no to the offer of alcohol or other drugs, and improving parenting skills or relationship communication skills. _____

13. Used positive reinforcement to help the client improve the use of a skill and achieve a goal. _____

14. Showed client how to manage contingencies (i.e., provide rewards or sanctions) to manage his or her own behavior (e.g., reward oneself for one month sobriety) or to influence another person in a positive way (e.g., improve a child's behavior, reduce conflict with a partner or coworker, resolve other disputes). _____

15. Collaborated with client on plans to cope with relapses of a problem (e.g., suicidal thoughts, psychotic symptoms, substance abuse, anxiety attacks, going off medication, anger- or impulse-control problems). _____

16. Coached client in specific lifestyle changes to enhance overall psychosocial well-being and physical health (e.g., stop smoking, reduce/abstain from substances and other high-risk behaviors, improve diet, engage in moderate exercise).   _____

Case Management Skills

1. Assessed and attended to the client's level of material resources (e.g., income, housing, food, medical, other basic needs).   _____

2. Made efforts to enhance social supports (e.g., improve the client's natural social network; link to other community resources, mutual help groups, family members, employers, landlords).   _____

3. Helped client to recruit significant others in his or her life to increase social supports.   _____

4. Advocated on the client's behalf (e.g., attempted to represent client's rights with landlord, court, other agencies, neighbor, other community member).   _____

5. Provided information and/or referral (e.g., health, substance abuse, social services).   _____

6. Networked with other providers and coordinated services for client with other agencies.   _____

7. Assessed the client's vocational potential (e.g., experience, abilities, strengths).   _____

8. Made at least one direct effort to link the client with a potential employer.   _____

The Comprehensive Service Plan

Use all available information from the client and significant others, your observations, and input from other professionals to conduct both quantitative and qualitative aspects of this multidimensional-functional assessment.

Client-Identification Data

Describe client-identification data (e.g., gender; age; marital status; sexual orientation; family composition; employment; racial, ethnic, cultural, religious, and spiritual affiliation and identity).

The Presenting Problem

Describe the client's problem from the client's view.

Describe the client's problem from your view as practitioner.

Describe the client's psychosocial history with an emphasis on problem trajectory.

Describe attempts to resolve the problems, previous treatment, and relevant outcomes.

The Individual Assessment

Mental Status: Cognitive Disturbances

Describe the client's level of hallucinations, delusions, disorientation, bizarre behavior or speech, memory problems, serious confusion or other symptoms of serious cognitive impairment. Include other troubling or dysfunctional beliefs or convictions.

How would you rate the client's overall mental status during the past month?

    Poor (0)   Impaired (1)   Marginal (2)   Good (3)   Excellent (4)

Mental Status: Emotional Distress

Describe the client's level of depression, anxiety, and overall ability to regulate his or her emotions.

How would you rate your client's emotional well-being over the past thirty days?

    Poor (0)   Impaired (1)   Marginal (2)   Good (3)   Excellent (4)

Behavioral Problems

Describe your client's overall ability to regulate his or her behavior. Consider things such as ability to express effectively; ability to work at things patiently; tendencies to verbally or physically lash out at others, to run away, or to cause harm to him- or herself; and proneness to impulsive, criminal, or substance-abusing behavior. How would you describe the client's overall impulse control?

How would you rate your client's impulse control generally over the past thirty days?

    Poor (0)   Impaired (1)   Marginal (2)   Good (3)   Excellent (4)

Adaptive Strengths and Coping Abilities

Describe your client's ability to cope with problems and everyday stressors. How would you describe the client's ability to assess problem situations, deal with triggers, cope with stress, solve problems, and reach out to others for help to deal effectively with difficulties?

How would you rate your client's overall adaptive strengths and coping abilities over the past thirty days?

    Poor (0)   Impaired (1)   Marginal (2)   Good (3)   Excellent (4)

Health Problems

Describe the client's overall health. Aside from normal, transient illnesses, think about the client's general health habits (e.g., smoking, heavy drinking, exercise, weight), chronic primary health disorders, the client's opinion of his or her own health, ability to engage in usual activities relatively free from discomfort, overall energy level, and hospitalizations and treatments for illness other than psychiatric ones. Consider the client's documented medical history and any ongoing treatments.

How would you rate your client's health over the past thirty days?

    Poor (0)   Impaired (1)   Marginal (2)   Good (3)   Excellent (4)

Use of Alcohol and Other Drugs

Describe the client's use of alcohol, illicit substances (e.g., cocaine, heroin, marijuana, hallucinogens) and abuse of prescription medication. What is the usage frequency? In what quantity? How serious are the associated psychological, physical, or social consequences?

How would you rate the client's functioning in the past month with regard to substance use?

    Poor (0)   Impaired (1)   Marginal (2)   Good (3)   Excellent (4)

Recreational Activities

Consider what the client does for fun (alone or with others), hobbies, relaxation (e.g., reading, watching television, playing video games or cards), and physical exercise (e.g., walking, jogging, biking). How would you describe the client's overall involvement in positive recreational activities?

How would you rate the adequacy of the client's participation in healthy recreational activities over the past thirty days?

   Poor (0)   Impaired (1)   Marginal (2)   Good (3)   Excellent (4)

Material Resources

Describe your client's current or (if institutionalized) most recent living situation. Consider such things as adequacy of food, clothing, shelter, and safety.
How would you rate the overall adequacy of the client's material resources over the past month?

   Poor (0)   Impaired (1)   Marginal (2)   Good (3)   Excellent (4)

Independent Living and Self-Care

Describe how well your client manages his or her household; takes care of personal hygiene; and eats, sleeps, and otherwise cares for basic needs.

How would you rate the client's ability to live independently and take care of his or her basic needs over the past thirty days?

   Poor (0)   Impaired (1)   Marginal (2)   Good (3)   Excellent (4)

Work (Role) Satisfaction

Describe the client's current work-related or other important role-related activities (e.g., employed, student, homemaker, volunteer, retired, disabled). Describe the activities and responsibilities that occupy the client in a productive manner.

How would you rate the client's work or role productivity over the past thirty days?

Poor (0)   Impaired (1)   Marginal (2)   Good (3)   Excellent (4)

Legal Problems

Describe any legal problems the client has had or continues to have, including minor infractions (e.g., public drunkenness, shoplifting inexpensive items, minor traffic violations, public disturbances) and more serious crimes (e.g., assault and battery, rape, burglary, driving under the influence). Consider the client's status (e.g., probation, awaiting imprisonment, parole). Consider any civil suits in which the client in involved, pending financial judgments against them, and so on. Overall, how would you describe the client's current legal situation?

How would you rate the client's legal situation over the past thirty days?

Poor (0)   Impaired (1)   Marginal (2)   Good (3)   Excellent (4)

DSM-IV Diagnosis

Axis I:

Axis II:

The Family and Social Assessment

Family Relations

Describe the client's current family structure, including authority, hierarchy, alliances, roles, rules, boundaries, subsystems (e.g., couple, siblings, parent-child alliances); patterns of interactions, and quality of communications. Describe specific problems within the family and specific adaptive strengths within the family. How does the family describe its own racial, ethnic, cultural, and religious identities?

How would you rate the quality of the client's immediate family relationships over the past thirty days?

Poor (0)   Impaired (1)   Marginal (2)   Good (3)   Excellent (4)

Immediate Social Relationships

With respect to close friends and acquaintances, describe the quality of your client's relationships with those available friends and acquaintances, as applicable. Over the past month, how would you describe the quality of the interaction overall between your client and friends and acquaintances with respect to closeness, intimacy, general interpersonal satisfaction, effective communications, degree of conflict, level of hostility, aggression, and evidence of any emotional or physical abuse?

How would you rate the quality of the client's immediate social relationships over the past thirty days?

Poor (0)   Impaired (1)   Marginal (2)   Good (3)   Excellent (4)

Extended Social Relationships

Describe the type and quality of relationships between your client and others in the client's community (other than close friends and family), including other families, law enforcement, human service agencies, school personnel, coworkers, and others from whom the client receives support or with whom the client is having serious conflict.

How would you rate the quality of the client's social relationships over the past thirty days?

Poor (0)   Impaired (1)   Marginal (2)   Good (3)   Excellent (4)

A Concise Summary of the MDF Assessment

Highlight the client's areas of distress and adaptive strengths. Emphasize those areas that are most likely to be emphasized in the intervention plan.

Recommendations for Further Focused Assessment

Note recommended referrals to consultants or additional instruments to be used.

THE COMPREHENSIVE SERVICE PLAN SUMMARY

Problems: Briefly describe key problems to be addressed	Goals: State desired outcome for each problem.	Objectives: Describe specific stepping stones toward each goal; update as client progresses.	Interventions: Describe intervention approaches to be used.	Assessment and evaluation: Describe indexes and scales used to track progress.

Guide to Reviewing Research Reports

Critically Reviewing Human Behavior and Practice Research: A Brief Guide

The Introduction

- Most studies open with a brief paragraph or two about the problem to be addressed.
- A literature review follows: key studies are carefully reviewed for content and for the quality of the methods employed. The authors summarize what is known, what the quality of the existing body of research is, and what gaps there are in both knowledge and quality of methodology in the current literature.
- A new research question should logically flow from the review, and specific hypotheses may be posed (although some authors report hypotheses in the "Methodology" section as "statistical analysis strategy").

Methods

Sample

- A description of the sample is presented here, detailing how it was obtained (e.g., random sample, convenience sample) and the sample characteristics (e.g., gender, age, race—using APA style for univariate statistics).
- If the investigation is an intervention study, how the sample was recruited and assigned to different treatment groups is discussed.

Design and Data Collection Procedure

- Design is primarily concerned with how the main variables of the study are configured relative to one another. Is it a survey (e.g., cross-sectional, longitudinal), a pre-experimental (e.g., uncontrolled pre-post study), quasi-experimental (e.g., comparison group with no random assignment), or true-experimental design? Is it an exploratory qualitative study?
- For survey research, did the authors use a convenience sample or random sampling? What size sample did they hope to obtain, and what was the actual response rate (i.e., the number of people who actually responded to the authors' request to participate in the study)?
- For a practice outcome or evaluation study, were cases assigned randomly or were cases in two groups matched by some other criterion?
- How were data collected? Face-to-face structured or unstructured interviews? Self-report questionnaires done at home? Mail, telephone, or Internet survey? Who collected the data? How was informed consent obtained? How was clients' confidentiality protected?

Instruments

- What type of instruments (e.g., scales, indexes) were used? What did they measure?
- Did the authors provide information regarding any relevant published psychometric data (e.g., reliability, validity, utility)?
- How were the scales scored?

Statistical Analysis Strategy

- As noted earlier, the authors might state (or restate) the study hypotheses here with specific reference to the relationship they expected to find between the key variables (no expected relationship is a *null hypothesis*).
- The authors should also discuss what types of statistical tests they plan to use and why they selected them.

Results

- Authors should report in text or tables all univariate descriptive data on the study sample (if this has not been done in the "Sample" section) and present univariate statistics (e.g., means, standard deviations, frequencies, percentages) for all key study variables.

- Authors should report any bivariate tests (e.g., chi square, t-tests, Pearson correlations) that test the relationship of two variables. These tests are often the first test of any study hypotheses. What are the basic findings?
- Last, authors should report the findings of any multivariate statistical tests (e.g., regression, analysis of variance, structural equation modeling). Try to find a clear verbal explanation of the results of those tests.

Discussion

- Some authors summarize their key findings briefly at the beginning of the "Discussion" section.
- Authors should then discuss what the findings mean with respect to theory, practice, or policy in the context of previous literature.
- Authors should discuss the limitations of their study (e.g., missing data, attrition in participant sample, small sample).
- Authors should then discuss questions for future research.

Critically Reviewing Human Behavior and Practice Research: A Longer Explanation

The following guidelines were generally developed by the American Psychological Association for the conducting and reporting of research, and they are accepted by most helping professions, including the National Association of Social Workers. Scholars who conduct research or critically review others' research to determine whether it merits publication use these guidelines.

The Introduction

Most research reports begin with an opening paragraph or two defining the problem or practice method of interest and then offer an argument to impress on the reader the importance of a particular social problem or psychosocial intervention. A review of the previous research on the subject area follows.

A representative review of the literature. Knowledge building does not happen in a vacuum. Researchers must build on and ideally improve on what has been done before. Therefore, all research begins with a reasonably representative review of prior research on the subject of the article. The subsequent discussion touches on the criteria that authors use to judge the quality of previous research.

Defining a theoretical framework, clarifying key concepts, and stating a research question and hypotheses. Whether studying a human behavior problem or studying the effectiveness of an intervention, researchers employ some kind of theoretical framework. In human behavior studies, a theoretical framework attempts to explain the relationship between two variables or among three or more variables. In a research study of expectancy theory, for example, an investigator may try to test the relationship between concepts related to adolescent drinking: (1) the expectancy that drinking results in enhanced social experience and (2) low self-esteem. Proponents of the theory might test the hypothesis that young people who have a strong belief that drinking enhances interpersonal skills (an idea derived, perhaps, from parental, peer, or cultural and media influences) are more likely to lack confidence in themselves in social situations (one aspect of low self-esteem). Theories that purport to explain human behavior should be testable; that is, stated in such a way that relevant research questions and hypotheses can be proved wrong (i.e., falsifiability). Whether this theory about beliefs in the effects of alcohol and interpersonal relations is valid depends on testing this theory many times with many different groups of people.

The general research question might be stated as follows: are young people with poor self-esteem more likely to drink abusively if they believe that drinking will enhance their social experience? To test this research question, it must be restated in the form of hypotheses, which are declarative statements that assert how two or more concepts are related. Hypotheses regarding human behavior usually come in one of two forms: (1) A (poor self-esteem) is correlated with B (the expectation of enhanced social relations); for example, a young person who scores high on a scale measuring belief in the positive effects of alcohol on social experience is significantly likely to have lower self-esteem; (2) A (poor self-esteem) causes B (the expectation of enhanced social relations): a young person with low self-esteem is significantly more likely to score higher on a scale measuring belief in the positive effects of alcohol on social experience *as a result of drinking.* Hypotheses such as these that test the relationship between two concepts are among the simplest. Other hypotheses can be much more complex and involve multiple concepts.

Each concept in the hypotheses must be clarified in the introduction.

Self-esteem, for example, is a fairly general concept about which there has been much research, and the authors of the study must stipulate how they will define it. In addition, each concept in human behavior research must be measurable; that is, quantifiable on some level with a scale. The specifics of the measurement of the main concepts in a study are typically explained in the "Methods" section of a research article.

If the study focuses on the efficacy of a type of intervention, it is essential that the authors define the actual intervention (as distinguished from an underlying theory). The authors should describe the practice interventions in the introduction and pose specific hypotheses to test their effectiveness. The hypotheses, however, will be of only the causal type: A (the intervention) causes B (a good outcome for the client). A hypothesis that tests an intervention might be stated as follows: with elderly, depressed clients, interpersonal psychotherapy plus medication will show a significantly greater reduction in depression (as measured by the Hamilton Depression Rating Scale) than will medication alone. The authors also give reasons why they believe this will, in fact, be the outcome in their study. Although research regarding interventions may be reviewed in the introduction, more details about how the intervention was carried out during the study are usually described in the "Methods" section of the article.

There is a subtle but important distinction between outcome research and evaluation research. Outcome research is designed to test and establish the efficacy of psychosocial practices; that is, to test whether interventions are effective when tested under controlled circumstances in which clients have been carefully recruited according to specific guidelines, practitioners are well trained in using well-defined interventions, and outcomes are carefully measured. Usually, the intervention of interest is compared with a control group (which receives treatment after a brief waiting period) or a treatment that is normally used in community treatment settings (i.e., treatment as usual). The purpose of evaluation, however, is to test the effectiveness of interventions; that is, to determine whether interventions can be implemented effectively under routine circumstances in everyday practice settings, environments that tend to be more fluid and less orchestrated than controlled trials. However, the difference between controlled outcome research and evaluation research is more a matter of degree. Both share the same goal of testing whether interventions actually result in improved outcomes for clients.

Methods

After posing a research question and one or more hypotheses, the authors then discuss how they will answer the research question and test their hypotheses. This section is referred to as the "Methods" or "Methodology" section of a research report. Methods include a sampling design, study design and data collection procedure, description of measurement instruments used in the study, and a description of the planned statistical strategy. If the study is a test of an intervention, then the interventions used in the study must be described in greater detail than in the introduction so readers understand the type of treatment being tested.

Sampling strategies. In human behavior research, the investigators must provide a thoughtful selection of study participants with a clear description of their characteristics (e.g., gender, age, race). Sampling designs are based on either nonprobability samples or probability samples. Nonprobability samples recruit participants who fit a certain predetermined criteria (e.g., twenty single mothers with a serious mental illness, forty-five young men recently released from prison, twenty-six homeless elderly men). Small nonprobability samples lend themselves to qualitative research and other small-sample survey studies (i.e., studies that often include both qualitative and quantitative measures). Other nonprobability samples may be larger: a survey of 400 recently graduated social workers, 350 mentally ill persons who attend a community support program, or 800 families served by a child welfare agency over the course of three years.

Probability samples are those that have been drawn randomly. *Random* means that every individual on a list of possible participants (e.g., all registered voters in the United States) has an equal chance of being selected. Using probability tables, statisticians have calculated how many people, if drawn randomly, are needed to approximate a sample that is representative of those people in the larger group. For example, to know how the typical registered social worker feels about evidence-based practices, one would identify all members of the National Association of Social Workers (say, 150,000) and randomly select about 1000 of them. This sample would provide a sound basis for generalization to all registered social workers, but only if the number of people who respond (i.e., the response rate) is sufficiently high. The response rate is the percentage of people from the sampled list who respond to the survey. What is acceptable? At least 50% of those 1000 people in the sample need to respond. However, even 50% may not be adequate if it can be demonstrated statistically that those who responded were in some way different in key aspects from those who did not. Such an analysis would, of course, assume that one had some information about those who did not respond (e.g., gender, age, race, years of MSW experience). A very good response rate is 60%, and 70% or greater is considered excellent. In short, the higher the response rate is, the stronger is the case the researcher can make that the sample is a representative picture of the larger group.

In practice outcome (efficacy) or evaluation (effectiveness) studies, characteristics of the client participants should be clearly described (e.g., age, sex, diagnosis, ethnicity, referral sources). Clients who participate in treatment studies are usually recruited through clinics and human services agencies. Clients in evaluation studies are often the actual clients of the agency being evaluated. In all theoretical research and intervention studies, clients should be voluntary participants, should be informed about the nature of the study, and should have their confidentiality protected. Researchers must apply for approval to conduct studies through institutional review boards to ensure that they followed sound procedures to obtain informed consent and to protect client confidentiality.

Design. The authors of a research article must select and describe a research design that can potentially answer a specific research question. Doing so assumes a clear understanding of the strengths and limitations of each respective design. In general, human behavior studies employ one of the following: uncontrolled qualitative observation, cross-sectional survey, and longitudinal survey. Research on the efficacy of psychosocial interventions usually employs some variation of the experimental design (using comparison or control groups), otherwise referred to as the "controlled trial." Evaluation studies often use either qualitative research with small samples or uncontrolled naturalistic evaluation with larger samples. Some evaluation studies use comparison groups. These different designs are explained subsequently.

A variety of data collection procedures are used in human behavior and intervention research. Questionnaires may be used in face-to-face interviews, mailed to participants, or filled out on the Internet. Other studies may employ direct observation (e.g., children in a classroom, practitioners behind a one-way window with clients). Some studies use more than one method of data collection: qualitative (e.g., recorded narrative accounts), quantitative (e.g., a scale that measures depression), or both. In any event, high priority is given to the selection of measures for the key study concepts (e.g., depression, posttraumatic stress). The scales selected should have a track record of reliability and validity (see chapter 4).

Research designs typically used in human behavior research. Qualitative studies of individuals and groups are generally used in exploratory research, an approach that lends itself to examining new or unusual phenomena (e.g., living with an apocalyptic cult for a year to better understand recruitment practices and worldview). It can also be used to examine new dimensions of commonly occurring problems (e.g., narrative accounts of living with agoraphobia or in abandoned subway tunnels for years, surveying key informants to examine mental health needs and services in the community). The researcher who conducts qualitative research is interested in the relatively unfiltered accounts of individuals who want to tell their stories. Thus, much of the data collected are written or recorded accounts of the participants who provide the information or narrate their experiences. Such data can provide clues to better understand a problem, raise new questions about a problem, and open new avenues of investigation in human behavior theory and research.

However, often in large qualitative studies, some coding scheme must be derived to categorize and even measure much of the content to reduce it to a more manageable data set. To draw some tentative conclusions from the data, some attempt must be made to summarize the accounts of, say, one hundred unstructured interviews with homeless people living on the street. Computer software has been developed to assist with these efforts. Although often emotionally compelling, qualitative research has some serious limitations: despite the best of intentions to be objective and not get in the way of participants, qualitative data are likely to be interpreted from the investigator's point of view. What is gained in textured and detailed accounts of individual lives may be lost in interpretive bias and the lack of generalizability to larger groups of people in similar circumstances. Nevertheless, qualitative research is a great place to begin investigating problem areas that are underrepresented in the research literature. However, these methods are a beginning point, not an end point, for human behavior research. Once major theoretical terms are defined and questions posed, survey methods with larger groups must be conducted to determine whether the insights gained through qualitative methods hold for more representative samples of the population.

Cross-sectional surveys (i.e., surveys with large samples at one point in time) are powerful ways to collect large amounts of data on representative groups of the general population. Because of the power of probability sampling, representative samples of participants can be surveyed by mail, phone, or Internet, or interviewed in person. Large cross-sectional surveys can provide invaluable descriptive data on the occurrence of mental disorders and other psychosocial problems nationally and internationally. They can also be used to study matters of theoretical interest, such as the relationship between beliefs about drinking and actual rate of alcohol use, race and use of mental health services, the association between poverty and child abuse and neglect, authoritarian beliefs and domestic violence, perceptions of media portrayals of women and severity of eating disorders, and so on. The subjects to be addressed by cross-sectional surveys are limitless, and students need merely employ a few keywords in a search engine that includes social science research journals to realize the extent of theory-driven cross-sectional research.

Longitudinal surveys may also include availability samples or randomly selected samples, but they are designed to follow a group of persons over time, sometimes for five, ten, or twenty years. Although cross-sectional surveys can be used to collect data on large groups of representative samples, they are generally limited to demonstrating correlational relationships among factors. The strength of longitudinal designs (because the passage of time becomes a measurable factor) is in determining cause-effect relationships. If, for example, one wishes to study the effects of early childhood trauma on adolescent and adult psychosocial well-being ten and twenty years in the future (in the same participants, over time), one can then measure both those events around the time they occur (or soon after) and a variety of other contributing factors (e.g., early temperament, socioeconomic level, parenting status, substance abuse, other family problems) throughout adolescence and into adulthood. Although challenging to conduct, longitudinal studies can provide powerful evidence to support or refute developmental theories.

Research designs used to demonstrate the practice efficacy and effectiveness. As noted earlier, research used to determine whether certain interventions actually help people with certain problems or disorders span the continuum from controlled outcome studies to naturalistic evaluation. Along this continuum are a range of design variations that can be used to either control for factors other than the intervention (to determine whether it is the intervention itself that makes a substantive difference for the client) or to determine how interventions work in a treatment-as-usual environment. There are good reasons for doing both types of studies: randomized controlled trials (discussed in Chapter 2) show whether interventions can work under carefully controlled circumstances, and program evaluations demonstrate whether interventions previously proved effective in controlled trials can be implemented cost-effectively in everyday practice.

Evaluating practice: Naturalistic program evaluation. Although controlled trials are important tools for testing whether interventions can work under well-controlled conditions, it is also important to evaluate the implementation of interventions in typical practice settings. Just because a practitioner claims to use an evidence-based practice does not mean that the practice will be implemented skillfully or effectively. Evaluating one's own practice is important to ensure that the intervention is implemented well and that the client improves. If, over time, the client does not improve, then modifications to the intervention plan or the whole program may be in order. Research reports of human service evaluations are fairly common in practice journals with an applied orientation. It should also be kept in mind that between controlled trials and naturalistic evaluation are studies that combine elements of both. For example, quasi-experimental designs can be used to compare different agency programs with clients that have a similar range of characteristics but some different program elements.

Controlled experimental trials are not used frequently as a method of routine evaluation in human service agencies. A much more feasible approach that accommodates everyday practice in human service agencies is naturalistic program evaluation (Hargreaves, Shumway, Hu, & Cuffel, 1998; Kazdin, 1998; O'Hare, 2005; Rossi & Freeman, 1993), otherwise referred to as *passive observational designs*. In naturalistic program evaluation, services are delivered without using control or comparison groups. Before engaging in evaluation, however, every effort is made to train staff in evidence-based practices (i.e., approaches already tested in controlled trials) and to incorporate the use of reliable and valid instruments to monitor client progress and evaluate whether clients benefit from the intervention. However, there is a cardinal rule of evaluation that is clear yet often ignored: before one can evaluate the intervention, one must define the intervention (a review of research reports of program evaluations reveals a frequent lack of clarity with regard to defining the intervention). Again, the intervention methods (i.e., combinations of skills) are to be distinguished from other aspects of practice theories, specifically change-process theories that purport to explain how the intervention works. These are different questions and require different research designs to answer them. Authors of research reports should take considerable pains to clearly define how the interventions were carried out; otherwise, the reader is left with the question, What are the researchers evaluating?

Naturalistic evaluation incorporates reliable, valid, and useful measures (e.g., scales and indexes) into routine practice as part of assessment and ongoing monitoring of client progress. Most social workers who have practiced in human service agencies are familiar with the myriad forms to fill out, including psychosocial assessments, progress notes, termination summaries, and so forth. Often, such forms are poorly designed and can be a costly administrative nuisance. Data collection in naturalistic evaluation is not much different in terms of execution, except that the standards for selecting quantitative instruments (e.g., scales for measuring psychiatric symptoms, substance abuse, and child and adolescent adjustment) are much higher than standards for typical agency forms. The scales must have a record of reliability (consistency) and validity (accuracy), and when well chosen they can be clinically useful. Such scales can help practitioners perform better assessments and service evaluations. The data are ideally collected at baseline (as part of the assessment), during the intervention at key intervals, and at termination. Some evaluators will also arrange for follow-up measures. These data are useful for monitoring progress with individual clients, and when data are aggregated, they can be used for program evaluation.

Guidelines for recruitment of participants are less stringent in routine evaluation. Most agencies obtain informed consent for clients at intake and let them know that data collection as part of routine record keeping may be used for program evaluation. Thus, most clients are automatically included in agency evaluation processes.

Thus, the guidelines for conducting naturalistic evaluation are simple: (1) use interventions that have been shown to be effective in controlled trials (this point may seem obvious, but many agencies continue to use untested intervention methods), (2) train staff in the use of the approach, (3) use reliable and valid instruments as part of routine monitoring, and (4) use the data from the multiple measures and qualitative reports over time to determine whether clients have improved. In this way, naturalistic evaluation fits seamlessly into the routine implementation of clinical processes and can provide a solid foundation for determining the quality of clinical programming. Authors of evaluative research reports should explicitly justify all these points in their description of the evaluation design.

Determining and Interpreting Results

An extensive discussion of statistics would go well beyond the purposes here. However, a brief discussion is in order to help students understand why critical interpretation of results is so important.

Statistical findings of human behavior and practice research generally fall into three categories: univariate, bivariate, or multivariate results. Univariate results are statistics that report the results of one variable at a time. These statistics usually include frequencies and percentages, means (i.e., average scores), and standard deviations (a measure of dispersal around the mean score). For example, in a human behavior study on the prevalence of drinking among a random sample of one thousand high school students, typical univariate results might include the frequency and percentage of males (450/45%) and females (550/55%) in the sample, the frequency and percentage of students who ever drink (650/65%), and the average amount of alcohol that a student consumes in a typical week (mean = 6.5 drinks). Univariate statistics are essentially used for description and thus are often referred to as *descriptive statistics.*

Human behavior and practice researchers, however, typically want to know more than descriptive information. As discussed earlier, researchers want to test hypotheses; that is, they want to make logical inferences from their data on, say, differences between groups or differences in clients' well-being between the beginning and the end of an intervention. Hence, bivariate and multivariate statistics are usually used to test hypotheses and thus are referred to as *inferential statistics* (as they test logical inferences about the relationship between variables and whether the differences are due to chance or to real differences in the general population). Commonly used bivariate statistics include the Pearson correlation coefficient, t-tests, and chi-square tests. Determining which statistic to use depends on how each variable is measured and whether the group is normally distributed; that is, whether the group statistics simulate those of the general population.

A typical use of bivariate statistics is to test a hypothesis to determine whether there is an important relationship or difference between two variables. For example, in an evaluation program, bivariate statistics show whether the average depression score for a group of women significantly improved from the time they start treatment to the time they finish treatment. Looking at the differences in scores for individual participants would not reveal whether the whole group benefited; it is necessary to compare the average group scores at the beginning and end of treatment. Comparison of the two mean scores requires a bivariate test of the hypothesis to show that there was a difference.

Multivariate statistics determine the relationships among more than two variables. For example, researchers are interested in more than just the relationship between gender and alcohol consumption in a group of high school students. A research question might be, Is stress in high school students related to alcohol consumption, and does this relationship vary by sex? Now there are three variables: sex, stress, and alcohol consumption. All of these factors can be measured, and how the three variables are related can be tested. It could be, for example, that stress has a greater impact on women's drinking that it does on men's drinking. Other factors could be added to the theoretical model, such as parental influence, participation in sports, overall quality of social relationships, and so on.

A multivariate research question in a program evaluation may focus on client characteristics (e.g., race, sex), services received (e.g., number of visits, type of intervention), and outcomes (e.g., changes in scores on depression and substance abuse scales). Several different questions could be asked: Do the number of visits differ across racial groups? Are there differences in rates of depression between men and women? Is one form of intervention more effective than another? These are interesting and important questions, but so far they only look at bivariate relationships. To complicate things (as researchers seem to enjoy), the researchers could ask more complex multivariate questions: Is one form of intervention more effective than another, and is the relationship between the intervention and outcome different by sex and race? Now there are four different variables: sex, race, type of intervention, and changes in score on a depression scale. To determine the answers, the researchers would use a multivariate statistical design that would examine changes in depression level while controlling (i.e., holding constant) the other factors. There are many multivariate statistical models available to researchers, but two of the more commonly used ones are multiple linear regression and variations on analysis of variance. Although detailed descriptions of these statistical approaches goes beyond the purposes here, readers should, at this point, develop a basic understanding of the purpose of these statistical models in their research courses to be better able to read and generally understand research reports. Most human behavior and intervention research uses these methods, and though an in-depth understanding of them is beyond the expertise of most practitioners, a basic understanding of their purpose and the ability to understand the results of such tests is now essential.

The Discussion

Researchers sometimes provide a summary of the results in either the "Results" section or in the first part of the "Discussion" or "Conclusion" section of a research report. Interpretations of the results should be balanced, and the researchers should avoid reading too much into their findings (i.e., going beyond the data) or overgeneralizing the results beyond the sample of study participants. In the discussion, the authors should examine the results in the context of existing theory and previous human behavior or intervention research. The authors should also discuss the extent to which the results can be generalized to other groups of clients or treatment environments. Generalization is a key point, because readers want to know the extent to which a theory applies to other groups or if an intervention is likely to work as well with similar groups of clients. The authors should also discuss the inherent limitations of the study design and any problems in carrying out the study (e.g., how many people dropped out or refused to answer questions). Last, most researchers offer suggestions for further research in their area of inquiry.

Learning how to critically read human behavior research requires considerable skill and is not a form of expertise that students typically develop early on in their social work careers. However, as one develops some basic skills in critiquing and understanding human behavior research, one can better distinguish theories for which there is a body of scientific evidence from those based mostly on ideology, tradition, or personal beliefs. However, most students (or experienced practitioners, for that matter) will not have to undertake the arduous task of reviewing human behavior research on their own. Fortunately, researchers and many practitioner-researchers have taken on the task of critically reviewing and summarizing human behavior and practice research findings to disseminate it for practitioners and other researchers. The findings of theory-driven research regarding child development, child abuse and neglect, major mental illnesses and substance abuse, aging, and so forth, are compiled in a wide array of excellent texts. The student need only seek them out. Being able to critically review human behavior research and practice outcome research is now an essential skill for social workers, as it allows them to collectively advance social work as a knowledge-based (rather than an ideology-based) profession.

Index

Page numbers followed by *f* refer to figures.